A HISTORY OF ENGLISH ROMANTICISM IN THE NINETEENTH CENTURY.

A HISTORY OF ENGLISH ROMANTICISM IN THE NINETEENTH CENTURY

BY

HENRY A. BEERS

Author of "A Suburban Pastoral," "The Ways of Yale," etc.

NEW YORK

HENRY HOLT AND COMPANY

1901

ROMANCE.

My love dwelt in a Northern land.
  A gray tower in a forest green
Was hers, and far on either hand
  The long wash of the waves was seen,
And leagues on leagues of yellow sand,
  The woven forest boughs between.

And through the silver Northern light
  The sunset slowly died away,
And herds of strange deer, lily-white,
  Stole forth among the branches grey;
About the coming of the light,
  They fled like ghosts before the day.

I know not if the forest green
  Still girdles round that castle grey;
I know not if the boughs between
  The white deer vanish ere the day;
Above my love the grass is green,
  My heart is colder than the clay.
ANDREW LANG.

PREFACE.

THE present volume is a sequel to " A History of English Romanticism in the Eighteenth Century" (New York: Henry Holt & Co., 1899). References in the footnotes to "Volume I." are to that work. The difficulties of this second part of my undertaking have been of a kind just opposite to those of the first. As it concerns my subject, the eighteenth century was an age of beginnings; and the problem was to discover what latent romanticism existed in the writings of a period whose spirit, upon the whole, was distinctly unromantic. But the temper of the nineteenth century has been, until recent years, prevailingly romantic in the wider meaning of the word. And as to the more restricted sense in which I have chosen to employ it, the mediævalising literature of the nineteenth century is at least twenty times as great as that of the eighteenth, both in bulk and in value. Accordingly the problem here is one of selection; and of selection not from a list of half-forgotten names, like Warton and Hurd, but from authors whose work is still the daily reading of all educated readers.

As I had anticipated, objection has been made to the narrowness of my definition of *romanticism*. But every writer has a right to make his own definitions; or, at least, to say what his book shall be about. I have not written a history of the "liberal movement in English literature"; nor of the "renaissance of wonder"; nor of the "emancipation of the ego." Why not have called the book, then, "A History of the Mediæval Revival in England"? Because I have a clear title to the use of *romantic* in one of its commonest acceptations; and, for myself, I prefer the simple dictionary definition, "pertaining to the style of the Christian and popular literature of the Middle Ages," to any of those more pretentious explanations which seek to express the true inwardness of romantic literature by analysing it into its elements, selecting one of these elements as essential, and rejecting all the rest as accidental.

M. Brunetière, for instance, identifies romanticism with lyricism. It is the "emancipation of the ego." This formula is made to fit Victor Hugo, and it will fit Byron. But M. Brunetière would surely not deny that Walter Scott's work is objective and dramatic quite as often as it is lyrical. Yet what Englishman will be satisfied with a definition of *romantic* which excludes Scott? Indeed, M. Brunetière himself is respectful to the traditional meaning of the word. "Numerous definitions," he says, "have been given of Romanticism, and still others are continually being offered; and all, or almost all of them, contain a part of the truth. Mme. de Staël was right when she asserted in her 'Allemagne' that Paganism and Christianity, the North and the South, antiquity and the Middle Ages, having divided between them the history of literature, Romanticism in consequence, in contrast to Classicism, was a combination of chivalry, the Middle Ages, the literatures of the North, and Christianity. It should be noted, in this connection, that some thirty years later Heinrich Heine, in the book in which he will rewrite Mme. de Staël's, will not give such a very different idea of Romanticism." And if, in an analysis of the romantic movement throughout Europe, any single element in it can lay claim to the leading place, that element seems to me to be the return of each country to its national past; in other words, mediævalism.

A definition loses its usefulness when it is made to connote too much. Professor Herford says that the "organising conception" of his "Age of Wordsworth" is romanticism. But if Cowper and Wordsworth and Shelley are romantic, then almost all the literature of the years 1798–1830 is romantic. I prefer to think of Cowper as a naturalist, of Shelley as an idealist, and of Wordsworth as a transcendental realist, and to reserve the name romanticist for writers like Scott, Coleridge, and Keats; and I think the distinction a serviceable one. Again, I have been censured for omitting Blake from my former volume. The omission was deliberate, not accidental, and the grounds for it were given in the preface. Blake was not discovered until rather late in the nineteenth century. He was not a link in the chain of influence which I was tracing. I am glad to find my justification in a passage of Mr. Saintsbury's "History of Nineteenth Century Literature" (p. 13): "Blake exercised on the literary *history* of his time no influence, and occupied in it no position. . . . The public had little opportunity of seeing his pictures, and less of reading his books. . . . He was practically an unread man."

But I hope that this second volume may make more clear the unity of my design and the limits of my subject.

It is scarcely necessary to add that no absolute estimate is attempted of the writers whose works are described in this history. They are looked at exclusively from a single point of view. H. A. B.

April, 1901.

TABLE OF CONTENTS.

A HISTORY OF ENGLISH
ROMANTICISM.

CHAPTER I.

Walter Scott.*

IT was reserved for Walter Scott, "the Ariosto of the North," "the historiographer royal of feudalism," to accomplish the task which his eighteenth-century forerunners had essayed in vain. He possessed the true enchanter's wand, the historic imagination. With this in his hand, he raised the dead past to life, made it once more conceivable, made it even actual. Before Scott no genius of the highest order had lent itself wholly or mainly to retrospection. He is the middle point and the culmination of English romanticism. His name is, all in all, the most important on our list. "Towards him all the lines of the romantic revival converge."† The popular ballad, the Gothic romance, the Ossianic poetry, the

---

* Scott's translations from the German are considered in the author's earlier volume, "A History of English Romanticism in the Eighteenth Century." Incidental mention of Scott occurs throughout the same volume; and a few of the things there said are repeated, in substance though not in form, in the present chapter. It seemed better to risk some repetition than to sacrifice fulness of treatment here.

† "The Development of the English Novel," by Wilbur L. Cross, p. 131.

new German literature, the Scandinavian discoveries, these and other scattered rays of influence reach a focus in Scott. It is true that his delineation of feudal society is not final. There were sides of mediæval life which he did not know, or understand, or sympathize with, and some of these have been painted in by later artists. That his pictures have a coloring of modern sentiment is no arraignment of him but of the *genre*. All romanticists are resurrectionists; their art is an elaborate make-believe. It is enough for their purpose if the world which they re-create has the look of reality, the *verisimile* if not the *verum*. That Scott's genius was *in extenso* rather than *in intenso;* that his work is largely improvisation; that he was not a miniature, but a distemper painter, splashing large canvasses with a coarse brush and gaudy pigments, all these are commonplaces of criticism. Scott's handling was broad, vigorous, easy, careless, healthy, free. He was never subtle, morbid, or fantastic, and had no niceties or secrets. He was, as Coleridge said of Schiller, "master, not of the intense drama of passion, but the diffused drama of history." Therefore, because his qualities were popular and his appeal was made to the people, the general reader, he won a hearing for his cause, which Coleridge or Keats or Tieck, with his closer workmanship, could never have won. He first and he alone *popularised* romance. No literature dealing with the feudal past has ever had the currency and the universal success of Scott's. At no time has mediævalism held so large a place in comparison with other literary interests as during the years of his greatest vogue, say from 1805 to 1830.

The first point to be noticed about Scott is the thoroughness of his equipment. While never a scholar in the academic sense, he was, along certain chosen lines, a really learned man. He was thirty-four when he published "The Lay of the Last Minstrel" (1805), the first of his series of metrical romances and the first of his poems to gain popular favour. But for twenty years he had been storing his mind with the history, legends, and ballad poetry of the Scottish border, and was already a finished antiquarian. The bent and limitations of his genius were early determined, and it remained to the end wonderfully constant to its object. At the age of twelve he had begun a collection of manuscript ballads. His education in romance dated from the cradle. His lullabies were Jacobite songs; his grandmother told him tales of moss-troopers, and his Aunt Janet read him ballads from Ramsay's "Tea-table Miscellany," upon which his quick and tenacious memory fastened eagerly. The ballad of "Hardiknute," in this collection, he knew by heart before he could read. "It was the first poem I ever learnt—the last I shall ever forget." Dr. Blacklock introduced the young schoolboy to the poems of Ossian and of Spenser, and he committed to memory "whole duans of the one and cantos of the other." "Spenser," he says, "I could have read forever. Too young to trouble myself about the allegory, I considered all the knights and ladies and dragons and giants in their outward and exoteric sense, and God only knows how delighted I was to find myself in such society." A little later Percy's "Reliques" fell into his hands, with results that have already been described.*

As soon as he got access to the circulating library in Edinburgh, he began to devour its works of fiction, char-

* Vol. i., p. 300.

acteristically rejecting love stories and domestic tales, but laying hold upon "all that was adventurous and romantic," and in particular upon "everything which touched on knight-errantry." For two or three years he used to spend his holidays with his schoolmate, John Irving, on Arthur's Seat or Salisbury Crags, where they read together books like "The Castle of Otranto" and the poems of Spenser and Ariosto; or composed and narrated to each other "interminable tales of battles and enchantments" and "legends in which the martial and the miraculous always predominated." The education of Edward Waverley, as described in the third chapter of Scott's first novel, was confessedly the novelist's own education. In the "large Gothic room" which was the library of Waverley Honour, the young book-worm pored over "old historical chronicles" and the writings of Pulci, Froissart, Brantome, and De la Noue; and became "well acquainted with Spenser, Drayton, and other poets who have exercised themselves on romantic fiction—of all themes the most fascinating to a youthful imagination."

Yet even thus early, a certain solidity was apparent in Scott's studies. "To the romances and poetry which I chiefly delighted in," he writes, "I had always added the study of history, especially as connected with military events." He interested himself, for example, in the art of fortification; and when confined to his bed by a childish illness, found amusement in modelling fortresses and "arranging shells and seeds and pebbles so as to represent encountering armies. . . . I fought my way thus through Vertot's ' Knights of Malta '—a book which, as it hovered between history and romance, was exceedingly dear to me."

Every genius is self-educated, and we find Scott from the first making instinctive selections and rejections among the various kinds of knowledge offered him. At school he would learn no Greek, and wrote a theme in which he maintained, to the wrath of his teacher, that Ariosto was a better poet than Homer. In later life he declared that he had forgotten even the letters of the Greek alphabet. Latin would have fared as badly, had not his interest in Matthew Paris and other monkish chroniclers " kept up a kind of familiarity with the language even in its rudest state." " To my Gothic ear, the ' Stabat Mater,' the ' Dies Iræ,'* and some of the other hymns of the Catholic Church are more solemn and affecting than the fine classical poetry of Buchanan." In our examination of Scott's early translations from the German,† it has been noticed how exclusively he was attracted by the romantic department of that literature, passing over, for instance, Goethe's maturer work, to fix upon his juvenile drama " Götz von Berlichingen." Similarly he learned Italian just to read in the original the romantic poets Tasso, Ariosto, Boiardo, and Pulci. When he first went to London in 1799, "his great anxiety," reports Lockhart, " was to examine the antiquities of the Tower and Westminster Abbey, and to make some researches among the MSS. of the British Museum." From Oxford, which he visited in 1803, he brought away only " a grand but indistinct picture of towers and chapels and oriels and vaulted halls "; having met there a recep-

---

* The sixth canto of the "Lay" closes with a few lines translated from the "Dies Iræ" and chanted by the monks in Melrose Abbey.
† Vol. i., pp. 389–404.

tion which, as he modestly acknowledges, " was more than
such a truant to the classic page as myself was entitled to
expect at the source of classic learning." Finally, in his
last illness, when sent to Rome to recover from the effects
of a paralytic stroke, his ruling passion was strong in
death. He examined with eagerness the remains of the
mediæval city, but appeared quite indifferent to that older
Rome which speaks to the classical student. It will be
remembered that just the contrary of this was true of Addison, when he was in Italy a century before.* Scott
was at no pains to deny or to justify the one-sidedness of
his culture. But when Erskine remonstrated with him
for rambling on

> "through brake and maze
> With harpers rude, of barbarous days,"

and urged him to compose a regular epic on classical
lines, he good-naturedly but resolutely put aside the ad-
vice.

> "Nay, Erskine, nay—On the wild hill
> Let the wild heath-bell † flourish still . . . .
> Though wild as cloud, as stream, as gale,
> Flow forth, flow unrestrained, my tale!" ‡

* Vol. i., pp. 48-49.
† "Scott was entirely incapable of entering into the spirit
of any classical scene. He was strictly a Goth and a Scot,
and his sphere of sensation may be almost exactly limited by
the growth of heather."—Ruskin, "Modern Painters," vol.
iii., p. 317.
‡ "Marmion": Introduction to Canto third. In the preface to "The Bridal of Triermain," the poet says: "According
to the author's idea of Romantic Poetry, as distinguished
from Epic, the former comprehends a fictitious narrative,
framed and combined at the pleasure of the writer; beginning
and ending as he may judge best; which neither exacts nor
refuses the use of supernatural machinery; which is free
from the technical rules of the *Epée.* . . . In a word, the
author is absolute master of his country and its inhabitants."

Scott's letters to Erskine, Ellis, Leyden, Ritson, Miss Seward, and other literary correspondents are filled with discussions of antiquarian questions and the results of his favourite reading in old books and manuscripts. He communicates his conclusions on the subject of " Arthur and Merlin " or on the authorship of the old metrical romance of " Sir Tristram." * He has been copying manuscripts in the Advocates' Library at Edinburgh. In 1791 he read papers before the Speculative Society on " The Origin of the Feudal System," " The Authenticity of Ossian's Poems," " The Origin of the Scandinavian Mythology." Lockhart describes two note-books in Scott's handwriting, with the date 1792, containing memoranda of ancient court records about Walter Scott and his wife, Dame Janet Beaton, the " Ladye " of Branksome in the " Lay "; extracts from " Guerin de Montglave "; copies of " Vegtam's Kvitha " and the " Death-Song of Regner Lodbrog," with Gray's English versions; Cnut's verses on passing Ely Cathedral; the ancient English " Cuckoo Song," and other rubbish of the kind.† When in 1803 he began to contribute articles to the *Edinburgh Review*, his chosen topics were such as " Amadis of Gaul," Ellis'

* Scott's ascription of "Sir Tristram " to Thomas the Rhymer, or Thomas of Erceldoune, was doubtless a mistake. His edition of the romance was printed in 1804. In 1800 he had begun a prose tale, "Thomas the Rhymer," a fragment of which is given in the preface to the General Edition of the Waverley Novels (1829). This old legendary poet and prophet, who flourished *circa* 1280, and was believed to have been carried off by the Queen of Faerie into Eildon Hill, fascinated Scott's imagination strongly. See his version of the "True Thomas'" story in the " Minstrelsy," as also the editions of this very beautiful romance in Child's "Ballads," in the publications of the E. E. Text So. ; and by Alois Brandl, Berlin : 1880.

† See vol. i., p. 390.

"Specimens of Ancient English Poetry," Godwin's "Chaucer," Sibbald's "Chronicle of Scottish Poetry," Evans' "Old Ballads," Todd's "Spenser," "The Life and Works of Chatterton," Southey's translation of "The Cid," etc.

Scott's preparation for the work which he had to do was more than adequate. His reading along chosen lines was probably more extensive and minute than any man's of his generation. The introductions and notes to his poems and novels are even overburdened with learn-ing. But this, though important, was but the lesser part of his advantage. "The old-maidenly genius of anti-quarianism" could produce a Strutt * or even perhaps a Warton; but it needed the touch of the creative imagi-nation to turn the dead material of knowledge into works of art that have delighted millions of readers for a hun-dred years in all civilised lands and tongues.

The key to Scott's romanticism is his intense local feeling.† That attachment to place which, in most men, is a sort of animal instinct, was with him a passion. To set the imagination at work some emotional stimulus is required. The angry pride of Byron, Shelley's revolt against authority, Keats' almost painfully acute sensitive-ness to beauty, supplied the nervous irritation which was wanting in Scott's slower, stronger, and heavier tempera-ment. The needed impetus came to him from his love of country. Byron and Shelley were torn up by the roots and flung abroad; but Scott had struck his roots deep

---

* See the General Preface to the Waverley Novels for some remarks on "Queenhoo Hall" which Strutt began and Scott completed.

† *Cf.* vol. i., p. 344.

into native soil. His absorption in the past and reverence for everything that was old, his conservative prejudices and aristocratic ambitions, all had their source in
this feeling. Scott's Toryism was of a different spring
from Wordsworth's and Coleridge's. It was not a reaction from disappointed radicalism; nor was it the result
of reasoned conviction. It was inborn and was nursed
into a sentimental Jacobitism by ancestral traditions and
by an early prepossession in favour of the Stuarts—a
Scottish dynasty—reinforced by encounters with men in
the Highlands who had been out in the '45. It did not
interfere with a practical loyalty to the reigning house
and with what seems like a somewhat exaggerated defer-
ence to George IV. Personally the most modest of men,
he was proud to trace his descent from "auld Wat of
Harden" * and to claim kinship with the bold Buccleuch.
He used to make annual pilgrimages to Harden Tower,
"the *incunabula* of his race"; and "in the earlier part of
his life," says Lockhart, "he had nearly availed himself
of his kinsman's permission to fit up the dilapidated *peel*
for his summer residence."

Byron wrote: "I twine my hope of being remembered
in my line with my land's language." But Scott wished
to associate his name with the land itself. Abbotsford
was more to him than Newstead could ever have been to
Byron; although Byron was a peer and inherited his
domain, while Scott was a commoner and created his.
Too much has been said in condemnation of Scott's

---

* "I am therefore descended from that ancient chieftain
whose name I have made to ring in many a ditty, and from
his fair dame, the Flower of Yarrow—no bad genealogy for
a Border minstrel."

weakness in this respect; that his highest ambition was
to become a *laird* and found a family; that he was more
gratified when the King made him a baronet than when
the public bought his books; that the expenses of Abbotsford and the hospitalities which he extended to all
comers wasted his time and finally brought about his
bankruptcy. Leslie Stephen and others have even made
merry over Scott's Gothic,* comparing his plaster-of-
Paris 'scutcheons and ceilings in imitation of carved oak
with the pinchbeck architecture of Strawberry Hill, and
intimating that the feudalism in his romances was only a
shade more genuine than the feudalism of "The Castle
of Otranto." Scott was imprudent; Abbotsford was his
weakness, but it was no ignoble weakness. If the ideal
of the life which he proposed to himself there was scarcely
a heroic one, neither was it vulgar or selfish. The artist
or the philosopher should perhaps be superior to the ambition of owning land and having "a stake in the country," but the ambition is a very human one and has its
good side. In Scott the desire was more social than
personal. It was not that title and territory were feathers
in his cap, but that they bound him more closely to the
dear soil of Scotland and to the national, historic past.

The only deep passion in Scott's poetry is patriotism,
the passion of place. In his metrical romances the rush
of the narrative and the vivid, picturesque beauty of the

* "He neither cared for painting nor sculpture, and was to-
tally incapable of forming a judgment about them. He had
some confused love of Gothic architecture because it was dark,
picturesque, old and like nature ; but could not tell the worst
from the best, and built for himself probably the most incongruous and ugly pile that gentlemanly modernism ever devised."—Ruskin, "Modern Painters," vol. iii., p. 271.

descriptions are indeed exciting to the imagination; but it is only when the chord of national feeling is touched that the verse grows lyrical, that the heart is reached, and that tears come into the reader's eyes, as they must have done into the poet's. A dozen such passages occur at once to the memory; the last stand of the Scottish nobles around their king at Flodden; the view of Edinburgh— "mine own romantic town "—from Blackford Hill:

> "Fitz-Eustace' heart felt closely pent:
>   As if to give his rapture vent,
> The spur he to his charger lent,
>   And raised his bridle-hand,
> And, making demi-volte in air,
> Cried, 'Where's the coward that would not dare
>   To fight for such a land?'"

and the still more familiar opening of the sixth canto in the "Lay"—"Breathes there the man," etc.:

> "O Caledonia! stern and wild,
>   Meet nurse for a poetic child!
> Land of brown heath and shaggy wood,
> Land of the mountain and the flood,
> Land of my sires! what mortal hand
> Can e'er untie the filial band
> That knits me to thy rugged strand?"

In such a mood geography becomes poetry and names are music.* Scott said to Washington Irving that if he did not see the heather at least once a year, he thought he would die.

Lockhart tells how the sound that he loved best of all sounds was in his dying ears—the flow of the Tweed over its pebbles.

Significant, therefore, is Scott's treatment of landscape, and the difference in this regard between himself and

* See vol. i., p. 200.

his great contemporaries. His friend, Mr. Morritt of Rokeby, testifies: "He was but half satisfied with the most beautiful scenery when he could not connect it with some local legend." Scott had to the full the romantic love of mountain and lake, yet "to me," he confesses, "the wandering over the field of Bannockburn was the source of more exquisite pleasure than gazing upon the celebrated landscape from the battlements of Stirling Castle. I do not by any means infer that I was dead to the feeling of picturesque scenery. . . . But show me an old castle or a field of battle and I was at home at once." And again: "The love of natural beauty, more especially when combined with ancient ruins or remains of our fathers' piety * or splendour, became with me an insatiable passion." It was not in this sense that high mountains were a "passion" to Byron, nor yet to Wordsworth. In a letter to Miss Seward, Scott wrote of popular poetry: "Much of its peculiar charm is indeed, I believe, to be attributed solely to its *locality*. . . . In some verses of that eccentric but admirable poet Coleridge † he talks of

> 'An old rude tale that suited well
> The ruins wild and hoary.'

I think there are few who have not been in some degree touched with this local sympathy. Tell a peasant an ordinary tale of robbery and murder, and perhaps you

* The *Abbey* of Tintern was irrelevant to Wordsworth.— Herford, "The Age of Wordsworth," Int., p. xx.

† "Dear Sir Walter Scott and myself were exact, but harmonious, opposites in this;—that every old ruin, hill, river or tree called up in his mind a host of historical or biographical associations; . . . whereas, for myself . . . I believe I should walk over the plain of Marathon without taking more interest in it than in any other plain of similar features."—Coleridge, "Table Talk," August 4, 1833.

may fail to interest him; but, to excite his terrors, you assure him it happened on the very heath he usually crosses, or to a man whose family he has known, and you rarely meet such a mere image of humanity as remains entirely unmoved. I suspect it is pretty much the same with myself."

Scott liked to feel solid ground of history, or at least of legend, under his feet. He connected his wildest tales, like "Glenfinlas" and "The Eve of St. John," with definite names and places. This Antæus of romance lost strength, as soon as he was lifted above the earth. With Coleridge it was just the contrary. The moment his moonlit, vapory enchantments touched ground, the contact "precipitated the whole solution." In 1813 Scott had printed "The Bridal of Triermain" anonymously, with a preface designed to mislead the public; having contrived, by way of a joke, to fasten the authorship of the piece upon Erskine. This poem is as pure fantasy as Tennyson's "Day Dream," and tells the story of a knight who, in obedience to a vision and the instructions of an ancient sage "sprung from Druid sires," enters an enchanted castle and frees the Princess Gyneth, a natural daughter of King Arthur, from the spell that has bound her for five hundred years. But true to his instinct, the poet lays his scene not *in vacuo*, but near his own beloved borderland. He found, in Burns' "Antiquities of Westmoreland and Cumberland" mention of a line of Rolands de Vaux, lords of Triermain, a fief of the barony of Gilsland; and this furnished him a name for his hero. He found in Hutchinson's "Excursion to the Lakes" the description of a cluster of rocks in the Vale of St. John's, which looked, at a distance, like a Gothic castle; this supplied him with a hint for the whole adventure. Meanwhile Coleridge had been living in the Lake Country. The wheels of his "Christabel" had got hopelessly mired, and he now borrowed a horse from Sir Walter and hitched it to his own wagon. He took over Sir Roland de Vaux of Triermain and made him the putative father of his mysterious Geraldine, although, in compliance with Scott's romance, the embassy that goes over the mountains to Sir Roland's castle can find no trace of it. In Part I. Sir Leoline's own castle stood nowhere in particular. In Part II. it is transferred to Cumberland, a mistake in art almost as grave as if the Ancient Mariner had brought his ship to port at Liverpool.

Wordsworth visited the "great Minstrel of the Border" at Abbotsford in 1831, shortly before Scott set out for Naples, and the two poets went in company to the ruins of Newark Castle. It is characteristic that in "Yarrow Revisited," which commemorates the incident, the Bard of Rydal should think it necessary to offer an apology for his distinguished host's habit of romanticising nature—that nature which Wordsworth, romantic neither in temper nor choice of subject, treated after so different a fashion.

> "Nor deem that localised Romance
>   Plays false with our affections ;
> Unsanctifies our tears—made sport
>   For fanciful dejections :
> Ah no ! the visions of the past
>   Sustain the heart in feeling
> Life as she is—our changeful Life,
>   With friends and kindred dealing."

The apology, after all, is only half-hearted. For while Wordsworth esteemed Scott highly and was careful to speak publicly of his work with a qualified respect, it is well known that, in private, he set little value upon it, and once somewhat petulantly declared that all Scott's poetry was not worth sixpence. He wrote to Scott, of "Marmion": "I think your end has been attained. That it is not the end which I should wish you to propose to yourself, you will be aware." He had visited Scott at Lasswade as early as 1803, and in recording his impressions notes that "his conversation was full of anecdote and averse from disquisition." The minstrel was a *raconteur* and lived in the past; the bard was a moralist and lived in the present.

There are several poems of Wordsworth's and Scott's touching upon common ground which serve to contrast their methods sharply and to illustrate in a striking way the precise character of Scott's romanticism. "Helvellyn" and "Fidelity" were written independently and celebrate the same incident. In 1805 a young man lost his way on the Cumberland mountains and perished of exposure. Three months afterwards his body was found, his faithful dog still watching beside it. Scott was a lover of dogs—loved them warmly, individually; so to speak, personally; and all dogs instinctively loved Scott.*

Wordsworth had a sort of tepid, theoretical benevolence towards the animal creation in general. Yet as between the two poets, the advantage in depth of feeling

---

* See the delightful anecdote preserved by Carlyle about the little Blenheim cocker who hated the "genus acrid-quack" and formed an immediate attachment to Sir Walter. Wordsworth was far from being an acrid quack, or even a solemn prig—another genus hated of dogs—but there was something a little unsympathetic in his personality. The dalesmen liked poor Hartley Coleridge better.

is, as usual, with Wordsworth. Both render, with perhaps equal power, though in characteristically different
ways, the impression of the austere and desolate grandeur
of the mountain scenery. But the thought to which
Wordsworth leads up is the mysterious divineness of instinct

> ". . . that strength of feeling, great
> Above all human estimate:"—

while Scott conducts his story to the reflection that Nature has given the dead man a more stately funeral than
the Church could have given, a comparison seemingly
dragged in for the sake of a stanzaful of his favourite
Gothic imagery.

> "When a Prince to the fate of the Peasant has yielded,
>   The tapestry waves dark round the dim-lighted hall;
> With 'scutcheons of silver the coffin is shielded,
>   And pages stand mute by the canopied pall:
> Through the courts at deep midnight the torches are gleam-
>   ing,
> In the proudly arched chapel the banners are beaming,
> Far adown the long aisle sacred music is streaming,
>   Lamenting a chief of the people should fall."

Wordsworth and Landor, who seldom agreed, agreed
that Scott's most imaginative line was the verse in
"Helvellyn":

> "When the wind waved his garment how oft didst thou
>   start!"

In several of his poems Wordsworth handled legendary
subjects, and it is most instructive here to notice his
avoidance of the romantic note, and to imagine how Scott
would have managed the same material. In the prefa-
tory note to "The White Doe of Rylstone," Wordsworth
himself pointed out the difference. "The subject being

taken from feudal times has led to its being compared to some of Sir Walter Scott's poems that belong to the same age and state of society. The comparison is inconsiderate. Sir Walter pursued the customary and very natural course of conducting an action, presenting various turns of fortune, to some outstanding point on which the mind might rest as a termination or catastrophe. The course I attempted to pursue is entirely different. Everything that is attempted by the principal personages in 'The White Doe' fails, so far as its object is external and substantial. So far as it is moral and spiritual it succeeds."

This poem is founded upon "The Rising in the North," a ballad given in the "Reliques," which recounts the insurrection of the Earls of Northumberland and Westmoreland against Elizabeth in 1569. Richard Norton of Rylstone, with seven stalwart sons, joined in the rising, carrying a banner embroidered with a red cross and the five wounds of Christ. The story bristled with opportunities for the display of feudal pomp, and it is obvious upon what points in the action Scott would have laid the emphasis; the muster of the tenantry of the great northern Catholic houses of Percy and Neville; the high mass celebrated by the insurgents in Durham Cathedral; the march of the Nortons to Brancepeth; the eleven days' siege of Barden Tower; the capture and execution of Marmaduke and Ambrose; and— by way of episode— the Battle of Neville's Cross in 1346.* But in conformity to the principle announced in the preface to the

---

* Scott could scarcely have forborne to introduce the figure of the Queen of Scots, to insure whose marriage with Norfolk was one of the objects of the rising.

2

" Lyrical Ballads "—that the feeling should give importance to the incidents and situation, not the incidents and
situation to the feeling—Wordsworth treats all this outward action as merely preparatory to the true purpose of
his poem, a study of the discipline of sorrow, of ruin and
bereavement patiently endured by the Lady Emily, the
only daughter and survivor of the Norton house.

> "Action is transitory—a step, a blow. . . .
>   Suffering is permanent, obscure and dark,
>   And has the nature of infinity.
>   Yet through that darkness (infinite though it seem
>   And irremoveable) gracious openings lie. . . .
>   Even to the fountain-head of peace divine."

With the story of the Nortons the poet connects a local
tradition which he found in Whitaker's " History of the
Deanery of Craven "; of a white doe which haunted the
churchyard of Bolton Priory.   Between this gentle creature and the forlorn Lady of Rylstone he establishes the
mysterious and soothing sympathy which he was always
fond of imagining between the soul of man and the things
of nature.*

Or take again the " Song at the Feast of Brougham
Castle," an incident in the Wars of the Roses.   Lord
Clifford, who had been hidden away in infancy from the
vengeance of the Yorkists and reared as a shepherd, is
restored to the estates and honours of his ancestors.
High in the festal hall the impassioned minstrel strikes
his harp and sings the triumph of Lancaster, urging the
shepherd lord to emulate the warlike prowess of his fore-
fathers.

* For a full review of "The White Doe" the reader should
consult Principal Shairp's "Aspects of Poetry," 1881.

"Armour rusting in his halls
On the blood of Clifford calls;
'Quell the Scot,' exclaims the Lance—
Bear me to the heart of France
Is the longing of the Shield."

Thus far the minstrel, and he has Sir Walter with
him; for this is evidently the part of the poem that he
liked and remembered, when he noted in his journal that
"Wordsworth could be popular* if he would—witness
the 'Feast at Brougham Castle'—'Song of the Cliffords,'
I think, is the name." But the exultant strain ceases
and the poet himself speaks, and with the transition in
feeling comes a change in the verse; the minstrel's song
was in the octosyllabic couplet associated with metrical
romance. But this Clifford was no fighter—none of
Scott's heroes. Nature had educated him.

"In him the savage virtue of the Race" was dead.

"Love had he found in huts where poor men lie;
His daily teachers had been woods and rills,
The silence that is in the starry sky,
The sleep that is among the lonely hills."

Once more, consider the pronounced difference in sentiment between the description of the chase in "Hart-
leap Well" and the opening passage of "The Lady of
the Lake":

"The stag at eve had drunk his fill.
Where danced the moon on Monan's rill," etc.†

* Scott averred that Wordsworth offended public taste on
system.
† This is incomparable, not only as a masterpiece of romantic narrative, but for the spirited and natural device by
which the hero is conducted to his adventure. R. L. Stevenson and other critics have been rather hard upon Scott's defects as an artist. He was indeed no stylist: least of all a
precieux. There are no close-set mosaics in his somewhat

Scott was a keen sportsman, and his sympathy was with the hunter.* Wordsworth's, of course, was with the quarry. The knight in his poem—who bears not unsuggestively the name of "Sir Walter"—has outstripped all his companions, like Fitz James, and is the only one in at the death. To commemorate his triumph he frames a basin for the spring whose waters were stirred by his victim's dying breath; he plants three stone pillars to mark the creature's hoof-prints in its marvellous leap from the mountain to the springside; and he builds a pleasure house and an arbour where he comes with his paramour to make merry in the summer days. But Nature sets her seal of condemnation upon the cruelty and vainglory of man. "The spot is curst"; no flowers or grass will grow there; no beast will drink of the fountain. Part I. tells the story without enthusiasm but without comment. Part II. draws the lesson

> "Never to blend our pleasure or our pride
> With sorrow of the meanest thing that feels."

The song of Wordsworth's "Solitary Reaper" derives a pensive sorrow from "old, unhappy, far-off things and battles long ago." But to Scott the battle is not far off, but a vivid and present reality. When he visited the

---

slip-shod prose, and he did not seek for the right word "with moroseness," like Landor. But, in his large fashion, he was skilful in inventing impressive effects. Another instance is the solitary trumpet that breathed its "note of defiance" in the lists of Ashby-de-la-Zouch, which has the genuine melodramatic thrill—like the horn of Hernani or the bell that tolls in "Venice Preserved."

* See the "Hunting Song" in his continuation of "Queen-hoo Hall"—

> "Waken, lords and ladies gay,
> On the mountain dawns the day."

Trosachs glen, his thought painly was, "What a place for a fight!" And when James looks down on Loch Katrine his first reflection is, "What a scene were here . . .

> "For princely pomp or churchman's pride!
> On this bold brow a lordly tower;
> In that soft vale a lady's bower;
> On yonder meadow, far away,
> The turrets of a cloister grey," etc.

The most romantic scene was not romantic enough for Scott till his imagination had peopled it with the life of a vanished age.

The literary forms which Scott made peculiarly his own, and in which the greater part of his creative work was done, are three: the popular ballad, the metrical romance, and the historical novel in prose. His point of departure was the ballad.* The material amassed in his Liddesdale "raids"—begun in 1792 and continued for seven successive years—was given to the world in the "Minstrelsy of the Scottish Border" (Vols. I. and II. in 1802; Vol. III. in 1803), a collection of ballads historical, legendary, and romantic, with an abundant apparatus in the way of notes and introductions, illustrating the history, antiquities, manners, traditions, and superstitions of the Borderers. Forty-three of the ballads in the "Minstrelsy" had never been printed before; and of the remainder the editor gave superior versions, choosing with sureness of taste the best among variant readings, and with a more intimate knowledge of local ways and language than any previous ballad-fancier had commanded. He handled his texts more faithfully than Percy, rarely substituting lines of his own. "From

---

* See vol. i., pp. 277 and 390.

among a hundred corruptions," says Lockhart, " he seized, with instinctive tact, the primitive diction and imagery, and produced strains in which the unbroken energy of half-civilised ages, their stern and deep passions, their daring adventures and cruel tragedies, and even their rude wild humour are reflected with almost the brightness of a Homeric mirror."

In the second volume of the "Minstrelsy" were included what Scott calls his "first serious attempts in verse," viz., "Glenfinlas" and "The Eve of St. John," which had been already printed in Lewis' "Tales of Wonder." Both pieces are purely romantic, with a strong tincture of the supernatural; but the first—Scott himself draws the distinction—is a "legendary poem," and the second alone a proper "ballad." "Glenfinlas," * founded on a Gaelic legend, tells how a Highland chieftain while hunting in Perthshire, near the scene of "The Lady of the Lake," is lured from his bothie at night and torn to pieces by evil spirits. There is no attempt here to preserve the language of popular poetry; stanzas abound in a diction of which the following is a fair example:

> "Long have I sought sweet Mary's heart,
>   And dropp'd the tear and heaved the sigh:
> But vain the lover's wily art
>   Beneath a sister's watchful eye."

" The Eve of St. John " employs common ballad stuff, the visit of a murdered lover's ghost to his lady's bedside—

"At the lone midnight hour, when bad spirits have power"—

but the poet, as usual, anchors his weird nightmares firmly to real names and times and places, Dryburgh

* The Glen of the Green Women.

Abbey, the black rood of Melrose, the Eildon-tree, the bold Buccleuch, and the Battle of Ancram Moor (1545). The exact scene of the tragedy is Smailholme Tower, the ruined keep on the crags above his grandfather's farm at Sandynowe, which left such an indelible impression on Scott's childish imagination.* "The Eve" is in ballad style and verse:

> "Thou liest, thou liest, thou little foot page,
>   Loud dost thou lie to me!
> For that knight is cold, and low laid in the mould,
>   All under the Eildon tree."

In his "Essay on the Imitation of Popular Poetry," Scott showed that he understood the theory of ballad composition. When he took pains, he could catch the very manner as well as the spirit of ancient minstrelsy; but if his work is examined under the microscope it is easy to detect flaws. The technique of the Pre-Raphaelites and other modern balladists, like Rossetti and Morris, is frequently finer; they reproduce more scrupulously the formal characteristics of popular poetry: the burden,

---

* "And still I thought that shattered tower
    The mightiest work of human power;
    And marvelled as the aged hind
    With some strange tale bewitched my mind,
    Of foragers who, with headlong force,
    Down from that strength had spurred their horse,
    Their Southern rapine to renew,
    Far in the distant Cheviots blue;
    And, home returning, filled the hall
    With revel, wassail-rout and brawl."—"Marmion." Introduction to Canto Third. See Lockhart for a description of the view from Smailholme, *à propos* of the stanza in "The Eve of St. John":

    "That lady sat in mournful mood;
        Looked over hill and vale:
    O'er Tweed's fair flood, and Mertoun's wood,
        And all down Teviot dale."

the sing-song repetitions, the quaint turns of phrase, the
imperfect rimes, the innocent, childlike air of the mediæval tale-tellers. Scott's vocabulary is not consist-
ently archaic, and he was not always careful to avoid
locutions out of keeping with the style of *Volkspoesie.**
He was by no means a rebel against eighteenth-century
usages.† In his prose he is capable of speaking of a lady
as an "elegant female." In his poetry he will begin a
ballad thus:

> "The Pope he was saying the high, high mass
>   All on St. Peter's day";

and then a little later fall into this kind of thing:

> "There the rapt poet's step may rove,
>   And yield the muse the day:
> There Beauty, led by timid Love,
>   May shun the tell-tale ray," etc. ‡

It is possible to name single pieces like "The Ancient
Mariner," and "La Belle Dame sans Merci," and "Rose-
Mary," of a rarer imaginative quality and a more perfect
workmanship than Scott often attains; yet upon the whole
and in the mass, no modern balladry matches the success
of his. The Pre-Raphaelites were deliberate artists, con-
sciously reproducing an extinct literary form; but Scott
had lived himself back into the social conditions out of
which ballad poetry was born. His best pieces of this
class do not strike us as imitations but as original, spon-

* See vol. i., pp. 394–395.
† Scott's verse "is touched both with the facile redundance
of the mediæval romances in which he was steeped, and with
the meretricious phraseology of the later eighteenth century,
which he was too genuine a literary Tory wholly to put aside."
—"The Age of Wordsworth," C. H. Herford, London, 1897.
‡ "The Gray Brother" in vol. iii. of the "Minstrelsy."

taneous, and thoroughly alive. Such are, to particularise but a few, "Jock o' Hazeldean," "Cadyow Castle," on the assassination of the Regent Murray; "The Reiver's Wedding," a fragment preserved in Lockhart's "Life"; "Elspeth's Ballad" ("The Red Harlow") in "The Antiquary"; Madge Wildfire's songs in "The Heart of Mid-Lothian," and David Gellatley's in "Waverley"; besides the other scraps and snatches of minstrelsy too numerous for mention, sown through the novels and longer poems. For in spite of detraction, Walter Scott remains one of the foremost British lyrists. In Mr. Palgrave's "Treasury" he is represented by a larger number of selections than either Milton, Byron, Burns, Campbell, Keats, or Herrick; making an easy fourth to Wordsworth, Shakspere, and Shelley. And in marked contrast with Shelley especially, it is observable of Scott's contributions to this anthology that they are not the utterance of the poet's personal emotion; they are coronachs, pibrochs, gathering songs, narrative ballads, and the like—objective, dramatic lyrics touched always with the light of history or legend.

The step from ballad to ballad-epic is an easy one, and it was by a natural evolution that the one passed into the other in Scott's hands. "The Lay of the Last Minstrel" (1805) was begun as a ballad on the local tradition of Gilpin Horner and at the request of the Countess of Dalkeith, who told Scott the story. But his imagination was so full that the poem soon overflowed its limits and expanded into a romance illustrative of the ancient manners of the Border. The pranks of the goblin page run in and out through the web of the tale, a slender and somewhat inconsequential thread of *diablerie*. Byron had his

laugh at it in "English Bards and Scotch Reviewers"; *
and in a footnote on the passage, he adds: "Never was
any plan so incongruous and absurd as the groundwork
of this production." The criticism was not altogether
undeserved; for the "Lay" is a typical example of romantic, as distinguished from classic, art both in its
strength and in its weakness; brilliant in passages, faulty
in architechtonic, and uneven in execution. Its supernatural machinery—Byron said that it had more "gram-
arye" than grammar—is not impressive, if due exception
be made of the opening of Michael Scott's tomb in Canto
Second.

When the "Minstrelsy" was published, it was remarked
that it "contained the elements of a hundred historical
romances." It was from such elements that Scott built
up the structure of his poem about the nucleus which the
Countess of Dalkeith had given him. He was less concerned, as he acknowledged, to tell a coherent story than
to paint a picture of the scenery and the old warlike life
of the Border; that *tableau large de la vie* which the
French romanticists afterwards professed to be the aim
of their novels and dramas. The feud of the Scotts and
Carrs furnished him with a historic background; with
this he enwove a love story of the Romeo and Juliet pattern. He rebuilt Melrose Abbey, and showed it by moonlight; set Lords Dacre and Howard marching on a
Warden-raid, and roused the border clans to meet them;
threw out dramatic character sketches of "stark moss-

---

* "And goblin brats, of Gilpin Horner's brood,
    Decoy young border-nobles through the wood,
    And skip at every step, Lord knows how high,
    And frighten foolish babes, the Lord knows why."

riding Scots " like Wat Tinlinn and William of Deloraine; and finally enclosed the whole in a *cadre* most happily invented, the venerable, pathetic figure of the old minstrel who tells the tale to the Duchess of Monmouth at Newark Castle.

The love story is perhaps the weakest part of the poem. Henry Cranstoun and Margaret of Branksome are nothing but lay figures. Scott is always a little nervous when the lover and the lady are left alone together. The fair dames in the audience expect a tender scene, but the harper pleads his age, by way of apology, gets the business over as decently as may be, and hastens on with comic precipitation to the fighting, which he thoroughly enjoys.*

The " light-horseman stanza " which Scott employed in his longer poems was caught from the recitation by Sir John Stoddart of a portion of Coleridge's " Christabel," then still in manuscript. The norm of the verse was the eight-syllabled riming couplet used in most of the English metrical romances of the thirteenth and fourteenth centuries. It is a form of verse which moves more swiftly than blank verse or the heroic couplet, and is perhaps better suited for romantic poetry.† But it is liable to grow monotonous in a long poem, and Coleridge's unsurpassed skill as a metrist was exerted to give it freedom, richness, and variety by the introduction of anapæstic lines and alternate rimes and triplets, breaking up the couplets into a series of irregular stanzas.

---

* "Now leave we Margaret and her knight
  To tell you of the approaching fight."
  —Canto Fifth, xiii.
† Landor says oddly of Warton that he "had lost his ear by laying it down on low swampy places, on ballads and sonnets."

With "The Lay of the Last Minstrel" romanticism
came of age and entered on its career of triumph.   One
wishes that Collins and Tom Warton might have lived
to hail it as the light, at last, towards which they had
struggled through the cold obstruction of the eighteenth
century.   One fancies Dr. Johnson's disgust over this
new Scotch monstrosity, which had every quality that he
disliked except blank verse; or Gray's delight in it, tempered by a critical disapproval of its loose construction
and irregularity.   Scott's romances in prose and verse
are still so universally known as to make any review of
them here individually an impertinence.   Their impact
on contemporary Europe was instantaneous and widespread.   There is no record elsewhere in literary history
of such success.   Their immense sales, the innumerable
editions and translations and imitations of them, are matters of familiar knowledge.   Poem followed poem, and
novel, novel in swift and seemingly exhaustless succession, and each was awaited by the public with unabated
expectancy.   Here once more was a poet who could tell
the world a story that it wanted to hear; a poet

> "Such as it had
> In the ages glad,
> Long ago."

The Homeric * quality which criticism has attributed
or denied to these poems is really there.   The difference,
the inferiority is obvious of course.   They are not in the
grand style; they are epic on a lower plane, ballad-epic,
bastard-epic perhaps, but they are epic.   No English verse

* Does not the quarrel of Richard and Philip in "The Talisman" remind one irresistibly of Achilles and Agamemnon in
the "Iliad"?

narrative except Chaucer's ranks, as a whole, above Scott's. Chaucer's disciple, William Morris, has an equal flow and continuity, and keeps a more even level of style; but his story-telling is languid compared with Scott's. The latter is greater in the dynamic than in the static department—in scenes of rapid action and keen excitement. His show passages are such as the fight in the Trosachs, Flodden Field, William of Deloraine's ride to Melrose, the trial of Constance, the muster on the Borough Moor, Marmion's defiance to Douglas, the combat of James and Roderick Dhu, the summons of the fiery cross, and the kindling of the need-fires—those romantic equivalents of the λαμπαδηφόροι in the "Agamemnon."

In the series of long poems which followed the "Lay," Scott deserted the Border and brought in new subjects of romantic interest, the traditions of Flodden and Bannockburn, the manners of the Gaelic clansmen, and the wild scenery of the Perthshire Highlands, the life of the Western Islands, and the rugged coasts of Argyle. Only two of these tales are concerned with the Middle Ages, strictly speaking: "The Lord of the Isles" (1813), in which the action begins in 1307; and "Harold the Dauntless" (1817), in which the period is the time of the Danish settlements in Northumbria. "Rokeby" (1812) is concerned with the Civil War. The scene is laid in Yorkshire. "Marmion" (1808), and "The Lady of the Lake" (1810), like "The Lay of the Last Minstrel," had to do with the sixteenth century, but the poet imported mediæval elements into all of these by the frankest anachronisms. He restored St. Hilda's Abbey and the monastery at Lindisfarne, which had been in ruins for centuries, and peopled them again with monks and nuns.

He revived in De Wilton the figure of the palmer and the ancient custom of pilgrimage to Palestine. And he transferred "the wondrous wizard, Michael Scott" from the thirteenth century to the end of the fifteenth. But, indeed, the state of society in Scotland might be described as mediæval as late as the middle of the sixteenth century. It was still feudal, and in great part Catholic. Particularly in the turbulent Borderland, a rude spirit of chivalry and a passion for wild adventure lingered among the Eliots, Armstrongs, Kerrs, Rutherfords, Homes, Johnstons, and other marauding clans, who acknowledged no law but march law, and held slack allegiance to "the King of Lothian and Fife." Every owner of a half-ruinous "peel" or border keep had a band of retainers within call, like the nine-and-twenty knights of fame who hung their shields in Branksome Hall; and he could summon them at short notice, for a raid upon the English or a foray against some neighbouring proprietor with whom he was at feud.

But the literary form under which Scott made the deepest impression upon the consciousness of his own generation and influenced most permanently the future literature of Europe, was prose fiction. As the creator of the historical novel and the ancestor of Kingsley, Ainsworth, Bulwer, and G. P. R. James; of Manzoni, Freytag, Hugo, Mérimée, Dumas, Alexis Tolstoi, and a host of others, at home and abroad, his example is potent yet. English fiction is directly or indirectly in his debt for "Romola," "Hypatia," "Henry Esmond," and "The Cloister and the Hearth." In several countries the historical novel had been trying for centuries to get itself born, but all its attempts had been abortive. "Waverley" is not only

vastly superior to "Thaddeus of Warsaw" (1803) and
"The Scottish Chiefs" (1809); it is something quite different in kind.* The Waverley Novels, twenty-nine in
number, appeared in the years 1814-31. The earlier
numbers of the series, "Waverley," "Guy Mannering,"
"The Antiquary," "Old Mortality," "The Black Dwarf,"
"Rob Roy," "The Heart of Mid-Lothian," "The Bride
of Lammermoor," and "A Legend of Montrose," were
Scotch romances of the seventeenth and eighteenth centuries. In "Ivanhoe" (1819) the author went to England
for his scene, and back to the twelfth century for his
period. Thenceforth he ranged over a wide region in
time and space; Elizabethan England ("Kenilworth"),
the France and Switzerland of Louis XI. and Charles
the Bold ("Quentin Durward" and "Anne of Geierstein"), Constantinople and Syria ("Count Robert of
Paris," "The Betrothed," and "The Talisman") in the
age of the Crusades. The fortunes of the Stuarts, interested him specially and engaged him in "Woodstock," "The Fortunes of Nigel," "The Monastery," and
its sequel, "The Abbot." He seems to have had, in the
words of Mr. R. H. Hutton, "something very like personal experience of a few centuries."

Scott's formula for the construction of a historical
romance was original with himself, and it has been followed by all his successors. His story is fictitious, his
hero imaginary. Richard I. is not the hero of "Ivanhoe," nor Louis XI. of "Quentin Durward." Shakspere dramatised history; Scott romanticised it. Still

---

*For a review of English historical fiction before Scott, con-
sult Professor Cross' "Development of the English Novel,"
pp. 110-114.

it is history; the private story is swept into the stream of large public events; the fate of the lover or the adventurer is involved with battles and diplomacies, with the rise and fall of kings, dynasties, political parties, nations. Stevenson says, comparing Fielding with Scott, that "in the work of the latter . . . we become suddenly conscious of the background. . . . It is curious enough to think that 'Tom Jones' is laid in the year '45, and that the only use he makes of the rebellion is to throw a troop of soldiers in his hero's way." * And it is this background which is, after all, the important thing in Scott—the leading impression; the broad canvas, the swarm of life, the spirit of the age, the reconstitution of an extinct society. This he was able to give with seeming ease and without any appearance of "cram." Chronicle matter does not lie about in lumps on the surface of his romance, but is decently buried away in the notes. In his comments on "Queenhoo Hall" he adverts to the danger of a pedantic method; and in his "Journal" (October 18th, 1826) he writes as follows of his own numerous imitators: "They have to read old books and consult antiquarian collections, to get their knowledge. I write because I have long since read such works and possess, thanks to a strong memory, the information which they have to seek for. This leads to a dragging in historical details by head and shoulders, so that the interest of the main piece is lost in minute description of events which do not affect its progress."

Of late the recrudescence of the historical novel has revived the discussion as to the value of the *genre*. It

* "Familiar Studies of Men and Books," by R. L. Stevenson. Article, "Victor Hugo's Romances."

may be readily admitted that Scott's best work is realistic, and is to be looked for in such novels as "The Antiquary," "Old Mortality," "The Heart of Mid-Lothian,"
and in characters like Andrew Fairservice, Bailie Nicol
Jarvie, Dandie Dinmont, Dugald Dalgetty, Jeanie Deans,
Edie Ochiltrie, which brought into play his knowledge
of men, his humour, observation of life, and insight into
Scotch human nature. Scott knew these people; he had
to divine James I., Louis XI., and Mary Stuart. The
historical novel is a *tour de force*. Exactly how knights-
templars, burgomasters, friars, Saracens, and Robin
Hood archers talked and acted in the twelfth century, we
cannot know. But it is just because they are strange to
our experience that they are dear to our imagination.
The justification of romance is its unfamiliarity—
"strangeness added to beauty"—"the pleasure of surprise" as distinguished from "the pleasure of recognition." Again and again realism returns to the charge
and demands of art that it give us the present and the
actual; and again and again the imagination eludes the
demand and makes an ideal world for itself in the blue
distance.

Two favourite arts, or artifices, of all romantic schools,
are "local colour" and "the picturesque." "Vers l'an
de grâce 1827," writes Prosper Mérimée, "j'étais *romantique*. Nous disions aux *classiques*; vos Grecs ne sont
pas des Grecs, vos Romains ne sont pas des Romains;
vous ne savez pas donner à vos compositions la *couleur
locale*. Point de salut sans la *couleur locale*." *

* "Le Roman Historique à l'Epoque Romantique." Essai
sur l'influence de Walter Scott. Par Louis Maigron. Paris
(Hachette), 1898, p. 331, *note*. And *ibid.*, p. 330: "Au

As to the picturesque—a word that connotes, in its
critical uses, some quality in the objects of sense which
strikes us as at once novel, and characteristic in its novelty—while by no means the highest of literary arts, it is
a perfectly legitimate one.* Creçy is not, at bottom, a
more interesting battle than Gettysburg because it was

lieu que les classiques s'efforçaient toujours, à travers les
modifications que les pays, les temps et les circonstances
peuvent apporter aux sentiments et aux passions des hommes,
d'atteindre à ce que ces passions et ces sentiments conservent
de permanent, d'immuable et d'éternel, c'est au contraire à
l'expression de l'accidentel et du relatif que les novateurs devaient les efforts de leur art. Plus simplement, à la place de
la vérité humaine, ils devaient mettre la vérité locale." Professor Herford says that what Scott "has in common with the
Romantic temper is simply the feeling for the picturesque, for
colour, for contrast." "Age of Wordsworth," p. 121.
    * De Quincey defines _picturesque_ as "the characteristic
pushed into a sensible excess." The word began to excite
discussion in the last quarter of the eighteenth century. See
vol. i., p. 185, for Gilpin's "Observations on Picturesque
Beauty." See also Uvedale Price, "Essays on the Picturesque
as Compared with the Sublime and the Beautiful," three
vols., 1794–96. Price finds the character of the picturesque to
consist in roughness, irregularity, intricacy, and sudden variation. Gothic buildings are more picturesque than Grecian,
and a ruin than an entire building. Hovels, cottages, mills,
interiors of old barns are picturesque. "In mills particularly,
such is the extreme intricacy of the wheels and the wood
work : such is the singular variety of forms and of lights and
shadows, of mosses and weather stains from the constant
moisture, of plants springing from the rough joints of the
stones—that, even without the addition of water, an old mill
has the greatest charm for a painter " (i., 55). He mentions,
as a striking example of picturesque beauty, a hollow lane or
by-road with broken banks, thickets, old neglected pollards,
fantastic roots bared by the winter torrents, tangled trailers
and wild plants, and infinite variety of tints and shades (i.,
23–29). He denounces the improvements of Capability Brown
(see "Romanticism," vol. i., p. 124) : especially the clump,
the belt and regular serpentine walks with smooth turf edges,
the made water with uniformly sloping banks—all as insip-
idly formal, in their way, as the old Italian gardens which
Brown's landscapes displaced.

fought with bows and arrows, but it is more picturesque to the modern imagination just for that reason. Why else do the idiots in "MacArthur's Hymn" complain that "steam spoils romance at sea"? Why did Ruskin lament when the little square at the foot of Giotto's Tower in Florence was made a stand for hackney coaches? Why did our countryman Halleck at Alnwick Towers resent the fact that "the Percy deals in salt and hides, the Douglas sells red herring"? And why does the picturesque tourist, in general, object to the substitution of naphtha launches for gondolas on the Venetian canals? Perhaps because the more machinery is interposed between man and the thing he works on, the more impersonal becomes his relation to nature.

Carlyle, in his somewhat grudging estimate of Scott, declares that "much of the interest of these novels results from contrasts of costume. The phraseology, fashion of arms, of dress, of life belonging to one age is brought suddenly with singular vividness before the eyes of another. A great effect this; yet by the very nature of it an altogether temporary one. Consider, brethren, shall not we too one day be antiques and grow to have as quaint a costume as the rest? . . . Not by slashed breeches, steeple hats, buff belts, or antiquated speech can romance-heroes continue to interest us; but simply and solely, in the long run, by being *men*. Buff belts and all manner of jerkins and costumes are transitory; man alone is perennial." * Carlyle's dissatisfaction with Scott arises from the fact that he was not a missionary nor a transcendental philosopher, but simply a teller of stories. Heine was not troubled in the same way, but he made the iden-

* "Essay on Walter Scott."

tical criticism. "Like the works of Walter Scott, so also do Fouqué's romances of chivalry * remind us of the fantastic tapestries known as Gobelins, whose rich texture and brilliant colors are more pleasing to our eyes than edifying to our souls. We behold knightly pageantry, shepherds engaged in festive sports, hand-to-hand combats, and ancient customs, charmingly intermingled. It is all very pretty and picturesque, but shallow; brilliant superficiality. Among the imitators of Fouqué, as among the imitators of Walter Scott, this mannerism of portraying—not the inner nature of men and things, but merely the outward garb and appearance—was carried to still greater extremes. This shallow art and frivolous style is still [1833] in vogue in Germany as well as in England and France. . . . In lieu of a knowledge of mankind, our recent novelists evince a profound acquaintance with clothes." †

---

* Andrew Lang reminds us that, after all, only three of the Waverley Novels are "chivalry romances." The following are the only numbers of the series that have to do with the Middle Ages: "Count Robert of Paris," *circa* 1090 A.D. ; "The Betrothed," 1187; "The Talisman," 1193; "Ivanhoe," 1194; "The Fair Maid of Perth," 1402; "Quentin Durward," 1470; "Anne of Geierstein," 1474-77.

† "The Romantic School in Germany," p. 187. *Cf.* Stendhal, "Walter Scott et la Princesse de Clèves." "Mes reflexions seront mal accueilles. Une immense troupe de littérateurs est intéressée à porter aux nues Sir Walter Scott et sa manière. L'habit et le collier de cuivre d'un serf du moyen âge sont plus facile à décrire que les mouvements du cœur humain. . . . N'oublions pas un autre avantage de l'école de Sir Walter Scott : la description d'un costume et la *pose* d'un personnage . . . prennent au moins deux pages. Les mouvements de l'âme fourniraient à peine quelques lignes. Ouvrez au hazard un des volumes de la ' Princesse de Clèves,' prenez dix pages au hasard, et ensuite comparez les aux dix pages d'" Ivanhoe ' ou de ' Quentin Durward ' : ces derniers ouvrages ont un *mérite historique.* Ils apprennent quelques petites

Elsewhere Heine acknowledges a deeper reason for the popularity of the Scotch novels. "Their theme . . . is the mighty sorrow for the loss of national peculiarities swallowed up in the universality of the newer culture— a sorrow which is now throbbing in the hearts of all peoples. For national memories lie deeper in the human breast than is generally thought." But whatever rank may be ultimately assigned to the historical novel as an art form, Continental critics are at one with the British in crediting its invention to Scott. "It is an error," says Heine, "not to recognise Walter Scott as the founder of the so-called historical romance, and to endeavour to trace it to German imitation." He adds that Scott was a Protestant, a lawyer and a Scotchman, accustomed to action and debate, in whose works the aristocratic and democratic elements are in wholesome balance; "whereas our German romanticists eliminated the democratic element entirely from their novels, and returned to the ruts of those crazy romances of knight-errantry that flour-

---

choses sur l'histoire aux gens qui l'ignorent ou qui le savent mal. Ce mérite historique a causé un grand plaisir : je ne le nie pas, mais c'est ce mérite historique qui se fanera le premier. . . . Dans 146 ans, Sir Walter Scott ne sera pas à la hauteur où Corneille nous apparaît 146 ans après sa mort." "To write a modern romance of chivalry," says Jeffrey, in his review of "Marmion" in the *Edinburgh*, "seems to be much such a phantasy as to build a modern abbey or an English pagoda. . . . [Scott's] genius, seconded by the omnipotence of fashion, has brought chivalry again into temporary favor. Fine ladies and gentlemen now talk, indeed, of donjons, keeps, tabards, 'scutcheons, tressures, caps of maintenance, portcullises, wimples, and we know not what besides ; just as they did, in the days of Dr. Darwin's popularity, of gnomes, sylphs, oxygen, gossamer, polygynia, and polyandria. That fashion, however, passed rapidly away, and Mr. Scott should take care that a different sort of pedantry," etc.

ished before Cervantes." *   " Quel est l'ouvrage littéraire," asks Stendhal in 1823,† " qui a le plus réussi en
France depuis dix ans? Les romans de Walter Scott.
. . . On s'est moqué à Paris pendant vingt ans du roman
historique; l'Académie a prouvé doctement le ridicule de
ce genre; nous y croyions tous, lorsque Walter Scott a
paru, son Waverley à la main; et Balantyne, son libraire
vient de mourir millionaire." ‡

Lastly the service of the Waverley Novels to history
was an important one. Palgrave says that historical fiction is the mortal enemy of history, and Leslie Stephen
adds that it is also the enemy of fiction. In a sense both
sayings are true. Scott was not always accurate as to
facts and sinned freely against chronology. But he
rescued a wide realm from cold oblivion and gave it
back to human consciousness and sympathy. It is treating the past more kindly to misrepresent it in some particulars, than to leave it a blank to the imagination.
The eighteenth-century historians were incurious of *life*.
Their spirit was general and abstract; they were in search
of philosophical formulas. Gibbon covers his subject
with a lava-flood of stately rhetoric which stiffens into a
uniform stony coating over the soft surface of life. Scott
is primarily responsible for that dramatic, picturesque

---

*For an exhaustive review of Scott's influence on the evo-
lution of historical fiction in France, consult Maigron, "Le
Roman Historique," etc. A longish passage from this work
will be found at the end of the present chapter. For English
imitators and successors of the Waverley Novels, see Cross,
"Development of the English Novel," pp. 136-48. See also
De Quincey's "Literary Reminiscences," vol. iii., for an
amusing account of "Walladmor" (1824), a pretended German translation of a non-existent Waverley novel.
  † " Racine et Shakespeare."   ‡ "Don Quixote."

treatment of history which we find in Michelet and Carlyle. "These historical novels," testifies Carlyle, "have
taught all men this truth, which looks like a truism, and
yet was as good as unknown to writers of history and
others, till so taught; that the bygone ages of the world
were actually filled by living men, not by protocols, state
papers, controversies, and abstractions of men. . . . It is
a great service, fertile in consequences, this that Scott
has done; a great truth laid open by him." *   In France,
too, historians like Barante and Augustin Thierry, were
Scott's professed disciples.   The latter confesses, in a
well-known passage, that "Ivanhoe" was the inspirer of
his "Conquête d'Angleterre," and styles the novelist "le
plus grand maître qu'il y ait jamais eu en fait de divi-
nation historique." †

Scott apprehended the Middle Ages on their spectacu-
lar, and more particularly, their military side.   He exhibits their large, showy aspects: battles, processions,
hunts, feasts in hall, tourneys,‡ sieges, and the like.   The
motley mediæval world swarms in his pages, from the
king on his throne down to the jester with his cap and
bells.   But it was the outside of it that he saw; the noise,
bustle, colour, stirring action that delighted him.   Into its
spiritualities he did not penetrate far; its scholasticisms,
strange casuistries, shuddering faiths, grotesque distor-

* "Sir Walter Scott."
† Dix ans d'études historiques": preface.
‡ Walter Bagehot says that "Ivanhoe" "describes the Middle Ages as we should have wished them to be," ignoring
their discomforts and harsh barbarism.   "Every boy has
heard of tournaments and has a firm persuasion that in an
age of tournaments life was thoroughly well understood.   A
martial society where men fought hand to hand on good
horses with large lances," etc. ("The Waverley Novels ").

tions of soul; its religious mysticisms, asceticisms, agonies; the ecstactic reveries of the cloister, terrors of hell, and visions of paradise. It was the literature of the knight, not of the monk, that appealed to him. He felt the awfulness and the beauty of Gothic sacred architecture and of Catholic ritual. The externalities of the mediæval church impressed him, whatever was picturesque in its ceremonies or august in its power. He pictured effectively such scenes as the pilgrimage to Melrose in the "Lay"; the immuring of the renegade nun in "Marmion"; the trial of Rebecca for sorcery by the Grand Master of the Temple in "Ivanhoe." Ecclesiastical figures abound in his pages, jolly friars, holy hermits, lordly prelates, grim inquisitors, abbots, priors, and priests of all descriptions, but all somewhat conventional and viewed *ab extra*. He could not draw a saint.* Significant, therefore, is his indifference to Dante, the poet *par excellence* of the Catholic Middle Age, the epitomizer of mediæval thought. "The plan" of the "Divine Comedy," "appeared to him unhappy; the personal malignity and strange mode of revenge presumptuous and uninteresting." Scott's genius was antipathetic to Dante's; and he was as incapable of taking a lasting imprint from his intense, austere, and mystical spirit, as from the nebulous gloom of the Ossianic poetry. Though conservative, he was not reactionary after the fashion of the German "throne-and-altar" romanticists, but remained always a good Church of England man and an obstinate opponent

---

* "Of enthusiasm in religion Scott always spoke very severely. . . . I do not think there is a single study in all his romances of what may be fairly called a pre-eminently spiritual character" (R. H. Hutton: "Sir Walter Scott," p. 126).

of Catholic emancipation.* "Creeds are data in his novels," says Bagehot; "people have different creeds, but each keeps his own."

Scott's interest in popular superstitions was constant. As a young man—in his German ballad period—they affected his imagination with a "pleasing horror." But as he grew older, they engaged him less as a poet than as a student of *Cultur geschichte.*

A wistful sense of the beauty of these old beliefs—a rational smile at their absurdity—such is the tone of his "Letters on Demonology and Witchcraft" (1830), a passage or two from which will give his attitude very precisely; an attitude, it will be seen, which is after all not so very different from Addison's, allowing for the distance in time and place, and for Scott's livelier imagination.† Scott had his laugh at Mrs. Radcliffe, and in his

---

* "Unopposed, the Catholic superstition may sink to dust, with all its absurd ritual and solemnities. Still it is an awful risk. The world is in fact as silly as ever, and a good competence of nonsense will always find believers" ("Diary" for 1829).

† See vol. i., p. 42. "We almost envy the credulity of those who, in the gentle moonlight of a summer night in England, amid the tangled glades of a deep forest, or the turfy swell of her romantic commons, could fancy they saw the fairies tracing their sportive ring. But it is in vain to regret illusions which, however engaging, must of necessity yield their place before the increase of knowledge, like shadows at the advance of morn" ("Demonology," p. 183). "Tales of ghosts and demonology are out of date at forty years of age and upward. . . . If I were to write on the subject at all, it should have been during a period of life when I could have treated it with more interesting vivacity. . . . Even the present fashion of the world seems to be ill-suited for studies of this fantastic nature; and the most ordinary mechanic has learning sufficient to laugh at the figments which in former times were believed by persons far advanced in the deepest knowledge of the age" (*Ibid.*, p. 398).

reviews of Hoffmann's "Tales" and Maturin's "Fatal Revenge" * he insists upon the delicacy with which the supernatural must be treated in an age of disbelief. His own management of such themes, however, though much superior to Walpole's or Mrs. Radcliffe's, has not the subtle art of Coleridge. The White Lady of Avenel, *e.g.*, in "The Abbot," is a notorious failure. There was too much daylight in his imagination for spectres to be quite at home. "The shapes that haunt thought's wildernesses"; the "night side of things"; the real shudder are not there, as in Hawthorne or in Poe. Walter Pater † says that Meinhold's "Amber Witch" has more of the true romantic spirit than Tieck, who was its professional representative. On the contrary, it has less of the romantic spirit, but more of the mediæval fact. It is a literal, realistic handling of the witch superstition, as Balzac's "Succube," in the "Contes Drolatiques" is a satirical version of similar material. But Tieck's "Märchen" are the shadows thrown by mediæval beliefs across a sensitive, modern imagination, and are in result, therefore, romantic. Scott's dealing with subjects of the kind is midway between Meinhold and Tieck. He does not blink the ugly, childish, stupid, and cruel features of popular superstition, but throws the romantic glamour over them, precisely as he does over his "Charlie over the water" Jacobites.‡

Again Scott's apprehension of the spirit of chivalry, though less imperfect than his apprehension of the spirit

* See vol. i., pp. 249 and 420.
† "Postscript" to "Appreciations."
‡ For the rarity of the real romantic note in mediæval writers see vol. i., pp. 26-28, and Appendix B to the present chapter.

of mediæval Catholicism, was but partial.   Of the themes
which Ariosto sang—

> "I e donne, i cavalier, l'arme, gli amori,
> Le cortesie, l'audaci imprese io canto"—

the northern Ariosto sang bravely the *arme* and the
audaci imprese; less confidently the *amori* and the *cortesie*.
He could sympathise with the knight-errant's high sense
of honour and his love of bold emprise; not so well with
his service of dames.   Mediæval courtship or "love-
drurye," the trembling self-abasement of the lover before
his lady, the fantastic refinements and excesses of gallantry, were alien to Scott's manly and eminently practical turn of mind.   It is hardly possible to fancy him
reading the "Roman de la Rose" with patience—he
thought "Troilus and Creseyde" tedious, which Rossetti
pronounces the finest of English love poems; or selecting
for treatment the story of Heloise or Tristram and Iseult,
or of "Le Chevalier de la Charette"; or such a typical
mediæval life as that of Ulrich von Liechtenstein.*
These were quite as truly beyond his sphere as a church
legend like the life of Saint Margaret or the quest of the
Sangreal.   In the "Talisman" he praises in terms only
less eloquent than Burke's famous words, "that wild
spirit of chivalry which, amid its most extravagant and
fantastic flights, was still pure from all selfish alloy—
generous, devoted, and perhaps only thus far censurable,
that it proposed objects and courses of action inconsistent
with the frailties and imperfections of man."   In "Ivanhoe," too, there is something like a dithyrambic lament

---

* See "Studies in Mediæval Life and Literature," by Edward T. McLaughlin, p. 34.

over the decay of knighthood—"The 'scutcheons have
long mouldered from the walls," etc.; but even here, enthusiasm is tempered by good sense, and Richard of the
Lion Heart is described as an example of the "brilliant
but useless character of a knight of romance." All this
is but to say that the picture of the Middle Age which
Scott painted was not complete. Still it was more nearly
complete than has yet been given by any other hand;
and the artist remains, in Stevenson's phrase, "the king
of the Romantics."

APPENDIX A.

"Jamais homme de génie n'a eu l'honneur et le bon-
heur d'être imité par plus d'hommes de génie, si tous les
grands écrivains de l'époque romantique depuis Victor
Hugo jusqu'à Balzac et depuis Alfred de Vigny jusqu'à
Mérimée, lui doivent tous et se sont tous glorifiés de
lui devoir quelque chose. . . . Il doit nous suffire pour
l'instant d'affirmer que l'influence de Walter Scott est à
la racine même des grandes œuvres qui ont donné au
nouveau genre tant d'éclat dans notre littérature; que
c'est elle qui les a inspirées, suscitées, fait éclore; que
sans lui nous n'aurions ni 'Hans d'Islande,' ni 'Cinq-
Mars,' ni 'Les Chouans,' ni la 'Chronique de Charles
IX.,' ni 'Notre Dame de Paris,' . . . Ce n'est rien moins
que le romantisme lui-même dont elle a hâté l'incubation,
facilité l'eclosion, aidé le développement."—MAIGRON,
"Le Roman Historique," p. 143.

"Il nous faut d'abord constater que c'est véritablement
de Walter Scott, et de Walter Scott seul, que commence
cette fureur des choses du moyen âge, cette manie de

couleur locale qui sévit avec tant d'intensité quelque
temps avant et longtemps après 1830, et donc qu'il reste,
au moins pour ce qui est de la description, le principal
initiateur de la génération nouvelle.   Sans doute et de
toute part, cette résurrection du moyen âge était des longtemps préparée.   Le ' Génie du Christianisme,' le ' Cours
de littérature dramatique ' de Schlegel, l'"Allemagne ' de
Mme. de Staël avaient fait des mœurs chrétiennes et
chevaleresques le fondement et la condition de renouvelle-
ment de l'art français.   Et, en effet, dès 1802, le moyen
âge était découvert, la cathédrale gothique restaurée, l'art
chrétien remis à la place éminente d'où il aurait fallu ne
jamais le laisser choir.   Mais où sont les œuvres exécu-
tées d'après ce modèle et ces principes?   S'il est facile
d'apercevoir et de déterminer la cathédrale religieuse de
Chateaubriand, est il donc si aisé de distinguer sa cathédrale poétique? . . . Un courant vigoureux, que le ' Genie
du Christianisme ' et les ' Martyrs ' ont puissamment
contribué à déterminer, fait dériver les imaginations vers
les choses gothiques; volontiers, l'esprit français se re-
tourne alors vers le passé comme vers la seule source de
poésie; et voici qu'un étranger vient se faire son guide
et fait miroiter, devant tous les yeux éblouis, la fantas-
magorie du moyen âge, donjons et créneaux, cuirasses et
belles armures, haquenées et palefrois, chevaliers re-
splendissants et mignonnes et délicates châtelaines. . . .
Sur ses traces, on se précipita avec furie dans la voie
qu'il venait subitement d'élargir.   Ce moyen âge, jusqu'à
lui si convoité et si infécond, devinait enfin une source
inépuisable d'émotions et de productions artistiques.
La ' cathédrale ' était bien restaurée cette fois.   Elle le
fut même trop, et borda trop obstinement tous les sentiers

littéraires.   Mais de cet excès, si vite fatigant, c'est
Walter Scott et non Chateaubriand, quoi qu'il en ait pu
dire, qui reste le grand coupable.   Il fit plus que dé-
couvrir le moyen âge; il le mit à la mode parmi les
Français."—*Ibid.*, pp. 195 *ff.*

APPENDIX B.

" The magical touch and the sense of mystery and all
the things that are associated with the name romance,
when that name is applied to ' The Ancient Mariner,' or
' La Belle Dame sans Merci,' or ' The Lady of Shalott,'
are generally absent from the most successful romances of
the great mediæval romantic age. . . . The true romantic interest is very unequally distributed over the works
of the Middle Ages, and there is least of it in the authors who are most representative of the ' age of chivalry.'
There is a disappointment prepared for any one who
looks in the greater romantic authors of the twelfth century for the music of ' The Faëry Queene ' or ' La Belle
Dame sans Merci.' . . . The greater authors of the
twelfth century have more affinity to the ' heroic romance '
of the school of the ' Grand Cyrus ' than to the dreams of
Spenser or Coleridge. . . . The magic that is wanting to
the clear and elegant narrative of Benoit and Chrestien
will be found elsewhere; it will be found in one form in
the mystical prose of the ' Queste del St. Graal '—a very
different thing from Chrestien's ' Perceval '—it will be
found, again and again, in the prose of Sir Thomas
Malory; it will be found in many ballads and ballad
burdens, in ' William and Margaret,' in ' Binnorie,' in
the ' Wife of Usher's Well,' in the ' Rime of the Count

Arnaldos,' in the ' Königskinder '; it will be found in the most beautiful story of the Middle Ages, ' Aucassin and Nicolette,' one of the few perfectly beautiful stories in the world."—" Epic and Romance," W. P. KER, London, 1897, p. 371 *ff.*

CHAPTER II.

Coleridge, Bowles, and the Pope Controversy.

WHILE Scott was busy collecting the fragments of Border minstrelsy and translating German ballads,* two other young poets, far to the south, were preparing their share in the literary revolution. In those same years (1795–98) Wordsworth and Coleridge were wandering together over the Somerset downs and along the coast of Devon, catching glimpses of the sea towards Bristol or Linton, and now and then of the skeleton masts and gossamer sails of a ship against the declining sun, like those of the phantom bark in "The Ancient Mariner." The first fruits of these walks and talks was that epoch-making book, the "Lyrical Ballads"; the first edition of which was published in 1798, and the second, with an additional volume and the famous preface by Wordsworth, in 1800. The genesis of the work and the allotment of its parts were described by Coleridge himself in the "Biographia Literaria" (1817), Chapter XIV.

"During the first year that Mr. Wordsworth and I were neighbours our conversations turned frequently on the two cardinal points of poetry, the power of exciting the sympathy of the reader by a faithful adherence to the truth

* For Coleridge's relations with German romance, see vol. i., pp. 419–21. For his early interest in Percy, Ossian, and Chatterton, *ibid.*, pp. 299, 328, 368–70.

of nature, and the power of giving the interest of novelty by the modifying colours of imagination. . . . The thought suggested itself that a series of poems might be composed of two sorts. In the one, the incidents and agents were to be, in part at least, supernatural; . . . for the second class, subjects were to be chosen from ordinary life. . . . It was agreed that my endeavours should be directed to persons and characters supernatural, or at least romantic. . . . With this view I wrote ' The Ancient Mariner,' and was preparing, among other poems, ' The Dark Ladie ' and the ' Christabel,' in which I should have more nearly realized my ideal than I had done in my first attempt."

Coleridge's contributions to romantic poetry are few though precious. Weighed against the imposing array of Scott's romances in prose and verse,* they seem like two or three little gold coins put into the scales to balance a handful of silver dollars. He stands for so much in the history of English thought, he influenced his own and the following generation on so many sides, that his romanticism shows like a mere incident in his intellectual history. His blossoming time was short at the best, and ended practically with the century. After his return from Germany in 1799 and his settlement at Keswick in 1800, he produced little verse of any importance beyond the second part of " Christabel " (written in 1800, published in 1816). His creative impulse failed him, and he became more and more involved in theology, metaphysics, political philosophy, and literary criticism.

* "There is as much difference between Coleridge's brief poem ' Christabel' and all the narrative poems of Walter Scott . . . as between a precious essence and a coarse imitation of it got up for sale" (Leigh Hunt's "Autobiography," p. 197).

It appears, therefore, at first sight, a little odd that Coleridge's German biographer, Professor Brandl, should have treated his subject under this special aspect,* and attributed to him so leading a place in the romantic movement. Walter Scott, if we consider his life-long and wellnigh exclusive dedication of himself to the work of historic restoration—Scott, certainly, and not Coleridge was the "high priest of Romanticism." † Brandl is dissatisfied with the term Lake School, or Lakers, commonly given to Wordsworth, Coleridge, and Southey, and proposes instead to call them the Romantic School, Romanticists (*Romantiker*), surely something of a misnomer when used of an eclectic versifier like Southey, or a poet of nature, moral reflection, and humble life like Wordsworth. Southey, in casting about him for a theme, sometimes became for the nonce and so far as subject goes, a romancer; as in "Joan of Arc" (1799), "Madoc" (1805), and "Roderick the Goth" (1814); not to speak of translations like "Amadis of Gaul," "Palmerin of England," and "The Chronicle of the Cid." But these were not due to the compelling bent of his genius, as in Scott. They were miscellaneous jobs, undertaken in the regular

---

* "Samuel Taylor Coleridge und die Englische Romantik," Alois Brandl, Berlin, 1886.

† It is in view of his critical attitude, not of his poetry, that Saintsbury applies this title to Coleridge. "The attitude was that of a mediævalism inspired by much later learning, but still more by that intermediate or decadent Greek philosophy which had so much influence on the Middle Ages themselves. This is, in other words, the Romantic attitude, and Coleridge was the high priest of Romanticism, which, through Scott and Byron, he taught to Europe, repreaching it even to Germany, from which it had partly come " ("A Short History of English Literature," by George Saintsbury, London, 1898, p. 656).

course of his business as a manufacturer of big, irregular epics, Oriental, legendary, mythological, and what not; and as an untiring biographer, editor, and hack writer of all descriptions. Southey was a mechanical poet, with little original inspiration, and represents nothing in particular. Wordsworth again, though innovating in practice and theory against eighteenth-century tradition, is absolutely unromantic in contrast with Scott and Coleridge.

But it will be fair to let the critic defend his own nomenclature; and the passage which I shall quote will serve not only as another attempt to define romanticism, but also to explain why Brandl regards the Lake poets as our romantic school *par excellence.* "'Lake School' is a name, but no designation. This was felt in England, where many critics have accordingly fallen into the opposite extreme, and maintained that the members of this group of poets had nothing in common beyond their personal and accidental conditions. As if they had only lived together, and not worked together! In truth they were bound together by many a strong tie, and above all by one of a polemical kind, namely, by the aversion for the monotony that had preceded them, and by the struggle against merely dogmatic rules. Unbending uniformity is death! Let us be various and individual as life itself is. . . . Away with dry Rationalism! Let us fight it with all the powers we possess; whether by bold Platonism or simple Bible faith; whether by enthusiastic hymns, or dreamy fairy tales; whether by the fabulous world of distant times and zones, or by the instincts of the children in the next village. Let us abjure the ever-recommended nostrum of imitation of the old masters in poetry, and rather attach ourselves to homely models, and endeavour, with their help, lovingly and organically to develop their inner life.　These were the aims of Walter Scott and his Scotch school, only with such changes as local differences demanded.　Individuality in person, nationality, and subject, and therefore the emphasis of all natural unlikeness, was the motto on both sides of the Tweed.　And, as these men, when confronted by elements peculiar, rare, and marvellous, designated such elements as ' romantic,' so may they themselves be justly called the ' Romantic School.'　But the term is much misused, and requires a little elucidation.　Shakespeare is usually called a romantic poet.　He, however, never used the expression, and would have been surprised if any one had applied it to him.　The term presupposes opposition to the classic style, to rhetorical deduction, and to measured periods, all of which were unknown in the time of the Renaissance, and first imported in that of the French Revolution.　On the other hand, Wordsworth, Coleridge, Southey, Lamb, and Walter Scott's circle all branched off from the classical path with a directness and consistency which sharply distinguish them from their predecessors, contemporaries, and successors.　Their predecessors had not broken with the Greek and Latin school, nor with the school of Pope; Chatterton copied Homer; Cowper translated him; Burns in his English verses, and Bowles in his sonnets, adhered to what is called the ' pig-tail period '!　The principal poems composed in the last decennium of the eighteenth century . . . adhered still more to classic tradition.　In London the satires of Mathias and Gifford renewed the style of the ' Dunciad,' and the moral poems of Rogers that of

the ' Essay on Man.' Landor wrote his youthful ' Gebir '
in the style of Virgil, and originally in Latin itself. The
amateur in German literature, William Taylor of Norwich, and Dr. Sayers, interested themselves especially for
those works by Goethe which bear an antique character
—for ' Iphigenia,' 'Proserpina,' 'Alexis and Dora.' Only
when the war with France drew near was the classical
feeling interrupted. Campbell, the Scotchman, and
Moore, the Irishman, both well schooled by translations
from the Greek, recalled to mind the songs of their own
people, and rendered them popular with the fashionable
world—though only by clothing them in classic garb.
How different to the ' artificial rust ' of ' Christabel '; to
the almost exaggerated homeliness of ' We Are Seven ';
and to the rude ' Lay of the Last Minstrel '! When at
last, with the fall of Napoleon, the great stars—Byron,
Shelley, Keats, and later the mature Landor—rose in the
hemisphere, they had all imbibed from the Romantic
school a warmer form of thought and feeling, and a number of productive impulses; though, Euphorion-like, they
still regarded the antique as their parent. They expressed
much appreciation of the Romantic school, but their hearts
were with Æschylus and Pindar. They contended for
national character, but only took pleasure in planting it
on classic soil. Byron's enthusiasm for Pope was not
only caprice; nor was it mere chance that Byron should
have died in Greece, and Shelley and Keats in Italy.
Compared with what we may call these classical members of the Romantic school, Wordsworth, Coleridge, and
Scott . . . may be said to have taken nothing, whether
in the form of translation or imitation, from classical
literature; while they drew endless inspiration from the

Middle Ages. In their eyes Pope was only a lucid, able, and clever journeyman. It is therefore fair to consider them, and them alone, as exponents of the Romantic school." *

As to Byron and Shelley this criticism may do; as to Chatterton and Keats it is misleading. Wordsworth more romantic than Chatterton! More romantic than Keats, because the latter often, and Wordsworth seldom, treats subjects from the antique! On the contrary, if "the name is graven on the workmanship," "Michael" and "The Brothers" are as classical as "Hyperion" or "Laodamia" or "The Hamadryad"; "bald as the bare mountain-tops are bald, with a baldness full of grandeur." Bagehot expressly singles Wordsworth out as an example of pure or classic art, as distinguished from the ornate art of such poets as Keats and Tennyson. And Mr. Colvin hesitates to classify him with Landor only because of his "suggestive and adumbrative manner"—not, indeed, he acknowledges, a romantic manner, and yet "quite distinct from the classical"; *i.e.*, because of the transcendental character of a portion of his poetry. But whatever may be true of the other members of the group, Coleridge at his best was a romantic poet. "Christabel" and "The Ancient Mariner," creations so exquisite sprung from the contact of modern imagination with mediæval beliefs, are enough in themselves to justify the whole romantic movement.

Among the literary influences which gave shape to Coleridge's poetry, Percy's ballads and Chatterton's

* "Samuel Taylor Coleridge and the English Romantic School," by Alois Brandl. Lady Eastlake's translation, London, 1887, pp. 219–23.

"Rowley Poems" are obvious and have already been mentioned. In his first volume of verse (1796), there is manifest a still stronger impulse from the sonnets of the Rev. William Lisle Bowles. We have noticed the reappearance of this discarded stanza form in the work of Gray, Mason, Edwards, Stillingfleet, and Thomas Warton, about the middle of the last century.* In 1782 Mrs. Charlotte Smith published a volume of sonnets, treating motives from Milton, Gray, Collins, Pope's "Eloisa" and Goethe's "Werther." But the writer who—through his influence upon Wordsworth more especially—contributed most towards the sonnet revival, was Bowles. In 1789 he had published a little collection of fourteen sonnets,† which reached a second edition with six pieces additional, in the same year. "His sonnets came into Wordsworth's hands (1793)," says Brandl, "just as he was leaving London with some friends for a morning's excursion; he seated himself in a recess on Westminster Bridge, and was not to be moved from his place till he had finished the little book. Southey, again, owned in 1832 that for forty years, he had taken the sweet and artless style of Bowles for a model." ‡ In the first chapter of his "Biographia Literaria" (1817) Coleridge tells how, when he had just entered on his seventeenth year, "the sonnets of Mr. Bowles, twenty in number and just then published in a quarto pamphlet, were first made known and presented" to him by his school-fellow at Christ's Hospital, Thomas

* See vol. i., pp. 160–61.
† "Fourteen Sonnets, written chiefly on Picturesque Spots," Bath, 1789.
‡ "Samuel Taylor Coleridge," p. 37. *Cf.* Wordsworth's Sonnets "Upon Westminster Bridge" (1802) and "Scorn Not the Sonnet."

Middleton, afterwards Bishop of Calcutta. "It was a double pleasure to me . . . that I should have received, from a friend so revered, the first knowledge of a poet by whose works, year after year, I was so enthusiastically delighted and inspired. My earliest acquaintances will not have forgotten the undisciplined eagerness and impetuous zeal with which I laboured to make proselytes, not only of my companions, but of all with whom I conversed, of whatever rank and in whatever place. As my school finances did not permit me to purchase copies, I made, within less than a year and a half, more than forty transcriptions, as the best presents I could offer to those who had in any way won my regard. And with almost equal delight did I receive the three or four following publications of the same author." To Bowles' poems Coleridge ascribes the credit of having withdrawn him from a too exclusive devotion to metaphysics and also a strengthened perception of the essentially unpoetic character of Pope's poetry. "Among those with whom I conversed there were, of course, very many who had formed their taste and their notions of poetry from the writings of Pope and his followers; or, to speak more generally, in that school of French poetry, condensed and invigorated by English understanding, which had predominated from the last century. I was not blind to the merits of this school, yet . . . they gave me little pleasure. . . . I saw that the excellence of this kind consisted in just and acute observations on men and manners in an artificial state of society, as its matter and substance; and in the logic of wit, conveyed in smooth and strong epigrammatic couplets, as its form. . . . The matter and diction seemed to me characterized not so much by poetic thoughts as by thoughts translated into the language of poetry." Coleridge goes on to say that, in a paper written during a Cambridge vacation, he compared Darwin's " Botanic Garden " to a Russian ice palace, " glittering, cold, and transitory "; that he expressed a preference for Collins' odes over those of Gray; and that in his " defence of the lines running into each other, instead of closing at each couplet; and of natural language . . . such as *I will remember thee*, instead of

> . . . Thy image on her wing
> Before my fancy's eye shall memory bring "

he had continually to appeal to the example of the older English poets from Chaucer to Milton. " The reader," he concludes, " must make himself acquainted with the general style of composition that was at that time deemed poetry, in order to understand and account for the effect produced on me by the sonnets, the ' Monody at Matlock ' and the ' Hope ' of Mr. Bowles; for it is peculiar to original genius to become less and less striking, in proportion to its success in improving the taste and judgment of its contemporaries. The poems of West, indeed, had the merit of chaste and manly diction, but they were cold, and, if I may so express it, only dead-coloured; while in the best of Warton's, there is a stiffness which too often gives them the appearance of imitations from the Greek. Whatever relation, therefore, of cause or impulse, Percy's collection of ballads may bear to the most popular poems of the present day, yet in the more sustained and elevated style of the then living poets, Cowper and Bowles were, to the best of my knowledge, the first who combined natural thoughts with natural diction; the first who reconciled the heart with the head." Coleridge adds in a note that he was not familiar with Cowper's "Task" till many years after the publication of Bowles' sonnets, though it had been published before them (1785).

It would be hard to account for the effect of Bowles' sonnets on Coleridge, did we not remember that it is not necessarily the greatest literature that comes home to us most intimately, but that which, for some reason, touches us where we are peculiarly sensitive. It is a familiar experience with every reader, that certain books make an appeal to him which is personal and individual, an appeal which they make to few other readers—perhaps to no other reader—and which no other books make to him. It is something in them apart from their absolute value or charm, or rather it is something in *him*, some private experience of his own, some occult association in depths below consciousness. He has a perfectly just estimate of their small importance in the abstract; they are not even of the second or third rank. Yet they speak to him; they seem written to him—are more to him, in a way, than Shakspere and Milton and all the public library of the world. In the line of light bringers who pass from hand to hand the torch of intelligential fire, there are men of most unequal stature, and a giant may stoop to take the precious flambeau from a dwarf. That Scott should have admired Monk Lewis, and Coleridge reverenced Bowles, only proves that Lewis and Bowles had something to give which Scott and Coleridge were peculiarly ready to receive.

Bowles' sonnets, though now little read, are not unreadable. They are tender in feeling, musical in verse, and pure in diction. They were mostly suggested by natural scenery, and are uniformly melancholy. Bowles could suck melancholy out of a landscape as a weasel sucks eggs. His sonnets continue the elegiac strain of Shenstone, Gray, Collins, Warton, and the whole " Il Penseroso " school, but with a more personal note, explained by a recent bereavement of the poet. " Those who know him," says the preface, " know the occasions of them to have been real; to the public he might only mention the sudden death of a deserving young woman with whom

> Sperabat longos heu ! ducere soles,
> Et fido acclinis consumuisse sinu. . . .

This is nothing to the public; but it may serve in some measure to obviate the common remark on melancholy poetry, that it has been very often gravely composed, when possibly the heart of the writer had very little share in the distress he chose to describe. But there is a great difference between *natural* and *fabricated* feelings even in poetry." Accordingly while the Miltonic group of last-century poets went in search of dark things—grots, caverns, horrid shades, and twilight vales; Bowles' mood bestowed its color upon the most cheerful sights and sounds of nature. The coming of summer or spring; the bells of Oxford and Ostend; the distant prospect of the Malvern Hills, or the chalk cliffs of Dover; sunrise on the sea, touching " the lifted oar far off with sudden gleam "; these and the like move him to tears equally with the glimmer of evening, the sequestered woods of Wensbeck, the ruins of Netley Abbey,* or the frowning battlements of Bamborough Castle, where

* *Cf.* vol. i., p. 182.

> "Pity, at the dark and stormy hour
>   Of midnight, when the moon is hid on high,
>   Keeps her lone watch upon the topmost tower."

In "English Bards and Scotch Reviewers" Byron calls
Bowles "the maudlin prince of mournful sonneteers,"
whose

> "   . . . muse most lamentably tells
> What merry sounds proceed from Oxford bells." *

Bowles' attitude had thus something more modern than
that of the eighteenth-century elegiacs, and in unison
with Coleridge's doctrine, that

> "   . . . we receive but what we give,
> And in our life alone does nature live :
> Ours is her wedding garment, ours her shroud." †

A number of Bowles' sonnets were addressed to rivers,
the Tweed, the Cherwell at Oxford, the Wensbeck, and
the Itchin near Winton, poems which stand midway between Thomas Warton's "To the River Lodon" and Coleridge's "To the River Otter," with Wordsworth's sonnet
sequence, "On the River Duddon."   A single sonnet of

---

* See Sonnet xvii., "On Revisiting Oxford."
See also Sonnet xi., "At Ostend : "

"The mournful magic of their mingled chimes
First waked my wondrous childhood into tears."

And *Cf.* Francis Mahony's "The Bells of Shandon"—

"Whose sounds so wild would, in the days of childhood,
Fling round my cradle their magic spells."

And Moore's "Those Evening Bells."   The twang of the
wind-harp also resounds through Bowles' Sonnets.   See for
the Æolus' harp, vol. i., p. 165, and *Cf.* Coleridge's poem,
"The Eolian Harp."

† "Dejection : An Ode" (1802).

Bowles will be enough to give a taste of his quality and to show what Coleridge got from him.*

Bowles was a disciple in the "School of Warton." He was "one of Joseph Warton's Winchester wonders," says Peter Cunningham, in a note in the second edition of Campbell's "Specimens of the British Poets"; "and the taste he imbibed there for the romantic school of poetry was strengthened and confirmed by his removal to Trinity College, Oxford, when Tom Warton was master there." Bowles was always prompt to own that he had learned his literary principles from the Wartons; and among his poems is a monody written on the death of his old teacher, the master of Winchester College. His verses abound in Gothic imagery quite in the Wartonian manner; the "castle gleaming on the distant steep"; "the pale moonlight in the midnight aisle"; "some convent's ancient walls," along the Rhine. Weak winds complain like spirits through the ruined arches of Netley Abbey:

> "The beam
> Of evening smiles on the gray battlement,
> And yon forsaken tower that time has rent."

* SONNET XX.

November, 1792.

> There is strange music in the stirring wind
>   When lowers the autumnal eve, and all alone
>   To the dark wood's cold covert thou art gone
> Whose ancient trees, on the rough slope reclined,
> Rock, and at times scatter their tresses sear.
>   If in such shades, beneath their murmuring,
>   Thou late hast passed the happier hours of spring,
> With sadness thou wilt mark the fading year;
>   Chiefly if one with whom such sweets at morn
>   Or eve thou'st shared, to distant scenes shall stray.
>   O Spring, return! return, auspicious May!
> But sad will be thy coming, and forlorn,
>   If she return not with thy cheering ray,
>   Who from these shades is gone, gone far away."

His lines on Shakspere recall Collins in their insistence upon the "elvish" things in the plays: "The
Tempest," "Midsummer Night's Dream," the weird sisters in "Macbeth," Ophelia's songs, the melancholy
Jacques. The lines to Burke on his "Reflections on the
Revolution in France," echo his celebrated dirge over
fallen chivalry:

> "Though now no more proud chivalry recalls
> The tourneys bright and pealing festivals;
> Though now on high her idle spear is hung,
> Though time her mouldering harp has half unstrung," etc.*

The "Hymn to Woden" alludes to Gray's "Fatal Sisters." "St. Michael's Mount" summons up the forms of
the ancient Druids, and sings how Fancy,

> "Sick of the fluttering fancies that engage
> The vain pursuits of a degenerate age, . . .
> Would fain the shade of elder days recall,
> The Gothick battlements, the bannered hall;
> Or list of elfin harps the fabling rhyme;
> Or, wrapt in melancholy trance sublime,
> Pause o'er the working of some wondrous tale,
> Or bid the spectres of the castle hail!"

Bowles' influence is traceable in Coleridge's earliest
volume of verse (1796) in a certain diffused softness and
gentle sensibility. This elegiac tone appears particularly
in effusions like "Happiness," "The Sigh," "To a
Young Ass," "To the Autumnal Moon," "Lines on an
Autumnal Evening," "To the Nightingale"; in "Melancholy: A Fragment" and "Elegy; imitated from Akenside," both in the "Sibylline Leaves" (1797); and in
numerous "lines," "monodies," "epitaphs," "odes," and

---

*Cf. Scott's "Harp of the North, that mouldering long hast
hung," etc. "Lady of the Lake," Canto I.

" stanzas." * Coleridge soon came to recognise the weakness of his juvenile verses, and parodied himself—and incidentally Bowles—in three sonnets printed at the end of Chapter I. of the " Biographia Literaria," designed to burlesque his own besetting sins, a " doleful egotism," an affected simplicity, and the use of " elaborate and swelling language and imagery." He never attained much success in the use of the sonnet form. A series of twelve sonnets in his first collection opens with one to Bowles:

"My heart has thanked thee, Bowles! for those soft strains
  Whose sadness soothes me, like the murmuring
  Of wild bees in the sunny showers of spring," etc.

More important to our inquiries than the poetry of Bowles is the occasion which he gave to the revival, under new conditions, of the Pope controversy. For it was over the body of Pope that the quarrel between classic and romantic was fought out in England, as it was fought out in France, a few years later, over the question of the dramatic unities and the mixture of tragedy and comedy in the *drame.* In 1806, just a half century after Joseph Warton published the first volume of his " Essay on Pope," Bowles' edition of the same poet appeared. In the life of Pope which was prefixed, the editor made some severe strictures on Pope's duplicity, jealousy, and other disagreeable traits, though not more severe than have been made by Pope's latest editor, Mr. Elwin, who has backed up his charges with an array of evidence fairly overwhelming. The edition contained likewise an

* "Shall gentle Coleridge pass unnoticed here,
  To turgid ode and tumid stanza dear?"
      —"English Bards and Scotch Reviewers."

essay on "The Poetical Character of Pope," in which
Bowles took substantially the same ground that had been
taken by his master, Joseph Warton, fifty years before.
He asserted in brief that, as compared with Spenser,
Shakspere, and Milton, Pope was a poet of the second
order; that in his descriptions of nature he was inferior
to Thomson and Cowper, and in lyrical poetry to Dryden
and Gray; and that, except in his "Eloisa" and one or
two other pieces, he was the poet of artificial manners
and of didactic maxims, rather than of passions.   Bowles'
chief addition to Warton's criticism was the following
paragraph, upon which the controversy that ensued chiefly
hinged: "All images drawn from what is beautiful or
sublime in the works of nature are more beautiful and
sublime than any images drawn from art, and they are
therefore *per se* (abstractedly) more poetical.   In like
manner those passions of the human heart, which belong
to nature in general, are *per se* more adapted to the higher
species of poetry than those derived from incidental and
transient manners."

The admirers of Pope were not slow in joining issue
with his critic, not only upon his general estimate of the
poet, but upon the principle here laid down.   Thomas
Campbell, in his "Specimens of the British Poets" (1819),
defended Pope both as a man and a poet, and maintained
that "exquisite descriptions of artificial objects are not
less characteristic of genius than the description of simple physical appearances."   He instanced Milton's description of Satan's spear and shield, and gave an ani-
mated picture of the launching of a ship of the line as
an example of the "sublime objects of artificial life."
Bowles replied in a letter to Campbell on "The Invari-

able Principles of Poetry." He claimed that it was the appearances of nature, the sea and the sky, that lent sublimity to the launch of the ship, and asked: " If images derived from art are as beautiful and sublime as those derived from nature, why was it necessary to bring your ship off the stocks? " He appealed to his adversary whether the description of a game of ombre was as poetical as that of a walk in the forest, and whether " the sylph of Pope, ' trembling over the fumes of a chocolate pot,' be an image as poetical as that of delicate and quaint Ariel, who sings ' Where the bee sucks, there lurk (*sic*) I.' " Campbell replied in the *New Monthly Magazine,* of which he was editor, and this drew out another rejoinder from Bowles. Meanwhile Byron had also attacked Bowles in two letters to Murray (1821), to which the indefatigable pamphleteer made elaborate replies. The elder Disraeli, Gifford, Octavius Gilchrist, and one Martin M'Dermot also took a hand in the fight—all against Bowles—and William Roscoe, the author of the "Life of Lorenzo de Medici," attacked him in an edition of Pope which he brought out in 1824. The rash detractor of the little Twitnam nightingale soon found himself engaged single-handed against a host; but he was equal to the occasion, in volubility if not in logic, and poured out a series of pamphlets, covering in all some thousand pages, and concluding with "A Final Appeal to the Literary Public" (1825), followed by "more last words of Baxter," in the shape of "Lessons in Criticism to William Roscoe" (1825).

The opponents of Bowles maintained, in general, that in poetry the subject is nothing, but the execution is all; that one class of poetry has, as such, no superiority over another; and that poets are to be ranked by their excellence as artists, and not according to some imaginary scale of dignity in the different orders of poetry, as epic, didactic, satiric, etc. "There is, in fact," wrote Roscoe, "no poetry in any subject except what is called forth by the genius of the poet. . . . There are no great subjects but such as are made so by the genius of the artist." Byron said that to the question "whether 'the description of a game of cards be as poetical, supposing the execution of the artists equal, as a description of a walk in a forest,' it may be answered that the materials are certainly not equal, but that the *artist* who has rendered the game of cards poetical is by far the greater of the two. But all this 'ordering' of poets is purely arbitrary on the part of Mr. Bowles. There may or may not be, in fact, different 'orders' of poetry, but the poet is always ranked according to his execution, and not according to his branch of the art." Byron also contended, like Campbell, that art is just as poetical as nature, and that it was not the water that gave interest to the ship but the ship to the water. "What was it attracted the thousands to the launch? They might have seen the poetical 'calm water' at Wapping or in the London lock or in the Paddington Canal or in a horse-pond or in a slop-basin." Without natural accessories—the sun, the sky, the sea, the wind—Bowles had said, the ship's properties are only blue bunting, coarse canvas, and tall poles. "So they are," admits Byron, "and porcelain is clay, and man is dust, and flesh is grass; and yet the two latter at least are the subjects of much poesy. . . . Ask the traveller what strikes him as most poetical, the Parthenon or the rock on which it stands. . . . Take away Stonehenge from Salisbury plain

and it is nothing more than Hounslow Heath òr any other
unenclosed down. . . . There can be nothing more poetical in its aspect than the city of Venice; does this de-
pend upon the sea or the canals? . . . Is it the Canal
Grande or the Rialto which arches it, the churches which
tower over it, the palaces which line and the gondolas
which glide over the waters, that render this city more
poetical than Rome itself? . . . Without these the water
would be nothing but a clay-coloured ditch. . . . There
would be nothing to make the canal of Venice more poetical than that of Paddington."

There was something futile about this whole discussion. It was marked with that fatally superficial and
mechanical character which distinguished all literary
criticism in Europe before the time of Lessing in Germany, and of Wordsworth and Coleridge in England. In
particular, the cardinal point on which Pope's rank as a
poet was made to turn was really beside the question.
There is no such essential distinction as was attempted
to be drawn between "natural objects" and "objects of
artificial life," as material for poetry. In a higher syn-
thesis, man and all his works are but a part of nature,
as Shakspere discerned:

> "Nature is made better by no mean
> But nature makes that mean: so over that art
> Which you say adds to nature, is an art
> That nature made: the art itself is nature."

Shakspere, as well as Pope, dealt with artificial life,
i.e., with the life of man in society, but how differently!
The reason why Pope's poetry fails to satisfy the heart
and the imagination resides not in his subjects—so far
Campbell and Byron were right—but in his mood; in his

imperfect sense of beauty and his deficiency in the highest qualities of the poet's soul. I may illustrate this by
an arrow from Byron's own quiver. To prove how much
poetry may be associated with "a simple, household,
'indoor,' artificial, and ordinary image," he cites the
famous stanza in Cowper's poem to Mrs. Unwin:

> "Thy needles, once a shining store,
> For my sake restless heretofore,
> Now rust disused and shine no more,
>   My Mary."

Let us contrast with this a characteristic passage from
"The Rape of the Lock," which also contains an artificial
image:

> "On her white breast a sparkling cross she wore
> Which Jews might kiss and infidels adore."

What is the difference? It is in the feeling of the poet.
Pope's couplet is very charming, but it is merely gallantry, a neatly turned compliment, playful, only half
sincere, a spice of mockery lurking under the sugared
words; while in Cowper's lines the humble domestic im-
plement is made sacred by the emotions of pity, sorrow,
gratitude, and affection with which it is associated. The
reason why Pope is not a high poet—or perhaps a poet at
all in the best sense of the word—is indicated by Coleridge with his usual acuteness and profundity in a sentence already quoted; that Pope's poetry both in matter
and diction was "characterised not so much by poetic
thoughts, as by thoughts *translated* into the language of
poetry."

Bowles, on the whole, had hold of the right end of the
controversy; his instinct was correct, but he was a
wretched controversialist. As a poet in the minor key,

he was tolerable; but as a prose writer, he was a very dull person and a bore. He was rude and clumsy; he tried to be sarcastic and couldn't; he had damnable iteration. Lowell speaks of his "peculiarly helpless way," and says: "Bowles, in losing his temper, lost also what little logic he had, and though, in a vague way, æsthetically right, contrived always to be argumentatively wrong. Anger made worse confusion in a brain never very clear, and he had neither the scholarship nor the critical faculty for a vigorous exposition of his own thesis. Never was wilder hitting than his, and he laid himself open to dreadful punishment, especially from Byron, whose two letters are masterpieces of polemic prose." Indeed, the most interesting feature of the Pope controversy is Byron's part in it and the light which it sheds on his position in relation to the classic and romantic schools. Before the definite outbreak of the controversy, Byron had attacked Bowles for his depreciation of Pope, in "English Bards and Scotch Reviewers" (1809), in a passage in which he wished that Bowles had lived in Pope's time, so that Pope might have put him into the "Dunciad."

It seems at first sight hard to reconcile Byron's evidently sincere admiration for Pope with the ultra-romantic cast of his own poetry—romantic, as Pater says, in mood if not in subject. In his early fondness for Ossian, his intense passion, his morbid gloom, his exaltation in wild and solitary places, his love of night and storm, of the desert and the ocean, in the careless and irregular outpour of his verse, in his subjectivity, the continual presence of the man in the work—in all these particulars Byron was romantic and would seem to have had little in common with Pope. But there was another side to Byron—and William Rossetti thinks his most characteristic side—viz., his wit and understanding; and this side sympathised heartily with Pope. It is well known that when Byron came back from the East he had in his trunk besides the manuscript of " Childe Harold," which he thought little of, certain " Hints from Horace " which the world thinks less of, but which he was eager to have published, while Dallas was urging him to print " Childe Harold." " English Bards and Scotch Reviewers " is a thoroughly Popeian satire; and " The Vision of Judgment," though not in couplets but in *ottava rima*, is one of the best personal satires in English. It has all of Pope's malicious wit, with a sweep and glow, which belonged to Byron as a poet rather than as a satirist, and which Pope never had. Lowell thinks, too, that what Byron admired in Pope was " that patience in careful finish which he felt to be wanting in himself and in most of his contemporaries."

With all this there probably mingled something of perversity and exaggeration in Byron's praises of Pope. He hated the Lakers, and he delighted to use Pope against them as a foil and a rod. He at least was everything that they were not. Doubtless in the Pope controversy, his " object was mainly mischief," as Lowell says. Byron loved a fight; he thought the Rev. W. L. Bowles an ass, and he determined to have some fun with him. Besides the two letters to Murray in 1821, an open letter of Byron's to Isaac Disraeli, dated March 15, 1820, and entitled " Some Observations upon an article in *Blackwood's Magazine*," * contains a long passage in vindication of Pope and in denunciation of contemporary poetry

* No. xxix., August, 1819, " Remarks on Don Juan."

—a passage which is important not only as showing Byron's opinions, but as testifying to the very general change in taste which had taken place since 1756, when Joseph Warton was so discouraged by the public hostility to his " Essay on Pope " that he withheld the second volume for twenty-six years. " The great cause of the present deplorable state of English poetry," writes Byron, " is to be attributed to that absurd and systematic depreciation of Pope in which, for the last few years, there has been a kind of epidemical concurrence. Men of the most opposite opinions have united upon this topic." He then goes on to praise Pope and abuse his own contemporaries, especially the Lake poets, both in the most extravagant terms. Pope he pronounces the most perfect and harmonious of poets. " Southey, Wordsworth, and Coleridge," he says, " had all of them a very natural antipathy to Pope . . . but they have been joined in it by . . . the whole heterogeneous mass of living English poets excepting Crabbe, Rogers, Gifford, and Campbell, who, both by precept and practice, have proved their adherence; and by me, who have shamefully deviated in practice, but have ever loved and honoured Pope's poetry with my whole soul." There is ten times more poetry, he thinks, in the " Essay on Man " than in the " Excursion "; and if you want passion, where is to be found stronger than in the " Epistle of Eloisa to Abelard "? To the sneer that Pope is only the " poet of reason " Byron replies that he will undertake to find more lines teeming with *imagination* in Pope than in any two living poets. " In the mean time," he asks, " what have we got instead? . . . The Lake school," and " a deluge of flimsy and unintelligible romances imitated from Scott and myself." He prophesies that all except the classical poets, Crabbe, Rogers, and Campbell, will survive their reputation, acknowledges that his own practice as a poet is not in harmony with his principles, and says: "I told Moore not very long ago, ' We are all wrong except Rogers, Crabbe, and Campbell.' " In the first of his two letters to Murray, Byron had taken himself to task in much the same way. He compared the romanticists to barbarians who had "raised a mosque by the side of a Grecian temple of the purest architecture"; and who were "not contented with their own grotesque edifice unless they destroy the prior and purely beautiful fabric which preceded, and which shames them and theirs for ever and ever. I shall be told that amongst those I *have* been (or it may be still *am*) conspicuous—true, and I am ashamed of it. I *have* been amongst the builders of this Babel . . . but never among the envious destroyers of the classic temple of our predecessor." "Neither time nor distance nor grief nor age can ever diminish my veneration for him who is the great moral poet of all times, of all climes, of all feelings, and of all stages of existence. The delight of my boyhood, the study of my manhood, perhaps he may be the consolation of my age. His poetry is the Book of Life." *

* " Time was, ere yet in these degenerate days
    Ignoble themes obtained mistaken praise.
    When sense and wit with poesy allied,
    No fabled graces, flourished side by side. . . .
    Then, in this happy isle, a Pope's pure strain
    Sought the rapt soul to charm, nor sought in vain ;
    A polished nation's praise aspired to claim,
    And raised the people's, as the poet's fame. . . .
    [But] Milton, Dryden, Pope, alike forgot,
    Resign their hallowed bays to Walter Scott."
        —" English Bards and Scotch Reviewers."

Strange language this from the author of "Childe Harold" and "The Corsair"! But the very extravagance of Byron's claims for Pope makes it plain that he was pleading a lost cause. When Warton issued the first volume of his "Essay on Pope," it was easy for leaders of literary opinion, like Johnson and Goldsmith, to pooh-pooh the critical canons of the new school. But when Byron wrote, the æsthetic revolution was already accomplished. The future belonged not to Campbell and Gifford and Rogers and Crabbe, but to Wordsworth and Scott and Coleridge and Shelley and Keats; to Byron himself, the romantic poet, but not to Byron the *laudator temporis acti.* The victory remained with Bowles, not because he had won it by argument, but because opinion had changed, and changed probably once and for all.*

*For the benefit of any reader who may wish to follow up the steps of the Pope controversy, I give the titles of Bowles' successive pamphlets. "The Invariable Principles of Poetry: A Letter to Thomas Campbell, Esq.," 1819. "A Reply to an 'Unsentimental Sort of Critic,'" Bath, 1820. [This was in answer to a review of "Spence's Anecdotes" in the *Quarterly* for October, 1820.] "A Vindication of the Late Editor of Pope's Works," London, 1821, second edition. [This was also a reply to the *Quarterly* reviewer and to Gilchrist's letters in the *London Magazine*, and was first printed in vol. xvii., Nos. 33, 34, and 35 of the *Pamphleteer.*] "An Answer to Some Observations of Thomas Campbell, Esq., in his Specimens of British Poets" (1822). "An Address to Thomas Campbell, Esq., Editor of the *New Monthly Magazine*, in Consequence of an Article in that Publication" (1822). "Letters to Lord Byron on a Question of Poetical Criticism," London, 1822. "A Final Appeal to the Literary Public Relative to Pope, in Reply to Certain Observations of Mr. Roscoe," London, 1825. "Lessons in Criticism to William Roscoe, Esq., with Further Lessons in Criticism to a Quarterly Reviewer," London, 1826. Gilchrist's three letters to Bowles were published in 1820–21. M'Dermot's "Letter to the Rev. W. L. Bowles in Reply to His Letter to Thomas Campbell, Esq., and to His Two Letters to Lord Byron," was printed at London, in 1822.

Coleridge's four contributions to the "Lyrical Ballads" included his masterpiece, "The Ancient Mariner." This is the high-water mark of romantic poetry; and, familiar as it is, cannot be dismissed here without full examination. As to form, it is a long narrative ballad in seven "fyts" or parts, and descends from that "Bible of the romantic reformation," Bishop Percy's "Reliques." The verse is the common ballad stanza—eights and sixes—enriched by a generous use of medial rhyme and alliteration:

> "The fair breeze blew, the white foam flew,
>   The furrow followed free:
> We were the first that ever burst
>   Into that silent sea";

varied and prolonged, moreover, by the introduction of additional lines with alternate riming, with couplets and sometimes with triplets. There are many five-lined and six-lined stanzas, and one—the longest in the poem —of nine lines. But these metric variations are used with temperance. The stanza form is never complex; it is built up naturally from the ballad stanza upon which it rests and to which it constantly returns as its norm and type. Of the one hundred and forty-two stanzas in the poem, one hundred and six are the ordinary four-lined stanzas of popular poetry. The language, too, is not obtrusively archaic as it is in Chatterton and some of the Spenserians; at most an occasional "wist" or "eftsoons"; now and then a light accent, in ballad fashion, on the final syllable of a rime-word like mariner or countrie. There is no definite burden, which would have been out of place in a poem that is narrative and not lyrical; but the ballad habits of phrase repeti-

tion and question and answer are sparingly employed.* In
reproducing the homely diction of old popular minstrelsy,
Coleridge's art was nicer than Scott's and more perfect
at every point. How skilfully studied, *e.g.*, is the simplicity of the following:

> "The moving moon went up the sky
> And nowhere did abide:
> *Softly she was going up.*"

> "Day after day, day after day
> *We stuck.*"

"The naive artlessness of the Middle Ages," says
Brandl, "became in the hands of the Romantic school,
an intentional form of art." The impression of antiquity
is heightened by the marginal gloss which the poet added
in later editions, composed in a prose that has a quaint
beauty of its own, in its mention of "the creatures of the
calm"; its citation of "the learned Jew Josephus and the
Platonic Constantinopilitan, Michael Psellus," as authorities on invisible spirits; and in passages like that
Dantesque one which tells how the mariner "in his lone-
liness and fixedness yearneth towards the journeying
moon, and the stars that still sojourn, yet still move onwards; and everywhere the blue sky belongs to them, and

---

* "With throats unslaked, with black lips baked,
  We could not laugh nor wail," etc.

"With throats unslaked, with black lips baked,
  Agape they heard me call," etc.

"Are those her sails that glance in the sun
  Like restless gossamers?
  Are those her ribs," etc.

Cf. "Christabel":

> "Is the night chilly and dark?
> The night is chilly, but not dark."

And see vol. i., p. 271.

is their appointed rest, and their native country, and their own natural homes, which they enter unannounced, as lords that are certainly expected, and yet there is a silent joy at their arrival."

In "The Ancient Mariner" there are present in the highest degree the mystery, indefiniteness, and strangeness which are the marks of romantic art. The period is not strictly mediæval, for mariners in the Middle Ages did not sail to the south polar regions or lie becalmed in the equatorial seas. But the whole atmosphere of the poem is mediæval. The Catholic idea of penance or expiation is the moral theme enwrought with the story. The hermit who shrives the mariner, and the little vesper bell which biddeth him to prayer are Catholic touches, and so are the numerous pious oaths and ejaculations:

> "By him who died on cross":
> "Heaven's mother send us grace":
> "The very deep did rot.   O Christ
>   That ever this should be!"

The albatross is hung about the mariner's neck instead of the crucifix, and drops off only when he blesses the creatures of the calm and is able to pray. The sleep which refreshes him is sent by "Mary Queen" from heaven. The cross-bow with which he shoots the bird is a mediæval property. The loud bassoon and the bride's garden bower and the procession of merry minstrels who go nodding their heads before her are straight out of the old land of balladry. One cannot fancy the wedding guest dressed otherwise than in doublet and hose, and perhaps wearing those marvellous pointed shoes and hanging sleeves which are shown in miniature paintings of the fifteenth century. And it is thus that illustrators

of the poem have depicted him.   Place is equally indefinite with time.   What port the ill-fated ship cleared from
we do not know or seek to know; only the use of the
word *kirk* implies that it was somewhere in "the north
countree"—the proper home of ballad poetry.

Coleridge's romances were very differently conceived
from Scott's.   He wove them out of "such stuff as
dreams are made on."   Industrious commentators have
indeed traced features of "The Ancient Mariner" to
various sources.   Coleridge's friend, Mr. Cruikshank.
had a dream of a skeleton ship.   Wordsworth told him
the incident, which he read in Shelvocke's voyages, of a
certain Captain Simon Hatley who shot a black albatross
south of Terra del Fuego, in hopes that its death might
bring fair weather.   Brandl thinks that the wedding ban-
quet in Monk Lewis' "Alonzo the Brave and the Fair
Imogene," furnished a hint; and surmises—what seems
unlikely—that Coleridge had read a certain epistle by
Paulinus, a bishop of the fourth century, describing a
vessel which came ashore on the coast of Lucania with
only one sailor on board, who reported that the ship had
been deserted, as a wreck, by the rest of the crew, and
had since been navigated by spirits.

But all this is nothing and less than nothing.   "The
Ancient Mariner" is the baseless fabric of a vision.   We
are put under a spell, like the wedding guest, and carried
off to the isolation and remoteness of mid-ocean.   Through
the chinks of the narrative, the wedding music sounds
unreal and far off.   What may not happen to a man alone
on a wide, wide sea?   The line between earthly and unearthly vanishes.   Did the mariner really see the spectral bark and hear spirits talking, or was it all but the

phantasmagoria of the calenture, the fever which attacks
the sailor on the tropic main, so that he seems to see
green meadows and water brooks on the level brine? No
one can tell; for he is himself the only witness, and the
ship is sunk at the harbour mouth. One conjectures that
no wreckers or divers will ever bring it to the top again.
Nay, was not the mariner, too, a spectre? Now he is
gone, and what was all this that he told me, thinks the
wedding guest, as he rises on the morrow morn. Or did
he tell me, or did I only dream it? A light shadow cast
by some invisible thing swiftly traverses the sunny face
of nature and is gone. Did we see it, or imagine it?
Even so elusive, so uncertain, so shadowy and phantom-
like is the spiriting of this wonderful poem. "Poetry,"
says Coleridge, "gives most pleasure when only generally and not perfectly understood. It was so by me with
Gray's ' Bard ' and Collins' odes. ' The Bard ' once intoxicated me, and now I read it without pleasure." *
There is no danger that his own poem will ever lose its
attractiveness in this way. Something inexplicable will
remain to tease us, like the white Pater Noster and St.
Peter's sister in Chaucer's night-spell.†

---

* "Anima Poetæ," 1895. p. 5. This recent collection of
marginalia has an equal interest with Coleridge's well-known
"Table Talk." It is the English equivalent of Hawthorne's
"American Note Books," full of analogies, images, and reflections—topics and suggestions for possible development
in future romances and poems. In particular it shows an
abiding prepossession with the psychology of dreams, apparitions, and mental illusions of all sorts.

    † "Jesu Crist and Seint Benedight
      Blisse this hous from every wicked wight,
      Fro the nightes mare, the white Pater Noster ;
      Where wonest thou, Seint Peter's suster."
             —"The Miller's Tale."

Pater subtly connects Coleridge's poetic method with his philosophical idealism. "The too palpable intruders from a spiritual world, in almost all ghost literature, in Scott and Shakespeare even, have a kind of coarseness or crudeness. . . . 'The Rime of the Ancient Mariner' has the plausibility, the perfect adaptation to reason and life, which belongs to the marvellous, when actually presented as part of a credible experience in our dreams. . . . The spectral object, so crude, so impossible, has become plausible, as 'the spot upon the brain that will show itself without,' and is understood to be but a condition of one's own mind, for which—according to the scepticism latent at least in so much of our modern philosophy—the so-called real things themselves are but *spectra* after all. It is this finer, more delicately marvellous supernaturalism, the fruit of his more delicate psychology, which Coleridge infuses into romantic narrative, itself also then a new or revived thing in English literature; and with a fineness of weird effect in 'The Ancient Mariner' unknown in those old, more simple, romantic legends and ballads. It is a flower of mediæval, or later German romance, growing up in the peculiarly compounded atmosphere of modern psychological speculation, and putting forth in it wholly new qualities."

In "The Ancient Mariner," as in most purely romantic poetry, the appeal is more to the imagination than to the heart or the conscience. Mrs. Barbauld complained that it was improbable and had no moral. Coleridge admitted its improbability, but said that it had too much moral; that, artistically speaking, it should have had no more moral than a fairy tale. The lesson of course is that of kindness to animals—" He prayeth well who lov-

eth well," etc.   But the punishment of the mariner, and
still more of the mariner's messmates, is so out of proportion to the gravity of the offence as to be slightly
ludicrous when stated by Leslie Stephen thus: "People
who approve of the unnecessary killing of an albatross
will die a lingering death by starvation." The moral, as
might be guessed, was foisted upon the poem by Wordsworth, and is identical with that of "Hart-Leap Well."
Wordsworth and Coleridge started to write "The Ancient Mariner" jointly; and two or three lines in the
poem, as it stands, were contributed by Wordsworth. But
he wanted to give the mariner himself "character and
profession"; and to have the dead seamen come to life
and sail the ship into port; and in other ways laid so
heavy a hand upon Coleridge's airy creation that it became plain that a partnership on these terms was out of
the question, and Wordsworth withdrew altogether. If
we must look for spiritual sustenence in the poem, we
shall find it perhaps not so much in any definite warning
against cruelty to creatures, as in the sentiment of the
blessedness of human companionship and the omnipres-
ence of God's mercy; in the passage, *e.g.*,

> "O wedding guest! this soul hath been
> Alone on a wide, wide sea," etc.—

where the thought is the same as in Cowper's "Soliloquy
of Alexander Selkirk," even to the detail of the "church-
going bell."

The first part of "Christabel" was written in 1797;
the second in 1800; and the poem, in its unfinished state,
was given to the press in 1816. Meanwhile it had become widely known in manuscript.   Coleridge used to

read it to literary circles, and copies of it had got about. We have seen its influence upon Scott. Byron too admired it greatly, and it was by his persuasion that Coleridge finally published it as a fragment, finding himself unable to complete it, and feeling doubtless that the public regarded him much as the urchins in Keats' poem regarded the crone

> "Who keepeth close a wondrous riddle book,
> As spectacled she sits in chimney nook."

"Christabel" is more distinctly mediæval than "The Ancient Mariner," and is full of Gothic elements: a moated castle, with its tourney court and its great gate

> . . . "ironed within and without,
> Where an army in battle array had marched out":

a feudal baron with a retinue of harpers, heralds, and pages; a lady who steals out at midnight into the moonlit oak wood, to pray for her betrothed knight; a sorceress who pretends to have been carried off on a white palfrey by five armed men, and who puts a spell upon the maiden. If "The Ancient Mariner" is a ballad, "Christabel" is, in form, a *roman d'aventures*, or metrical chivalry tale, written in variations of the octosyllabic couplet. These variations, Coleridge said, were not introduced wantonly but "in correspondence with some transition, in the nature of the imagery or passion." A single passage will illustrate this:

> "They passed the hall that echoes still,
> Pass as lightly as you will.
> The brands were flat, the brands were dying
> Amid their own white ashes lying;

> But when the lady passed, there came
> A tongue of light, a fit of flame ;
> And Christabel saw the lady's eye,
> And nothing else saw she thereby,
> Save the boss of the shield of Sir Leoline tall,
> Which hung in a murky old niche in the wall.
> O softly tread, said Christabel,
> My father seldom sleepeth well."

When, after the hurrying anapæsts, the verse returns to the strict iambic measure in the last couplet, the effect is a hush, in harmony with the meaning of the words.*

"Christabel" is not so unique and perfect a thing as "The Ancient Mariner," but it has the same haunting charm, and displays the same subtle art in the use of the supernatural. Coleridge protested that it "pretended to be nothing more than a common fairy tale." † But Lowell asserts that it is "tantalising in the suggestion of deeper meanings than were ever there." There is, in truth, a hint of allegory, like that which baffles and fascinates in Christina Rossetti's "Goblin Market"; a hint so elusive that the comparison often made between Geraldine and Spenser's Duessa, is distressing to a reader of sensitive nerves. That mystery which is a favourite weapon in the romanticist armoury is used again here with consummate skill. What was it that Christabel saw on the lady's bosom? We are left to conjecture. It was "a sight to dream of, not to tell," ‡ and the poet keeps his secret. Lamb, whose taste was very fine in these matters, advised Coleridge never to finish the poem. Brandl thinks that the idea was taken from the curtained

---

* *Vide supra*, p. 27.
† "Biographia Literaria," chap. xxiv.
‡ Keats quotes this line in a letter about Edmund Kean. Forman's ed., vol. iii., p. 4.

picture in the "Mysteries of Udolpho"; and he also con-
siders that the general situation—the castle, the forest,
the old father and his young daughter, and the strange
lady—are borrowed from Mrs. Radcliffe's "Romance
of the Forest"; and that Bürger's "Lenore," Lewis'
"Alonzo," and some of the Percy ballads contributed a
detail here and there. But *Quellenforschungen* of this
kind are very unimportant. It is more important to note
the superior art with which the poet excites curiosity and
suspends—not simply, like Mrs. Radcliffe, postpones—
the gratification of it to the end, and beyond the end, of
the poem. Was Geraldine really a witch, or did she only
seem so to Christabel? The angry moan of the mastiff
bitch and the tongue of flame that shot up as the lady
passed—were they omens, or accidents which popular
superstition interprets into omens? Was the malignant
influence which Geraldine exerted over the maiden supernatural possession, or the fascination of terror and repug-
nance? Did she really utter the words of a charm, or
did her sweet bedfellow dream them? And once more,
what was that upon her breast—"that bosom old—that
bosom cold"? Was it a wound, or the mark of a serpent, or some foul and hideous disfigurement—or was it
only the shadows cast by the swinging lamp?

That isolation and remoteness, that preparation of the
reader's mind for the reception of incredible things, which
Coleridge secured in "The Ancient Mariner" by cutting
off his hero from all human life amid the solitude of the
tropic sea, he here secured—in a less degree, to be sure
—by the lonely midnight in Sir Leoline's castle. Geraldine and her victim are the only beings awake except
the hooting owls. There is dim moonlight in the wood,

dim firelight in the hall, and in Christabel's chamber "the silver lamp burns dead and dim."

The second part of the poem was less successful, partly for the reason, as the reviewers pointed out, that it undertakes the hardest of tasks, "witchery by daylight." But there were other reasons. Three years had passed since the poem was begun. Coleridge had been to Germany and had settled at Keswick. The poet had been lost in the metaphysician, and he took up his interrupted task without inspiration, putting force upon himself. The signs of effort are everywhere visible, and it is painfully manifest that the poet cannot recover the genial, creative mood in which he had set out. In particular it is observable that, while there is no mention of place in the first part, now we have frequent references to Windermere, Borrowdale, Dungeon Ghyll, and other Lake Country localities familiar enough in Wordsworth's poetry, but strangely out of place in "Christabel." It was certainly an artistic mistake to transfer Sir Leoline's castle from fairyland to Cumberland.* There is one noble passage in the second part, the one which Byron prefixed to his "Farewell" to Lady Byron:

"Alas! they had been friends in youth," etc.

But the stress of personal emotion in these lines is not in harmony with the romantic context. They are like a patch of cloth of gold let into a lace garment and straining the delicate tissue till it tears.

The example of "The Ancient Mariner," and in a still greater degree of "Christabel," was potent upon all subsequent romantic poetry. It is seen in Scott, in Byron,

* *Vide supra*, p. 14.

and in Keats, not only in the modelling of their tales, but in single lines and images. In the first stanza of the "Lay" Scott repeats the line which occurs so often in "Christabel"—"Jesu Maria shield her well!" In the same poem, the passage where the Lady Margaret steals out of Branksome Tower at dawn to meet her lover in the wood, gliding down the secret stair and passing the bloodhound at the portal, will remind all readers of "Christabel." The dialogue between the river and mountain spirits will perhaps remind them of the ghostly antiphonies which the "Mariner" hears in his trance. The couplet

> "The seething pitch and molten lead
> Reeked like a witch's caldron red."

is, of course, from Coleridge's

> "The water, like a witch's oils,
> Burned green and blue and white."

In "The Lord of the Isles" Scott describes the "elvish lustre" and "livid flakes" of the phosphorescence of the sea, and cites, in a note, the description, in "The Ancient Mariner," of the sea snakes from which

> "The elvish light
> Fell off in hoary flakes."

The most direct descendant of "Christabel" was "The Eve of St. Agnes." Madeline's chamber, "hushed, silken, chaste," recalls inevitably the passage in the older poem:

> "The moon shines dim in the open air,
> And not a moonbeam enters here.
> But they without its light can see
> The chamber carved so curiously,

> Carved with figures strange and sweet,
> All made out of the carver's brain,
> For a lady's chamber meet :
> The lamp with twofold silver chain
> Is fastened to an angel's feet."

The rest of Coleridge's ballad work is small in quantity and may be dismissed briefly. " Alice du Clos " has good lines, but is unimportant as a whole. The very favourite poem " Love " is a modern story enclosing a mediæval one. In the moonshine by the ruined tower the guileless Genevieve leans against the statue of an armed man, while her lover sings her a tale of a wandering knight who bore a burning brand upon his shield and went mad for the love of " The Lady of the Land." *

The fragment entitled " The Dark Ladie " was begun as a " sister tale " to " Love." The hero is a " knight that wears the griffin for his crest." There are only fifteen stanzas of it, and it breaks off with a picture of an imaginary bridal procession, whose " nodding minstrels " recall " The Ancient Mariner," and incidentally some things of Chatterton's. Lines of a specifically romantic colouring are of course to be found scattered about nearly everywhere in Coleridge; like the musical little song that follows the invocation to the soul of Alvar in " Remorse " :

> "And at evening evermore,
> In a chapel on the shore,
> Shall the chanters sad and saintly—
> Yellow tapers burning faintly—
> Doleful masses chant for thee,
> *Miserere Domine !* "

* Brandl thinks that this furnished Keats with a hint or two for his " Belle Dame sans Merci." Coleridge's " Dejection : An Ode " is headed with a stanza from " the grand old ballad of Sir Patrick Spence."

or the wild touch of folk poesy in that marvellous opium dream, "Kubla Khan"—the "deep romantic chasm":

> "A savage place, as holy and enchanted
> As e'er beneath a waning moon was haunted
> By woman wailing for her demon lover."

Or the well-known ending of "The Knight's Grave":

> "The knight's bones are dust,
> And his good sword rust;
> His soul is with the saints, I trust."

In taking account of Coleridge's services to the cause of romanticism, his critical writings should not be overlooked. Matthew Arnold declared that there was something premature about the burst of creative activity in English literature at the opening of the nineteenth century, and regretted that the way had not been prepared, as in Germany, by a critical movement. It is true that the English romantics put forth no body of doctrine, no authoritative statement of a theory of literary art. Scott did not pose as the leader of a school, or compose prefaces and lectures like Hugo and Schlegel.* As a

---

* "The English Romantic critics did not form a school. Like everything else in the English Romantic movement, its criticism was individual, isolated, sporadic, unsystematised. It had no official mouthpiece, like Sainte-Beuve and the *Globe;* its members formed no compact phalanx like that which, towards the close of our period, threw itself upon the 'classiques' of Paris. Nor did they, with the one exception of Coleridge, approach the Romantic critics of Germany in range of ideas, in grasp of the larger significance of their own movement. It was only in Germany that the ideas implicit in the great poetic revival were explicitly thought out in all their many-sided bearing upon society, history, philosophy, religion ; and that the problem of criticism, in particular, was presented in its full depth and richness of meaning. . . . As English Romanticism achieved greater things on its creative than on its critical side, so its criticism was more remarkable

contributor to the reviews on his favourite topics, he was no despicable critic; shrewd, good-natured, full of special knowledge, anecdote, and illustration. But his criticism was never polemic, and he had no quarrel with the classics. He cherished an unfeigned admiration for Dryden, whose life he wrote and whose works he edited. Doubtless he would cheerfully have admitted the inferiority of his own poetry to Dryden's and Pope's. He had no programme to announce, but just went ahead writing romances; in practice an innovator, but in theory a literary conservative.

Coleridge, however, was fully aware of the scope of the new movement. He represented, theoretically as well as practically, the reaction against eighteenth-century academicism, the Popean tradition* in poetry, and the maxims of pseudo-classical criticism. In his analysis and vindication of the principles of romantic art, he brought to bear a philosophic depth and subtlety such as had never before been applied in England to a merely belletristic subject. He revolutionised, for one thing, the critical view of Shakspere, devoting several lecture courses to the exposition of the thesis that "Shakspere's judgment was commensurate with his genius." These lectures borrowed a number of passages from A. W. von Schlegel's "Vorlesungen über Dramatische Kunst

on that side which is akin to creation—in the subtle appreciation of literary quality—than in the analysis of the principles on which its appreciation was founded" (C. H. Herford: "The Age of Wordsworth," p. 50).

* See "Biographia Literaria," chap. i. "From the common opinion that the English style attained its greatest perfection in and about Queen Anne's reign, I altogether dissent" (Lecture "On Style," March 13, 1818).

und Litteratur," delivered at Vienna in 1808, but en-
grafted with original matter of the highest value. Compared with these Shakspere notes, with the chapters on
Wordsworth in the "Biographia Literaria," and with the
obiter dicta sown through Coleridge's prose, all previous
English criticism appears crude and superficial, and the
contemporary squabble over Pope like a scolding match
in the nursery.

Coleridge's acute and sympathetic insight into the
principles of Shaksperian drama did not save him from
producing his abortive "Zapolya" in avowed imitation
of the "Winter's Tale." What curse is on the English
stage that men who have done work of the highest grade
in other departments, as soon as they essay playwriting,
become capable of failures like "The Borderers" and
"John Woodville" and "Manfred" and "Zapolya"?
As for "Remorse," with its Moorish sea-coasts, wild
mountains, chapel interiors with painted windows, torch-
light and moonlight, dripping caverns, dungeons, daggers
and poisoned goblets, the best that can be said of it is
that it is less bad than "Zapolya." And of both it may
be said that they are romantic not after the fashion of
Shakspere, but of those very German melodramas which
Coleridge ridiculed in his "Critique on Bertram." *

* See vol. i., p. 421 ff.

CHAPTER III.

Keats, Leigh Hunt, and the Dante Revival.

IN the interchange of literary wares between England and Germany during the last years of the eighteenth century, it is observable that the English romantics went no further back than to their own contemporaries for their knowledge of the *Deutsche Vergangenheit.* They translated or imitated robber tragedies, chivalry tales, and ghost ballads from the modern restorers of the Teutonic *Mittelalter;* but they made no draughts upon the original storehouse of German mediæval poetry. There was no such reciprocity as yet between England and the Latin countries. French romanticism dates, at the earliest, from Chateaubriand's "Génie du Christianisme" (1802), and hardly made itself felt as a definite force, even in France, before Victor Hugo's "Cromwell" (1828). But in the first quarter of the nineteenth century, Italy, Spain, and France began to contribute material to the English movement in the shape of translations like Cary's "Divine Comedy" (1814); Lockhart's "Spanish Ballads" (1824); Southey's "Amadis of Gaul" (1803), "Palmerin of England" (1807), and "The Chronicle of the Cid" (1808); and Rose's* "Partenopex of Blois" (1807). By far the most influential of these was Cary's "Dante."

---

* Scott's friend, William Stewart Rose—to whom the first verse epistle in "Marmion" is addressed. He also translated the "Orlando Furioso" (1823–31). His "Partenopex" was made from a version in modern French.

Hitherto the Italian Middle Age had impressed itself
upon the English imagination not directly but through
the richly composite art of the Renaissance schools of
painting and poetry; through Raphael and his followers;
through the romances of Ariosto and Tasso and their
English scholar, Spenser.   Elizabethan England had been
supplied with versions of the "Orlando Furioso"* and
the "Gierusalemme Liberata," by Harrington and Fair-
fax—the latter still a standard translation and a very accomplished piece of versification.   Warton and Hurd and
other romanticising critics of the eighteenth century were
perpetually upholding Ariosto and Tasso against French
detraction :

> "In face of all his foes, the Cruscan quire,
>   And Boileau, whose rash envy could allow
>   No strain which shamed his country's creaking lyre,
>   That whetstone of the teeth—monotony in wire!" †

Scott's eager championship of Ariosto has already been
mentioned.‡   But the stuff of the old Charlemagne epos is
sophisticated in the brilliant pages of Ariosto, who
follows Pulci and Boiardo, if not in burlesquing chivalry
outright, yet in treating it with a half irony.   Tasso is
serious, but submits his romantic matter—Godfrey of
Boulogne and the First Crusade—to the classical epic
mould.   It was pollen from Italy, but not Italy of the
Middle Ages, that fructified English poetry in the six-

---

* A new translation of the "Orlando," by Hoole, appeared
in 1773-83 ; of Tasso's "Jerusalem" in 1763 ; and of Metasta-
sio's dramas in 1767.   These were in the heroic couplets of
Pope.

† "Childe Harold," Canto iv., xxxviii.   And *Cf.* vol. i., pp.
25, 49, 100, 170, 219, 222–26.

‡ *Vide supra*, p. 5.

teenth century. Two indeed of *gli antichi*, "the all Etruscan three," communicated an impulse both earlier and later. Love sonneteering, in emulation of Petrarca, began at Henry VIII.'s court. Chaucer took the substance of "Troilus and Creseyde" and "The Knightes Tale" from Boccaccio's "Filostrato" and "Teseide"; and Dryden, who never mentions Dante, versified three stories from the "Decameron." But Petrarch and Boccaccio were not mediæval minds. They represent the earlier stages of humanism and the new learning. Dante was the genuine *homme du moyen âge*, and Dante was the latest of the great revivals. "Dante," says Carlyle, "was the spokesman of the Middle Ages; the thought they lived by stands here in everlasting music."

The difficulty, not to say obscurity, of the "Divine Comedy"; its allusive, elliptical style; its scholasticism and allegorical method; its multitudinous references to local politics and the history of thirteenth-century Italy, defied approach. Above all, its profound, austere, mystical spirituality was abhorrent to the clear, shallow rationalism of the eighteenth century, as well as to the religious liberalism of the seventeenth and the joyous sensuality of the sixteenth. Goethe the pagan disliked Dante, no less than Scott the Protestant.* In particular, deistic France, *arbiter elegantiarum*, felt with a shiver of repulsion,

"How grim the master was of Tuscan song."

"I estimate highly," wrote Voltaire to an Italian correspondent, "the courage with which you have dared to

* *Vide supra*, p. 40. Goethe pronounced the "Inferno" abominable, the "Purgatorio" doubtful, and the "Paradiso" tiresome (Plumptre's "Dante," London, 1887, vol. ii., p. 484).

say that Dante was a madman * and his work a monster.
. . . There are found among us and in the eighteenth
century, people who strive to admire imaginations so
stupid and barbarous." A French translation of the
"Divine Comedy" had been printed by the Abbé Gran-
gier† at Paris in 1596; but Rivarol, whose "Inferno"
was published in 1783, was the first Frenchman, says
Lowell, to divine Dante's greatness. The earliest German version was Bachenschwanz's prose translation of
the "Commedia" (Leipsic, 1767–69),‡ but the German
romantic school were the first to furnish a sympathetic
interpretation of Dante to their countrymen.

Chaucer was well acquainted with the work of "the
grete poet of Florence," and drew upon him occasionally,
though by no means so freely as upon Boccaccio. Thus
in "The Monkes Tale" he re-tells, in a very inferior
fashion, the tragedy of Ugolino. In "The Parliament of
Foules" and "The Hous of Fame" there are distinct
imitations of Dante. A passage from the "Purgatory"
is quoted in the "Wif of Bathes Tale," etc. Spenser
probably, and Milton certainly, knew their Dante. Milton's sonnet to Henry Lawes mentions Dante's encounter with the musician Casella "in the milder shades
of Purgatory." Here and there a reference to the "Divine Comedy" occurs in some seventeenth-century English prose writer like Sir Thomas Browne or Jeremy Taylor. It is thought that the description of Hell in
Sackville's "Mirror for Magistrates" shows an acquaint-

* See Walpole's opinion, vol. i., p. 235.
† For early manuscript renderings see "Les Plus Anciennes
Traductions Françaises de la Divine Comédie," par C. Morel,
Paris, 1897.
‡ Lowell says Kannegiesser's, 1809.

ance with the "Inferno." But Dante had few readers in England before the nineteenth century. He was practically unknown there and in all of Europe outside of Italy. "His reputation," said Voltaire, "will go on increasing because scarce anybody reads him." And half a century later Napoleon said the same thing in the same words: "His fame is increasing and will continue to increase because no one ever reads him."

In the third volume of his "History of English Poetry" (1781), Thomas Warton had spoken of the "Divine Comedy" as "this wonderful compound of classical and romantic fancy, of pagan and Christian theology, of real and fictitious history, of tragical and comic incidents, of familiar and heroic manners, and of satirical and sublime poetry. But the grossest improprieties of this poem discover an originality of invention, and its absurdities often border on sublimity. We are surprised that a poet should write one hundred cantos on hell, paradise, and purgatory. But this prolixity is partly owing to the want of art and method, and is common to all early compositions, in which everything is related circumstantially and without rejection, and not in those general terms which are used by modern writers." Warton is shocked at Dante's "disgusting fooleries" and censures his departure from Virgilian grace. Milton "avoided the childish or ludicrous excesses of these bold inventions . . . but rude and early poets describe everything." But Warton felt Dante's greatness. "Hell," he wrote, "grows darker at his frown." He singled out for special mention the Francesca and Ugolino episodes.

If Warton could write thus it is not surprising to discover among classical critics either a total silence as to

Dante, or else a systematic depreciation. Addison does
not mention him in his Italian travels; and in his "Saturday papers" misses the very obvious chance for a comparison between Dante and Milton such as Macaulay
afterwards elaborated in his essay on Milton. Goldsmith, who knew nothing of Dante at first hand, wrote
of him with the usual patronising ignorance of eighteenth-
century criticism as to anything outside of the Greek
and Latin classics: "He addressed a barbarous people
in a method suited to their apprehension; united purgatory and the river Styx, St. Paul and Virgil, heaven
and hell together; and shows a strange mixture of good
sense and absurdity. The truth is, he owes most of his
reputation to the obscurity of the times in which he
lived." *

In 1782, William Hayley, the biographer of Cowper
and author of that very mild poem "The Triumphs of
Temper," published a verse "Essay on Epic Poetry"
in five epistles. In his notes to the third epistle, he
gave an outline of Dante's life with a translation of
his sonnet to Guido Cavalcanti and of the first three cantos of the "Inferno." "Voltaire," he says, has spoken
of Dante "with that precipitate vivacity which so frequently led the lively Frenchman to insult the reputation
of the noblest writers." He refers to the "judicious and
spirited summary" of the "Divine Comedy" in Warton,
and adds, "We have several versions of the celebrated
story of Ugolino; but I believe no entire canto of Dante
has hitherto appeared in our language. . . . The author
has been solicited to execute an entire translation of
Dante, but the extreme inequality of this poet would render

* "Present State of Polite Learning" (1759).

such a work a very laborious undertaking; and it appears very doubtful how far such a version would interest our country. Perhaps the reception of these cantos may discover to the translator the sentiments of the public." Hayley adopted "triple rhyme," *i.e.*, the *terza rima*, and said that he did not recollect it had ever been used before in English. His translation is by no means contemptible—much better than Boyd's,—but fails entirely to catch Dante's manner or to keep the strange precision and picturesqueness of his phrase. Thus he renders

"Chi per lungo silenzio parea fioco,"

"Whose voice was like the whisper of a lute";

and the poet is made to address Beatrice—O donna di virtu—as "bright fair," as if she were one of the belles in "The Rape of the Lock." In this same year a version of the "Inferno" was printed privately and anonymously by Charles Rogers, a book and art collector and a friend of Sir Joshua Reynolds. But the first complete translation of the "Comedy" into English was made by Henry Boyd, a clergyman of the Irish Church; the "Inferno" in 1785 (with a specimen from Ariosto); the whole in 1802. Boyd was a quite obscure person, author among other things of a Spenserian poem entitled "The Woodman's Tale," and his translation attracted little notice. In his introduction he compares Dante with Homer, and complains that "the venerable old bard . . . has been long neglected"; perhaps, he suggests, because his poem could not be tried by Aristotle's rules or submitted to the usual classical tests.

"Since the French, the restorers of the art of criticism, cast a damp upon original invention, the character of

Dante has been thrown under a deeper shade. That agreeable and volatile nation found in themselves an insuperable aversion to the gloomy and romantic bard, whose genius, ardent, melancholy, and sublime, was so different from their own."

Boyd used a six-lined stanza, a singularly ill chosen medium for rendering the *terza rima;* and his diction was as wordy and vague as Dante's is concise and sharp of edge. A single passage will illustrate his manner:

> "So full the symphony of grief arose,
>   My heart, responsive to the lovers' woes,
>   With thrilling sympathy convulsed my breast.
> Too strong at last for life my passion grew,
> And, sickening at the lamentable view,
>   I fell like one by mortal pangs oppressed." *

The first opportunity which the mere English reader had to form any real notion of Dante, was afforded by Henry Francis Cary's translation in blank verse (the "Inferno," with the Italian text in 1805; the entire "Commedia" in 1814, with the title "The Vision of Hell, Purgatory, and Paradise"). This was a work of talent, if not of genius; and in spite of the numerous versions in prose and verse that have since appeared, it continues the most current and standard Dante in England, if not in America, where Longfellow naturally challenges precedence. The public was as yet so unprepared to appreciate Dante that Cary's work received little attention until brought into notice by Coleridge; and the translator was deeply chagrined by the indiffer-

---

* "Mentre che l'uno spirto questo disse,
  L'altro piangeva sì, che di pietade
I venni men, così com' io morisse :
  E cadde come corpo morte cade."
                    —"Inferno," Canto v.

ence, not to say hostility, with which his labours were acknowledged. In the memoir * of Cary by his son there is a letter from Anne Seward—the Swan of Lichfield—which throws a singular light upon the critical taste of the "snug coterie and literary lady" of the period. She writes: "How can you profess to be charmed with the few faint outlines of landscape painting in Dante, who are blind to the beautiful, distinct, and profuse scenery in the pages of Ossian?" She goes on to complain that the poem, in its English dress, is vulgar and obscure.

Coleridge devoted to Dante a part of his series of lectures given at London in 1818, reading copious selections from Cary's version. The translator had claimed, in his introduction, that the Florentine poet "leaves to Homer and Shakespeare alone the power of challenging the pre-eminence or equality." Coleridge emphasized the "end-less, subtle beauties of Dante"; the vividness, logical connection, strength, and energy of his style. In this he pronounced him superior to Milton; and in picturesque-ness he affirmed that he surpassed all other poets ancient or modern. With characteristic penetration he indicated the precise position of Dante in mediæval literature; his poetry is "the link between religion and philosophy"; it is "christianized, but without the further Gothic accession of proper chivalry"; it has that "inwardness which . . . distinguishes all the classic from all the modern poetry." It was perhaps in consequence of Coleridge's praise that Cary's translation went into its second edition in 1819, the year following this lecture course. A third was published in 1831. Italians used to complain that the foreign reader's knowledge of the "Divine Comedy"

* Vol. i., p. 236.

was limited to the " Inferno," and generally to the Ugolino and Francesca passages. Coleridge's quotations are all from the "Inferno," and Lowell thinks that he had not read beyond it. He testified that the Ugolino and Francesca stories were already "so well known and admired that it would be pedantry to analyse them." Sir Joshua Reynolds had made a painting of the former subject. In 1800 William Blake produced a series of seven engravings in illustration of the "Inferno." In 1817 Flaxman began his illustrations of the whole "Commedia," extending to a hundred plates.*

In 1819–20 Byron was living at Ravenna, the place of Dante's death and burial † and of the last years of his exile. He used to ride for hours together through Ravenna's "immemorial wood," ‡ and the associations of the scene prompted him to put into English (March, 1820) the Francesca episode, that "thing woven as out of rainbows on a ground of eternal black." In the letter to Murray, sent with his translation, he wrote: " Enclosed you will find, line for line, in third rhyme (*terza rima*), of which your British blackguard reader as yet understands nothing, Fanny of Rimini. You know that she was born here, and married and slain, from Cary, Boyd, and such people." In his diary, Byron commented scornfully on Frederick Schlegel's assertions that Dante had never been a favourite with his own countrymen; and

* Plumptre's "Dante," vol. ii., p. 439.
† "Ungrateful Florence ! Dante sleeps afar,
　　Like Scipio, buried by the upbraiding shore."
　　　　　　　　　　—"Childe Harold," iv., 57.
‡ See vol. i., p. 49 ; and "Purgatorio," xxviii., 19–20.

　　"Tal, qual di ramo in ramo si raccoglie
　　Per la pineta in sul lito di Chiassi."

that his main defect was a want of gentle feelings. "*Not* a favourite! Why they talk Dante—write Dante—and think and dream Dante at this moment (1821) to an excess which would be ridiculous, but that he deserves it. . . . Of gentle feelings!—and Francesca of Rimini—and the father's feelings in Ugolino—and Beatrice—and ' La Pia '! Why there is a gentleness in Dante beyond all gentleness." Byron had not the patience to be a good translator. His rendering is closer and, of course, more spirited than Hayley's; but where long search for the right word was needed, and a delicate shading of phrase to reproduce without loss the meaning of this most meaning and least translatable of masters, Byron's work shows haste and imperfection.

> "Love, who to none beloved to love again
>   Remits."

is neither an idiomatic nor in any way an adequate eng-lishing of

> "Amor, che a nullo amato amar perdona."

Nor does

> "*Accursed* was the book and he who wrote,"

fully give the force of the famous

> "Galeotto fu il libro, e chi lo scrisse." *

The year before Byron had composed "The Prophecy of Dante," an original poem in four cantos, in *terza rima,*

---

* He did better in free paraphrase than in literal translation. *Cf.* Stanza cviii., in "Don Juan," Canto iii.—
"Soft hour! which wakes the wish and melts the heart "—
with its original in the "Purgatorio," viii., 1–6.

> " . . . imitative rhyme,
> Harsh Runic copy of the South's sublime." *

The poem foretells "the fortunes of Italy in the ensuing centuries," and is a rheotorical piece, diffuse and declamatory, and therein quite the opposite of Dante. It manifests Byron's self-conscious habit of submitting his theme to himself, instead of losing himself in his theme. *He* is Dante in exile, and Gemma Donati is Lady Byron—

> "That fatal she,
> Their mother, the cold partner who hath brought
> Destruction for a dowry—this to see
> And feel and know without repair, hath taught
> A bitter lesson ; but it leaves me free :
> I have not vilely found nor basely sought,
> They made an exile not a slave of me."

Dante's bitter and proud defiance found a response in Byron's nature, but his spirit, as a whole, the English poet was not well fitted to interpret. In the preface to "The Prophecy," Byron said that he had not seen the *terza rima* tried before in English, except by Hayley, whose translation he knew only from an extract in the notes to Beckford's "Vathek."

Shelley's knowledge and appreciation of Dante might be proved from isolated images and expressions in many parts of his writings. He translated the sonnet to Guido Cavalcanti with greater freedom and elegance than Hayley, and wrote a short copy of verses on the Hunger Tower at Pisa, the scene of Ugolino's sufferings. In the preface to "Epipsychidion" he cites the "Vita Nuova" as the utterance of an idealised and spiritualised love like that which his own poem records. In the "Defence of Poetry" he pays a glowing tribute to Dante as the

* Dedication to La Guiccioli.

second of epic poets and "the first awakener of entranced Europe." His poetry is the bridge "which unites the modern and the ancient world." Contrary to the prevailing critical tradition, Shelley preferred the "Purgatory" and the "Paradise" to the "Hell." Shelley also employed *terza rima* in his fragmentary pieces, "Prince Athanase," "The Triumph of Life," "The Woodman and the Nightingale," and in one of his best lyrics, the "Ode to the West Wind," * written in 1819 "in a wood that skirts the Arno, near Florence." This linked measure, so difficult for the translator and which gives a hampered movement to Byron's and Hayley's specimens of the "Inferno," Shelley may be said to have really domesticated in English verse by his splendid handling of it in original work:

> "Make me thy lyre even as the forest is:
> What if my leaves are falling, like its own?
> The tumult of thy mighty harmonies
> Will take from both a deep autumnal tone,
> Sweet though in sadness. Be thou, spirit fierce,
> My spirit! Be thou me, impetuous one!"

Shelley expressed to Medwin his dissatisfaction with all English renderings from Dante—even with Cary—and announced his intention, or desire, to translate the whole of the "Divine Comedy" in *terza rima*. Two specimens of this projected version he gave in "Ugolino," and "Matilda Gathering Flowers" ("Purg.," xxviii., 1–51). He also made a translation of the first canzone of the "Convito."

After the appearance of Cary's version, critical com-

* But in this poem each thirteenth and fourteenth line make a couplet, thus breaking up the whole into a series of loose sonnets.

prehension of Dante grew rapidly. In the same year when Coleridge gave his lectures, Hallam published his "Middle Ages," which contained a just though somewhat coldly worded estimate of the great Italian. This was amplified in his later work, "The Literature of Europe" (1838–39). Hallam said that Dante was the first name in the literature of the Middle Ages, the creator of his nation's poetry, and the most original of all writers, and the most concise. But he blamed him for obscurity, forced and unnatural turns of expression, and barbarous licenses of idiom. The "Paradise" seemed to him tedious, as a whole, and much of the "Purgatory" heavy. Hallam repeated, if he did not originate that nice bit of discernment, that in his "Paradise" Dante uses only three leading ideas—light, music, and motion. Then came Macaulay's essay "Milton," in the *Edinburgh* for 1825, with the celebrated parallel between the "Divine Comedy" and the "Paradise Lost," and the contrast between Dante's "picturesque" and Milton's "imaginative" method. Macaulay's analysis has been questioned by Ruskin and others; some of his positions were perhaps mistaken, but they were the most advanced that English Dante criticism had as yet taken up. And finally came Carlyle's vivid piece of portrait painting in "Hero Worship" (1841). The first literal prose translation of any extent from the "Commedia" was the "Inferno" by Carlyle's brother John (1849).

Since the middle of the century Dante study and Dante literature in English-speaking lands have waxed enormously. Dante societies have been founded in England and America. Almost every year sees another edition, a new commentary or a fresh translation in prose, in blank verse, in *terza rima*, or in some form of stanza. It is not exaggerating to say that there is more public mention of Dante now in a single year than in all the years of the eighteenth century together. It would be interesting, if it were possible, to count the times that Dante's name occurs in English writings of the eighteenth and then of the nineteenth century; afterwards to do the same with Ariosto and Tasso and compare the results. It would be found that, while the eighteenth century set no very high value on Ariosto and Tasso, it ignored Dante altogether; and that the nineteenth has put aside the superficial mediævalism of the Renaissance romancers and gone back to the great religious romancer of the Italian Middle Age. There is no surer plummet than Dante's to sound the spiritual depth of a time. It is in the nineteenth century first that Shakspere and Dante took possession of the European mind. In 1800 Shakspere was an English, or at most an English and German poet, and Dante exclusively an Italian. In 1900 they had both become world poets. Shakspere's foreign conquests were the earlier and are still the wider, as wide perhaps as the expanse—

"That deep-browed Homer ruled as his demesne."

But the ground that Dante has won he holds with equal secureness. Not that he will ever be popular, in Shakspere's way; and yet it is far gone when the æsthete in a comic opera is described as a " Francesca da Rimini young man."

As a stimulus to creative work the influence of Dante, though not entirely absent, is not conspicuous in the first half of the century. It is not until the time of the Rossettis in England and of Longfellow and Dr. Parsons in America that any poetry of a really Dantesque inspiration and, at the same time, of high original value was added to our literature.*

The first fruits of the Dante revival in England, in the shape of original production, was Leigh Hunt's "Story of Rimini" (1816)—"Mr. Hunt's smutty story of Rimini," as the Tory wits of *Blackwood* were fond of calling it in their onslaughts upon the Cockney school. This was a romaunt in four cantos upon the already familiar episode of Francesca, that "lily in the mouth of Tartarus." Hunt took Dryden's "Fables" as his model in versification, employing the heroic couplet with the frequent variation of the triplet and the alexandrine. The poem is not at all Dantesque in its lax and fluent sweetness, and in that colloquial, familiar manner which is constant in all Hunt's writing, both prose and verse; reminding one, at its best, of Chaucer, who was, indeed, one of his favourite masters. Hunt softens the ferocity of the tale as given by Boccaccio, according to whom the husband Giovanni Malatesta was a cripple, and killed the lovers *in flagrante delicto.* Hunt makes him a personable man, though of proud and gloomy temper. He slays his brother Paolo in chivalrous fashion and in single combat, and Francesca dies of a broken heart. The descriptive portions of the "Story of Rimini" are charming: the

---

* T. W. Parsons' "Lines on a Bust of Dante" appeared in the Boston *Advertiser* in 1841. His translation of the first ten cantos of the "Inferno" was published in 1843: later instalments in 1867 and 1893. Longfellow's version of the "Divine Comedy" with the series of sonnets by the translator came out in 1867–70. For the Dante work of the Rossettis, *vide infra,* pp. 282 *ff.*

feudal procession with trumpeters, heralds, squires, and
knights, sent to escort home the bride; the pine forest
outside Ravenna; and the garden at Rimini in which the
lovers used to meet—

> "Places of nestling green for poets made."

Hunt had a quick eye for colour; a fondness, not altogether free from affectation, for dainty phrases; and
a feminine love of little niceties in dress, tapestry,
needlework, and furnishings. The poem was written
mostly in prison where its author spent two years for a
libel on the Prince Regent. Byron used to visit him
there and bring him books bearing on Francesca's history. Hunt brought into the piece romantic stuff from
various sources, including a summary of the book which
betrayed the lovers to their fatal passion, the romance of
"Lancelot du Lac." And Giovanni speaks to his dying
brother a paraphrase of the celebrated eulogy pronounced
over Lancelot by Sir Ector in the "Morte Darthur":

> "And, Paulo, thou wert the completest knight
> That ever rode with banner to the fight;
> And thou wert the most beautiful to see,
> That ever came in press of chivalry:
> And of a sinful man thou wert the best
> That ever for his friend put spear in rest;
> And thou wert the most meek and cordial
> That ever among ladies eat in hall;
> And thou wert still, for all that bosom gored,
> The kindest man that ever struck with sword."

Hunt makes the husband discover his wife's infidelity
by overhearing her talking in her sleep. In many other
particulars he enfeebles, dandifies, and sentimentalises
Dante's fierce, abrupt tragedy; holding the reader by the

button while he prattles in his garrulous way of Paulo's
" taste "—

> " The very nose, lightly yet firmly wrought,
>   Showed taste "—

and of

> " The two divinest things in earthly lot,
>   A lovely woman in a rural spot ! "

a couplet which irresistibly suggests suburban picnics.

Yet no one in his generation did more than Leigh
Hunt to familiarise the English public with Italian romance. He began the study of Italian when he was a
schoolboy at Christ Hospital, being attracted to Ariosto
by a picture of Angelica and Medoro, in West's studio.
Like his friend Keats, on whose " Eve of St. Agnes " he
wrote an enthusiastic commentary,* Hunt was eclectic in
his choice of material, drawing inspiration impartially
from the classics and the romantics; but, like Keats, he
became early a declared rebel against eighteenth-century
traditions and asserted impulse against rule.   " In antiquarian corners," he says, in writing of the influences of
his childish days, " Percy's 'Reliques' were preparing a
nobler age both in poetry and prose."   At school he fell
passionately in love with Collins and Gray, composed a
" Winter " in imitation of Thomson, one hundred stanzas
of a " Fairy King " in emulation of Spenser, and a long
poem in Latin inspired by Gray's odes and Malet's
" Northern Antiquities."   In 1802 [ætate 18] he published a volume of these *juvenilia*—odes after Collins and
Gray, blank verse after Thomson and Akenside, and a
" Palace of Pleasure " after Spenser's " Bower of Bliss." †

---

* " The Seer."
 † He named a daughter, born while he was in prison, after
Spenser's Florimel.

It was in this same year that on a visit to Oxford, he was introduced to Kett, the professor of poetry, who expressed a hope that the youthful bard might be inspired by "the muse of Warton," whom Hunt had never read. There had fallen in Hunt's way when he was a young man, Bell's edition of the poets, which included Chaucer and Spenser. "The omission of these in Cooke's edition," he says, "was as unpoetical a sign of the times as the present familiarity with their names is the reverse. It was thought a mark of good sense; as if good sense, in matters of literature, did not consist as much in knowing what was poetical poetry, as brilliant wit." Of his "Feast of the Poets" (1814) he writes: * "I offended all the critics of the old or French school, by objecting to the monotony of Pope's versification, and all the critics of the new or German school by laughing at Wordsworth." In the preface to his collected poems [1832] occurs the following interesting testimony to the recentness of the new criticism. "So long does fashion succeed in palming its petty instincts upon the world for those of a nation and of nature, that it is only of late years that the French have ceased to think some of the most affecting passages in Shakespeare ridiculous. . . . Yet the English themselves, no great while since, half blushed at these criticisms, and were content if the epithet ' bizarre ' (' *votre bizarre Shakespeare* ') was allowed to be translated into ' a wild, irregular genius.' Everything was wild and irregular except rhymesters in toupees. A petty conspiracy of decorums took the place of what was becoming to humanity." In the summer of 1822 Hunt went by sailing vessel through the Mediterranean to Italy. The

* "Autobiography," p. 200 (ed. of 1870).

books which he read chiefly on board ship were "Don Quixote," Ariosto, and Berni; and his diary records the emotion with which he coasted the western shores of Spain, the ground of Italian romance, where the Paynim chivalry used to land to go against Charlemagne: the scene of Boiardo's "Orlando Inamorato" and Ariosto's "Orlando Furioso." "I confess I looked at these shores with a human interest, and could not help feeling that the keel of our vessel was crossing a real line, over which knights and lovers had passed. And so they have, both real and fabulous; the former not less romantic, the latter scarcely less real. . . . Fair speed your sails over the lucid waters, ye lovers, on a lover-like sea! Fair speed them, yet never land; for where the poet has left you, there ought ye, as ye are, to be living forever— forever gliding about a summer sea, touching at its flowery islands and reposing beneath its moon."

Hunt's sojourn in Italy, where he lived in close association with Byron and Shelley, enabled him to *préciser* his knowledge of the Italian language and literature. In 1846 he published a volume of "Stories from the Italian Poets," containing a summary or free paraphrase in prose of the "Divine Comedy" and the poems of Pulci, Boiardo, Ariosto, and Tasso, "with comments throughout, occasional passages versified and critical notices of the lives and genius of the authors." Like our own romanticist poet Longfellow, who rediscovered Europe for America, Leigh Hunt was a sympathetic and interpretative rather than a creative genius; and like Longfellow, an admirable translator. Among his collected poems are a number of elegant and spirited versions from various mediæval literatures. "The Gentle Armour" is a playful adaptation of a French fabliau "Les Trois Chevaliers et la Chemise," which tells of a knight whose hard-hearted lady set him the task of fighting his two rivals in the lists, armed only in her smock; and, in contrition for this harsh imposure, went to the altar with her faithful champion, wearing only the same bloody sark as her bridal garment. At least this is the pretty turn which Hunt gave to the story. In the original it had a coarser ending. There are also, among these translations from mediæval sources, the Latin drinking song attributed to Walter Map—

Mihi est propositum in taberna mori—

and Andrea de Basso's terrible "Ode to a Dead Body," in fifteenth-century Italian; which utters, with extraordinary power, the ascetic thought of the Middle Age, dwelling with a kind of gloomy exultation on the foulness of the human frame in decay.

In the preface to his "Italian Poets," Hunt speaks of "how widely Dante has re-attracted of late the attention of the world." He pronounces him "the greatest poet for intensity that ever lived," and complains that his metrical translators have failed to render his "passionate, practical, and creative style—a style which may be said to write things instead of words." Hunt's introduction is a fine piece of critical work. His alert, sparkling, and nimble intellect—somewhat lacking in concentration and seriousness—but sensitive above all things to the picturesque, was keenly awake to Dante's poetic greatness. On the other hand, his cheerful philosophy and tolerant, not to say easy-going moral nature, was shocked by the Florentine's bitter pride, and by what he conceives to be

his fanaticism, bigotry, superstition, and personal vindic-
tiveness, when

> "Hell he peoples with his foes,
>   Dark scourge of many a guilty line."

Hunt was a Universalist, and Dante was a Catholic
Calvinist.   There was a determined optimism about
Hunt, and a buoyancy as of a cork or other light body,
sometimes a little exasperating to men of less sanguine
temperament.*   He ends by protesting that Dante is a
semi-barbarian and his "Divine Comedy" too often an
infernal tragedy.   "Such a vision as that of his poem
(in a theological point of view) seems no better than the
dream of an hypochondriacal savage."   It was some
years before this, in his lecture on "The Hero as Poet,"
delivered in 1840, that a friend of Leigh Hunt, of a temperament quite the opposite of his, had spoken a very
different word touching this cruel scorn—this *sæva indig-
natio* of Dante's.   Carlyle, like Hunt, discovered *intensity*
to be the prevailing character of Dante's genius, em-
blemed by the pinnacle of the city of Dis; that "red-hot
cone of iron glowing through the dim immensity of
gloom."   Hunt, the Universalist, said of Dante, "when
he is sweet-natured once he is bitter a hundred times."
"Infinite pity," says Carlyle, the Calvinist, "yet also infinite rigour of law; it is so nature is made; it is so
Dante discerned that she was made.   What a paltry notion is that of his 'Divine Comedy's' being a poor sple-
netic, impotent terrestrial libel; putting those into hell
whom he could not be avenged upon on earth!   I suppose

---

* See Dickens' caricature of him as Harold Skimpole in
"Bleak House."

if ever pity tender as a mother's was in the heart of any
man, it was in Dante's.   But a man who does not know
rigour cannot pity either.   His very pity will be cowardly,
egoistic—sentimentality, or little better. . . . Morally
great above all we must call him; it is the beginning of
all.   His scorn, his grief are as transcendent as his love;
as, indeed, what are they but the *inverse* or *converse* of
his love?"

It is interesting to note that, antipathetic as Hunt's
nature was, in many ways, not only to the individual
Dante but to the theological thought of which he was the
spokesman, in his view of the sacred art of the Italian
Middle Age he anticipated the Pre-Raphaelites and the
modern interpreters of Dante.   Here is a part of what
he says of the paintings in the Campo Santo at Pisa:
"The best idea, perhaps, which I can give an Englishman of the general character of the painting is by refer-
ring him to the engravings of Albert Durer and the serious parts of Chaucer.   There is the same want of proper
costume—the same intense feeling of the human being,
both in body and soul—the same bookish, romantic, and
retired character—the same evidences, in short, of antiquity and commencement, weak (where it is weak) for
want of a settled art and language, but strong for that
very reason in first impulses, and in putting down all
that is felt. . . . The manner in which some of the hoary
saints in these pictures pore over their books and carry
their decrepit old age, full of a bent and absorbed feeble-
ness—the set limbs of the warriors on horseback—the
sidelong unequivocal looks of some of the ladies playing
on harps and conscious of their ornaments—the people
of fashion seated in rows, with Time coming up unawares

to destroy them—the other rows of elders and doctors of the Church, forming part of the array of heaven—the uplifted hand of Christ denouncing the wicked at the day of judgment—the daring satires occasionally introduced against monks and nuns—the profusion of attitudes, expressions, incidents, broad draperies, ornaments of all sorts, visions, mountains, ghastly looking cities, fiends, angels, sibylline old women, dancers, virgin brides, mothers and children, princes, patriarchs, dying saints; it would be simply blind injustice to the superabundance and truth of conception in all this multitude of imagery not to recognize the real inspirers as well as harbingers of Raphael and Michael Angelo, instead of confining the honour to the Masaccios and Peruginos, [who] . . . are no more to be compared with them than the sonneteers of Henry VIII. 's time are to be compared with Chaucer. Even in the very rudest of the pictures, where the souls of the dying are going out of their mouths, in the shape of little children, there are passages not unworthy of Dante and Michael Angelo. . . . Giotto, be thou one to me hereafter, of a kindred brevity, solidity, and stateliness with that of thy friend, Dante! " *

Among all the writers of his generation, Keats was most purely the poet, the artist of the beautiful. His

---

* "When I was last at Haydon's," wrote Keats to his brother George in 1818-19, "I looked over a book of prints taken from the fresco of the church at Milan, the name of which I forget. In it were comprised specimens of the first and second age of art in Italy. I do not think I ever had a greater treat out of Shakespeare; full of romance and the most tender feeling; magnificence of drapery beyond everything I ever saw, not excepting Raphael's—but grotesque to a curious pitch—yet still making up a fine whole, even finer to me than more accomplished works, as there was left so much room for imagination."

sensitive imagination thrilled to every touch of beauty from whatever quarter. That his work is mainly retrospective and eclectic in subject is because a young poet's mind responds more readily to books than to life, and this young poet did not outlive his youth. In the Greek mythology he found a world of lovely images ready to his hand; in the poetry of Spenser, Chaucer, and Ariosto he found another such world. Arcadia and Faeryland— "the realms of gold"—he rediscovered them both for himself, and he struck into the paths that wound through their enchanted thickets with the ardour of an explorer. This was the very mood of the Renaissance—this genial heat which fuses together the pagan and the Christian systems—this indifference of the creative imagination to the mere sources and materials of its creations. Indeed, there is in Keats' style a "natural magic" which forces us back to Shakspere for comparison; a noticeable likeness to the diction of the Elizabethans, when the classics were still a living spring of inspiration, and not a set of copies held *in terrorem* over the head of every new poet.

Keats' break with the classical tradition was early and decisive. In his first volume (1817) there is a piece entitled "Sleep and Poetry," composed after a night passed at Leigh Hunt's cottage near Hampstead, which contains his literary declaration of faith. After speaking of the beauty that fills the universe, and of the office of Imagination to be the minister and interpreter of this beauty, as in the old days when "here her altar shone, even in this isle," and "the muses were nigh cloyed with honours," he asks:

"Could all this be forgotten? Yes, a schism
Nurtured by foppery and barbarism,

Made great Apollo blush for this, his land.
Men were thought wise who could not understand
His glories: with a puling infant's force,
They swayed about upon a rocking horse
And thought it Pegasus. Ah, dismal-souled!
The winds of heaven blew, the ocean rolled
Its gathering waves—ye felt it not. The blue
Bowed its eternal bosom, and the dew
Of summer night collected still, to make
The morning precious. Beauty was awake!
Why were ye not awake? But ye were dead
To things ye knew not of—were closely wed
To musty laws, lined out with wretched rule
And compass vile: so that ye taught a school
Of dolts to smooth, inlay and clip and fit;
Till, like the certain wands of Jacob's wit,
Their verses tallied. Easy was the task:
A thousand handicraftsmen wore the mask
Of Poesy. Ill-fated, impious race!
That blasphemed the bright Lyrist to his face,
And did not know it,—no, they went about,
Holding a poor decrepit standard out,
Marked with most flimsy mottoes, and, in large,
The name of one Boileau!"

This complaint, so far as it relates to the *style* of the
rule-ridden eighteenth-century poetry, had been made
before: by Cowper, by Wordsworth, by Coleridge. But
Keats, with his instinct for beauty, pierces to the core of
the matter. It was because of Pope's defective sense of
the beautiful that the doubt arose whether he was a poet
at all. It was because of its

" . . . forgetting the great end
Of Poetry, that it should be a friend
To soothe the cares and lift the thoughts of man,"

that the poetry of the classical school was so unsatisfying.
This is one of the very few passages of Keats that are at
all doctrinal* or polemic; and as such it has been re-

*Against the hundreds of maxims from Pope, Keats fur-
nishes a single motto—the first line of "Endymion"—
"A thing of beauty is a joy forever."

peatedly cited by biographers and essayists and literary historians. Lowell quotes it, in his essay on Dryden, and adds: " Keats was the first resolute and wilful heretic, the true founder of the modern school, which admits no cis-Elizabethan authority save Milton." Mr. Gosse quotes it and says, "in these lines he has admirably summed up the conceptions of the first half of the present century with regard to classical poetry." * The passage was still fresh when Byron, in the letter to Disraeli already quoted † (March 15th, 1820), held it up to scorn as the opinion of " a young person learning to write poetry and beginning by teaching the art. . . . The writer of this is a tadpole of the Lakes, a young disciple of the six or seven new schools, in which he has learned to write such lines and such sentiments as the above. He says ' easy were the task' of imitating Pope, or it may be of equalling him, I presume. I recommend him to try before he is so positive on the subject, and then compare what he will have *then* written, and what he has *now* written, with the humblest and earliest compositions of Pope, produced in years still more youthful than those of Mr. Keats when he invented his new ' Essay on Criticism,' entitled ' Sleep and Poetry ' (an ominous title) from whence the above canons are taken."

In a manuscript note on this passage made after Keats' death, Byron wrote: " My indignation at Mr. Keats' depreciation of Pope has hardly permitted me to do justice to his own genius. . . . He is a loss to our literature; and the more so, as he himself, before his death, is said

---

* "From Shakespeare to Pope." See also Sidney Colvin's "Keats," New York, 1887, pp. 61–64.

† *Vide supra*, p. 70.

to have been persuaded that he had not taken the right line, and was reforming his style upon the more classical models of the language." Keats made a study of Dryden's versification before writing "Lamia"; but had he lived to the age of Methusaleh, he would not have "reformed his style" upon any such classical models as Lord Byron had in mind. Classical he might have become, in the sense in which "Hyperion" is classical; but in the sense in which Pope was classical—never. Pope's Homer he deliberately set aside for Chapman's—

> "Yet did I never breathe its pure serene
> Till I heard Chapman speak out loud and bold." *

Keats had read Virgil, but seemingly not much Latin poetry besides, and he had no knowledge of Greek. He made acquaintance with the Hellenic world through classical dictionaries and a study of the casts in the British Museum. But his intuitive grasp of the antique ideal of beauty stood him in as good stead as Landor's scholarship. In such work as "Hyperion" and the "Ode on a Grecian Urn" he mediates between the ancient and the modern spirit, from which Landor's clear-cut marbles stand aloof in chill remoteness. As concerns his equipment, Keats stands related to Scott in romance learning much as he does to Landor in classical scholarship. He was no antiquary, and naturally made mistakes of detail. In his sonnet "On First Looking into Chapman's Homer," he makes Cortez, and not Balboa, the

* That he knew Pope's version is evident from a letter to Haydon of May, 1817, given in Lord Houghton's "Life."

discoverer of the Pacific. *À propos* of a line in "The Eve of St. Agnes"—

"And the long carpets rose along the gusty floor"—

Leigh Hunt called attention to the fact that rushes and not carpets covered the floors in the Middle Ages. In the same poem, Porphyro sings to his lute an ancient ditty,

"In Provençe called 'La Belle Dame sans Merci.'"

The ditty was by Alain Chartier, who was not a troubadour, but a Norman by birth and a French court poet of the fifteenth century. The title, which Keats found in a note in an edition of Chaucer, pleased his fancy and suggested his ballad,* of the same name, which has nothing in common with Chartier's poem. The latter is a conventional love *estrif* in the artificial taste of the time. But errors of this sort, which any encyclopædia can correct, are perfectly unimportant.

Byron's sneer at Keats, as "a tadpole of the Lakes," was ridiculously wide of the mark. He was nearly of the second generation of romantics; he was only three years old when "The Ancient Mariner" was published; "Christabel" and Scott's metrical romances had all been issued before he put forth his first volume. But though

* He could have known extremely little of mediæval literature ; yet there is nothing anywhere, even in the far more instructed Pre-Raphaelite school which catches up the whole of the true mediæval romantic spirit—the spirit which animates the best parts of the Arthurian legend, and of the wild stories which float through mediæval tale-telling, and make no small figure in mediæval theology—as does the short piece of 'La Belle Dame sans Merci'" (Saintsbury: "A Short History of English Literature," p. 673).

he owes much to Coleridge * and more perhaps to Chatterton, he took no imprint from Wordsworth, and cared nothing for Scott. Keats, like his friend Hunt, turned instinctively away from northern to southern Gothic; from rough border minstrelsy to the mythology and romance of the races that dwelt about the midland sea. Keats' sensuous nature longed for "a beaker full of the warm South." "I have tropical blood in my veins," wrote Hunt, deprecating "the criticism of a Northern climate" as applied to his "Story of Rimini." Keats' death may be said to have come to him from Scotland, not only by reason of the brutal attacks in *Blackwood's* —to which there is some reason for believing that Scott was privy—but because the hardships and exposure of his Scotch tour laid the foundation of his fatal malady. He brought back no literary spoils of consequence from the North, and the description of the journey in his letters makes it evident that his genius could not find itself there. This uncomfortable feeling of alienation is expressed in his "Sonnet on Visiting the Tomb of Burns." The Scotch landscape seems "cold—strange."

> "The short-lived paly Summer is but won
> From Winter's ague."

And in the letter from Dumfries, enclosing the sonnet he writes: "I know not how it is, the clouds, the sky, the houses, all seem anti-Grecian and anti-Charlemagnish." *Charlemagnish* is Keats' word for the true mediæval-romantic. It is noteworthy that Keats avoided Scott's favourite verse forms. "La Belle Dame sans Merci" is not in the minstrel ballad measure; and when Keats

* *Vide supra*, p. 85. And for Keats' interest in Chatterton see vol. i., pp. 370–72.

uses the eight-syllabled couplet, he uses it very differently from Scott, without the alternate riming which prevails in "The Lay of the Last Minstrel" and all the rest of the series.

A spark from Spenser kindled the flame of poetry in Keats. His friend, Cowden Clarke, read him the "Epithalamium" one day in 1812 in an arbour in the old school garden at Enfield, and lent him a copy of "The Faëry Queene" to take home with him. "He romped through the scenes of the romance," reports Mr. Clarke, "like a young horse turned into a spring meadow." There is something almost uncanny—like the visits of a spirit—about these recurrent appearances of Spenser in English literary history. It must be confessed that nowadays we do not greatly romp through "The Faëry Queene." There even runs a story that a certain professor of literature in an American college, being consulted about Spenser by one of his scholars, exclaimed impatiently, "Oh, damn Spenser!" But it is worth while to have him in the literature, if only as a starter for young poets. Keats' earliest known verses are an "Imitation of Spenser" in four stanzas. His allusions to him are frequent, and his fugitive poems include a "Sonnet to Spenser" and a number of "Spenserian Stanzas." But his only really important experiment in the measure of "The Faëry Queene" was "The Eve of St. Agnes." It was with fine propriety that Shelley chose that measure for his elegy on Keats in "Adonais." Keats made a careful study of Spenser's verse, the

"Spenserian vowels that elope with ease"—

and all the rest of it. His own work in this kind is

thought to resemble most closely the "Psyche" of the Irish poetess, Mary Tighe, published in 1805 * on the well-known fable of Cupid and Psyche in Apuleius. It is inferred that Keats knew the poem from a mention of the author in one of his pieces. He also wrote an "Ode to Psyche," which seems, however, to have been inspired by an engraving in Spenser's "Polymetis." Mrs. Tighe was one of the latest and best of the professed imitators of Spenser. There is beauty of a kind in her languidly melodious verse and over-profuse imagery, but it is not the passionate and quintessential beauty of Keats. She is quite incapable of such choice and pregnant word effects as abound in every stanza of "St. Agnes":

> "Unclasps her *warmed* jewels, one by one":
>   "*Buttressed* from moonlight":
>   "The music, *yearning* like a God in pain":
>   "The boisterous, *midnight*, festive clarion."

Keats' intimate association with Leigh Hunt, whose acquaintance he made in 1816, was not without influence on his literary development. He admired the "Story of Rimini," † and he adopted in his early verse epistles and in "Endymion" (1818), that free ante-Popean treatment of the couplet with *enjambement*, or overflow, double rimes, etc., which Hunt had practised in the poem itself and advocated in the preface. Many passages in "Rimini" and in Keats' couplet poems anticipate, in their easy flow, the relaxed versification of "The Earthly Paradise." This was the Elizabethan type of heroic couplet,

---

* The Dict. Nat. Biog. mentions doubtfully an earlier edition in 1795.

‡ See "Sonnet on Leigh Hunt's Poem 'The Story of Rimini.'" Forman's ed., vol. ii., p. 229.

and its extreme instance is seen in William Chamberlayne's "Pharonnida" (1659). There is no proof of
Keats' alleged indebtedness to Chamberlayne, though
he is known to have been familiar with another specimen
of the type, William Browne's "Britannia's Pastorals."
Hunt also confirmed Keats in the love of Spenser,
and introduced him to Ariosto whom he learned to
read in the Italian, five or six stanzas at a time. Dante
he read in Cary's translation, a copy of which was the
only book that he took with him on his Scotch trip.
"The fifth canto of Dante," he wrote (March, 1819),
"pleases me more and more; it is that one in which he
meets with Paulo and Francesca." He afterwards
dreamed of the story and wrote a sonnet upon his dream,
which Rossetti thought "by far the finest of Keats' sonnets" next to that on Chapman's "Homer." * Mr. J. M.
Robertson thinks that the influence of Cary's "Dante" is
visible in "Hyperion," especially in the recast version
"Hyperion: A Vision." † And Leigh Hunt suggests
that in the lines in "The Eve of St. Agnes"—

> "The sculptured dead on each side seem to freeze,
>   Emprisoned in black, purgatorial rails:
> Knights, ladies, praying in dumb orat'ries,
> He passeth by; and his weak spirit fails
>   To think how they may ache in icy hoods and mails"—

the germ of the thought is in Dante.‡   Keats wished

* See Forman's ed., vol. ii., p. 334.
† "New Essays toward a Critical Method," London, 1897,
p. 256.
‡ "Come, per sostentar solaio o tetto,
    Per mensola talvolta una figura
  Si vede giunger le ginocchia al petto,
    La qual fa del non ver vera rancura
  Nascere in chi la vede."
              —"Purgatorio," Canto x., 130-34.

that Italian might take the place of French in English schools. To Hunt's example was also due, in part, that fondness for neologisms for which the latter apologises in the preface to "Rimini," and with which Keats was wont to enrich his diction, as well as with Chattertonian archaisms, Chapmanese compounds, "taffeta phrases, silken terms precise" from Elizabethan English, and coinages like *poesied, follying, eye-earnestly*—licenses and affectations which gave dire offence to Gifford and the classicals generally.

In the 1820 volume, which includes Keats' maturest work, there was a story from the "Decameron," "Isabella, or the Pot of Basil," which tells how a lady exhumes the body of her murdered lover, cuts off the head and buries it in a pot of sweet basil, which she keeps in her chamber and waters with her tears. It was perhaps symptomatic of a certain morbid sensibility in Keats to select this subject from so cheerful a writer as Boccaccio. This intensity of love surviving in face of leprosy, torment, decay, and material horrors of all kinds; this passionate clinging of spirit to body, is a mediæval note, and is repeated in the neo-romantic school which derives from Keats; in Rossetti, Swinburne, Morris, O'Shaughnessy, Marzials, and Paine. Think of the unshrinking gaze which Dante fixes upon the tortures of the souls in pain; of the wasted body of Christ upon the cross; of the fasts, flagellations, mortifications of penitents; the unwashed friars; the sufferings of martyrs. Keats apologises for his endeavour "to make old prose in modern rime more sweet," and for his departure from the even, unexcited narrative of his original:

"O eloquent and famed Boccaccio,
    Of thee we now should ask forgiving boon. . . .
For venturing syllables that ill beseem
    The quiet glooms of such a piteous theme. . . .

Ah! wherefore all this wormy circumstance?
    Why linger at the yawning tomb so long?
O for the gentleness of old Romance,
    The simple plaining of the minstrel's song."

But it is just this wormy circumstance that rivets the poet's attention; his imagination lingers over Isabella kissing the dead face, pointing each eyelash, and washing away the loam that disfigures it with her tears; over the basil tufts growing rankly from the mouldering head.

"The thing was vile with green and livid spot,"

but Keats' tenderness pierces the grave.

It is instructive to compare "Isabella" with Dryden's "Sigismonda and Guiscardo," also from the "Decameron" and surcharged with the physically horrible. In this tale Tancred sends his daughter her lover's heart in a golden goblet. She kisses the heart, fills the cup with poison, drinks, and dies. The two poems are typical examples of romantic and classical handling, though neither is quite a masterpiece in its kind. The treatment in Dryden is cool, unimpassioned, objective—like Boccaccio's, in fact. The story is firmly told, with a masculine energy of verse and language. Sigismonda and Tancred are characters, confronted wills, as in drama, and their speeches are like _tirades_ from a tragedy of Racine. But here Dryden's rhetorical habit and his fondness for reasoning in rime run away with him, and make his art inferior to Boccaccio's. Sigismonda argues her case like counsel for the defendant. She even enjoys her own argument and carries it out with a gusto into abstractions.

> "But leaving that : search we the secret springs,
> And backward trace the principles of things ;
> There shall we find, that when the world began
> One common mass composed the mould of man," etc.

Dryden's grossness of taste mars his narrative at several points. The satirist in him will not let him miss the chance for a sneer at priests and another at William III.'s standing army. He makes his heroine's love ignobly sensual. She is a widow, who having "tasted marriage joys," is unwilling to live single. Dryden's *bourgeois* manner is capable even of ludicrous descents.

> "The sudden bound awaked the sleeping sire,
> And showed a sight no parent can desire."

In Keats' poem there are no characters dramatically opposed. Lorenzo and Isabella have no individuality apart from their love; passion has absorbed character. The tale is not evolved firmly and continuously, but with lyrical outbursts, a poignancy of sympathy at the points of highest tragic tensity and a swooning sensibility all through, that sometimes breaks into weakness. There can be no question, however, which poem is the more *felt ;* no question, either, as to which method is superior—at least as between these two artists, and as applied to subjects of this particular kind.

"Isabella" is in *ottava rima,* "The Eve of St. Agnes" in the Spenserian stanza. This exquisite creation has all the insignia of romantic art and has them in a dangerous degree. It is brilliant with colour, richly ornate, tremulous with emotion. Only the fine instinct of the

artist saved it from the overladen decoration and cloying
sweetness of "Endymion," and kept it chaste in its
warmth.   As it is, the story is almost too slight for its
descriptive mantle "rough with gems and gold."   Such
as it is, it is of Keats' invention and of the "Romeo and
Juliet" variety of plot.   A lover who is at feud with his
mistress' clan ventures into his foemen's castle while a
revel is going on, penetrates by the aid of her nurse to
his lady's bower, and carries her off while all the household are sunk in drunken sleep.   All this in a night of
wild weather and on St. Agnes' Eve, when, according to
popular belief, maidens might see their future husbands
in their dreams, on the performance of certain conditions.
The resemblance of this poem to "Christabel" at several
points, has already been mentioned,* and especially in
the description of the heroine's chamber.   But the differences are even more apparent.   Coleridge's art is tem-
perate and suggestive; spiritual, too, with an unequalled
power of haunting the mind with a sense of ghostly pres-
ences.   In his scene the touches are light and few; all
is hurried, mysterious, shadowy.   But Keats was a word
painter, his treatment more sensuous than Coleridge's,
and fuller of imagery.   He lingers over the figure of the
maiden disrobing, and over the furnishings of her room.
The Catholic elegancies of his poem, as Hunt called
them, and the architectural details are there for their own
sake—as pictures; the sculptured dead in the chapel, the
foot-worn stones, the cobwebbed arches, broad hall pillar,
and dusky galleries; the "little moonlight room, pale,
latticed, chill"; the chain-drooped lamp:

> "The carven angels ever eager-eyed"

* *Vide supra*, p. 85.

that

> "Stared, where upon their heads the cornice rests,
>   With hair blown back and wings put crosswise on their
>   breasts."

Possibly "La Belle Dame sans Merci" borrows a hint from the love-crazed knight in Coleridge's "Love," who is haunted by a fiend in the likeness of an angel; but here the comparison is to Keats' advantage. Not even Coleridge sang more wildly well than the singer of this weird ballad strain, which has seemed to many critics * the masterpiece of this poet, wherein his "natural magic" reaches its most fascinating subtlety and purity of expression.

The famous picture of the painted "casement, high and triple-arched" in Madeline's chamber, "a burst of richness, noiseless, coloured, suddenly enriching the moonlight, as if a door of heaven were opened," † should be compared with Scott's no less famous description of the east oriel of Melrose Abbey by moonlight, and the comparison will illustrate a distinction similar to that already noted between the romanticism of Coleridge and Scott. The latter is here depicting an actual spot, one of the great old border abbeys; national pride and the pathos of historic ruins mingle with the description. Madeline's castle stood in the country of dream; and it was an "elfin storm from fairyland" that came to aid the

---

* Rossetti, Colvin, Gates, Robertson, Forman, and others.

† Leigh Hunt. It has been objected to this passage that moonlight is not strong enough to transmit *colored* rays, like sunshine (see Colvin's "Keats," p. 160). But the mistake—if it is one—is shared by Scott.

> "The moonbeam kissed the holy pane
>   And threw on the pavement a bloody stain."
>
>   —"Lay of the Last Minstrel," Canto ii., xi.

lovers' flight,* and all the creatures of his tale are but the

> "Shadows haunting fairily
> The brain new stuffed in youth with triumphs gay
> Of old Romance."

In Keats is the romantic escape, the longing to

> "leave the world unseen,
> And with thee fade away into the forest dim."†

Keats cared no more for history than he did for contemporary politics.   Courthope ‡ quotes a passage from " Endymion " to illustrate his indifference to everything but art:

> "Hence, pageant history!   Hence, gilded cheat! . . .
> Many old rotten-timbered boats there be
> Upon thy vaporous bosom, magnified
> To goodly vessels; many a sail of pride,
> And golden-keeled, is left unlaunched and dry.
> But wherefore this?   What care, though owl did fly
> About the great Athenian admiral's mast?
> What care though striding Alexander past
> The Indus with his Macedonian numbers?
>   . . . Juliet leaning
> Amid her window-flowers,—sighing,—weaning
> Tenderly her fancy from its maiden snow,
> Doth more avail than these: the silver flow
> Of Hero's tears, the swoon of Imogen,
> Fair Pastorella in the bandit's den,
> Are things to brood on with more ardency
> Than the death-day of empires."

* It is interesting to learn that the line
> "For o'er the Southern moors
> I have a home for thee"

read in the original draught "Over the bleak Dartmoor," etc. Dartmoor was in sight of Teignmouth where Keats once spent two months; but he cancelled the local allusion in obedience to a correct instinct.
  † " Ode to a Nightingale."
  ‡ "The Liberal Movement in English Literature," London, 1885, p. 181.

This passage should be set beside the complaint in "Lamia" of the disenchanting touch of science:

"There was an awful rainbow once in heaven," etc.

Keats is the poet of romantic emotion, as Scott of romantic action. Professor Gates says that Keats' heroes never *do* anything.* It puzzles the reader of "The Eve of St. Agnes" to know just why Porphyro sets out the feast of cates on the little table by Madeline's bedside, unless it be to give the poet an opportunity for his luscious description of "the lucent syrups tinct with cinnamon" and other like delicacies. In the early fragment "Calidore," the hero—who gets his name from Spenser —does nothing in some hundred and fifty lines but assist two ladies to dismount from their palfreys. To revert, as before, to Ariosto's programme, it was not the *arme* and *audaci imprese* which Keats sang, but the *donne*, the *amori*, and the *cortesie*. Feudal war array was no concern of his, but the "argent revelry" of masque and dance, and the "silver-snarling trumpets" in the musicians' gallery. He was the poet of the lute and the nightingale, rather than of the shock of spear in tourney and crusade. His "Specimen of an Induction to a Poem" begins

"Lo! I must tell a tale of chivalry."

But he never tells it. The piece evaporates in visions of pure loveliness; "large white plumes"; sweet ladies on the worn tops of old battlements; light-footed damsels standing in sixes and sevens about the hall in courtly talk. Meanwhile the lance is resting against the wall.

* "Studies and Appreciations." Lewis G. Gates. New York, 1890, p. 17.

"Ah ! shall I ever tell its cruelty,
   When the fire flashes from a warrior's eye,
   And his tremendous hand is grasping it? "

"No," answers the reader, "I don't think you ever will.   Leave that sort of thing to Walter Scott, and go on and finish your charming fragment of 'The Eve of St. Mark,' which stops provokingly just where Bertha was reading the illuminated manuscript, as she sat' in her room of an April evening, when

   'On the western window panes,
   The chilly sunset faintly told
   Of unmatured green valleys cold.' " *

This quaintly attractive fragment of Keats was written while he was living in the old cathedral and college city of Winchester.   "Some time since," he writes to his brother George, September, 1819, "I began a poem called ' The Eve of St. Mark,' quite in the spirit of town quietude. I think it will give you the sensation of walking about an old country town in a coolish evening."   The letter describes the maiden-lady-like air of the side streets, with doorsteps fresh from the flannel, the doors themselves black, with small brass handles and lion's head or ram's head knockers, seldom disturbed.   He speaks of his walks through the cathedral yard and two college-like squares, grassy and shady, dwelling-places of deans and prebendaries, out to St. Cross Meadows with their Gothic tower and Alms Square.   Mr. Colvin thinks that Keats "in this piece anticipates in a remarkable degree the feeling and method of the modern pre-Raphaelite schools"; and that it is "perfectly in the spirit of Ros-

* See vol. i., p. 371, and for Cumberland's poem, on the same superstition, *ibid.*, 177.

setti (whom we know that the fragment deeply impressed and interested)." Mr. Forman, indeed, quotes Rossetti's own *dictum* (works of John Keats, vol. ii., p. 320) that the poem " shows astonishingly real mediævalism for one not bred as an artist."

It is in the Pre-Raphaelites that Keats' influence on our later poetry is seen in its most concentrated shape. But it is traceable in Tennyson, in Hood, in the Brownings, and in many others, where his name is by no means written in water. " Wordsworth," says Lowell, " has influenced most the ideas of succeeding poets; Keats their forms."

CHAPTER IV.

The Romantic School in Germany.*

CROSS-FERTILIZATION, at least in these modern eras, is as necessary in the life of a literature as in that of an animal or a plant. English romanticism, though it started independently, did not remain an isolated phe-

* Besides the authorities quoted or referred to in the text, the materials used in this chapter are drawn mainly from the standard histories of German literature; especially from Georg Brandes' "Hauptströmungen in der Litteratur des Neunzehnten Jahrhunderts" (1872–76) ; Julian Schmidt's "Geschichte der Deutschen Litteratur" (Berlin, 1890) ; H. J. T. Hettner's "Litteraturgeschichte" (Braunschweig, 1872) ; Wilhelm Scherer's "History of German Literature" (Conybeare's translation, New York, 1886) ; Karl Hillebrand's "German Thought" (trans., New York, 1880) ; Vogt und Koch's "Geschichte der Deutschen Litteratur" (Leipzig and Wien, 1897). My own reading in the German romantics is by no means extensive. I have read, however, a number of Tieck's "Märchen" and of Fouqué's romances; Novalis' "Hymns to the Night" and "Heinrich von Ofterdingen" ; A. W. Schlegel's "Lectures on Dramatic Literature" and F. Schlegel's "Lucinde" ; all of Uhland's ballads and most of Heine's writings in verse and prose; a large part of "Des Knaben Wunderhorn," and the selections from Achim von Arnim, Clemens Brentano, and Joseph Görres contained in Koch's "Deutsche National Litteratur," 146 Band (Stuttgart, 1891). These last include Brentano's "Die Erfindung des Rosenkranzes," "Kasperl und Annerl," "Gockel und Hinkerl," etc., and Arnim's "Kronenwächter," a scene from "Die Päpstin Johanna," etc. I have, of course, read Madame de Staël's "L'Allemagne" ; all of Carlyle's papers on German literature, with his translations; the Grimm fairy tales and the like.

132

nomenon; it was related to the general literary movement in Europe. Even Italy had its romantic movement;
Manzoni began, like Walter Scott, by translating Bürger's
" Lenore " and " Wild Huntsman "; and afterwards, like
Schlegel in Germany and Hugo in France, attacked the
classical entrenchments in his " Discourse of the Three
Unities." It is no part of our undertaking to write the
history of the romantic schools in Germany and France.
But in each of those countries the movement had points
of likeness and unlikeness which shed light upon our
own; and an outline sketch of the German and French
schools will help the reader better to understand both
what English romanticism was, and what it was not.

In Germany, as in England, during the eighteenth century, the history of romanticism is a history of arrested
development. Romanticism existed in solution, but was
not precipitated and crystallised until the closing years
of the period. The current set flowing by Bürger's ballads and Goethe's " Götz," was met and checked by a
counter-current, the new enthusiasm for the antique promoted by Winckelmann's * works on classic art, by the
neo-paganism of Goethe's later writings, and by the influence of Lessing's † clear, rationalising, and thoroughly
Protestant spirit.‡

We may note, at the outset, the main features in which
the German romanticism differed from the English.
First, then, it was more definitely a *movement*. It was
organised, self-conscious, and critical. Indeed, it was

---

*" Gedanken über die Nachahmung der Griechischen Werke
in der Malerei und Bildhauerkunst," 1755. " Geschichte der
Kunst des Alterthums," 1764.

† " Laocoon," 1766.

‡ See vol. i., chap. xi. ; and particularly pp. 383–87.

in criticism and not in creative literature that its highest successes were won. Coleridge, Scott, and Keats, like their English forerunners in the eighteenth century,* worked independently of one another. They did not conspire to a common end; had little personal contact— were hardly acquaintances, and in no sense a "school." But the German romanticists constituted a compact group with coherent aims. They were intimate friends and associates; travelled, lived, and worked together; edited each other's books and married each other's sisters.† They had a theory of art, a programme, and a propaganda; were aggressive and polemical, attacking their adversaries in reviews, and in satirical tales,‡ poems, and plays. Their headquarters were at Jena, "the central point," says Heine, "from which the new æsthetic dogma radiated. I advisedly say dogma, for this school began with a criticism of the art productions of the past, and with recipes for the art works of the future." Their organ was the *Athenæum,* established by Friedrich Schlegel at Berlin in 1798, the date of Wordsworth's and Coleridge's "Lyrical Ballads," and the climacteric year of English and German romanticism.

The first number of the *Athenæum* contained the manifesto of the new school, written by Friedrich Schlegel, the seminal mind of the coterie. The terms of this pronunciamento are somewhat rapt and transcendental; but through its mist of verbiage, one discerns that the ideal

---

* See vol. i., pp. 422–23.

† Novalis' and Wackenroder's remains were edited by Tieck and F. Schlegel. Arnim married Brentano's sister Bettina— Goethe's Bettina.

‡ *E.g.,* Tieck's "Der Gestiefelte Kater," against Nicolai and the *Aufkiärung.*

of romantic art is announced to be: beauty for beauty's sake, the union of poetry and life, and the absolute freedom of the artist to express himself. "Romantic poetry," says Schlegel—"and, in a certain sense, all poetry ought to be romantic—should, in representing outward objects, also represent itself." There is nothing here to indicate the precise line which German romantic poetry was to take; but there is the same rejection of authority, the same assertion of the right of original genius to break a path for itself, which was made, in their various ways, by Wordsworth and Coleridge in the "Lyrical Ballads," by Keats in "Sleep and Poetry," and by Victor Hugo in the preface to "Cromwell."

A second respect in which German romanticism differed from English was in its thoroughgoing character. It is the disposition of the German mind to synthesise thought and life, to carry out theory into practice. Each of those imposing systems of philosophy, Kant's, Fichte's, Schelling's, Hegel's, has its own *æsthetik* as well as its own *ethik*. It seeks to interpret all human activities from a central principle; to apply its highest abstractions to literature, government, religion, the fine arts, and society. The English mind is practical rather than theoretical. It is sensible, cautious, and willing to compromise; distrusting alike the logical habit of the French to push out premises into conclusions at all hazards; and the German habit of system-building. The Englishman has no system; he has his whim, and is careless of consistency. It is quite possible for him to have an æsthetic liking for the Middle Ages, without wishing to restore them as an actual state of society. It is hard for an Englishman to understand to what degree a literary man, like Schiller,

was influenced in his writings by the critical philosophy
of Kant; or how Schelling's transcendental idealism was
used to support Catholicism, and Hegel made a prop to
Protestant orthodoxy and Junkerism. "Tragedies and
romances," wrote Mme. de Staël, "have more importance
in Germany than in any other country. They take them
seriously there; and to read such and such a book, or
see such and such a play, has an influence on the destiny
and the life. What they admire as art, they wish to introduce into real life; and poetry, philosophy, the ideal,
in short, have often an even greater empire over the Germans than nature and the passions." In proof of this,
she adduces the number of young Germans who committed suicide in consequence of reading "Werther";
or took to highway robbery in emulation of "Die Räu-
ber."

In England, accordingly, romanticism was a merely
literary revolution and kept strictly within the domain of
art. Scott's political conservatism was indeed, as we
have seen, not unrelated to his antiquarianism and his
fondness for the feudal past; but he remained a Protestant Tory. And as to his Jacobitism, if a Stuart pre-
tender had appeared in Scotland in 1815, we may be
sure that the canny Scott would not have taken arms in
his behalf against the Hanoverian king. Coleridge's
reactionary politics had nothing to do with his romanticism; though it would perhaps be going too far to deny
that his reverence for what was old and tested by time
in the English church and constitution may have had its
root in the same temper of mind which led him to compose archaic ballad-romances like "Christabel" and
"The Dark Ladye." But in Germany "throne and altar"

became the shibboleth of the school; half of the romanticists joined the Catholic Church, and the new literature rallied to the side of aristocracy and privilege.

A third respect in which the German movement differed
from the English is partly implied in what has been said
above.   In Germany the romantic revival was contempo-
raneous with a great philosophical development which
influenced profoundly even the lighter literature of the
time.   Hence the mysticism which is found in the work
of many of the romanticists, and particularly in the writings of Novalis.   Novalis was a disciple of Schelling,
and Schelling the continuator of Fichte.   Fichte's "Wis-
senschaftslehre" (1794) is the philosophical corner-stone
of the German romantic school.   The freedom of the
fancy from the thraldom of the actual world; the right of
the Ego to assert itself fully; the principle formulated
by Friedrich Schlegel, that "the caprice of the poet knows
no law"; all these literary doctrines were corollaries of
Fichte's objective idealism.*   It is needless to say that,
while romantic art usually partakes of the mysterious, there

---

* As to the much-discussed romantic irony, the theory of
which played a part in the German movement corresponding
somewhat to Hugo's doctrine of the grotesque, it seems to
have made no impression in England.   I can discover no
mention of it in Coleridge.   Carlyle, in the first of his two
essays on Richter (1827), expressly distinguishes true humour
from irony, which he describes as a faculty of caricature,
consisting "chiefly in a certain superficial distortion or rever-
sal of objects"—the method of Swift or Voltaire.   That is,
Carlyle uses irony in the common English sense; the Socratic
irony, the irony of the "Modest Proposal."   The earliest attempt that I have encountered to interpret to the English
public what Tieck and the Schlegels meant by "irony" is an
article in *Blackwood's* for September, 1835, on "The Modern
German School of Irony"; but its analysis is not very *einge-
hend.*

is nothing of this philosophical or transcendental mysticism in the English romanticists. If we were to expect it anywhere it would be in Coleridge, who became the mediator between German and English thought. But Coleridge's poetry was mainly written before he visited Germany and made acquaintance with the systems of Kant and Schelling; and in proportion as his speculative activity increased, his creative force declined. There is enough of the marvellous and the unexplained in "Christabel," and "The Ancient Mariner"; but the "mystic ruby" and the "blue flower" of the Teutonic symbolists are not there.

The German romantic school, in the limited and precise sense of the term, consisted of the brothers August Wilhelm and Friedrich Schlegel, Ludwig Tieck, Friedrich von Hardenberg (Novalis), Johann Dietrich Gries, Tieck's friend Wackenroder, and—at a distance—Zacharias Werner, the dramatist; besides a few others, their associates or disciples, whose names need not here be mentioned. These were, as has been said, personal friends; they began to be heard of about 1795; and their quarters were at Jena and Berlin. A later or younger group (*Spätromantiker*) gathered in 1808 about the *Zeitung für Einsiedler*, published at Heidelberg. These were Clemens Brentano, Achim von Arnim, Ludwig Uhland, Joseph Görres, and the brothers Jacob and Wilhelm Grimm. Arnim, Brentano, and Görres were residing at the time at Heidelberg; the others contributed from a distance. Arnim edited the *Einsiedler;* Görres was teaching in the university. There were, of course, many other adherents of the school, working individually at different times and places, scattered indeed all over Germany, and of various degrees of importance or unimportance, of whom I need mention only Friedrich de la Motte Fouqué, the popular novelist and author of " Undine."

The history of German romanticism has been repeatedly told. There are exhaustive treatments of the subject by Julian Schmidt, Koberstein, Hettner (" Die Romantische Schule," Braunschweig, 1850); Haym (" Die Romantische Schule," Berlin, 1870); by the Danish critic, Georg Brandes (" Den Romantiske Skole i Tydskland "). But the most famous review of this passage of literary history is the poet Heine's brilliant little book, " Die Romantische Schule," * published at Paris in 1833. This was written as a kind of supplement to Mme. de Staël's " L'Allemagne " (1813), and was intended to instruct the French public as to some misunderstandings in Mme. de Staël's book, and to explain what German romanticism really was. Professor Boyesen cautions us to be on our guard against the injustice and untrustworthiness of Heine's report. The warning is perhaps not needed, for the animus of his book is sufficiently obvious. Heine had begun as a romantic poet, but he had parted company with the romanticists because of the reactionary direction which the movement took. He had felt the spell, and he renders it with wonderful vividness in his history of the school. But, at the same time, the impatience of the political radical and the religious sceptic— the " valiant soldier in the war for liberty "—and the bitterness of the exile for opinion's sake, make them-

---

* An English translation was published in this country in 1882. See also H. H. Boyesen's " Essays on German Literature " (1892) for three papers on the " Romantic School in Germany."

selves felt. His sparkling and malicious wit turns the
whole literature of romanticism into sport; and his abuse
of his former teacher, A. W. Schlegel, is personal and
coarse beyond description. Twenty years ago, he said,
when he was a lad, what overflowing enthusiasm he would
have lavished upon Uhland! He used to sit on the ruins
of the old castle at Düsseldorf declaiming Uhland's poem

> "A wandering shepherd young and fair
> Beneath the royal castle strayed."

"But so much has happened since then! What then
seemed to me so grand; all that chivalry and Catholicism; those cavaliers that hack and hew at each other in
knightly tournaments; those gentle squires and virtuous
dames of high degree; the Norseland heroes and minnesingers; the monks and nuns; ancestral tombs thrilling
with prophetic powers; colourless passion, dignified by the
high-sounding title of renunciation, and set to the accompaniment of tolling bells; a ceaseless whining of the
'Miserere'; how distasteful all that has become to me
since then!" And—of Fouqué's romances—"But our
age turns away from all fairy pictures, no matter how
beautiful. . . . This reactionary tendency, this continual
praise of the nobility, this incessant glorification of the
feudal system, this everlasting knight-errantry balderdash
. . . this everlasting sing-song of armours, battle-steeds,
high-born virgins, honest guild-masters, dwarfs, squires,
castles, chapels, minnesingers, faith, and whatever else
that rubbish of the Middle Ages may be called, wearied
us."

It is a part of the irony of things that this satirist of
romance should have been precisely the one to compose

the most popular of all romantic ballads; and that the most current of all his songs should have been the one in which he sings of the enchantress of the Rhine,

> "Ich weiss nicht was soll es bedeuten
> Dass Ich so traurig bin."

The "Loreley" is translated into many tongues, and is sung everywhere. In Germany it is a really national song. And yet the tale on which it is founded is not an ancient folk legend—"ein Mährchen aus alten Zeiten"—but a modern invention of Clemens Brentano, who first published it in 1802 in the form of a ballad inserted in one of his novels:

> "Zu Bacharach am Rheine
> Wohnt' eine Zanberin:
> Sie war so schön und feine
> Und riss viel Herzen hin."

A certain forgotten romanticist, Graf Loeben, made a lyrical tale out of it in 1821, and Heine composed his ballad in 1824, afterwards set to the mournful air in which it is now universally familiar.

It has been mentioned that Heine's "Romantische Schule" was a sort of continuation and correction of Mme. de Staël's "L'Allemagne." That very celebrated book was the result of the distinguished lady's residence in Germany, and of her determination to reveal Germany to France. It has been compared in its purpose to the "Germania" of Tacitus, in which the historian held up the primitive virtues of the Teutonic race as a lesson and a warning to corrupt Rome. Mme. de Staël had arranged to publish her book in 1810, and the first impression of ten thousand copies had already been printed, when the whole edition was seized and destroyed by the police, and the author was ordered to quit France within twenty-four hours. All this, of course, was at the instance of Napoleon, who was by no means above resenting the hostility of a lady author. But the Minister of Police, General Savary, assumed the responsibility of the affair; and to Mme. de Staël's remonstrance he wrote in reply: "It appeared to me that the air of this country did not agree with you, and we are not yet reduced to seek for models amongst the people you admire [the Germans]. Your last work is not French." It was not, accordingly, until 1813 that Mme. de Staël's suppressed work on Germany saw the light.

The only passages in it that need engage our attention are those in which the author endeavours to interpret to a classical people the literature of a Gothic race. In her chapter entitled "Of Classic and Romantic Poetry," she says: "The word romantic has been lately introduced in Germany to designate that kind of poetry which is derived from the songs of the troubadours; that which owes its birth to the union of chivalry and Christianity." She mentions the comparison—evidently derived from Schlegel's lectures which she had attended—of ancient poetry to sculpture and modern to painting; explains that the French incline towards classic poetry, and the English— "the most illustrious of the Germanic nations"—towards "that which owes its birth to chivalry and romance." "The English poets of our times, without entering into concert with the Germans, have adopted the same system. Didactic poetry has given place to the fictions of the Middle Ages." She observes that simplicity and definiteness, that a certain corporeality and externality—or what in modern critical dialect we would call objectivity—are notes of antique art; while variety and shading of colour, and a habit of self-reflection developed by Christianity [subjectivity], are the marks of modern art. "Simplicity in the arts would, among the moderns, easily degenerate into coldness and abstraction, while that of the ancients was full of life and animation. Honour and love, valour and pity, were the sentiments which distinguished the Christianity of chivalrous ages; and those dispositions of the soul could only be displayed by dangers, exploits, love, misfortunes—that romantic interest, in short, by which pictures are incessantly varied." Mme. de Staël's analysis here does not go very deep, and her expression is lacking in precision; but her meaning will be obvious to those who have well considered the various definitions and expositions of these contrasted terms with which we set out. Without deciding between the comparative merits of modern classic and romantic work, Mme. de Staël points out that the former must necessarily be imitative. "The literature of the ancients is, among the moderns, a transplanted literature; that of chivalry and romance is indigenous. . . . The literature of romance is alone capable of further improvement, because, being rooted in our own soil, that alone can continue to grow and acquire fresh life; it expresses our religion; it recalls our history." Hence she notes the fact that while the Spaniards of all classes know by heart the verses of Calderon; while Shakspere is a popular and national poet among the English; and the ballads of Goethe and Bürger are set to music and sung all over Germany; the French classical poets are quite unknown to the common people, "because the arts in France are not, as elsewhere, natives

of the very country in which their beauties are displayed."
In her review of German poetry she gives a brief description, among other things, of the " Nibelungen Lied," and
a long analysis of Bürger's "Leonora" and "Wilde
Jäger." She says that there are four English translations
of " Leonora," of which William Spenser's is the best.
"The analogy between the English and German allows a
complete transfusion of the originality of style and versification of Bürger. . . . It would be difficult to obtain
the same result in French, where nothing strange or odd
seems natural." She points out that terror is "an in-
exhaustible source of poetical effect in Germany. . . .
Stories of apparitions and sorcerers are equally well received by the populace and by men of more enlightened
minds." She notes the fondness of the new school for
Gothic architecture, and describes the principles of
Schlegelian criticism. She transcribes A. W. Schlegel's
praises of the ages of faith and the generous brotherhood
of chivalry, and his lament that "the noble energy of
ancient times is lost," and that "our times alas! no
longer know either faith or love." The German critics
affirm that the best traits of the French character were
effaced during the reign of Louis XIV.; that "literature,
in ages which are called classical, loses in originality
what it gains in correctness"; that the French tragedies
are full of pompous affectation; and that from the middle
of the seventeenth century, a constrained and affected
manner had prevailed throughout Europe, symbolised by
the wig worn by Louis XIV. in pictures and bas-reliefs,
where he is portrayed sometimes as Jupiter and sometimes as Hercules clad only in his lion's skin—but always with the perruque. Heine complains that Mme. de

Staël fell into the hands of the Schlegels, when in Germany, and that her account of German literature was coloured by their prejudices; that William Schlegel, in particular, became her escort at all the capitals of Europe and won great *éclat* thereby

Schlegel's elegiac lament over the decay of chivalry may remind the English reader of the famous passage in Burke * about Marie Antoinette. "Little did I dream that I should have lived to see such disasters fallen upon her in a nation of gallant men, in a nation of men of honour and of cavaliers. I thought ten thousand swords must have leaped from their scabbards to avenge even a look that threatened her with insult. But the age of chivalry is gone. That of sophisters, economists, and calculators has succeeded; and the glory of Europe is extinguished forever. Never, never more shall we behold that generous loyalty to rank and sex, that proud submission, that dignified obedience, that subordination of the heart, which kept alive, even in servitude itself, the spirit of an exalted freedom. The unbought grace of life, the cheap defence of nations, the nurse of manly sentiment and heroic enterprise is gone! It is gone, that sensibility of principle, that chastity of honour, which felt a stain like a wound, which inspired courage whilst it mitigated ferocity, which ennobled whatever it touched, and under which vice itself lost half its evil by losing all its grossness." †

But Burke's reaction against the levelling spirit of

* Gentz, "The German Burke," translated the "Reflections on the Revolution in France" into German in 1796.
† See also in the same tract, Burke's tribute to the value of hereditary nobility, and remember that these were the words of a Whig statesman.

French democracy was by no means so thoroughgoing as the romanticist protest in Germany. It was manifestly impossible to revive the orders of chivalry, as a practical military system; or to recreate the feudal tenures in their entirety. Nor did even the most romantic of the German romanticists dream of this. They appealed, however, to the knightly principles of devotion to church and king, of honour, of religious faith, and of personal loyalty to the suzerain and the nobility. It was these political and theological aspects of the movement that disgusted Heine. He says that just as Christianity was a reaction against Roman materialism; and the Renaissance a reaction against the extravagances of Christian spiritualism; and romanticism in turn a reaction against the vapid imitations of antique classic art; "so also do we now behold a reaction against the re-introduction of that Catholic, feudal mode of thought, of that knight-errantry and priestdom, which were being inculcated through literature and the pictorial arts. . . . For when the artists of the Middle Ages were recommended as models . . . the only explanation of their superiority that could be given was that these men believed in that which they depicted. . . . Hence the artists who were honest in their devotion to art, and who sought to imitate the pious distortions of those miraculous pictures, the sacred uncouthness of those marvel-abounding poems, and the inexplicable mysticisms of those olden works . . . made a pilgrimage to Rome, where the vicegerent of Christ was to re-invigorate consumptive German art with asses' milk."

A number of the romanticists were Catholic by birth. There was Joseph von Eichendorff, *e.g.*, who had a strong admiration for the Middle Ages, wrote sacred poetry, and published in 1815 a novel entitled "Ahnung und Gegenwart," the hero of which ends by retiring to a monastery. And Joseph Görres, who published a work on German *Volksbücher* * (1807); a follower of Schelling and editor of *Der Rheinische Merkur*, a violent anti-Gallican journal during the war of liberation. Görres, according to Heine, "threw himself into the arms of the Jesuits," and became the "chief support of the Catholic propaganda at Munich"; lecturing there on universal history to an audience consisting chiefly of pupils from the Romish seminaries. Another *Spätromantiker*, born Catholic, was Clemens Brentano, whom Heine describes in 1833 as having lived at Frankfort for the last fifteen years in hermit-like seclusion, as a corresponding member of the propaganda. For six years (1818–24) Brentano was constantly at the bedside of the invalid nun, Anna Katharina Emmerich, at Dülmen. She was a "stigmatic," afflicted, *i.e.*, with a mysterious disease which impressed upon her body marks thought to be miraculous counterfeits of the wounds of Christ. She had trances and visions, and uttered revelations which Brentano recorded and afterwards published in several volumes, that were translated into French and Italian and widely circulated among the faithful.

As adherents of the romantic school who were born and bred Protestants, but became converts to the Catholic faith, Heine enumerates Friedrich Schlegel, Tieck, Novalis, Werner, Schütz, Carové, Adam Müller, and Count

---

* Dream books, medicine books, riddle books, almanacs, craftsmen's proverbs, fabulous travels, prophecies, legends, romances and the like, hawked about at fairs.

Stolberg. This list, he says, includes only authors; "the number of painters who in swarms simultaneously abjured Protestantism and reason was much larger." But Tieck and Novalis never formally abjured Protestantism. They detested the Reformation and loved the mediæval Church, but looked upon modern Catholicism as a degenerate system. Their position here was something like that of the English Tractarians in the earlier stages of the Oxford movement. Novalis composed "Marienlieder." Tieck complained of the dryness of Protestant ritual and theology, and said that in the Middle Ages there was a unity (*Einheit*) which ought to be again recovered. All Europe was then one fatherland with a single faith. The period of the Arthursage was the blossoming time of romance, the vernal season of love, religion, chivalry, and—sorcery! He pleaded for the creation of a new Christian, Catholic mythology.

In 1808 Friedrich Schlegel became a Roman Catholic —or, as Heine puts it—"went to Vienna, where he attended mass daily and ate broiled fowl." His wife, a daughter of Moses Mendelssohn, a Jewess by race, followed her husband into the Catholic Church. Zacharias Werner, author of a number of romantic melodramas, the heroes of which are described as monkish ascetics, religious mystics, and "spirits who wander on earth in the guise of harp-players"—Zacharias Werner also went to Vienna and joined the order of Ligorians. This conversion made a prodigious noise in Germany. It occurred at Rome in 1811, and the convert afterwards witnessed the liquefaction of the blood of St. Januarius at Naples, that annual miracle in which Newman expresses so firm a belief. Werner then spent two years in the study of theology, visited Our Lady's Chapel at Loretto in 1813; was ordained priest at Aschaffenburg in 1814; and preached at St. Stephen's Church, Vienna, on the vanity of worldly pleasures, with fastings many, with castigations and mortifications of the flesh. The younger Voss declared that Werner's religion was nothing but a poetic coquetting with God, Mary, the wounds of Christ, and the holy carbuncle (*Karfunkelstein*). He had been a man of dissolute life and had been divorced from three wives. "His enthusiasm for the restoration of the Middle Ages," says Heine, "was one-sided; it applied only to the hierarchical, Catholic phase of mediævalism; feudalism did not so strongly appeal to his fancy. . . . Pater Zacharias died in 1823, after sojourning for fifty-four years in this wicked, wicked world." Carlyle contributed to the *Foreign Review* in 1828 an essay on "Werner's Life and Writings," with translations of passages from his drama, "The Templars in Cyprus."

But the conversion which caused the greatest scandal was that of Count Friedrich Stolberg, whose apostasy was denounced by his early friend Voss, the translator of Homer, in a booklet entitled "Wie ward Fritz Stolberg ein Unfreier?" Voss showed, says Heine, that "Stolberg had secretly joined an association of the nobility which had for its purpose to counteract the French ideas of liberty; that these nobles entered into a league with the Jesuits; that they sought, through the re-establishment of Catholicism, to advance also the interests of the nobility." *

The German literary historians agree that the fresh outbreak of romanticism in the last decade of the eigh-

* For Stolberg see also vol. i., pp. 376–77.

teenth century was the resumption of an earlier movement which had been interrupted; that it was furthered by the new feeling of German nationality aroused by the Bonapartist tyranny; and finally that it was a protest against the flat mediocrity which ruled in the ultra-evangelical circle headed by Nicolai, the Berlin bookseller and editor. Into this mere Philistinism had narrowed itself the nobler rationalism of Lessing, with its distrust of *Träumerei* and *Schwärmerei*—of superstition and fanaticism. "Dry light is best," says Bacon, but the eye is hungry for colour, that has looked too steadily on the *lumen siccum* of the reason; and then imagination becomes the prism which breaks the invisible sunbeam into beauty. Hence the somewhat extravagant romantic love of colour, and the determination to *believe*, at all hazards and even in the teeth of reason. Hence the imperfectly successful attempt to force back the modern mind into a posture of child-like assent to the marvellous. Tieck's "Mährchen" and the Grimm brothers' nursery tales belong to this "renascence of wonder," like Lewis' "Tales of Terror," Scott's "Demonology," and Coleridge's "Christabel" in England. "The tendencies of 1770 to 1780," says Scherer, "which had now quite disappeared, asserted themselves with new and increased force. The nations which were groaning under Napoleon's oppression sought comfort in the contemplation of a fairer and grander past. Patriotism and mediævalism became for a long time the watchwords and the dominating fashion of the day."

Allowing for the differences mentioned, the romantic movements in England and Germany offer, as might be expected, many interesting parallels. Carlyle, writing

in 1827,* says that the recent change in German literature is only a part of a general change in the whole literature of Europe. "Among ourselves, for instance, within
the last thirty years, who has not lifted up his voice with
double vigour in praise of Shakespeare and nature, and
vituperation of French taste and French philosophy?
Who has not heard of the glories of old English literature; the wealth of Queen Elizabeth's age; the penury of
Queen Anne's; and the inquiry whether Pope was a poet?
A similar temper is breaking out in France itself, her-
metically sealed as that country seemed to be against all
foreign influences; and doubts are beginning to be enter-
tained, and even expressed, about Corneille and the three
unities. It seems to be substantially the same thing
which has occurred in Germany, and been attributed to
Tieck and his associates; only that the revolution which
is here proceeding, and in France commencing, appears
in Germany to be completed."

In Germany, as in England—in Germany more than
in England—other arts beside literature partook of the
new spirit. The brothers Boisserée agitated for the com-
pletion of the "Kölner Dom," and collected their famous
picture gallery to illustrate the German, Dutch, and Flemish art of the fifteenth century; just as Gothic came into
fashion in England largely in consequence of the writings of Walpole, Scott, and Ruskin. Like our own later
Pre-Raphaelite group, German art critics began to praise
the naïve awkwardness of execution and devout spirituality of feeling in the old Florentine painters, and German
artists strove to paint like Fra Angelico. Friedrich
Schlegel gave a strong impulse to the study of mediæval

* "Ludwig Tieck": Introductions to "German Romance."

art, and Heine scornfully describes him and his friend
Joseph Görres, rummaging about "among the ancient
Rhine cities for the remains of old German pictures and
statuary which were superstitiously worshipped as holy
relics." Tieck and his friend Wackenroder brought back
from their pilgrimage to Dresden in 1796 a devotion, a
kind of sentimental Mariolatry, to the celebrated Madon-
nas of Raphael and Holbein in the Dresden gallery;
and from their explorations in Nürnberg, that *Perle des
Mittelalters*, an enthusiasm for Albrecht Dürer. This
found expression in Wackenroder's "Herzensergiessungen eines Kunstliebenden Klosterbruders"; and in
Tieck's novel, "Sternbald's Wanderungen," in which he
accompanies a pupil of Dürer to Rome. Wackenroder,
like Tieck's other friend, Novalis, was of a consumptive,
emotional, and somewhat womanish constitution of mind
and body, and died young. Tieck edited his remains,
including letters on old German art. The standard editions of their joint writings are illustrated by engravings
after Dürer, one of which in particular, the celebrated
"Knight, Death, and the Devil," symbolizes the mysterious terrors of Tieck's own tales, and of German romance
in general. The knight is in complete armour, and is
riding through a forest. On a hilltop in the distance are
the turrets of a castle; a lean hound follows the knight;
on the ground between his horse's hoofs sprawls a lizard-
like reptile; a figure on horseback approaches from the
right, with the face half obliterated or eaten away to the
semblance of a skull, and snakes encircling the temples.
Behind comes on a demon or goblin shape, with a tall
curving horn, which is "neither man nor woman, neither
beast nor human," but one of those grotesque and ob-

scene monsters which the mediæval imagination sculptured upon the cathedrals. This famous copperplate
prompted Fouqué's romance, "Sintram and his Companions." He had received a copy of it for a birthday
gift, and brooded for years over its mysterious significance; which finally shaped itself in his imagination into
an allegory of the soul's conflict with the powers of darkness. His whole narrative leads up to the description
of Dürer's picture, which occupies the twenty-seventh and
climacteric chapter. The school of young German Pre-
Raphaelite art students, associated at Rome in 1810 under
the leadership of Overbeck and Cornelius, was considerably influenced by Wackenroder's "Herzensergiessungen."

Music, too, and particularly church music, was affected
by the new taste. The ancient music of the "Dies Iræ"
and other Latin hymns was revived; and it would not be
far wrong to say that the romantic school sowed the seed
of Wagner's great music-dramas, profoundly Teutonic and
romantic in their subject matter and handling and in their
application of the united arts of poetry, music, and scene-
painting to old national legends such as "Parzival,"
"Tannhäuser," * "The Knight of the Swan," and the
"Nibelungen Hoard."

History, too, and Germanic philology took impulse
from this fresh interest in the past. Johannes Müller, in
his "History of the Swiss Confederation" (1780–95),
drew the first appreciative picture of mediæval life, and
caught, in his diction, something of the manner of the
old chroniclers. As in England ancient stores of folklore and popular poetry were gathered and put forth by

* Brentano's fragment "Die Erfindung des Rosenkranzes,"
begun in 1803, deals with the Tannhäuser story.

Percy, Ritson, Ellis, Scott, and others, so in Germany the Grimm brothers' universally known collections of fairy tales, legends, and mythology began to appear.* Tieck published in 1803 his "Minnelieder aus dem Schwabischen Zeitalter." Karl Simrock made modern versions of Middle High German poetry. Uhland, whose "Walther von der Vogelweide," says Scherer, "gave the first complete picture of an old German singer," carried the war into Africa by going to Paris in 1810 and making a study of the French Middle Age. He introduced the old French epics to the German public, and is regarded, with A. W. Schlegel, as the founder of romance philology in Germany.

A pupil of Bodmer,† the Swiss Christian Heinrich Myller, had issued a complete edition of the "Nibelungenlied" in 1784–85. The romantic school now took up this old national epic and praised it as a German Iliad, unequalled in sublimity and natural power. Uhland gave a great deal of study to it, and A. W. Schlegel lectured upon it at Berlin in 1801–2. Both Schlegel and Tieck made plans to edit it; and Friedrich von der Hagen, inspired by the former's lectures, published four editions of it, and a version in modern German. "For a long time," testifies Heine, "the 'Nibelungenlied' was the sole topic of discussion among us. . . . It is difficult for a Frenchman to form a conception of this work, or even of the language in which it is written. It is a language of stone, and the verses are, as it were, blocks of granite." By way of giving his French readers a notion

* " Kinder und Hausmährchen " (1812–15). "Deutsche Sagen" (1816). "Deutsche Mythologie" (1835).
† See vol. i., pp. 375–76.

of the gigantic passions and rude, primitive strength of the poem, he imagines a battle of all the Gothic cathedrals of Europe on some vast plain, and adds, "But no! even then you can form no conception of the chief characters of the ' Nibelungenlied '; no steeple is so high, no stone so hard as the fierce Hagen, or the revengeful Chrimhilde."

Another work which corresponds roughly with Percy's "Reliques," as the "Nibelungenlied" with Macpherson's "Ossian," was "Des Knaben Wunderhorn" (The Boy's Magic Trumpet), published in 1806–8 by Clemens Brentano and Achim von Arnim, with a dedication to Goethe. This was a three-volume collection of German songs, and although it came much later than Percy's, and after the imitation of old national balladry in Germany was already well under way, so that its relation to German romanticism is not of an initial kind, like that of Percy's collection in England; still its importance was very great. It influenced all the lyrical poetry of the Romantic school, and especially the ballads of Uhland. "I cannot sufficiently extol this book," says Heine. "It contains the sweetest flowers of German poesy. . . . On the title page . . . is the picture of a lad blowing a horn; and when a German in a foreign land views this picture, he almost seems to hear the old familiar strains, and homesickness steals over him. . . . In these ballads one feels the beating of the German popular heart. Here is revealed all its sombre merriment, all its droll wit. Here German wrath beats furiously the drum; here German satire stings; here German love kisses. Here we behold the sparkling of genuine German wine, and genuine German tears."

The German romantic school, like the English, but more learnedly and systematically, sought to reinforce its native stock of materials by *motifs* drawn from foreign literatures, and particularly from Norse mythology and from Spanish romance. Percy's translation of Malet: Gray's versions from the Welsh and the Scandinavian: Southey's "Chronicles of the Cid" and Lockhart's trans- lations of the Spanish ballads are paralleled in Germany by William Schlegel's, and Uhland's, and others' studies in old Norse mythology and poetry; by Tieck's transla- tion of "Don Quixote"* and by Johann Dietrich Gries' of Calderon. The romanticists, indeed, and especially Tieck and A. W. Schlegel, were most accomplished trans- lators. Schlegel's great version of Shakspere is justly esteemed one of the glories of the German tongue. Heine affirms that it was undertaken solely for polem- ical purposes and at a time (1797) when the enthusiasm for the Middle Ages had not yet reached an extravagant height. "Later, when this did occur, Calderon was translated and ranked far above Shakespeare. . . . For the works of Calderon bear most distinctly the impress of the poetry of the Middle Ages, particularly of the two principal epochs, knight-errantry and monasticism. The pious comedies of the Castilian priest-poet, whose poet- ical flowers had been besprinkled with holy water and canonical perfumes . . . were now set up as models, and Germany swarmed with fantastically pious, insanely pro- found poems, over which it was the fashion to work one's

* "If Cervantes' purpose," says Heine, "was merely to de- scribe the fools who sought to restore the chivalry of the Mid- dle Ages, . . . then it is a peculiarly comic irony of accident that the romantic school should furnish the best translation of a book in which their own folly is most amusingly ridiculed."

self into a mystic ecstasy of admiration, as in ' The Devotion to the Cross'; or to fight in honour of the Madonna, as in ' The Constant Prince.' . . . Our poetry,
said the Schlegels, is superannuated. . . . Our emotions
are withered; our imagination is dried up. . . . We must
seek again the choked-up springs of the naïve, simple
poetry of the Middle Ages, where bubbles the elixir of
youth." Heine adds that Tieck, following out this prescription, drank so deeply of the mediæval folk tales
and ballads that he actually became a child again and
fell to lisping.

There is a suggestive analogy between the position of
the Warton brothers in England and the Schlegel brothers
in Germany. The Schlegels, like the Wartons, were
leaders in the romantic movement of their time and country, and were the inspirers of other men. The two pairs
were alike also in that their best service was done in the
field of literary history, criticism, and exposition, while
their creative work was imitative and of comparatively
small value. Friedrich Schlegel's scandalous romance
"Lucinde" is of much less importance than his very
stimulating lectures on the "History of Literature" and
the "Wisdom and Languages of India"; * and his elder
brother, though an accomplished metrist and translator,
was not successful in original verse. But this resemblance between the Wartons and the Schlegels must not
be pressed too far. Here, as at many other points, the
German movement had greater momentum. The Wartons
were men of elegant scholarship after their old-fashioned

* F. Schlegel's declamations against printing and gun powder in his Vienna lectures of 1810 foretoken Ruskin's philip-
pics against railways and factories.

kind, a kind which joined the usual classical culture of the English universities to a liberal—and in their century somewhat paradoxical—enthusiasm in antiquarian pursuits. But the Schlegels were men of really wide learning and of depth in criticism. Compared with their scientific method and grasp of principles, the "Observations" and "Essays" of the Wartons are mere dilettantism. To the influence of the Schlegels is not unfairly attributed the origin in Germany of the sciences of comparative philology and comparative mythology, and the works of scholars like Bopp, Diez, and the brothers Grimm. Herder * had already traced the broad cosmopolitan lines which German literary scholarship was to follow, with German thoroughness and independence. And Heine acknowledges that "in reproductive criticism, where the beauties of a work of art were to be brought out clearly; where a delicate perception of individualities was required; and where these were to be made intelligible, the Schlegels were far superior to Lessing." The one point at which the English movement outweighed the German was Walter Scott, whose creative vigour and fertility made an impact upon the mind of Europe to which the romantic literature of the Continent affords no counterpart.

The principles of the Schlegelian criticism were first communicated to the English public by Coleridge; who, in his lectures on Shakspere and other dramatists, helped himself freely to William Schlegel's " Vorlesungen über dramatische Kunst und Litteratur." †   Heine

* See vol. i., pp. 300, 337, 416.

† *Vide supra*, p. 88. A. W. Schlegel was in England in 1823. Tieck met Coleridge in England in 1818, having made his acquaintance in Italy some ten years before.

denounces the shallowness of these principles and their failure to comprehend the modern mind. "When Schlegel seeks to depreciate the poet Bürger, he compares his ballads with the old English ballads of the Percy collection, and he shows that the latter are more simple, more naïve, more antique, and consequently more poetical. . . . But death is not more poetical than life. The old English ballads of the Percy collection exhale the spirit of their age, and Bürger's ballads breathe the spirit of *our* time. The latter, Schlegel never understood. . . . What increased Schlegel's reputation still more was the sensation which he excited in France, where he also attacked the literary authorities of the French, . . . showed the French that their whole classical literature was worthless, that Molière was a buffoon and no poet, that Racine likewise was of no account . . . that the French are the most prosaic people of the world, and that there is no poetry in France." It is well known that Coleridge detested the French, as "a light but cruel race"; that he undervalued their literature and even affected an ignorance of the language. The narrowness of Schlegelian criticism was only the excess of Teutonism reacting against the previous excesses of Gallic classicism.

The deficiency of creative imagination in the Schlegels was supplied by their disciple Ludwig Tieck, who made the "Mährchen," or popular traditionary tale, his peculiar province. It was Wackenroder who first drew his attention to "those old, poorly printed *Volksbücher*, with their coarse wood-cuts which had for centuries been circulating among the peasantry, and which may still be picked up at the book-stalls of the Leipzig fairs." *

* Boyesen: "Aspects of the Romantic School."

Tieck's volume of "Volksmährchen" (1797) gave repro-
ductions of a number of these old tales, such as the
"Haimonskinder," the "Schöne Magelone," "Tannhäuser," and the "Schildbürger." His "Phantasus"
(1812) contained original tales conceived in the same
spirit. Scherer says that Tieck uttered the manifesto of
German romanticism in the following lines from the
overture of his "Kaiser Octavianus":

> "Mondbeglänzte Zaubernacht,
> Die den Sinn gefangen hält,
> Wundervolle Mährchenwelt,
> Steig auf in der alten Pracht!"

"Forest solitude" [*Waldeinsamkeit*], says Boyesen,*
"churchyards at midnight, ruins of convents and baron-
ial castles; in fact, all the things which we are now apt
to call romantic, are the favourite haunts of Tieck's muse.
. . . Tieck was excessively fond of moonlight and liter-
ally flooded his tales with its soft, dim splendour; therefore moonlight is now romantic. . . . He never allows a
hero to make a declaration of love without a near or distant accompaniment of a bugle (*Schalmei* or *Waldhorn*);
accordingly the bugle is called a romantic instrument."

"The true tone of that ancient time," says Carlyle,†
"when man was in his childhood, when the universe
within was divided by no wall of adamant from the universe without, and the forms of the Spirit mingled and
dwelt in trustful sisterhood with the forms of the Sense,
was not easy to seize and adapt with any fitness of application to the feelings of modern minds. It was to
penetrate into the inmost shrines of Imagination, where

---

* *Ibid.*
† "Ludwig Tieck," in "German Romance."

human passion and action are reflected in dim and fitful, but deeply significant resemblances, and to copy these with the guileless, humble graces which alone can become them. . . . The ordinary lovers of witch and fairy matter will remark a deficiency of spectres and enchantments, and complain that the whole is rather dull. Cultivated free-thinkers, again, well knowing that no ghosts or elves exist in this country, will smile at the crack-brained dreamer, with his spelling-book prose and doggerel verse, and dismiss him good-naturedly as a German Lake poet." "In these works," says Heine, "there reigns a mysterious intenseness, a peculiar sympathy with nature, especially with the vegetable and mineral kingdoms. The reader feels himself transported into an enchanted forest; he hears the melodious gurgling of subterranean waters; at times he seems to distinguish his own name in the rustling of the trees. Ever and anon a nameless dread seizes upon him as the broad-leaved tendrils entwine his feet; strange and marvellous wild flowers gaze at him with their bright, languishing eyes; invisible lips mockingly press tender kisses on his cheeks; gigantic mushrooms, which look like golden bells, grow at the foot of the trees; large silent birds sway to and fro on the branches overhead, put on a sapient look and solemnly nod their heads. Everything seems to hold its breath; all is hushed in awed expectation; suddenly the soft tones of a hunter's horn are heard, and a lovely female form, with waving plumes on head and falcon on wrist, rides swiftly by on a snow-white steed. And this beautiful damsel is so exquisitely lovely, so fair; her eyes are of the violet's hue, sparkling with mirth and at the same time earnest, sincere, and yet ironical; so chaste and yet so full of tender passion, like the fancy of our excellent Ludwig Tieck. Yes, his fancy is a charming, high-born maiden, who in the forests of fairyland gives chase to fabulous wild beasts; perhaps she even hunts the rare unicorn, which may only be caught by a spotless virgin."

In 1827 Carlyle * published translations of five of Tieck's "Mährchen," viz.: "The Fair-Haired Eckbert," "The Trusty Eckart," "The Elves," "The Runenberg," and "The Goblet." He mentioned that another tale had been already Englished—"The Pictures" (Die Gemälde). This version was by Connop Thirwall, who had also rendered "The Betrothal" in 1824. In spite of Carlyle's recommendations, Tieck's stories seem to have made small impression in England. Doubtless they came too late, and the romantic movement, by 1827, had spent its first force in a country already sated with Scott's poems and novels. Sarah Austin, a daughter of William Taylor of Norwich, went to Germany to study German literature in this same year 1827. In her "Fragments from German Prose Writers" (1841), she speaks of the small success of Tieck's stories in England, but testifies that A. W. Schlegel's dramatic lectures had been translated early and the translation frequently reprinted. Another of the Norwich Taylors—Edgar—was the translator of Grimm's "Haus- und Kinder-Mährchen." Julius Hare, who was at school at Weimar in the winter of 1804–5, rendered three of Tieck's tales, as well as Fouqué's "Sintram" (1820).

It is interesting to note that Tieck was not unknown to Hawthorne and Poe. The latter mentions his "Journey into the Blue Distance" in his "Fall of the House of

* "German Romance," four vols., Edinburgh.

Usher"; and in an early review of Hawthorne's "Twice-
Told Tales" (1842) and "Mosses from an Old Manse"
(1846), at a time when their author was still, in his own
words, "the obscurest man of letters in America," Poe
acutely pointed out a resemblance between Hawthorne
and Tieck; "whose manner," he asserts, "in some of his
works, is absolutely identical with that *habitual* to Hawthorne." One finds a confirmation of this *aperçu*—or
finds, at least, that Hawthorne was attracted by Tieck—
in passages of the "American Note-Books," where he
speaks of grubbing out several pages of Tieck at a sit-
ting, by the aid of a German dictionary. Colonel Hig-
ginson ("Short Studies"), *à propos* of Poe's sham learning and his habit of mystifying the reader by imaginary
citations, confesses to having hunted in vain for this fas-
cinatingly entitled "Journey into the Blue Distance";
and to having been laughed at for his pains by a friend
who assured him that Poe could scarcely read a word of
German. But Tieck did really write this story, "Das
Alte Buch: oder Reise ins Blaue hinein," which Poe
misleadingly refers to under its alternate title. There
is, indeed, a hint of allegory in Tieck's "Mährchen"—
which are far from being mere fairy tales—that reminds
one frequently of Hawthorne's shadowy art—of such
things as "Ethan Brand," or "The Minister's Black
Veil," or "The Great Carbuncle of the White Mountains." There is, *e.g.*, "The Elves," in which a little
girl does but step across the foot-bridge over the brook
that borders her father's garden, to find herself in a
magic land where she stays, as it seems to her, a few
hours; but returns home to learn that she has been absent
seven years. Or there is "The Runenberg," where a

youth wandering in the mountains, receives from a sorceress, through the casement of a ruined castle, a wondrous
tablet set with gems in a mystic pattern; and years afterward wanders back into the mountains, leaving home
and friends to search for fairy jewels, only to return again
to his village, an old and broken-down man, bearing a
sackful of worthless pebbles which appear to him the
most precious stones.   And there is the story of " The
Goblet," where the theme is like that of Hawthorne's
" Shaker Bridal," a pair of lovers whose union is thwarted
and postponed until finally, when too late, they find that
only the ghost or the memory of their love is left to mock
their youthful hope.

But the mystic, *par excellence*, among the German romanticists was Novalis, of whose writings Carlyle gave
a sympathetic account in the *Foreign Review* for 1829.
Novalis' " Hymns to the Night," written in Ossianic
prose, were perhaps not without influence on Longfellow
(" Voices of the Night "), but his most significant work
was his unfinished romance " Heinrich von Ofterdingen."
The hero was a legendary poet of the time of the Crusades, who was victor in a contest of minstrelsy on the
Wartburg.   But in Novalis' romance there is no firm
delineation of mediæval life—everything is dissolved
in a mist of transcendentalism and allegory.   The story
opens with the words: " I long to see the blue flower;
it is continually in my mind, and I can think of nothing
else."   Heinrich falls asleep, and has a vision of a wondrous cavern and a fountain, beside which grows a tall,
light blue flower that bends towards him, the petals showing " like a blue spreading ruff in which hovered a lovely
face."   This blue flower, says Carlyle, is poetry, " the

real object, passion, and vocation of young Heinrich."
Boyesen gives a subtler interpretation. "This blue
flower," he says, "is the watchword and symbol of the
school. It is meant to symbolise the deep and nameless
longings of a poet's soul. Romantic poetry invariably
deals with longing; not a definite formulated desire for
some attainable object, but a dim mysterious aspiration,
a trembling unrest, a vague sense of kinship with the
infinite,* a consequent dissatisfaction with every form of
happiness which the world has to offer. The object of
the romantic longing, therefore, so far as it has any object, is the ideal. . . . The blue flower, like the absolute
ideal, is never found in this world; poets may at times
dimly feel its nearness, and perhaps even catch a brief
glimpse of it in some lonely forest glade, far from the
haunts of men, but it is in vain to try to pluck it. If for
a moment its perfume fills the air, the senses are intoxicated and the soul swells with poetic rapture." † It
would lead us too far afield to follow up the traces of this
mystical symbolism in the writings of our New England
transcendentalists. One is often reminded of Novalis'
blue flower in such a poem as Emerson's "Forerunners,"
or Lowell's "Footpath," or Whittier's "Vanishers," or
in Thoreau's little parable about the horse, the hound,
and the dove which he had long ago lost and is still
seeking. And again one is reminded of Tieck when
Thoreau says: "I had seen the red election birds brought
from their recesses on my comrades' strings and fancied
that their plumage would assume stranger and more daz-

---

* A. W. Schlegel says that romantic poetry is the representation (*Darstellung*) of the infinite through symbols.
† "Novalis and the Blue Flower."

zling colours in proportion as I advanced farther into the
darkness and solitude of the forest." Heinrich von
Ofterdingen travels to Augsburg to visit his grandfather,
conversing on the way with various shadowy persons, a
miner, a hermit, an Eastern maiden named Zulma, who
represent respectively, according to Boyesen, the poetry
of nature, the poetry of history, and the spirit of the
Orient. At Augsburg he meets the poet Klingsohr (the
personification, perhaps, of poetry in its full development). With his daughter Matilda he falls in love,
whose face is that same which he had beheld in his
vision, encircled by the petals of the blue flower. Then
he has a dream in which he sees Matilda sink and disappear in the waters of a river. Then he encounters her in
a strange land and asks where the river is. "Seest thou
not its blue waves above us?" she answers. "He looked
up and the blue river was flowing softly over their heads."
"This image of Death, and of the river being the sky in
that other and eternal country" *—does it not once more
remind us of the well-known line in Channing's "A
Poet's Hope"—

> "If my bark sink, 'tis to another sea";

or of Emerson's "Two Rivers":

> "Thy summer voice, Musketaquit,
>   Repeats the music of the rain,
>   But sweeter rivers pulsing flit
>   Through thee, as thou through Concord plain"?

But transcendentalism is one thing and romanticism is
another, and we may dismiss Novalis with a reminder of
the fact that the *Journal of Speculative Philosophy*, once
published at Concord, took for its motto a sentence from

* Carlyle.

his "Blüthenstaub" (Flower-pollen): "Philosophy can bake no bread, but she can procure for us God, freedom, and immortality." *

Brentano and Von Arnim have had practically no influence in England. Brentano's most popular story was translated by T. W. Appell, under the title, "Honour, or the Story of the Brave Casper and the Fair Annerl: With an Introduction and Biographical Notice" (London, 1847). The same story was rendered into French in the *Correspondant* for 1859 ("Le Brave Kasperl et la Belle Annerl"). Three tales of Arnim were translated by Théophile Gautier, as "Contes Bizarres" (Paris, 1856). Arnim's best romance is "Die Kronenwächter" (1817). Scherer testifies that this "combined real knowledge of the Reformation period with graphic power"; and adds: "It was Walter Scott's great example which, in the second decade of this century, first made conscientious faithfulness and study of details the rule in historical novel-writing." Longfellow's "German Poets and Poetry" (1845) includes nothing from Arnim or Brentano. Nor did Thomas Roscoe's "German Novelists" (four volumes), nor George Soane's "Specimens of German Romance," both of which appeared in 1826.

The most popular of the German romanticists was Friedrich Baron de la Motte Fouqué, the descendant of a family exiled from France by the Revocation of the Edict of Nantes, and himself an officer in the Prussian army in the war of liberation. Fouqué's numerous romances, in all of which he upholds the ideal of Christian knighthood, have been, many of them, translated into

---

* Selections from Novalis in an English translation were published at London in 1891.

English. "Aslauga's Knight" appeared in Carlyle's
"Specimens of German Romance" (1827); "Sintram,"
"Undine," and "Der Zauberring" had been translated
even earlier. "Thiodolf the Icelander" and others have
also been current in English circulating libraries.
Carlyle acknowledges that Fouqué's notes are few, and
that he is possessed by a single idea. "The chapel and
the tilt yard stand in the background or the foreground
in all the scenes of his universe. He gives us knights,
soft-hearted and strong-armed; full of Christian self-
denial, patience, meekness, and gay, easy daring; they
stand before us in their mild frankness, with suitable
equipment, and accompaniment of squire and dame. . . .
Change of scene and person brings little change of subject; even when no chivalry is mentioned, we feel too
clearly the influence of its unseen presence. Nor can it
be said that in this solitary department his success is of
the very highest sort. To body forth the spirit of
Christian knighthood in existing poetic forms; to wed
that old *sentiment* to modern *thoughts*, was a task which
he could not attempt. He has turned rather to the fictions and machinery of former days." Heine says that
Fouqué's Sigurd the Serpent Slayer has the courage of
a hundred lions and the sense of two asses. But Fouqué's
"Undine" (1811) is in its way a masterpiece and a
classic. This story of the lovely water-sprite, who received a soul when she fell in love with the knight, and
with a soul, a knowledge of human sorrow, has a slight
resemblance to the conception of Hawthorne's "Marble
Faun." Coleridge was greatly fascinated by it. He
read the original several times, and once the American
translation, printed at Philadelphia. He said that it was

beyond Scott, and that Undine resembled Shakspere's
Caliban in being a literal *creation*.

But in general Fouqué's chivalry romances, when
compared with Scott's, have much less vigour, variety,
and dramatic force, though a higher spirituality and a
softer sentiment. The Waverley novels are solid with a
right materialistic treatment. It was Scott's endeavour
to make the Middle Ages real. The people are there,
as well as chevaliers and their ladies. The history of
the times is there. But in Fouqué the Middle Ages become even more unreal, fairy-like, fantastic than they
are in our imaginations. There is nothing but tourney-
ing, love-making, and enchantment. Compare the rumour
of the Crusades and Richard the Lion Heart in "Der
Zauberring" with the stalwart flesh-and-blood figures in
"Ivanhoe" and "The Talisman." A wavering moonshine lies all over the world of the Fouqué romances, like
the magic light which illumines the Druda's castle in
"Der Zauberring," on whose battlements grow tall white
flowers, and whose courts are filled with unearthly music
from the perpetual revolution of golden wheels. "On
the romantic side," wrote Richter, in his review of
"L'Allemagne" in the Heidelberg *Jahrbücher* for 1815,
"we could not wish the Briton to cast his first glance
at us; for the Briton—to whom nothing is so poetical as
the common weal—requires (being used to the weight of
gold), even for a golden age of poetry, the thick golden
wing-cases of his epithet-poets; not the transparent gossamer wings of the Romanticists; no many-coloured but-
terfly dust; but, at lowest, flower-dust that will grow to
something."

Another *Spätromantiker* who has penetrated to the English literary consciousness is the Swabian Ludwig Uhland, the sweetest lyric poet of the romantic school. Uhland studied the poems of Ossian, the Norse sagas, the "Nibelungenlied" and German hero legends, the Spanish romances, the poetry of the trouveres and the troubadours, and treated motives from all these varied sources. His true field, however, was the ballad, as Tieck's was the popular tale; and many of Uhland's ballads are favourites with English readers, through excellent translations. Sarah Austin's version of one of them is widely familiar:

> "Many a year is in its grave
> Since I crossed this restless wave," etc.

Longfellow translated three: "The Black Knight," "The Luck of Edenhall," and "The Castle by the Sea." It is to be feared that the last-named belongs to what Scherer calls that "trivial kind of romanticism, full of sadness and renunciation, in which kings and queens with crimson mantles and golden crowns, kings' daughters and beautiful shepherds, harpers, monks, and nuns play a great part." But it has a haunting beauty, and a dreamy melody like Goethe's "Es war ein König in Thule." The mocking Heine, who stigmatises Fouqué's knights as combinations of iron and sentimentality, complains that in Uhland's writings too "the naïve, rude, powerful tones of the Middle Ages are not reproduced with idealised fidelity, but rather they are dissolved into a sickly, sentimental melancholy. . . . The women in Uhland's poems are only beautiful shadows, embodied moonshine; milk flows in their veins, and sweet tears in their eyes, *i.e.*, tears which lack salt. If we compare Uhland's knights with the knights in the old ballads, it seems to us as if the former were composed of suits of leaden armour, entirely filled with flowers, instead of flesh and bones. Hence Uhland's knights are more pleasing to delicate nostrils than the old stalwarts, who wore heavy iron trousers and were huge eaters and still huger drinkers."

Upon the whole it must be concluded that this second invasion of England by German romance, in the twenties and early thirties of the nineteenth century, made a lesser impression than the first irruption in, say, 1795 to 1810, in the days of Bürger and "Götz," and "The Robbers," and Monk Lewis and the youthful Scott. And the reason is not far to seek. The newcomers found England in possession of a native romanticism of a very robust type, by the side of which the imported article showed like a delicate exotic. Carlyle affirms that Madame de Staël's book was the precursor of whatever acquaintance with German literature exists in England. He himself worked valiantly to extend that acquaintance by his articles in the *Edinburgh* and *Foreign Review*, and by his translations from German romance. But he found among English readers an invincible prejudice against German mysticism and German sentimentality. The romantic *chiaroscuro*, which puzzled Southey even in "The Ancient Mariner," became dimmest twilight in Tieck's "Mährchen" and midnight darkness in the visionary Novalis. The *Weichheit, Wehmuth,* and *Sehnsucht nach der Unendlichkeit* of the German romanticists were moods not altogether unfamiliar in English poetry. "Now stirs the feeling infinite," sings Byron.

> "Now more than ever seems it rich to die,
> To cease upon the midnight with no pain,"

cries Keats.   But when Novalis, in his *Todessehnsucht*, exclaims, "Death is the romance of life," the sentiment has an alien sound.   There was something mutually repellent between the more typical phases of English and German romanticism.   Tieck and the Schlegels, we know, cared little for Scott.   We are told that Scott read the *Zeitung für Einsiedler*, but we are not told what he thought of it.   Perhaps romanticism, like transcendentalism, found a more congenial soil in New than in Old England.   Longfellow spent the winter of 1835–36 in Heidelberg, calling on A. W. Schlegel at Bonn, on his way thither.   "Hyperion" (1839) is saturated with German romance.   Its hero, Paul Flemming, knew "Des Knaben Wunderhorn" almost by heart.   No other German book had ever exercised such "wild and magic influence upon his imagination."

CHAPTER V.

The Romantic Movement in France.*

FRENCH romanticism had aspects of its own which distinguished it from the English and the German alike. It differed from the former and agreed with the latter in being organised. In France, as in Germany, there was a romantic *school*, whose members were united by common literary principles and by personal association. There were sharply defined and hostile factions of classics and romantics, with party cries, watchwords, and shibboleths; a propaganda carried on and a polemic waged in pamphlets, prefaces, and critical journals. Above all there was a leader. Walter Scott was the great romancer of Europe, but he was never the head of a school in his own country in the sense in which Victor Hugo was in France, or even in the sense in which the Schlegels were in Germany. Scott had imitators, but Hugo had disciples.

* It is scarcely necessary to say that no full-length picture of the French romantic movement is attempted in this chapter, but only such a sketch as should serve to illustrate its relation to English romanticism. For the history of the movement, besides the authorities quoted or referred to in the text, I have relied principally upon the following: Petit de Julleville: "Histoire de la Littérature Française," Tome vii., Paris, 1899. Brunetière: "Manual of the History of French Literature" (authorized translation), New York, 1898. L. Bertrand: "La Fin du Classicisme," Paris, 1897. Adolphe Jullien: "Le Romantisme et L'Editeur Renduel," Paris, 1897. I have also read somewhat widely, though not exhaus-

One point in which the French movement differed from both the English and the German was in the suddenness and violence of the outbreak. It was not so much a gradual development as a revolution, an explosion. The reason of this is to be found in the firmer hold which academic tradition had in France, the fountainhead of eighteenth-century classicism. Romanticism had a special work to do in the land of literary convention in asserting the freedom of art and the unity of art and life. Everything that is in life, said Hugo, is, or has a right to be in art. The French, in political and social matters the most revolutionary people of Europe, were the most conservative in matters of taste. The Revolution even intensified the reigning classicism by giving it a republican turn. The Jacobin orators appealed constantly to the examples of the Greek and Roman democracies. The Goddess of Reason was enthroned in place of God. Sunday was abolished, and the names of the months and of the days of the week were changed. Dress under the Directory was patterned on antique modes—the liberty cap was Phrygian—and children born under the Repub-

---

tively, in the writings of the French romantics themselves, including Hugo's early poems and most of his dramas and romances; Nodier's "Contes en prose et en verse"; nearly all of Musset's works in prose and verse; ditto of Théophile Gautier's; Stendhal's "La Chartreuse de Parme," "Le Rouge et le Noir," "Racine et Shakespeare," "Lord Byron en Italie," etc.; Vigny's "Chatterton," "Cinq-Mars," and many of his Scriptural poems; Balzac's "Les Chouans"; Mérimée's "Chronique de Charles IX.," and most of his "Nouvelles"; Chateaubriand's "Le Génie du Christianisme"; some of Lamartine's "Meditations"; most of George Sand's novels, and a number of Dumas'; many of Sainte-Beuve's critical writings; and the miscellanies of Gérard de Nerval (Labrunie). Of many of these, of course, no direct use or mention is made in the present chapter.

lic were named after Roman patriots, Brutus, Cassius, etc. The great painter of the Revolution was David,* who painted his subjects in togas, with backgrounds of Greek temples. Voltaire's classicism was monarchical and held to the Louis XIV. tradition; David's was republican. And yet the recognised formulæ of taste and criticism were the same in 1800 as in 1775, or in 1675.

A second distinction of the French romanticism was its local concentration at Paris. The centripetal forces have always been greater in France than in England and Germany. The earlier group of German *Romantiker* was, indeed, as we have seen, united for a time at Jena and Berlin; and the *Spätromantiker* at Heidelberg. But this was dispersion itself as compared with the intense focussing of intellectual rays from every quarter of France upon the capital. In England, I hardly need repeat, there was next to no cohesion at all between the widely scattered men of letters whose work exhibited romantic traits.

In one particular the French movement resembled the English more nearly than the German. It kept itself almost entirely within the domain of art, and did not carry out its principles with German thoroughness and consistency into politics and religion. It made no efforts towards a practical restoration of the Middle Ages. At the beginning, indeed, French romanticism exhibited something analogous to the Toryism of Scott, and the reactionary *Junkerism* and neo-Catholicism of the Schle-

* "Il a pour l'art du moyen âge, un mepris voisin de la demence et de la frénésie. . . . Voir le discours où il propose de mutiler les statues des rois de la façade de Notre-Dame, pour en former un piédestal à la statue du peuple français." Bertrand : "La Fin du Classicisme," pp. 302–3 and *note.*

gels. Chateaubriand in his "Génie du Christianisme" attempted a sort of æsthetic revival of Catholic Christianity, which had suffered so heavily by the deistic teachings of the last century and the atheism of the Revolution. Victor Hugo began in his "Odes et Ballades" (1822) as an enthusiastic adherent of monarchy and the church. "L'histoire des hommes," he wrote, "ne présente de poésie que jugée du haut des idées monarchiques et religieuses." But he advanced quite rapidly towards liberalism both in politics and religion. And of the young men who surrounded him, like Gautier, Labrunie, Sainte-Beuve, Musset, De Vigny, and others, it can only be affirmed that they were legitimist or republican, Catholic or agnostic, just as it happened and without affecting their fidelity to the literary canons of the new school.* The German romanticism was philosophical; the French was artistic and social. The Parisian *ateliers* as well as the Parisian *salons* were nuclei of revolt against classical traditions. "This intermixture of art with poetry," says Gautier,† "was and remains one of the characteristic marks of the new school, and enables us to understand why its earliest recruits were found more among artists than among men of letters. A multitude of objects, images, comparisons, which were believed to be irreducible to words, entered into the language and have stayed there. The sphere of literature was enlarged, and now includes the sphere of art in its measureless circle." "At that time painting and poetry fraternised. The artists read the poets and the poets visited the artists.

---

* But see, for the Catholic reaction in France, the writings of Joseph de Maistre, especially "Du Pape" (1819).
† "Histoire du Romantisme" (1874).

Shakspere, Dante, Goethe, Lord Byron, and Walter Scott were to be found in the studio as in the study. There were as many splotches of colour as of ink on the margins of those beautiful volumes that were so incessantly thumbed. Imaginations, already greatly excited by themselves, were heated to excess by the reading of those foreign writings of a colouring so rich, of a fancy so free and so strong. Enthusiasm mounted to delirium. It seemed as if we had discovered poetry, and that was indeed the truth. Now that this fine flame has cooled and that the positive-minded generation which possesses the world is preoccupied with other ideas, one cannot imagine what dizziness, what *éblouissement* was produced in us by such and such a picture or poem, which people nowadays are satisfied to approve by a slight nod of the head. It was so new, so unexpected, so lively, so glowing!" *

The romantic school in France had not only its poets, dramatists, and critics, but its painters, architects, sculptors, musical composers, and actors. The romantic artist *par excellence* was Eugène Delacroix, the painter of "The Crusaders Entering Jerusalem. "The Greeks and Romans had been so abused by the decadent school of David that they fell into complete disrepute at this time. Delacroix's first manner was purely romantic, that is to say, he borrowed nothing from the recollections or the forms of the antique. The subjects that he treated were relatively modern, taken from the history of the Middle Ages, from Dante, Shakspere, Goethe, Lord Byron, or Walter Scott." He painted "Hamlet," "The Boat of Dante," "Tasso in Bedlam," "Marino Faliero," "The Death of Sardanapalus," "The Combat of the Giaour and

* *Ibid.*, 210.

the Pasha," "The Massacre of the Bishop of Liége," and similar subjects. Goethe in his conversations with Eckerman expressed great admiration of Delacroix's interpretations of scenes in "Faust" (the brawl in Auerbach's cellar, and the midnight ride of Faust and Mephistopheles to deliver Margaret from prison). Goethe hoped that the French artist would go on and reproduce the whole of "Faust," and especially the sorceress' kitchen and the scenes on the Brocken. Other painters of the romantic school were Camille Roqueplan, who treated motives drawn from "The Antiquary" and other novels of Walter Scott; * and Eugène Devéria, whose "Birth of Henry IV.," executed in 1827, when the artist was only twenty-two years of age, was a masterpiece of colouring and composition. The house of the Devéria brothers was one of the rallying points of the Parisian romanticists. And then there was Louis Boulanger, who painted "Mazeppa" and "The Witches' Sabbath" ("La Ronde du Sabbat" †); and the water-colour painter and engraver, Celestin Nanteuil, who furnished innumerable designs for vignettes, frontispieces, and book illustrations to the writers of the romantic school.

"Of all the arts," says Gautier, "the one that lends itself least to the expression of the romantic idea is certainly sculpture. It seems to have received from antiquity its definitive form. . . . What can the statuary art do without the gods and heroes of mythology who furnish it with plausible pretexts for the nude, and for such

* Heine counted, in the Salon of 1831, more than thirty pictures inspired by Scott.

† Also "Le Roi Lear" (Salon of 1836) and "La Procession du Pape des Fous" (aquarelle) for Hugo's "Notre-Dame de Paris."

drapery as it needs; things which romanticism prescribes, or did at least prescribe at that time of its first fervour? Every sculptor is of necessity a classic." * Nevertheless, he says that the romantic school was not quite unprovided of sculptors. "In our inner circle (*cénacle*), Jehan du Seigneur represented this art, austere and rebellious to the fancy. . . . Jehan du Seigneur—let us leave in his name of Jean this mediæval *h* which made him so happy and made him believe that he wore the apron of Ervein of Steinbach at work on the sculptures of Strasburg minster." Gautier mentions among the productions of this Gothic-minded statuary an "Orlando Furioso," a bust of Victor Hugo, and a group from the latter's romance, "Notre Dame de Paris," the gipsy girl Esmeralda giving a drink to the humpback Quasimodo. It was the endeavour of the new school, in the arts of design as well as in literature, to introduce colour, novelty, picturesqueness, character. They studied the great Venetian and Flemish colourists, neglected under the reign of David, and "in the first moments of their fury against *le poncif classique*, they seemed to have adopted the theory of art of the witches in 'Macbeth'—Fair is foul and foul is fair"; † *i.e.*, they neglected a traditional beauty in favour of the *characteristic*. "They sought the true, the new, the picturesque perhaps more than the ideal; but this reaction was certainly permissible after so many Ajaxes, Achilleses, and Philocteteses."

It is not quite so easy to understand what is meant by romanticism in music as in literature. But Gautier

* Recall Schlegel's saying that the genius of the classic drama was plastic and that of the romantic picturesque.
† Gautier, 192.

names a number of composers as adhering to the romantic school, among others, Hippolyte Monpon, who set to
music "the leaping metres, the echo-rimes, the Gothic
counter-points of Hugo's 'Odes et Ballades' and songs
like Musset's 'L'Andalouse'—

'Avez vous vu dans Barcelone,'

He believed like us in serenades, alcaldes, mantillas,
castinets; in all that Italy and that Spain, a trifle conventional, which was brought into fashion by the author
of 'Don Paëz,' of 'Portia,' and of the 'Marchioness of
Amalgui,' . . . 'Gastibelza, the Man with the Cara-
bine,' and that guitar, so profoundly Spanish, of Victor
Hugo, had inspired Monpon with a savage, plaintive air,
of a strange character, which long remained popular, and
which no romanticist—if any such is left—has forgotten."
A greater name than Monpon was Hector Berlioz, the
composer of "Romeo and Juliette" and "The Damnation
of Faust." Gautier says that Berlioz represented the romantic idea in music, by virtue of his horror of common
formulæ, his breaking away from old models, the complex
richness of his orchestration, his fidelity to local colour
(whatever that may mean in music), his desire to make
his art express what it had never expressed before, "the
tumultuous and Shaksperian depth of the passions, reveries amorous or melancholy, the longings and demands
of the soul, the indefinite and mysterious feelings which
words cannot render." Berlioz was a passionate lover of
German music and of the writings of Shakspere, Goethe,
and Scott. He composed overtures to "Waverley,"
"King Lear," and "Rob Roy"; a cantata on "Sardanapalus," and music for the ghost scene in "Hamlet" and

for Goethe's ballad, "The Fisher." He married an English actress whom he had seen in the parts of Ophelia,
Portia, and Cordelia. Berlioz *en revanche* was better
appreciated in Germany than in France, where he was
generally considered mad; where his "Symphonie fan-
tastique" produced an effect analogous to that of the
first pieces of Richard Wagner; and where "the sympho-
nies of Beethoven were still thought barbarous, and pronounced by the classicists not to be music, any more than
the verses of Victor Hugo were poetry, or the pictures of
Delacroix painting." And finally there were actors and
actresses who came to fill their rôles in the new romantic dramas, of whom I need mention only Madame Dor-
val, who took the part of Hugo's Marion Delorme. What
Gautier tells us of her is significant of the art that she
interpreted; that her acting was by sympathy, rather than
calculation; that it was intensely emotional; that she
owed nothing to tradition; her tradition was essentially
modern, dramatic rather than tragic.*

Romanticism in France was, in a more special sense
than in Germany and England, an effort for freedom,
passion, originality, as against rule, authority, convention. "Romanticism," says Victor Hugo,† "so many
times poorly defined, is nothing else than *liberalism* in
literature. . . . Literary liberty is the child of political
liberty. . . . After so many great things which our fathers have done and which we have witnessed, here we are,
issued forth from old forms of society; why should we
not issue out of the old forms of poetry? A new people,

---

* This is a distinction more French than English: *la tragédie* vs. *le drame*.
† Preface to "Hernani."

a new art.   While admiring the literature of Louis XIV.,
so well adapted to his monarchy, France will know how to
have its own literature, peculiar, personal, and national—
this actual France, this France of the nineteenth century
to which Mirabeau has given its freedom and Napoleon
its power."   And again : *   "What I have been pleading
for is the liberty of art as against the despotism of systems, codes, and rules.   It is my habit to follow at all
hazards what I take for inspiration, and to change the
mould as often as I change the composition.   Dogmatism
in the arts is what I avoid above all things.   God forbid
that I should aspire to be of the number of those, either
romantics or classics, who make works *according to their
system ;* who condemn themselves never to have more than
one form in mind, to always be *proving* something, to
follow any other laws than those of their organization
and of their nature.   The artificial work of such men as
those, whatever talents they may possess, does not exist for
art.   It is a theory, not a poetry."   It is manifest that a
literary reform undertaken in this spirit would not long
consent to lend itself to the purposes of political or
religious reaction, or to limit itself to any single influence
like mediævalism, but would strike out freely in a multitude of directions; would invent new forms and adapt old
ones to its material; and would become more and more
modern, various, and progressive.   And such, in fact,
was the history of Victor Hugo's intellectual development and of the whole literary movement in France which
began with him and with De Stendhal (Henri Beyle).
This assertion of the freedom of the individual artist was
naturally accompanied with certain extravagances.   "To

* Preface to "Cromwell."

develop freely all the caprices of thought," says Gautier,* "even if they shocked taste, convention, and rule; to hate and repel to the utmost what Horace calls the *profanum vulgus*, and what the moustached and hairy *rapins* call grocers, philistines, or bourgeois; to celebrate love with warmth enough to burn the paper (that they wrote on); to set it up as the only end and only means of happiness; to sanctify and deify art, regarded as a second creator; such are the *données* of the programme which each sought to realise according to his strength; the ideal and the secret postulations of the young romanticists."

Inasmuch as the French romantic school, even more than the English and the German, was a breach with tradition and an insurrection against existing conditions, it will be well to notice briefly what the particular situation was which the romanticists in France confronted. "To understand what this movement was and what it did," says Saintsbury,† "we must point out more precisely what were the faults of the older literature, and especially of the literature of the late eighteenth century. They were, in the first place, an extremely impoverished vocabulary, no recourse being had to the older tongue for picturesque archaisms, and little welcome being given to new phrases, however appropriate and distinct. In the second place, the adoption, especially in poetry, of an exceedingly conventional method of speech, describing everything where possible by an elaborate periphrasis, and avoiding direct and simple terms. Thirdly, in all forms of literature, but especially in poetry and drama, the acceptance for almost every kind of work of cut-and-dried

* "Histoire du Romantisme," p. 64.
† "Primer of French Literature," p. 115.

patterns,* to which it was bound to conform. We have already pointed out that this had all but killed the tragic drama, and it was nearly as bad in the various accepted forms of poetry, such as fables, epistles, odes, etc. Each piece was expected to resemble something else, and originality was regarded as a mark of bad taste and insufficient culture. Fourthly, the submission to a very limited and very arbitrary system of versification, adapted only to the production of tragic alexandrines, and limiting even that form of verse to one monotonous model. Lastly, the limitation of the subject to be treated to a very few classes and kinds." If to this description be added a paragraph from Gautier's "Histoire du Romantisme," we shall have a sufficient idea of the condition of French literature and art before the appearance of Victor Hugo's "Odes et Ballades" (1826). "One cannot imagine to what a degree of insignificance and paleness literature had come. Painting was not much better. The last pupils of David were spreading their wishywashy colours over the old Græco-Roman patterns. The classicists found that perfectly beautiful; but in the presence of these masterpieces, their admiration could not keep them from putting their hands before their mouths to cover a yawn; a circumstance, however, that failed to make them any more indulgent to the artists of the new school, whom they called tattooed savages and accused of painting with a drunken broom." One is reminded by Mr. Saintsbury's summary of many features which we have observed in the English academicism of the eighteenth

---

* One of the principles of the romanticists was the *mélange des genres*, whereby the old lines between tragedy and comedy, *e.g.*, were broken down, lyricism admitted into the drama, etc.

century; the impoverished vocabulary, *e.g.*, which makes
itself evident in the annotations on the text of Spenser
and other old authors; the horror of common terms, and
the constant abuse of the periphrasis—the "gelid cis-
tern," the "stercoraceous heap," the "spiculated pal-
ings," and the "shining leather that encased the limb."
And the heroic couplet in English usage corresponds very
closely to the French alexandrine. In their dissatisfaction with the paleness and vagueness of the old poetic
diction, and the monotony of the classical verse, the new
school innovated boldly, introducing archaisms, neologisms, and all kinds of exotic words and popular locutions,
even *argot* or Parisian slang; and trying metrical experiments of many sorts. Gautier mentions in particular one
Théophile Dondey (who, after the fashion of the school,
anagrammatised his name into Philothée O'Neddy) as presenting this *caractère d'outrance et de tension.* "The word
paroxyste, employed for the first time by Nestor Roqueplan, seems to have been invented with an application to
Philothée. Everything is *poussé* in tone, high-coloured,
violent, carried to the utmost limits of expression, of an
aggressive originality, almost dripping with the unheard-
of (*ruissilant d'inouïsme*); but back of the double-horned
paradoxes, sophistical maxims, incoherent metaphors,
swoln hyperboles, and words six feet long, are the poetic
feeling of the time and the harmony of rhythm." One
hears much in the critical writings of that period, of the
mot propre, the *vers libre*, and the *rime brisé*. It was in
tragedy especially that the periphrasis reigned most
tyrannically, and that the introduction of the *mot propre*,
i.e., of terms that were precise, concrete, familiar, technical even, if needful, horrified the classicists. It was

beneath the dignity of the muse—the elegant muse of the Abbé Delille—Hugo tells us, to speak naturally. "She underlines," in sign of disapprobation, "the old Corneille for his way of saying crudely

> 'Ah, ne me brouillez pas avec la république.'

She still has heavy on her heart his *Tout beau, monsieur.* And many a *seigneur* and many a *madame* was needed to make her forgive our admirable Racine his *chiens* so monosyllabic. . . . History in her eyes is in bad tone and taste. How, for example, can kings and queens who swear be tolerated? They must be elevated from their royal dignity to the dignity of tragedy. . . . It is thus that the king of the people (Henri IV.) polished by M. Legouvé, has seen his *ventre-saint-gris* shamefully driven from his mouth by two sentences, and has been reduced, like the young girl in the story, to let nothing fall from this royal mouth, but pearls, rubies, and sapphires—all of them false, to say the truth." It seems incredible to an Englishman, but it is nevertheless true that at the first representations of "Hernani" in 1830, the simple question and answer

> "Est il minuit?—Minuit bientot"

raised a tempest of hisses and applause, and that the opposing factions of classics and romantics "fought three days over this hemistich. It was thought trivial, familiar, out of place; a king asks what time it is like a common citizen, and is answered, as if he were a farmer, *midnight.* Well done! Now if he had only used some fine periphrasis, *e.g.:*

> ——l'heure
> Atteindra bientot sa dernière demeure.*

* Stendhal, writing in 1823 ("Racine et Shakspere"), com-

If they could not away with definite words in the verse, they endured very impatiently, too, epithets, metaphors, comparisons, poetic words—lyricism, in short; those swift escapes into nature, those soarings of the soul above the situation, those openings of poetry athwart drama, so frequent in Shakspere, Calderon, and Goethe, so rare in our great authors of the eighteenth century." Gautier gives, as one reason for the adherence of so many artists to the romantic school, the circumstance that, being accustomed to a language freely intermixed with technical terms, the *mot propre* had nothing shocking for them; while their special education as artists having put them into intimate relation with nature, "they were prepared to feel the imagery and colours of the new poetry and were not at all repelled by the precise and picturesque details so disagreeable to the classicists. . . . You cannot imagine the storms that broke out in the parterre of the Théâtre Français, when the 'Moor of Venice,' translated by

plains that "it will soon be thought bad form to say, on the French stage, '*Fermez cette fenêtre*' [window] : we shall have to say, '*Fermez cette croisée*' [casement]. Two-thirds of the words used in the parlours of the best people (*du meilleur ton*) cannot be reproduced in the theatre. M. Legouvé, in his tragedy 'Henri IV.,' could not make use of the patriot king's finest saying, 'I could wish that the poorest peasant in my kingdom might, at the least, have a chicken in his pot of a Sunday.' English and Italian verse allows the poet to say everything; and this good French word *pot* would have furnished a touching scene to Shakspere's humblest pupil. But *la tragédie racinienne*, with its *style noble* and its artificial dignity, has to put it thus,—in four alexandrines :

> "' Je veux enfin qu'au jour marqué pour le repos,
> L'hôte laborieux des modestes hameaux,
> Sur sa table moins humble, ait, par ma bienfaisance,
> Quelques-uns de ces mets réservés à l'aisance.'"

It was Stendhal (whose real name was Henri Beyle) who said that Paris needed a chain of mountains on its horizon.

Alfred de Vigny, grinding his teeth, reiterated his demands for that handkerchief (*mouchoir*) prudently denominated *bandeau* (head-band, fillet) in the vague Shakspere imitation of the excellent Ducis. A bell was called 'the sounding brass'; the sea was 'the humid element,' or 'the liquid element,' and so on. The professors of rhetoric were thunderstruck by the audacity of Racine, who in the 'Dream of Athalie' had spoken of dogs as dogs—molossi would have been better—and they advised young poets not to imitate this license of genius. Accordingly the first poet who wrote bell (*cloche*) committed an enormity; he exposed himself to the risk of being cut by his friends and excluded from society." *

As to the alexandrine, the recognised verse of French tragedy, Victor Hugo tells us,† that many of the reformers, wearied by its monotony, advocated the writing of plays in prose. He makes a plea, however, for the retention of the alexandrine, giving it greater richness and suppleness by the displacement of the cæsura, and the free use of *enjambement* or run-over lines; just as Leigh Hunt and Keats broke up the couplets of Pope into a freer and looser form of verse. "Hernani" opened with an *enjambement*

> "Serait ce déja lui? C'est bien à l'escalier
> Dérobé."

This was a signal of fight—a challenge to the classicists —and the battle began at once, with the very first lines of the play.‡ In his dramas Hugo used the alexandrine, but in his lyric poems, his wonderful resources as a

* Gautier, 188.
† "Cromwell," 1827.
‡ Gautier, 107.

metrist were exhibited to the utmost in the invention of the most bizarre, eccentric, and original verse forms. An example of this is the poem entitled "The Djinns" included in "Les Orientales" (1829). The coming and going of the flying cohort of spirits is indicated by the crescendo effect of the verse, beginning with a stanza in lines of two syllables, rising gradually to the middle stanza of the poem in lines of ten syllables, and then dying away by exactly graded diminutions to the final stanza:

> "On doute
> La nuit—
> J'écoute
> Tout fuit,
> Tout passe :
> L'espace
> Efface
> Le bruit." *

But the earlier volume of "Odes et Ballades" (1826) offers many instances of metrical experiments hardly less ingenious. In "La Chasse du Burgrave" every rime is followed by an echo word, alike in sound but different in sense:

> "Il part, et Madame Isabelle,
> Belle,
> Dit gaiement du haut des remparts :
> 'Pars !'
> Tous las chasseurs sont dans la plaine,
> Pleine
> D'ardents seigneurs, de sénéchaux
> Chauds."

The English reader is frequently reminded by Hugo's verses of the queer, abrupt, and *outré* measures, and fan-

---

* Musset's fantastic "Ballade à la Lune," exaggerates the romantic so decidedly as to seem ironical. It is hard to say whether it is hyperbole or parody. See Petit de Julleville, vol. vii., p. 652.

tastic rimes of Robert Browning. Compare with the
above, *e.g.*, his " Love among the Ruins."

> "Where the quiet coloured end of evening smiles
> Miles and miles
> On the solitary pastures where our sheep,
> Half asleep," etc.

From the fact, already pointed out, that the romantic
movement in France was, more emphatically than in England and Germany, a breach with the native literary tradition, there result several interesting peculiarities.   The
first of these is that the new French school, instead of
fighting the classicists with weapons drawn from the old
arsenal of mediæval France, went abroad for allies; went
especially to the modern writers of England and Germany. This may seem strange when we reflect that
French literature in the Middle Ages was the most influential in Europe; and that, from the old heroic song of
Roland in the eleventh century down to the very popular
court allegory, the " Roman de la Rose ", in the fourteenth
and to the poems of Villon in the fifteenth, it afforded a
rich treasure-house of romantic material in the shape of
chronicles, *chansons de geste*, *romans d'aventures*, *fabliaux*,
lais, legends of saints, homilies, miracles, songs, farces,
jeuspartis, *pastourelles*, *ballades*—of all the literary forms
in fact which were then cultivated. Nor was this mass
of work entirely without influence on the romanticists of
1830. Théophile Dondey, wrote a poem on Roland
and Gérard de Nerval (Labrunie) hunted up the old popular songs and folklore of Touraine and celebrated their
naïveté and truly national character. Attention was directed to the Renaissance group of poets who preceded
the Louis XIV. writers—to Ronsard and " The Pleiade."

Later the Old French Text Society was founded for the preservation and publication of mediæval remains. But in general the innovating school sought their inspiration in foreign literatures. Antony Deschamps translated the "Inferno"; Alfred de Vigny translated "Othello" as the "Moor of Venice" (1829), and wrote a play on the story of Chatterton,* and a novel, "Cinq Mars," which is the nearest thing in French literature to the historical romances of Scott.† Chateaubriand and Victor Hugo were both powerfully impressed by Macpherson's "Ossian." Gérard de Nerval made, at the age of eighteen, a translation of "Faust" (1828), which Goethe read with admiration, and wrote to the translator, saying that he had never before understood his own meaning so well. "It was a difficult task at that time," says Gautier, "to render into our tongue, which had become excessively timid, the bizarre and mysterious beauties of this ultra-romantic drama. . . . From his familiarity with Goethe, Uhland, Bürger and L. Tieck, Gérard retained in his turn of mind a certain dreamy tinge which sometimes made his own works seem like translations of unknown poets beyond the Rhine. . . . The sympathies and the studies of Gérard de Nerval drew him naturally towards Germany, which he often visited and where he made fruitful sojourns; the shadow of the old Teutonic oak hovered more than once above his brow with confidential murmurs; he walked under the lindens with their heart-shaped leaves; on the margin of fountains he saluted the elf whose white robe trails a hem bedewed by the green grass; he saw the ravens circling around the moun-

* See vol. i., pp. 372–73.
† Gautier, 163.

tain of Kyffhausen; the kobolds came out before him
from the rock clefts of the Hartz, and the witches of the
Brocken danced their grand Walpurgisnight round about
the young French poet, whom they took for a Jena student. . . . He knows how to blow upon the postillion's
horn,* the enchanted melodies of Achim von Arnim and
Clement Brentano; and if he stops at the threshold of
an inn embowered in hop vines, the *Schoppen* becomes
in his hands the cup of the King of Thule." Among
the French romanticists of Hugo's circle there was a
great enthusiasm for wild German ballads like Bürger's
"Lenore" and Goethe's "Erl-King." The translation
of A. W. Schlegel's "Vorlesungen über Dramatische
Kunst und Litteratur," by Madame Necker de Saussure,
in 1814, was doubtless the first fruits of Madame de
Staël's "Allemagne," published the year before. Gautier himself and his friend Augustus Mac-Keat (Auguste
Maguet) collaborated in a drama founded on Byron's
"Parisina." "Walter Scott was then in the full flower
of his success. People were being initiated into the
mysteries of Goethe's 'Faust,' . . . and discovering
Shakspere under the translation, a little dressed up, of
Letourneur; and the poems of Lord Byron, 'The Corsair,'
'Lara,' 'The Giaour,' 'Manfred,' 'Beppo,' 'Don Juan,'
were coming to us from the Orient, which had not yet
grown commonplace." Gautier said that in *le petit cénacle*—the inner circle of the initiated—if you admired
Racine more than Shakspere and Calderon, it was an
opinion that you would do well to keep to yourself.
"Toleration is not the virtue of neophytes." As for
himself, who had set out as a painter—and only later de-

* "Des Knaben Wunderhorn."

viated into letters—he was all for the Middle Ages: "An old iron baron, feudal, ready to take refuge from the encroachments of the time, in the castle of Goetz von Berlichingen." Of Bouchardy, the extraordinary author of "Le Sonneur de Saint Paul," who "was to Hugo what Marlowe was to Shakspere"—and who was playfully accused of making wooden models of the plots of his melodramas—Gautier says that he "planned his singular edifice in advance, like a castle of Anne Radcliffe, with donjon, turrets, underground chambers, secret passages, corkscrew stairs, vaulted halls, mysterious closets, hiding places in the thickness of the walls, *oubliettes*, charnel-houses, crypts where his heroes and heroines were to meet later on, to love, hate, fight, set ambushes, assassinate, or marry. . . . He cut masked doors in the walls for his expected personage to appear through, and trap doors in the floor for him to disappear through."

The reasons for this resort to foreign rather than native sources of inspiration are not far to seek. The romantic movement in France was belated; it was twenty or thirty years behind the similar movements in England and Germany. It was easier and more natural for Stendhal or Hugo to appeal to the example of living masters like Goethe and Scott, whose works went everywhere in translation and who held the ear of Europe, than to revive an interest all at once in Villon or Guillaume de Lorris or Chrestien de Troyes. Again, in no country had the divorce between fashionable and popular literature been so complete as in France; in none had so thick and hard a crust of classicism overlain the indigenous product of the national genius. It was not altogether easy for Bishop Percy in 1765 to win immediate recognition from the educated class for Old English minstrelsy; nor for Herder and Bürger in 1770 to do the same thing for the German ballads. In France it would have been impossible before the Bourbon restoration of 1815. In England and in Germany, moreover, the higher literature had always remained more closely in touch with the people. In both of those countries the stock of ballad poetry and folklore was much more extensive and important than in France, and the habit of composing ballads lasted later. The only French writers of the classical period who produced anything at all analogous to the German "Mährchen" were Charles Perrault, who published between 1691–97 his famous fairy tales, including "Blue Beard," "The Sleeping Beauty," "Little Red Riding-Hood," "Cinderella," and "Puss in Boots"; and the Countess d'Aulnoy (died 1720), whose "Yellow Dwarf" and "White Cat" belong to the same department of nursery tales.*

A curious feature of French romanticism was the way in which the new-found liberty of art asserted itself in manners, costume, and personal habits. Victor Hugo himself was scrupulously correct and subdued in dress, but his young disciples affected bright colours and rich stuffs. They wore Spanish mantillas, coats with large velvet lapels, pointed doublets or jerkins of satin or damask velvet in place of the usual waistcoat; long hair after the Merovingian fashion, and pointed beards. We have seen that Shenstone was regarded as an eccentric, and perhaps somewhat dangerous, person when at the university, because he wore his own hair instead of a wig. In France, half a century later, not only the *per-*

* Charles Nodier vindicated the literary claims of Perrault.

ruque, but the *menton glabre* was regarded as symptomatic of the classicist and the academician; while the
beard became a badge of romanticism. At the beginning
of the movement, Gautier informs us, "there were only
two full beards in France, the beard of Eugène Devéria
and the beard of Petrus Borel. To wear them required
a courage, a coolness, and a contempt for the crowd truly
heroic. . . . It was the fashion then in the romantic
school to be pale, livid, greenish, a trifle cadaverous, if
possible. It gave one an air of doom, Byronic, *giaourish*,
devoured by passion and remorse." It will be remembered that the rolling Byronic collar, open at the throat,
was much affected at one time by young persons of romantic temperament in England; and that the conservative classes, who adhered to the old-fashioned stock and
high collar, looked askance upon these youthful innova-
tors as certainly atheists and libertines, and probably
enemies to society—would-be corsairs or banditti. It is
interesting, therefore, to discover that in France, too, the
final touch of elegance among the romantics was not to
have any white linen in evidence; the shirt collar, in
particular, being "considered as a mark of the grocer,
the bourgeois, the philistine." A certain *gilet rouge*
which Gautier wore when he led the *claque* at the first
performance of "Hernani" has become historic. This
flamboyant garment—a defiance and a challenge to the
academicians who had come to hiss Hugo's play—was,
in fact, a *pourpoint* or jerkin of cherry-coloured satin, cut
in the shape of a Milanese cuirass, pointed, busked, and
arched in front, and fastened behind the back with hooks
and eyes. From the imperturbable disdain with which
the wearer faced the opera-glasses and laughter of the

assembly it was evident that it would not have taken much urging to induce him to come to the second night's performance decked in a daffodil waistcoat.* The young enthusiasts of *le petit cénacle* carried their Byronism so far that, in imitation of the celebrated revels at Newstead, they used to drink from a human skull in their feasts at *le Petit Moulin Rouge*. It had belonged to a drum-major, and Gérard de Nerval got it from his father, who had been an army surgeon. One of the neophytes, in his excitement, even demanded that it be filled with sea water instead of wine, in emulation of the hero of Victor Hugo's novel, "Han d'Islande," who "drank the water of the seas in the skull of the dead." Another *caput mortuum* stood on Hugo's mantelpiece in place of a clock.† "If it did not tell the hour, at least it made us think of the irreparable flight of time. It was the verse of Horace translated into romantic symbolism." There was a decided flavour of Bohemianism about the French romantic school, and the spirit of the lives which many of them led may best be studied in Murger's classic, "La Vie de Boheme." ‡

As another special feature of French romanticism, we may note the important part taken by the theatre in the history of the movement. The stage was the citadel of classical prejudice, and it was about it that the fiercest battles were fought. The climacteric year was 1830, in which year Victor Hugo's tragedy, "Hernani, or Castilian Honour," was put on at the Théâtre Français on February 25th, and ran for thirty nights. The representation was a fight between the classics and the romantics, and

---

* Gautier, 92.

† Rue Jean-Gougon, where the *cénacle* met often.

‡ Nerval hanged himself at Paris, in January, 1855, in the rue de la Vielle Lanterne.

there was almost a mob in the theatre. The dramatic censorship under Charles X., though strict, was used in the interest of political rather than æsthetic orthodoxy. But it is said that some of the older Academicians actu· ally applied to the king to forbid the acting of "Her- nani." Gautier has given a mock-heroic description of this famous literary battle *quorum pars magna fuit*. He had received from his college friend, Gérard de Nerval —who had been charged with the duty of drumming up recruits for the Hugonic *claque*—six tickets to be dis- tributed only to tried friends of the cause—sure men and true. The tickets themselves were little squares of red paper, stamped in the corner with a mysterious counter- sign—the Spanish word *hierro*, iron, not only symbolizing the hero of the drama, but hinting that the ticket-holder was to bear himself in the approaching fray frankly, bravely, and faithfully like the sword. The proud recip- ient of these tokens of confidence gave two of them to a couple of artists—ferocious romantics, who would gladly have eaten an Academician, if necessary; two he gave to a brace of young poets who secretly practised *la rime riche, le mot propre*, and *la métaphore exacte :* the other two he reserved for his cousin and himself. The general at- titude of the audience on the first nights was hostile, "two systems, two parties, two armies, two civilizations even—it is not saying too much—confronted one an- other, . . . and it was not hard to see that yonder young man with long hair found the smoothly shaved gentle- man opposite a disastrous idiot; and that he would not long be at pains to conceal his opinion of him." The classical part of the audience resented the touches of Spanish local colour in the play, the mixture of pleas-

antries and familiar speeches with the tragic dialogue,
and of heroism and savagery in the character of Hernani;
and they made all manner of fun of the species of pun
—*de ta suite, j'en suis*—which terminated the first act.
"Certain lines were captured and recaptured, like dis-
puted redoubts, by each army with equal obstinacy. On
one day the romantics would carry a passage, which the
enemy would retake the next day, and from which it became necessary to dislodge them. What uproar, what
cries, cat-calls, hisses, hurricanes of bravos, thunders of
applause! The heads of parties blackguarded each other
like Homer's heroes before they came to blows. . . . For
this generation ' Hernani ' was what the ' Cid ' was for the
contemporaries of Corneille. All that was young, brave,
amorous, poetic, caught the inspiration of it. Those fine
exaggerations, heroic, Castilian; that superb Spanish
emphasis; that language so proud and high even in its
familiarity; those images of a dazzling strangeness, threw
us into an ecstasy and intoxicated us with their heady
poetry." The victory in the end was with the new school.
Musset, writing in 1838, says that the tragedies of Corneille and Racine had disappeared from the French stage
for ten years.

Another triumphant battlefield—a veritable *fête romantique*—was the first representation in 1831 of Alex-
andre Dumas' "Anthony." "It was an agitation, a
tumult, an effervescence. . . . The house was actually
delirious; it applauded, sobbed, wept, shouted. A certain famous green coat was torn from the author's back
and rent into shreds by his too ardent admirers, who
wanted pieces of it for memorabilia." *

*Gautier, 167.

The English reader who hears of the stubborn resistance offered to the performance of ' Hernani ' will naturally suppose that there must have been something about it contrary to public policy—some immorality, or some political references, at least, offensive to the government; and he will have a difficulty in understanding that the trouble was all about affairs purely literary. " Hernani " was fought because it violated the unities of place and time; because its hero was a Spanish bandit; because in the dialogue a spade was called a spade, and in the verse the lines overlap. The French are often charged with frivolity in matters of conduct, but to the discussion of matters of art they bring a most serious conscience. The scene in " Hernani " shifts from Saragossa to the castle of Don Ruy Gomez de Silva in the mountains of Arragon, and to the tomb of Charlemagne at Aix-la-Chapelle. The time of the action, though not precisely indicated, covers at least a number of months. The dialogue is, in many parts, nervous, simple, direct, abrupt; in others running into long *tirades* and soliloquies, rich with all the poetic resources of the greatest poet who has ever used the French tongue. The spirit of the drama, as well as its form, is romantic. The point of honour is pushed to a fantastic excess; all the characters display the most delicate chivalry, the noblest magnanimity, the loftiest Castilian pride. Don Ruy Gomez allows the King to carry off his bride, rather than yield up the outlaw who has taken refuge in his castle; and that although he has just caught this same outlaw paying court to this same bride, whose accepted lover he is. Hernani, not to be outdone in generosity, offers his life to his enemy and preserver, giving him his horn and promising to come to

meet his death at its summons. There is the same fault
here which is felt in Hugo's novels. Motives are exaggerated, the *dramatis personæ* strut. They are rather
over-dramatic in their poses—melodramatic, in fact—
and do unlikely things. But this fault is the fault of a
great nature, grandeur exalted into grandiosity, till the
heroes of these plays, "Hernani," "Marion Delorme,"
"Le Roi d'Amuse," loom and stalk across the scene like
epic demigods of more than mortal stature and mortal
passions. But Hugo was not only a great dramatist and
a great poet, but a most clever playwright. "Hernani"
is full of effective stage devices, crises in the action
which make an audience hold its breath or shudder;
moments of intense suspense like that in the third act,
where the old hidalgo pauses before his own portrait,
behind which the outlaw is hidden; or that in the fifth,
where Hernani hears at first, faint and far away, the blast
of the fatal horn that summons him to leave his bride at
the altar and go to his death. The young romantics of
the day all got "Hernani" by heart and used to rehearse
it at their assemblies, each taking a part; and the famous
trumpet, the *cor d'Hernani*, became a symbol and a rallying call.

No such scene would have been possible in an English playhouse as that which attended the first representation of "Hernani" at the Théâtre Français. For not
only is an English audience comparatively indifferent to
rules of art and canons of taste, but the unities had never
prevailed in practice in England, though constantly recommended in theory. The French had no Shakspere,
and the English no Academy. We may construct an
imaginary parallel to such a scene if we will suppose

that all reputable English tragedies from 1600 down to 1830 had been something upon the model of Addison's "Cato" and Johnson's "Irene"; or better still upon the model of Dryden's heroic plays in rimed couplets; and that then a drama like "Romeo and Juliet" had been produced upon the boards of Drury Lane, and a warm spurt of romantic poetry suddenly injected into the icy current of classic declamation.

Having considered the chief points in which the French romantic movement differed from the similar movements in England and Germany, let us now glance at the history of its beginnings, and at the work of a few of its typical figures. The presentation of "Hernani" in 1830 was by no means the first overt act of the new school. Discussion had been going on for years in the press. De Stendhal says that the classicists had on their side two-thirds of the Académie Française, and all of the French journalists; that their leading organ, however, was the very influential *Journal des Débats* and its editor, M. Dussant, the general-in-chief of the classical party. The romanticists, however, were not without organs of their own; among which are especially mentioned *Le Conservateur Littéraire*, begun in 1819, *Le Globe* in 1824, and the *Annales Romantiques* in 1823, the last being "practically a kind of annual of the *Muse Française* (1823–24), which had pretty nearly the same contributors." All of these journals were Bourboniste, except *Le Globe*, which was liberal in politics.* The Academy denounced the new literary doc-

* The romanticism of the *Globe* was of a more conservative stripe than that of the *Muse Française*, which was the organ of the group of young poets who surrounded Hugo. The motto of the latter was *Jam nova progenies cœlo demittitur*

trine as a heresy and its followers as a sect, but it made
head so rapidly that as early as 1829, a year before
" Hernani " was acted, a " Histoire du Romantisme en
France " appeared, written by a certain M. de Toreinx.*
It agrees with other authorities in dating the beginning
of the movement from Chateaubriand's " Le Génie du
Christianisme " (1802). " Chateaubriand," says Gautier,
" may be regarded as the grandfather, or, if you prefer it,
the sachem of romanticism in France.   In the ' Genius
of Christianity ' he restored the Gothic cathedral; in the
' Natchez ' he reopened the sublimity of nature, which
had been closed; in ' René ' he invented melancholy and
modern passion."

Sprung from an ancient Breton family, Chateaubriand
came to America in 1790 with the somewhat singular and
very French idea of travelling overland to the northwest
passage.   He was diverted from this enterprise, however,

alto.   The *Globe* defined romanticism as Protestantism in letters.   The critical battle was on as early as 1824.   On April
24, in that year, Auger, director of the Academy, read at the
annual session of the Institute a discourse on romanticism,
which he denounced as a literary schism.   The prospectus of
the *Globe*, an important document on the romantic side, dates
from the same year.   The *Constitutionnel*, the most narrowly
classical of the opposing journals, described romanticism as an
epidemic malady.   To the year 1825, when the *Cénacle* had
its headquarters at Victor Hugo's house, belong, among others, the following manifestoes on both sides of the controversy :
" Les Classiques Vengés," De la Touche ; " Le Temple du
Romantisme," Morel ; " Le Classique et le Romantique " (a
satirical comedy in the classical interest), Baour-Lormian.
Cyprien Desmarais' " Essais sur les classiques et les romantiques " had appeared at Paris in 1823.   At Rouen was printed
in 1826 " Du Classique et du Romantique," a collection of papers read at the Rouen Academy during the year, rather
favorable, on the whole, to the new movement.

* This is now a somewhat rare book ; I have never seen a
copy of it ; but it was reviewed in *The Saturday Review* (vol.
lxv., p. 369).

fell in with an Indian tribe and wandered about with them in the wilderness. He did not discover the north-west passage, but, according to Lowell, he invented the forest primeval. Chateaubriand gave the first full utterance to that romantic note which sounds so loudly in Byron's verse; the restless dissatisfaction with life as it is, the longing for something undefined and unattainable, the love for solitude and the desert, the "passion incapable of being converted into action"—in short, the *maladie du siècle*—since become familiar in "Childe Harold" and in Sénancour's "Obermann." In one of the chapters* of "Le Génie du Christianisme" he gives an analysis of this modern melancholy, this Byronic satiety and discontent, which he says was unknown to the ancients. "The farther nations advance in civilization, the more this unsettled state of the passions predominates; for then our imagination is rich, abundant, and full of wonders; but our existence is poor, insipid, and destitute of charms. With a full heart we dwell in an empty world." "Penetrate into those forests of America coeval with the world; what profound silence pervades these retreats when the winds are husht! What unknown voices when they begin to rise! Stand still and everything is mute; take but a step and all nature sighs. Night approaches, the shades thicken; you hear herds of wild beasts passing in the dark; the ground murmurs under your feet; the pealing thunder rebellows in the deserts; the forest bows, the trees fall, an unknown river rolls before you. The moon at length bursts forth in the east; as you proceed at the foot of the trees, she seems to move before you on their tops and solemnly to accompany your

* Part ii., Book iii., chap ix.

steps. The wanderer seats himself on the trunk of an oak to await the return of day; he looks alternately at the nocturnal luminary, the darkness, and the river; he feels restless, agitated, and in expectation of something extraordinary; a pleasure never felt before, an unusual fear, cause his heart to throb, as if he were about to be admitted to some secret of the Divinity; he is alone in the depth of the forests, but the mind of man is equal to the expanse of nature, and all the solitudes of the earth are not too vast for the contemplations of his heart. There is in man an instinctive melancholy, which makes him harmonise with the scenery of nature. Who has not spent whole hours seated on the bank of a river, contemplating its passing waves? Who has not found pleasure on the seashore in viewing the distant rock whitened by the billows? How much are the ancients to be pitied, who discovered in the ocean naught but the palace of Neptune and the cavern of Proteus; it was hard that they should perceive only the adventures of the Tritons and the Nereids in the immensity of the seas, which seems to give an indistinct measure of the greatness of our souls, and which excites a vague desire to quit this life, that we may embrace all nature and taste the fulness of joy in the presence of its Author." *

The outbreak of the Revolution recalled Chateaubriand to France. He joined the army of the *emigrées* at Coblentz, was wounded at the siege of Thionville, and escaped into England where he lived (1793–1800) until the time of the Consulate, when he made his peace with Napoleon and returned to France. He had been a freethinker, but was converted to Christianity by a dying

* Part ii., Book iv., chap. i.

message from his mother who was thrown into prison by the revolutionists. "I wept," said Chateaubriand, "and I believed." "Le Génie du Christianisme" was an expression of that reactionary feeling which drove numbers of Frenchmen back into the Church, after the blasphemies and horrors of the Revolution. It came out just when Napoleon was negotiating his *Concordat* with the Pope, and was trying to enlist the religious and conservative classes in support of his government; and it reinforced his purposes so powerfully that he appointed the author, in spite of his legitimism, to several diplomatic posts. "Le Génie du Christianisme" is indeed a plea for Christianity on æsthetic grounds—an attempt, as has been sneeringly said, to recommend Christianity by making it look pretty. Chateaubriand was not a close reasoner; his knowledge was superficial and inaccurate; his character was weakened by vanity and shallowness. He was a sentimentalist and a rhetorician, but one of the most brilliant of rhetoricians; while his sentiment, though not always deep or lasting, was for the nonce sufficiently sincere. He had in particular a remarkable talent for pictorial description; and his book, translated into many tongues, enjoyed an extraordinary vogue. The English version, made in 1815, was entitled "The Beauties of Christianity." For Chateaubriand undertook to show that the Christian religion had influenced favorably literature and the fine arts; that it was more poetical than any other system of belief and worship. He compared Homer and Vergil with Dante, Tasso, Milton, and other modern poets, and awarded the palm to the latter in the treatment of the elementary relations and stock characters, such as husband and wife, father and child,

the priest, the soldier, the lover, etc.; preferring Pope's
Eloisa, *e.g.*, to Vergil's Dido, and "Paul and Virginia"
to the idyls of Theocritus. He pronounced the Christian mythology—angels, devils, saints, miracles—superior to the pagan; and Dante's Hell much more
impressive to the imagination than Tartarus. He dwelt
eloquently upon the beauty and affecting significance of
Gothic church architecture, of Catholic ritual and symbolism, the dress of the clergy, the crucifix, the organ, the
church bell, the observances of Christian festivals, the
monastic life, the orders of chivalry, the country churchyards where the dead were buried, and even upon the
superstitions which the last century had laughed to scorn;
such as the belief in ghosts, the adoration of relics, vows
to saints and pilgrimages to holy places. In his chapter on "The Influence of Christianity upon Music," he
says that the "Christian religion is essentially melodious
for this single reason, that she delights in solitude"; the
forests are her ancient abode, and her musician "ought
to be acquainted with the melancholy notes of the waters
and the trees; he ought to have studied the sound of the
winds in cloisters, and those murmurs that pervade the
Gothic temple, the grass of the cemetery, and the vaults
of death." He repeats the ancient fable that the designers of the cathedrals were applying forest scenery to
architecture: "Those ceilings sculptured into foliage of
different kinds, those buttresses which prop the walls and
terminate abruptly like the broken trunks of trees, the
coolness of the vaults, the darkness of the sanctuary, the
dim twilight of the aisles, the chapels resembling grottoes,
the secret passages, the low doorways, in a word everything in a Gothic church reminds you of the labyrinths

of a wood, everything excites a feeling of religious awe, of mystery, and of the Divinity." The birds perch upon the steeples and towers as if they were trees, and "the Christian architect, not content with building forests, has been desirous to retain their murmurs, and by means of the organ and of bells, he has attached to the Gothic temple the very winds and the thunders that roll in the recesses of the woods. Past ages, conjured up by these religious sounds, raise their venerable voices from the bosom of the stones and sigh in every corner of the vast cathedral. The sanctuary re-echoes like the cavern of the ancient Sibyl; loud-tongued bells swing over your head; while the vaults of death under your feet are profoundly silent." He praises the ideals of chivalry; gives a sympathetic picture of the training and career of a knight-errant, and asks: "Is there then nothing worthy of admiration in the times of a Roland, a Godfrey, a Coucey, and a Joinville; in the times of the Moors and the Saracens; . . . when the strains of the Troubadours were mingled with the clash of arms, dances with religious ceremonies, and banquets and tournaments with sieges and battles?" Chateaubriand says that the finest Gothic ruins are to be found in the English lake country, on the Scotch mountains, and in the Orkney Islands; and that they are more impressive than classic ruins because in the latter the arches are parallel with the curves of the sky, while in the Gothic or pointed architecture the arches "form a contrast with the circular arches of the sky and the curvatures of the horizon. The Gothic being, moreover, entirely composed of *voids*, the more readily admits of the decoration of herbage and flowers than the fulness of the Grecian orders. The clustered columns, the domes carved into foliage, or scooped out in the form of a fruit-basket, offered so many receptacles into which the winds carry, with the dust, the seeds of vegetables. The house-leek fixes itself in the mortar; the mosses cover rugged masses with their elastic coating; the thistle projects its brown burrs from the embrasure of a window; and the ivy creeping along the northern cloisters falls in festoons over the arches."

All this is romantic enough; we have the note of Catholic mediævalism and the note of Ossianic melancholy combined; and this some years before " The Lay of the Last Minstrel," and when Byron was a boy of fourteen and still reading his Ossian.* But we are precluded from classifying Chateaubriand among full-fledged romanticists. His literary taste was by no means emancipated from eighteenth-century standards. In speaking of Milton, *e.g.*, he says that if he had only been born in France in the reign of Louis XIV., and had "combined with the native grandeur of his genius the taste of Racine and Boileau," the "Paradise Lost" might have equalled the " Iliad."

Chateaubriand never called himself a romantic. It is agreed upon all hands that the expressions *romantisme* and *littérature romantique* were first invented or imported by Madame de Staël in her "L'Allemagne" (1813), "pour exprimer l'affranchissement des vieilles formes littéraires." † Some ten years later, or by 1823, when Stendhal published his " Racine et Shakspere," the issue between the schools had been joined and the question

---

* For Chateaubriand and Ossian see vol. i., pp. 332–33. He made translations from Ossian, Gray, and Milton.

† "Victor Hugo," par Paul Boudois, p. 32.

quite thoroughly agitated in the Parisian journals. Stendhal announced himself as an adherent of the new, but his temper was decidedly cool and unromantic. I have quoted his epigrammatic definition of romanticism.*

In this *brochure* Stendhal announces that France is on the eve of a literary revolution and that the last hour of classicism has struck, although as yet the classicists are in possession of the theatres, and of all the salaried literary positions under government; and all the newspapers of all shades of political opinion are shut to the romanticists. A company of English actors who attempted to give some of Shakspere's plays at the Porte-Saint-Martin in 1822 were mobbed. "The hisses and cat-calls began before the performance, of which it was impossible to hear a single word. As soon as the actors appeared they were pelted with apples and eggs, and from time to time the audience called out to them to talk French, and shouted, '*À bas Shakspere! c'est un aide de camp du duc de Wellington.*'" It will be remembered that in our own day the first representations of Wagner's operas at Paris were interrupted with similar cries: "*Pas de Wagner!*" "*À bas les Allemands!*" etc.

In 1827 Kemble's company visited Paris and gave, in English, "Hamlet," "Romeo and Juliet," "Othello," and "The Merchant of Venice." Dumas went to see them and described the impression made upon him by Shakspere, in language identical with that which Goethe used about himself.† He was like a man born blind and suddenly restored to sight. Dumas' "Henry III." (1829), a *drame* in the manner of Shakspere's historical plays,

* Vol. i., p. 10.
† See vol. i., p. 379.

though in prose, was the immediate result of this new vision.   English actors were in Paris again in 1828 and 1829; and in 1835 Macready presented "Hamlet," "Othello," and "Henry IV." with great success.   Previous to these performances, the only opportunities that the French public had to judge of Shakspere's dramas as acting plays were afforded by the wretched adaptations of Ducis and other stage carpenters.   Ducis had read Shakspere only in Letourneur's very inadequate translation (revised by Guizot in 1821).   His "Hamlet" was played in 1769; "Macbeth," 1784; "King John," 1791; "Othello" (turned into a comedy), 1792.   Mercier's "Timon" was given in 1794; and Dejaure's "Imogènes" —an "arrangement" of "Cymbeline"—in 1796.   The romanticists labored to put their countrymen in possession of better versions of Shakspere.   Alfred de Vigny rendered "Othello" (1827), and Emile Deschamps, "Romeo and Juliet" and "Macbeth."

Stendhal interviewed a director of one of the French theatres and tried to persuade him that there would be money in it for any house which would have the courage to give a season of romantic tragedy.   But the director, who seemed to be a liberal-minded man, assured him that until some stage manager could be found rich enough to buy up the dramatic criticism of the *Constitutionnel* and two or three other newspapers, the law students and medical students, who were under the influence of those journals, would never suffer the play to get as far as the third act.   "If it were otherwise," he said, "don't you suppose that we would have tried Schiller's 'William Tell'?   The police would have cut out a quarter of it; one of our adapters another quarter; and what was left would reach a hundred representations, *provided it could once secure three.*"

To this the author replied that the immense majority of young society people had been converted to romanticism by the eloquence of M. Cousin.

"Sir," said the director, "your young society people don't go into the parterre to engage in fisticuffs [*faire le coup de poing*], and at the theatre, as in politics, we despise philosophers who don't fight." Stendhal adds that the editors of influential journals found their interest in this state of things, since many of them had pieces of their own on the stage, written of course in alexandrine verse and on the classic model; and what would become of these masterpieces if Talma should ever get permission to play in a prose translation of "Macbeth," abridged, say, one-third? "I said one day to one of these gentlemen, 28,000,000 men, *i.e.*, 18,000,000 in England and 10,000,000 in America, admire ' Macbeth ' and applaud it a hundred times a year. ' The English,' he answered me with great coolness, ' cannot have real eloquence or poetry truly admirable; the nature of their language, which is not derived from the Latin, makes it quite impossible.'" A great part of "Racine et Shakspere" is occupied with a refutation of the doctrine of the unities of time and place, and with a discussion of the real nature of dramatic illusion, on which their necessity was supposed to rest. Stendhal maintains that the illusion is really stronger in Shakspere's tragedies than in Racine's. It is not essential here to reproduce his argument, which is the same that is familiar to us in Lessing and in Coleridge, though he was an able controversialist, and his logic and irony give a freshness to the treatment of this hack-

neyed theme which makes his little treatise well worth
the reading. To illustrate the nature of *real* stage illusion, he says that last year (August, 1822) a soldier in a
Baltimore theatre, seeing Othello about to kill Desde-
mona, cried out, "It shall never be said that a damned
nigger killed a white woman in my presence," and at the
same moment fired his gun and broke an arm of the actor
who was playing Othello. "*Eh bien*, this soldier had
illusion: he believed that the action which was passing
on the stage was true."

Stendhal proposes the following as a definition of romantic tragedy: "It is written in prose; the succession
of events which it presents to the eyes of the spectators
lasts several months, and they happen in different places."
He complains that the French comedies are not funny,
do not make any one laugh; and that the French tragic
dialogue is epic rather than dramatic. He advises his
readers to go and see Kean in "Richard" and "Othello";
and says that since reading Schlegel and Dennis (!)
he has a great contempt for the French critics. He ap-
peals to the usages of the German and English stage in
disregarding the rules of Aristotle, and cites the great
popularity of Walter Scott's romances, which, he says,
are nothing more than romantic tragedies with long descriptions interspersed, to support his plea for a new
kind of French prose-tragedy; for which he recommends
subjects taken from national history, and especially from
the mediæval chroniclers like Froissart. Nevertheless,
he does not advise the direct imitation of Shakspere.
He blames Schiller for copying Shakspere, and eulogizes
Werner's "Luther" as nearer to the masterpieces of
Shakspere than Schiller's tragedies are. He wants the

new French drama to resemble Shakspere only in dealing freely with modern conditions, as the latter did with the conditions of his time, without having the fear of Racine or any other authority before its eyes.

In 1824 the Academy, which was slowly constructing its famous dictionary of the French language, happened to arrive at the new word *romanticism* which needed defining. This was the signal for a heated debate in that venerable body, and the director, M. Auger, was commissioned to prepare a manifesto against the new literary sect, to be read at the meeting of the Institute on the 24th of April next. It was in response to this manifesto that Stendhal wrote the second part of his "Racine et Shakspere" (1825), attached to which is a short essay entitled "Qu'est ce que le Romanticisme?"* addressed to the Italian public, and intended to explain to them the literary situation in France, and to enlist their sympathies on the romantic side. "Shakspere," he says, "the hero of romantic poetry, as opposed to Racine, the god of the classicists, wrote for strong souls; for English hearts which were what Italian hearts were about 1500, emerging from that sublime Middle Age *questi tempi della virtu sconosciutta.*" Racine, on the contrary, wrote for a slavish and effeminate court. The author disclaims any wish to impose Shakspere on the Italians. The day will come, he hopes, when they will have a national tragedy of their own; but to have that, they will do better to follow in the footprints of Shakspere than, like Alfieri, in the footprints of Racine. In spite of the pedants, he predicts that Germany and England will carry it over France; Shakspere, Schil-

---

* The use of this form instead of *romantisme* is perhaps worth noticing.

ler, and Lord Byron will carry it over Racine and Boileau. He says that English poetry since the French Revolution has become more enthusiastic, more serious, more passionate. It needed other subjects than those required by the witty and frivolous eighteenth century, and sought its heroes in the rude, primitive, inventive ages, or even among savages and barbarians. It had to have recourse to time or countries when it was permitted to the higher classes of society to have passions. The Greek and Latin classics could give no help; since most of them belonged to an epoch as artificial, and as far removed from the naïve presentation of the passions, as the eighteenth century itself. The court of Augustus was no more natural than that of Louis XIV. Accordingly the most successful poets in England, during the past twenty years, have not only sought deeper emotions than those of the eighteenth century, but have treated subjects which would have been scornfully rejected by the age of *bel esprit.* The anti-romantics can't cheat us much longer. " Where, among the works of our Italian pedants, are the books that go through seven editions in two months, like the romantic poems that are coming out in London at the present moment? Compare, *e.g.,* the success of Moore's ' Lalla Rookh,' which appeared in June, 1817, and the eleventh edition of which I have before me, with the success of the ' Camille ' of the highly classical Mr. Botta ! ' "

In 1822, a year before the appearance of Stendhal's " Racine et Shakspere," Victor Hugo had published his " Odes et Poésies Diverses," and a second collection followed in 1824. In the prefaces to these two volumes he protests against the use of the terms classic and romantic, as *mots de guerre* and vague words which every one defines in accordance with his own prejudices. If romanticism means anything, he says, it means the literature of the nineteenth century; and all the anathemas launched at the heads of contemporary writers reduce themselves to the following method of argument. "We condemn the literature of the nineteenth century because it is romantic. And why is it romantic? Because it is the literature of the nineteenth century." As to the false taste which disfigured the eighteenth-century imitations of Racine and Boileau, he would prefer to distinguish that by the name *scholastic*, a style which is to the truly classic what superstition and fanaticism are to religion. The intention of these youthful poems of Hugo was partly literary and partly political and religious: "The history of mankind affords no poetry," he says, "except when judged from the vantage-ground of monarchical ideas and religious beliefs. . . . He has thought that . . . in substituting for the outworn and false colours of pagan mythology the new and truthful colours of the Christian theogony, one could inject into the ode something of the interest of the drama, and could make it speak, besides, that austere, consoling, and religious language which is needed by an old society that issues still trembling from the saturnalia of atheism and anarchy. . . . The literature of the present, the actual literature, is the expression, by way of anticipation, of that religious and monarchical society which will issue, doubtless, from the midst of so many ancient débris, of so many recent ruins. . . . If the literature of the great age of Louis XIV. had invoked Christianity in place of worshipping heathen gods . . . the triumph of the sophistical doctrines of the last century would have been much more difficult, perhaps even impossible. . . . But France had not that good fortune; its national poets were almost all pagan poets; and our literature was rather the expression of an idolatrous and democratic, than of a monarchical and Christian society." The prevailing note, accordingly, in these early odes is that of the Bourbon Restoration of 1815–30, and of the Catholic reaction against the sceptical *Éclaircissement* of the eighteenth century. The subjects are such as these: "The Poet in the Times of Revolution"; "La Vendée"; "The Maidens of Verdun," which chants the martyrdom of three young royalist sisters who were put to death for sending money and supplies to the *emigrés;* "Quibiron," where a royalist detachment which had capitulated under promise of being treated like prisoners of war, were shot down in squads by the Convention soldiery; "Louis XVII."; "The Replacement of the Statue of Henry IV."; "The Death of the Duke of Berry"; "The Birth of the Duke of Bourdeaux" and his "Baptism"; "The Funeral of Louis XVIII."; "The Consecration of Charles X."; "The Death of Mlle. de Sombreuil," the royalist heroine who saved her father's life by drinking a cupful of human blood in the days of the Terror; and "La Bande Noire," which denounces with great bitterness the violation of the tombs of the kings of France by the regicides, and pleads for the preservation of the ruins of feudal times:

> "O murs! ô créneaux! ô tourelles!
> Remparts, fossés aux ponts mouvants!
> Lourds faisceaux de colonnes frêles!
> Fiers châteaux! modestes couvents!
> Cloîtres poudreux, salles antiques,
> Où gémissaient les saints cantiques,
> Où riaient les banquets joyeux!
> Lieux où le cœur met ses chimères!

Églises où priaient nos mères
Tours où combattaient nos aïeux ! "

In these two ode collections, though the Catholic and legitimist inspiration is everywhere apparent, there is nothing revolutionary in the language or verse forms. But in the "Odes et Ballades" of 1826, "the romantic challenge," says Saintsbury, "is definitely thrown down. The subjects are taken by preference from times and countries which the classical tradition had regarded as barbarous. The metres and rhythm are studiously broken, varied, and irregular; the language has the utmost possible glow of colour, as opposed to the cold correctness of classical poetry, the completest disdain of conventional periphrasis, the boldest reliance on exotic terms and daring neologisms." This description applies more particularly to the Ballades, many of which, such as "La Ronde du Sabbat," "La Légende de la Nonne," "La Chasse du Burgrave," and "Le Pas d'Armes du Roi Jean" are mediæval studies in which the lawless *grotesquerie* of Gothic art runs riot. "The author, in composing them," says the preface, "has tried to give some idea of what the poems of the first troubadours of the Middle Ages might have been; those Christian rhapsodists who had nothing in the world but their swords and their guitars, and went from castle to castle paying for their entertainment with their songs." To show that liberty in art does not mean disorder, the author draws an elaborate contrast between the garden of Versailles and a primitive forest, in a passage which will remind the reader of similar comparisons in the writings of Shenstone, Walpole, and other English romanticists of the eighteenth century. There is as much order, he asserts, in the forest as in the garden, but it is a live order, not a dead regularity. "Choose then," he exclaims, "between the masterpiece of gardening and the work of nature; between that which is beautiful by convention and that which is beautiful without rule; between an artificial literature and an original poetry. . . . In two words—and we shall not object to have judgment passed in accordance with this observation on the two kinds of literature that are called *classic* and *romantic*,—regularity is the taste of mediocrity, order is the taste of genius. . . . It will be objected to us that the virgin forest hides in its magnificent solitudes a thousand dangerous animals, while the marshy basins of the French garden conceal at most a few harmless creatures. That is doubtless a misfortune; but, taking it all in all, we like a crocodile better than a frog; we prefer a barbarism of Shakspere to an insipidity of Campistron." But above all things—such is the doctrine of this preface —do not imitate anybody—not Shakspere any more than Racine. "He who imitates a *romantic* poet becomes thereby a *classic*, and just because he imitates." In 1823 Hugo had published anonymously his first prose romance, "Han d'Islande," the story of a Norwegian bandit. He got up the local colour for this by a careful study of the Edda and the Sagas, that "poésie sauvage" which was the admiration of the new school and the horror of the old. But it was in the preface to "Cromwell," published in 1827, that Hugo issued the full and, as it were, official manifesto of romanticism. The play itself is hardly actable. It is modelled, in a sense, upon the historical plays of Shakspere, but its Cromwell is a very melodramatic person, and its Puritans and Cavaliers strike the English reader with the same sense of absurdity produced by the pictures of English society in "L'Homme qui Rit." But of the famous preface Gautier says: "The Bible among Protestants, the Koran among Mahometans are not the object of a deeper veneration. It was, indeed, for us the book of books, the book which contained the pure doctrine." It consisted in great part of a triumphant attack upon the unities, and upon the verse and style which classic usage had consecrated to French tragedy. I need not repeat the argument here. It is already familiar, and some sentences * from this portion of the essay I have quoted elsewhere.

The preface also contained a plea for another peculiarity of the romantic drama, its mixture, viz., of tragedy and comedy. According to Hugo, this is the characteristic trait, the fundamental difference, which separates modern from ancient art, romantic from classical literature. Antique art, he says, rejected everything which was not purely beautiful, but the Christian and modern spirit feels that there are many things in creation besides that which is, humanly speaking, beautiful; and that everything which is in nature is—or has the right to be —in art. It includes in its picture of life the ugly, the misshapen, the monstrous. Hence results a new type, the grotesque, and a new literary form, romantic comedy. He proceeds to illustrate this thesis with his usual wealth of imaginative detail and pictorial language. The Middle Ages, more than any other period, are rich in instances of that intimate blending of the comic and the horrible which we call the grotesque; the witches' Sabbath, the hoofed and horned devil, the hideous figures of Dante's hell; the Scaramouches, Crispins, Harlequins

* See vol. i., pp. 19–20.

of Italian farce; "grimacing silhouettes of man, quite unknown to grave antiquity"; and "all those local dragons of our legends, the gargoyle of Rouen, the Taras of Tarascon, etc. . . . The contact of deformity has given to the modern sublime something purer, grander, more sublime, in short, than the antique beauty. . . . Is it not because the modern imagination knows how to set prowling hideously about our churchyards, the vampires, the ogres, the erl-kings, the *psylles*, the ghouls, the *brucolaques*, the *aspioles*, that it is able to give its fays that bodiless form, that purity of essence which the pagan nymphs approach so little? The antique Venus is beautiful, admirable, no doubt; but what has spread over the figures of Jean Goujon that graceful, strange, airy elegance? What has given them that unfamiliar character of life and grandeur, unless it be the neighbourhood of the rude and strong carvings of the Middle Ages? . . . The grotesque imprints its character especially upon that wonderful architecture which in the Middle Ages takes the place of all the arts. It attaches its marks to the fronts of the cathedrals; enframes its hells and purgatories under the portal arches, and sets them aflame upon the windows; unrolls its monsters, dogs, demons around the capitals, along the friezes, on the eaves." We find this same bizarre note in the mediæval laws, social usages, church institutions, and popular legends, in the court fools, in the heraldic emblems, the religious processions, the story of "Beauty and the Beast." It explains the origin of the Shaksperian drama, the high-water mark of modern art.

Shakspere does not seem to me an artist of the grotesque. He is by turns the greatest of tragic and the greatest of comic artists, and his tragedy and comedy lie close together, as in life, but without that union of the terrible and the ludicrous in the same figure, and that element of deformity which is the essence of the proper grotesque. He has created, however, one specimen of true grotesque, the monster Caliban. Caliban is a comic figure, but not purely comic; there is something savage, uncouth, and frightful about him. He has the dignity and the poetry which all rude, primitive beings have: which the things of nature, rocks and trees and wild beasts have. It is significant, therefore, that Robert Browning should have been attracted to Caliban. Browning had little comic power, little real humour; in him the grotesque is an imperfect form of the comic. The same criticism applies to Hugo. He gave a capital example of the grotesque in the four fools in the third act of "Cromwell" and in Triboulet, the Shaksperian jester of "Le Roi s'Amuse." Their songs and dialogues are bizarre and fantastic in the highest degree, but they are not funny; they do not make us laugh like the clowns of Shakspere—they are not comic, but merely queer. Hugo's defective sense of humour is shown in the way in which he frequently takes that one step which, Napoleon said, separates the sublime from the ridiculous— exaggerating character and motive till the heroic passes into melodrama and melodrama into absurdity. This fault is felt in his great prose romance "Notre-Dame de Paris" (1831), a picture of mediæval Paris, in which the humpback Quasimodo affords an exact illustration of what the author meant by the grotesque; another of the same kind is furnished by the hero of his later romance "L'Homme qui Rit."

Gautier has left a number of sketches, written in a vein

lovingly humorous, of some of the eccentrics—the *curiosités romantiques*—whose oddities are perhaps even more instructive as to the many directions which the movement took, than the more ordered enthusiasm of the less extreme votaries.   There was the architect Jule Vabre, *e.g.*, whose specialty was Shakspere. Shakspere "was his god, his idol, his passion, a wonder to which he could never grow accustomed." Vabre's life-project was a French translation of his idol, which should be absolutely true to the text, reproducing the exact turn and movement of the phrase, following the alternations of prose, rime, and blank verse in the original, and shunning neither its euphemistic subtleties nor its barbaric roughnesses. To fit himself for this task, he went to London and lived there, striving to submit himself to the atmosphere and the *milieu*, and learning to think in English; and there Gautier encountered him about 1843, in a tavern at High-Holborn, drinking stout and eating *rosbif* and speaking French with an English accent. Gautier told him that all he had to do now, to translate Shakspere, was to learn French. "I am going to work at it," he answered, more struck with the wisdom than the wit of the suggestion. A few years later Vabre turned up in France with a project for a sort of international seminary. "He wanted to explain ' Hernani ' to the English and ' Macbeth ' to the French. It made him tired to see the English learning French in ' Télémaque,' and the French learning English in the ' Vicar of Wakefield.' " Poor Vabre's great Shakspere translation never materialised; but François-Victor Hugo, the second son of the great romancer, carried out many of Vabre's principles of translation in his version of Shakspere.

Another curious figure was the water-colour painter, Célestin Nanteuil, who suggested to Gautier the hero of an early piece of his own, written to accompany an engraving in an English keepsake, representing the Square of St. Sebald at Nuremberg.   This hero, Elias Wildman-stadius, or l'Homme Moyen-âge, was " in a sort, the Gothic genius of that Gothic town "—a *retardataire* or man born out of his own time—who should have been born in 1460, in the days of Albrecht Dürer.   Célestin Nanteuil " had the air of one of those tall angels carrying a censer or playing on the *sambucque*, who inhabit the gable ends of cathedrals; and he seemed to have come down into the city among the busy townsfolk, still wearing his nimbus plate behind his head in place of a hat, and without having the least suspicion that it is not perfectly natural to wear one's aureole in the street." He is described as resembling in figure "the spindling columns of the church naves of the fifteenth century. . . . The azure of the frescoes of Fiesole had furnished the blue of his eyes; his hairs, of the blond of an aureole, seemed painted one by one, with the gold of the illuminators of the Middle Ages. . . . One would have said, that from the height of his Gothic pinnacle Célestin Nanteuil overlooked the actual town, hovering above the sea of roofs, regarding the eddying blue smoke, perceiving the city squares like a checkerboard, the streets like the notches of a saw in a stone bench, the passers-by like mice; but all that confusedly athwart the haze, while from his airy observatory he saw, close at hand and in all their detail, the rose windows, the bell towers bristling with crosses, the kings, patriarchs, prophets, saints, angels of all the orders, the whole monstrous army of demons or chimeras, nailed, scaled, tushed, hideously winged; *guivres*, taresques, gargoyles, asses' heads, apes' muzzles, all the strange bestiary of the Middle Age." Nanteuil furnished illustrations for the books of the French romanticists. "Hugo's 'Notre-Dame de Paris' was the object of his most fervent admiration, and he drew from it subjects for a large number of designs and aquarelles." Gautier mentions, as among his rarest vignettes, the frontispiece of "Albertus," recalling Rembrandt's manner; and his view of the Palazzo of San Marc in Royer's "Venezia la bella." Gautier says that one might apply to Nanteuil's aquarelles what Joseph Delorme* said of Hugo's ballads, that they were Gothic window paintings. "The essential thing in these short fantasies is the carriage, the shape, the clerical, monastic, royal, seignorial *awkwardness* of the figures and their high colouring. . . . Célestin had made his own the angular anatomy of coats-of-arms, the extravagant contours of the mantles, the chimerical or monstrous figures of heraldry, the branchings of the emblazoned skirts, the lofty attitude of the feudal baron, the modest air of the chatelaine, the sanctimonious physiognomy of the big Carthusian Carmelite, the furtive mien of the young page with parti-coloured pantaloons. . . . He excelled also in setting the persons of poem, drama, or romance in ornamented frames like the Gothic shrines with triple colonettes, arches, canopied and bracketed niches, with statuettes, figurines, emblematic animals, male and female saints on a background of gold. He entered so deeply into the sentiment of the old Gothic imagery that he could make a Lady of the Pillar in a brocade dalmatica, a Mater Dolorosa with the seven

* Sainte-Beuve's "Confessions de Joseph Delorme," 1829.

swords in her breast, a St. Christopher with the child
Jesus on his shoulder and leaning on a palm tree, worthy
to serve as types to the Byzantine painters of Epinal. . . .
Nothing resembled less the clock face and troubadour
Middle Age which flourished about 1825. It is one of
the main services of the romantic school to have thoroughly disembarrassed art from this." Gautier describes
also a manuscript piece of Nerval, for which he furnished
a prologue, and which was an imitation of one of the
Diableries, or popular farces of the Middle Ages, in which
the devil was introduced. It contained a piece within
the piece, in the fashion of an old mystery play, with
scenery consisting of the mouth of hell, painted red and
surmounted by a blue paradise starred with gold. An
angel came down to play at dice with the devil for souls.
In his excess of zeal, the angel cheated and the devil
grew angry and called him a "big booby, a celestial
fowl," and threatened to pull his feathers out (" Le Prince
des Sots ").

In France, as in England and Germany, the romantic
revival promoted and accompanied works of erudition like
Raynouard's researches in Provençal and old French
philology and the poetry of the troubadours (1816);
Creuzé de Lesser's "Chevaliers de la Table Ronde";
Marchangy's "La Gaule Poétique." History took new
impulse from that *sens du passé* which romanticism did so
much to awaken. Augustin Thierry's obligations to Scott
have already been noticed. It was the war chant of the
Frankish warriors in Chateaubriand's "Les Martyrs"—

"Pharamond ! Pharamond ! nous avons combattu avec
    l'épée "—

which first excited his historical imagination and started

him upon the studies which issued in the "Récits Méro-vingiens" and the "Conquête d'Angleterre." Barante's "Ducs de Bourgogne" (1814–28) confessedly owes much of its inception to Scott. Michaud's "History of the Crusades" (1811–22) and the "History of France" (1833–67) by that most romantic of historians, Michelet, may also be credited to the romantic movement. The end of the movement, as a definite period in the history of French literature, is commonly dated from the failure upon the stage of Victor Hugo's "Les Burgraves" in 1843. The immediate influence of the French romantic school upon English poetry or prose was slight. Like the German school, it came too late. The first genera-tion of English romantics was drawing to its close. Scott died two years after "Hernani" stormed the French the-atre. Two years later still died Coleridge, long since fallen silent — as a poet — and always deaf to Gallic charming. We shall find the first impress of French romance among younger men and in the latter half cen-tury.

In France itself the movement passed on into other phases. Many early adherents of Hugo's *cénacle* and *entourage* fell away from their allegiance and, like Sainte-Beuve and Musset, took up a critical or even antagonis-tic attitude. Musset's "Lettres de Dupuis et Cotonet" * turns the whole romantic contention into mockery. Yet no work more fantastically and gracefully romantic, more Shaksperian in quality, was produced by any member of the school than Musset produced in such dramas as "Fantasio" and "Lorenzaccio."

* See vol. i., pp. 18–23.

CHAPTER VI.

Diffused Romanticism in the Literature of the Nineteenth Century.

Most of the poetry of the century that has just closed has been romantic in the wider or looser acceptation of the term. Emotional stress, sensitiveness to the pictur-esque, love of natural scenery, interest in distant times and places, curiosity of the wonderful and mysterious, subjectivity, lyricism, intrusion of the ego, impatience of the limits of the *genres*, eager experiment with new forms of art—these and the like marks of the romantic spirit are as common in the verse literature of the nineteenth century as they are rare in that of the eighteenth. The same is true of imaginative prose, particularly during the first half of the century, the late Georgian and early Victorian period. In contrast with Addison, Swift, and Goldsmith, De Quincey, Carlyle, and Ruskin are romanticists. In contrast with Hume, Macaulay is romantic, concrete, pic-torial. The critical work of Hazlitt and Lamb was in line with Coleridge's. They praised the pre-Augustan writers, the Elizabethan dramatists, the seventeenth-century humorists and moralists, the Sidneian amourists and fanciful sonneteers, at the expense of their classical successors.

But in the narrower sense of the word—the sense which controls in these inquiries—the great romantic generation ended virtually with the death of Scott in 1832. Coleridge followed in 1834, Wordsworth in 1850. Both had long since ceased to contribute anything of value to imaginative literature. Byron, Shelley, and Keats had died some years before Coleridge; Leigh Hunt survived until 1859. The mediævalism of Coleridge, Scott, and Keats lived on in dispersed fashion till it condensed itself a second time, and with redoubled intensity, in the work of the Pre-Raphaelite Brotherhood, which belongs to the last half of the century. The direct line of descent was from Keats to Rossetti; and the Pre-Raphaelites bear very much such a relation to the elder group, as the romantic school proper in Germany bears to Bürger and Herder, and to Goethe and Schiller in their younger days. That is to say, their mediævalism was more concentrated, more exclusive, and more final.

We have come to a point in the chronology of our subject where the material is so abundant that we must narrow the field of study to creative work, and to work which is romantic in the strictest meaning. Henceforth we may leave out of account all works of mere erudition as such; all those helps which the scholarship of the century has furnished to a knowledge of the Middle Ages: histories, collections, translations, reprints of old texts, critical editions, Middle English lexicons and grammars, studies of special subjects, such as popular myths or miracle plays or the Arthurian legends, and the like. Numerous and valuable as these publications have been, they concern us only indirectly. They have swelled the material available for the student; they have not necessarily stimulated the imagination of the poet; which sometimes—as in the case of Chatterton and of Keats—

goes off at a touch and carries but a light charge of learning. In literary history it is the beginnings that count. Child's great ballad collection is, beyond comparison, more important from the scholar's point of view than Percy's "Reliques." But in the history of romanticism it is of less importance, because it came a century later. Mallet's "Histoire de Dannemarc" has been long since superseded, and the means now accessible in English for a study of Norse mythology are infinitely greater than when Gray read and Percy translated the "Northern Antiquities." But it is not the history of the revival of the *knowledge* of mediæval life that we are following here; it is rather the history of that part of our modern creative literature which has been kindled by contact— perhaps a very slight and casual contact—with the transmitted *image* of mediæval life.

Nor need we concern ourselves further with literary criticism or the history of opinion. This was worth considering in the infancy of the movement, when Warton began to question the supremacy of Pope; when Hurd asserted the fitness for the poet's uses of the Gothic fictions and the institution of chivalry; and when Percy ventured to hope that cultivated readers would find something deserving attention in old English minstrelsy. It was still worth considering a half-century later, when Coleridge explained away the dramatic unities, and Byron once more took up the lost cause of Pope. But by 1832 the literary revolution was complete. Romance was in no further need of vindication, when all Scott's library of prose and verse stood back of her, and

> "High-piled books in characterly
> Held, like rich garners, the full-ripened grain."

As to Scott's best invention, the historical romance, I
shall not pursue its fortunes to the end.   The formula
once constituted, its application was easy, whether the
period chosen was the Middle Ages or any old period
B.C. or A.D.   Here and there an individual stands forth
from the class, either for its excellent conformity with
the Waverley type or for its originality in deviation.   Of
the former kind is Charles Reade's "The Cloister and
the Hearth" (1861); and of the latter Mr. Maurice
Hewlett's "The Forest Lovers" (1898).   The title page
of Reade's novel describes the book as " a
romance."   It is as well documented as any of Scott's
and reposes especially upon the "Colloquies" of Eras
mus, the betrothal of whose parents, with their subse
quent separation by the monastic vow of celibacy, is the
subject of the story.   This is somewhat romanticised
but keeps a firm grip upon historical realities.   The
period of the action is the fifteenth century, yet the work
is as far as possible from being a chivalry tale, like the
diaphanous fictions of Fouqué.   "In that rude age,"
writes the novelist, "body prevailing over mind, all sen
timents took material forms.   Man repented with scourges
prayed by bead, bribed the saints with wax tapers, pu
fish into the body to sanctify the soul, sojourned in cold
water for empire over the emotions, and thanked God for
returning health in 1 cwt., 2 stone, 7 lbs., 3 oz., 1 dwt
of bread and cheese."   There is no lack in "The Clois
ter and the Hearth" of stirring incident and bold adven
ture; encounters with bears and with bandits, sieges
witch trials, gallows hung with thieves, archery with long
bow and arbalest—everywhere fighting enough, as in
Scott; and, also as in Scott, behind the private drama of

true love, intrigue, persecution, the broad picture of society. It is no idealised version of the Middle Ages.
The ugly, sordid side of mediæval life is turned outwards;
its dirt, discomfort, ignorance, absurdity, brutality, un-
reason and insecurity are rendered with crass realism.
The burgher is more in evidence than the chevalier.
Less after the manner of the Waverley novels, and more
after that of "Hypatia," "Romola," and "Fathers and
Sons," it depicts the intellectual unrest of the time, the
conflicting ideals of the old and new generations. The
printing-press is being set up, and the hero finds his art
of calligraphy, learned in the scriptorium, no longer in
request. The Pope and many of the higher clergy are
infected with the religious scepticism and humanitarian
enthusiasm of the Renaissance. The child Erasmus is
the new birth of reason, destined to make war on monkery
and superstition and thereby avenge his parents' wrongs.
Of quite another fashion of mediævalism is Mr. Hewlett's
story—sheer romance. The wonderful wood of Morgraunt, with its charcoal burners and wayside shrines,
black meres frowned over by skeleton castles, and gentle
hinds milked by the heroine to get food for her wounded
lover, is of no time or country, but almost as unreal as
Spenser's fairy forest. Through its wild ways Isoult la
Desirous and Prosper le Gai go adventuring like Una
and her Red Cross knight, or Enid and Geraint. Or,
again, Isoult in her page's dress, and forsaken by her
wedded lord, is like Viola or Imogen or Rosalind, or
Constance in "Marmion," or any lady of old romance.
Or sometimes again she is like a wood spirit, or an elemental creature such as was Undine. The invented
place names, High March, Wanmeeting, Market Basing,

etc., with their transparent air of actuality, sound an echo
from William Morris' prose romances, like "The House
of the Wolfings" and "The Sundering Flood." As in
the last named, and in Thomas Hardy's "Return of the
Native," the reader's imagination is assisted by a map of
the Morgraunt forest and the river Wan. Mr. Hewlett
has evidently profited, too, by recent romances of various
schools: by "Prince Otto," *e.g.*, and "The Prisoner of
Zenda," and possibly by others. His Middle Ages are
not the Middle Ages of history, but of poetic convention;
a world where anything may happen and where the facts
of any precise social state are attenuated into "atmosphere" for the use of the imagination. "The Forest
Lovers" is nearer to "Christabel" or "La Belle Dame
sans Merci" than to "Ivanhoe": is, indeed, a prose poem,
though not quite an allegory like "Sintram and his
Companions."

Among Scott's contemporaries, Byron and Shelley,
profoundly romantic in temper, were not retrospective in
their habit of mind; and the Middle Ages, in particular,
had little to say to them. Scott stood for the past; Byron
—a man of his time, a modern man—for the present;
Shelley—a visionary, with a system of philosophical per-
fectionism—for the future. Memory, Mnemosyne, mother
of the muses, was the nurse of Scott's genius. Byron
lived intensely in the world which he affected to despise.
Shelley prophesied, with eyes fixed upon the coming age.
We have found, in Byron's contributions to the Pope
controversy, one expression of his instinctive sympathy
with the classical and contempt for the Gothic. Shelley,
too, was a Hellenist; and to both, in their angry break
with authority and their worship of liberty, the naked

freedom, the clear light, the noble and harmonious forms
of the antique were as attractive as the twilight of the
"ages of faith," with their mysticism, asceticism, and
grotesque superstitions, were repulsive. Remote as their
own feverish and exuberant poetry was from the unexcited
manner of classical work, the latter was the ideal towards
which they more and more inclined. The points at which
these two poets touch our history, then, are few. Byron,
to be sure, cast "Childe Harold" into Spenserian verse,
and gave it a ballad title.* In the first canto there are
a few archaisms; words like *fere*, *shent*, and *losel* occur,
together with Gothic properties, such as the "eremite's
sad cell" and "Paynim shores" and Newstead's "monastic dome." The ballad "Adieu, adieu my native
shore," was suggested by "Lord Maxwell's Good-Night"
in the "Border Minstrelsy," and introduces some romantic appurtenances: the harp, the falcon, and the little
foot-page. But this kind of falsetto, in the tradition of
the last-century Spenserians, evidently hampered the
poet; so he shook himself free from imitation after the
opening stanzas, and spoke in his natural voice.† "Lara"
is a tale of feudal days, with a due proportion of knights,
dames, vassals, and pages; and an ancestral hall with
gloomy vaults and portrait galleries, where

> "—the moonbeam shone
> Through the dim lattice o'er the floor of stone,

* "It is almost superfluous to mention that the appellation
'Childe,' as 'Childe Waters,' 'Childe Childers,' etc., is used
as more consonant with the old structure of versification which
I have adopted."—Preface to "Childe Harold." Byron ap-
peals to a letter of Beattie relating to "The Minstrel," to justify his choice of the stanza.
† See vol. i., p. 98.

> And the high fretted roof and saints that there
> O'er Gothic windows knelt in pictured prayer. . . .
> The waving banner and the clapping door,
> The rustling tapestry and the echoing floor;
> The long dim shadows of surrounding trees,
> The flapping bats, the night-song of the breeze,
> Aught they behold or hear their thought appalls,
> As evening saddens o'er the dark grey walls."

But these things are unimportant in Byron—mere commonplaces of description inherited from Scott and Lewis and Mrs. Radcliffe. Neither is it of importance that "Parisina" is a tale of the year 1405, and has an echo in it of convent bells and the death chant of friars; nor that the first scene of "Manfred" passes in a "Gothic gallery," and includes an incantation of spirits upon the model of "Faust"; nor that "Marino Faliero" and "The Two Foscari" are founded on incidents of Venetian history which happened in the fourteenth and fifteenth centuries respectively; nor yet that Byron translated the Spanish ballad "Woe is me Alhama" and a passage from Pulci's "Morgante Maggiore." * Similarly Shelley's experimental versions of the "Prolog im Himmel," and "Walpurgisnacht" in "Faust," and of scenes from Calderon's "Magico Prodigioso" are felt to be without special significance in comparison with the body of his writings. "Faust" impressed him, as it did Byron, and he urged Coleridge to translate it, speaking of the current English versions as wretched misrepresentations of the original. But in all of Shelley's poetry the scenery, architecture, and imagery in general are sometimes Italian, sometimes Asiatic, often wholly fantastic, but never mediæval. Their splendour is a classic splendour, and

* For Byron's and Shelley's dealings with Dante, *vide supra*, pp. 99-102.

not what Milton contemptuously calls "a Hunnish and Norwegian stateliness." His favourite names are Greek: Cythna, Ianthe, and the like. The ruined cathedral in "Queen Mab"—a poem only in its title romantic—is coupled with the ruined dungeon, in whose courts the children play; both alike "works of faith and slavery," symbols of the priestcraft and kingcraft which Shelley hated, now made harmless by the reign of Reason and Love in a regenerated universe. How different is the feeling which the empty cathedral inspires in Lowell; once thronged with worshippers, now pathetically lonely —a cliff, far inland, from which the sea of faith has forever withdrawn! At the time when "Queen Mab" was written, Coleridge, Southey, and Landor's "Gebir" were Shelley's favourite reading. "He was a lover of the wonderful and wild in literature," says Mrs. Shelley, in her notes on the poem; "but had not fostered these tastes at their genuine sources—the romances and chivalry of the Middle Ages—but in the perusal of such German works as were current in those days.* . . . Our earlier English poetry was almost unknown to him."

"Queen Mab" begins with a close imitation of the opening lines of Southey's "Thalaba the Destroyer." The third member of the Lake School is a standing illustration of Mr. Colvin's contention that the distinction between classic and romantic is less in subject than in treatment. Southey regarded himself as, equally with Wordsworth and Coleridge, an innovator and a rebel against poetic conventions. His big Oriental epics, "Thalaba" and "The Curse of Kehama," are written in

* For the type of prose romance essayed by Shelley, see vol. i., p. 403.

verse purposely irregular, but so inferior in effect to the irregular verse of Coleridge and Scott as to prove that irregularity, as such, is only tolerable when controlled by the subtly varying lyric impulse—not when it is adopted as a literary method. Southey's worth as a man, his indefatigable industry, his scholarship, and his excellent work in prose make him an imposing figure in our literature. But his poetical reputation has faded more rapidly than that of his greater contemporaries. He ranged widely in search of subjects and experimented boldly in forms of verse; but his poems are seldom inspired; they are manufactures rather than creations, and to-day Southey, the poet, represents nothing in particular.

But, like Taylor of Norwich, Southey, by his studies in foreign literature, added much to the romantic material constantly accumulating in the English tongue. In his two visits to the Peninsula he made acquaintance with Spanish and Portuguese; and afterwards by his translations and otherwise, helped his countrymen to a knowledge of the old legendary poetry of Spain, the country above all others of chivalry and romance. Mention has already been made of his versions of " Amadis of Gaul," " Palmerin of England," and the " Chronicle of the Cid." The last named was not a translation from any single source, but was put together from the " Poem of the Cid," which the translator considered to be " unquestionably the oldest poem in the language " and probably by a writer contemporary with the great Campeador himself; from the prose " Chronicle " assigned to the thirteenth century; and from the ballads, which Southey thought mainly worthless, *i.e.*, from the historical point of view.

Southey's long blank verse poems on mediæval subjects, partly historical, partly legendary, "Joan of Arc" (1795), "Madoc" (1805), and "Roderick, the Last of the Goths" (1814), like his friend Landor's "Gebir," are examples of romantic themes with classical or, at least, unromantic handling. The last of them was the same in subject, indeed, with Landor's drama, "Count Julian." I have spoken of "Thalaba" and "The Curse of Kehama" as epics; but Southey rejected "the degraded title of epic" and scouted the rules of Aristotle. Nevertheless, the best qualities of these blank verse narratives are of the classic-epic kind. The story is not badly told; the measure is correct if not distinguished; and the style is simple, clear, and in pure taste. But the spell of romance, the witchery of Coleridge and Keats is absent; and so are the glow and movement of Scott.

Southey got up his history and local colour conscientiously, and his notes present a formidable array of authorities. While engaged upon "Madoc," he went to Wales to verify the scenery and even came near to leasing a cottage and taking up his residence there. "The manners of the poem," he asserted, "will be found historically true." The hero of "Madoc" was a legendary Welsh prince of the twelfth century who led a colony to America. The *motif* of the poem is therefore nearly the same as in William Morris's "Earthly Paradise," and it is curious to compare the two. In Southey's hands the blank verse, which in the last century had been almost an ear-mark of the romanticising schools, is far more classical than the heroic couplet which Morris writes. In the Welsh portion of "Madoc" the historical background is carefully studied from Giraldus Cambrensis, Evans' "Specimens," the "Triads of Bardism," the

"Cambrian Biography," and similar sources; and in the Aztec portion, from old Spanish chronicles of the conquest of Mexico and the journals of modern travellers in America. In "The Earthly Paradise" nothing is historical except the encounter with Edward III.'s fleet in the channel. Over all, the dreamlike vagueness and strangeness of romance. Yet the imaginative impression is more distinct; not an impression of reality, but as of a soft, bright miniature painting in an old manuscript.

In common with his literary associates, Southey was prompted by Percy's "Reliques" to try his hand at the legendary ballad and at longer metrical tales like "All for Love" and "The Pilgrim to Compostella." Most of these pieces date from the last years of the century. One of them, "St. Patrick's Purgatory," was inserted by Lewis in his "Tales of Wonder." Another of the most popular, and a capital specimen of grotesque, "The Old Woman of Berkeley," was upon a theme which was also undertaken by Taylor of Norwich and Dr. Sayers of the same city, when Southey was on a visit to the former in 1798. The story, told by Olaus Magnus as well as by William of Malmesbury, was of a witch whose body was carried off by the devil, though her coffin had been sprinkled with holy water and bound with a triple chain. For material Southey drew upon Spanish chronicles, French *fabliaux*, the "Acta Sanctorum," Matthew of Westminster, and many other sources. His ballads do not compare well with those of Scott and Coleridge. They abound in the supernatural—miracles of saints, sorceries, and apparitions; but the matter-of-fact narrative, commonplace diction, and jog-trot verse are singularly out of keeping with the subject matter. The most wildly romantic situations become tamely unromantic under Southey's handling. Though in better taste than Lewis' grisly compositions, yet, as in Lewis, the want of "high seriousness" or any finer imagination in these legendary tales makes them turn constantly towards the comic; so that Southey was scandalised to learn that Mr. Payne Collier had taken his "Old Woman of Berkeley" for a "mock ballad" or parody. He affected especially a stanza which he credited to Lewis' invention:

> "Behind a wide column, half breathless with fear
>   She crept to conceal herself there;
> That instant the moon o'er a dark cloud shone clear,
> And she saw in the moonlight two ruffians appear,
>   And between them a corpse did they bear." *

Southey employs no archaisms, no refrains, nor any of the stylistic marks of ancient minstrelsy. His ballads have the metrical roughness and plain speech of the old popular ballads, but none of their frequent, peculiar beauties of thought and phrase.

Spain, no less than Germany and Italy, was laid under contribution by the English romantics. Southey's work in this direction was followed by such things as Lockhart's "Spanish Ballads" (1824), Irving's "Alhambra," and Bryant's and Longfellow's translations from Spanish lyrical poetry. But these exotics did not stimulate original creative activity in England in equal degree with the German and Italian transplantings. They were imported, not appropriated. Of all European countries Spain had remained the most Catholic and mediæval. Her eight centuries of struggle against the Moors had given her a rich treasure of legendary song and story.

* "Mary, the Maid of the Inn."

She had a body of popular ballad poetry larger than either England's or Germany's.* But Spain had no modern literature to mediate between the old and new; nothing at all corresponding with the schools of romance in Germany, from Herder to Schlegel, which effected a revival of the Teutonic Middle Age and impressed it upon contemporary England and France. Neither could the Spanish Middle Age itself show any such supreme master as Dante, whose direct influence on English poetry has waxed with the century. There was a time when, for the greater part of a century, England and Spain were in rather close contact, but it was mainly a hostile contact, and its tangential points were the ill-starred marriage of Philip and Mary, the Great Armada of 1588, and the abortive "Spanish Marriage" negotiations of James I.'s reign. Readers of our Elizabethan literature, however, cannot fail to remark a knowledge of, and interest in, Spanish affairs now quite strange to English writers. The dialogue of the old drama is full of Spanish phrases of convenience like *bezo los manos, paucas palabras,* etc., which were evidently quite as well understood by the audience as was later the colloquial French—*savoir faire, coup de grâce,* etc.—which began to come in with Dryden, and has been coming ever since. The comedy Spaniard, like Don Armado in "Love's Labour's Lost," was a familiar figure on the English boards. Middleton took the double plot of his "Spanish Gipsy" from two novels of Cervantes; and his "Game of Chess," a political allegorical play, aimed against Spanish intrigues, made a popular hit and was stopped, after a then unex-

* Duran's great collection, begun in 1828, embraces nearly two thousand pieces.

ampled run, in consequence of the remonstrances of Gon-
domar, the Spanish ambassador. Somewhat later the
Restoration stage borrowed situations from the Spanish
love-intrigue comedy, not so much directly as by way of
Molière, Thomas Corneille, and other French playwrights;
and the duenna and the *gracioso* became stock figures in
English performances. The direct influence of Calderon
and Lope de Vega upon our native theatre was infinites-
imal. The Spanish national drama, like the English, was
self-developed and unaffected by classical rules. Like
the English, it was romantic in spirit, but was more
religious in subject and more lyrical in form. The land
of romance produced likewise the greatest of all satires
upon romance. "Don Quixote," of course, was early
translated and imitated in England; and the *picaro* romances had an important influence upon the evolution of
English fiction in De Foe and Smollett; not only directly through books like "The Spanish Rogue," but by
way of Le Sage.* But upon the whole, the relation between
English and Spanish literature had been one of distant
respect rather than of intimacy. There was never any
such inrush of foreign domination from this quarter as
from Italy in the sixteenth century, or from France in the
thirteenth, fourteenth, and latter half of the seventeenth.

The unequalled wealth of Spanish literature in popular
ballads is partially explained by the facility with which
such things were composed. The Spanish ballad, or
romance, was a stanza (*redondilla*, roundel) of four eight-

---

* It is hardly necessary to mention early English translations of "Palmerin of England" (1616) and "Amadis de Gaul"
(1580), or to point out the influence of Montemayor's "Diana
Enamorada" upon Sidney, Shakspere, and English pastoral
romance in general.

syllable lines with a prevailing trachaic movement—just
the metre, in short, of "Locksley Hall." Only the second and fourth lines rimed, and the rime was merely
assonant or vowel rime. Given the subject and the
lyrical impulse, and verses of this sort could be produced
to order and in infinite number by poets of the humblest
capacity. The subjects were furnished mainly by Spanish history and legend, the exploits of national heroes
like the Cid (Ruy Diaz de Bivar), the seven Princes of
Lara, Don Fernán Gonzalez, and Bernaldo del Carpio, the
leader in the Spanish versions of the great fight by Fon-
tarabbia

> "When Rowland brave and Olivier,
> And every paladin and peer
> On Roncesvalles died."

Southey thought the Spanish ballads much inferior to
the English and Scotch, a judgment to which students of
Spanish poetry will perhaps hardly agree.* The Spanish ballads, like the British, are partly historical and
legendary, partly entirely romantic or fictitious. They
record not only the age-long wars against the Saracen,

* "The English and Scotch ballads, with which they may
most naturally be compared, belong to a ruder state of society, where a personal violence and coarseness prevailed
which did not, indeed, prevent the poetry it produced from
being full of energy, and sometimes of tenderness; but which
necessarily had less dignity and elevation than belong to the
character, if not the condition, of a people who, like the Spanish, were for centuries engaged in a contest ennobled by a
sense of religion and loyalty—a contest which could not fail
sometimes to raise the minds and thoughts of those engaged
in it far above such an atmosphere as settled round the bloody
feuds of rival barons or the gross maraudings of a border
warfare. The truth of this will at once be felt, if we compare
the striking series of ballads on Robin Hood with those on the
Cid and Bernardo de Carpio; or if we compare the deep tragedy of Edom O'Gordon with that of the Conde Alarcos; or,

the common enemy, but the internecine feuds of the Spanish Christian kingdoms, the quarrels between the kings
and their vassals, and many a dark tale of domestic
treachery or violence. In these respects their resemblance to the English and Scotch border ballads is obvious; and it has been pointed out that they sprang from
similar conditions, a frontier war for national independence, maintained for centuries against a stubborn foe.
The traditions concerning Wallace and the Bruce have
some analogy with the chronicles of the Cid; but as to
the border fights celebrated in Scott's " Minstrelsy," they
were between peoples of the same race, tongue, and
faith; and were but petty squabbles in comparison with
that epic crusade in which the remnants of the old Gothic
conquerors slowly made head against, and finally over-
threw and expelled, an Oriental religion, a foreign blood,
and a civilisation in many respects more brilliant than
anything which Europe could show. The contrast between Castile and Granada is more picturesque than the
difference between Lothian and Northumberland. The
Spanish ballads have the advantage, then, of being connected with imposing passages of history. In spirit they
are intensely national. Three motives animate them all:
loyalty to the king, devotion to the cross, and the *pun-
donor:* that sensitive personal honour—the " Castilian
pride " of " Hernani,"—which sometimes ran into fantas-

what would be better than either, if we should sit down to the
' Romancero General,' with its poetical confusion of Moorish
splendours and Christian loyalty, just when we have come
fresh from Percy's ' Reliques ' or Scott's ' Minstrelsy ' " ("History of Spanish Literature," George Ticknor, vol. i., p. 141,
third American ed., 1866). The " Romancero General " was
the great collection of some thousand ballads and lyrics published in 1602-14.

tic excess. A rude chivalry occasionally softens the feroc
ity of feudal manners in Northern ballad-poetry, as in the
speech of Percy over the dead Douglas in " Chevy Chase.'
But in the Spanish *romances* the knightly feeling is all-
pervading. The warriors are *hidalgos*, gentlemen of a
lofty courtesy; the Moorish chieftains are not "heathen
hounds," but chivalrous adversaries, to be treated, in de-
feat, with a certain generosity. This refinement and
magnanimity are akin to that ideality of temper which
makes Don Quixote at once so noble and so ridiculous,
and which is quite remote from the sincere realism of
the British minstrelsy. In style the Spanish ballads
are simple, forcible, and direct, but somewhat monotonous in their facility. The English and Scotch have
a wider range of subject; the best of them have a condensed energy of expression and a depth of tragic feeling
which is more potent than the melancholy grace of the
Spanish. Women take a more active part in the former,
the Christians of the Peninsula having caught from their
Saracen foes a prejudice in favour of womanly seclusion
and retirement. There is also a wilder imagination in
Northern balladry; a much larger element of the mythological and supernatural. Ghosts, demons, fairies, en-
chanters are rare in the Spanish poems. Where the
marvellous enters into them at all, it is mostly in the
shape of saintly miracles. St. James of Compostella
appears on horseback among the Christian hosts battling
with the Moors, or even in the army of the Conquista-
dores in Mexico—an incident which Macaulay likens to
the apparition of the "great twin Brethren" in the Roman
battle of Lake Regillus. The mediæval Spaniards were
possibly to the full as superstitious as their Scottish con-

temporaries, but their superstitions were the legends of the Catholic Church, not the inherited folklore of Gothic and Celtic heathendom. I will venture to suggest, as one reason of this difference, the absence of forests in Spain. The shadowy recesses of northern Europe were the natural haunts of mystery and unearthly terrors. The old Teutonic forest, the Schwarzwald and the Hartz, were peopled by the popular imagination with were-wolves, spectre huntsmen, wood spirits, and all those nameless creatures which Tieck has revived in his "Mährchen" and Hauptmann in the Rautendelein of his "Versunkene Glocke." The treeless plateaus of Spain, and her stony, denuded sierras, all bare and bright under the hot southern sky, offered no more shelter to such beings of the mind than they did to the genial life of Robin Hood and his merry men "all under the greenwood tree." And this mention of the bold archer of Sherwood recalls one other difference—the last that need here be touched upon —between the ballads of Spain and of England. Both constitute a body of popular poetry, *i.e.*, of folk poetry. They recount the doings of the upper classes, princes, nobles, knights, and ladies, as seen from the angle of observation of humble minstrels of low degree. But the people count for much more in the English poems. The Spanish are more aristocratic, more public, less domestic, and many of them composed, it is thought, by lordly makers. This is perhaps, in part, a difference in national character; and, in part, a difference in the conditions under which the social institutions of the two countries were evolved.

Spain collected her ballads early in numerous song-books—*cancioneros*, *romanceros*—the first of which, the

"Cancionero" of 1510, is "the oldest collection o. popular poetry, properly so-called, that is to be found i. any European literature." *   But modern Spain had gone through her classic period, like England and Germany She had submitted to the critical canons of Boileau, and was in leading-strings to France till the end of the eighteenth century.   Spain, too, had her romantic move ment, and incidentally her ballad revival, but it came later than in England and Germany, later even than in France.   Historians of Spanish literature inform us that the earliest entry of French romanticism into Spain took place in Martinez de la Rosa's two dramas, "The Con spiracy of Venice" (1834) and "Aben-Humeya," first written in French and played at Paris in 1830; and that the representation of Duke de Rivas' play, "Don Alvaro' (1835), was "an event in the history of the modern Span ish drama corresponding to the production of 'Hernani at the Théâtre Français" in 1830.†   Both of these authors had lived in France and had there made acquaintance with the works of Chateaubriand, Byron, and Walter Scott.   Spain came in time to have her own Byron and her own Scott; the former in José de Espronceda, author of "The Student of Salamanca," who resided for a time in London; the latter in José Zorrilla, whose "Granada,' "Legends of the Cid," etc., "were popular for the same reason that 'Marmion' and 'The Lady of the Lake' were popular; for their revival of national legends in a form both simple and picturesque" ‡   Scott himself is reported

* "The Ancient Ballads of Spain."   R. Ford, in Edinburgh Review, No. 146.
† "A History of Spanish Literature."   By James Fitz Maurice Kelly, New York, 1898, pp. 366-67.
‡ *Ibid.*, pp. 368-73.

to have said that if he had come across in his younger
days Perez de Hita's old historical romance, "The Civil
Wars of Granada" (1595), "he would have chosen Spain
as the scene of a Waverley novel." *

But when Lockhart, in 1824, set himself to

> "—relate
> In high-born words the worth of many a knight
> From tawny Spain, lost in the world's debate "—

her ballad poetry had fallen into disfavour at home, and
"no Spanish Percy, or Ellis, or Ritson," he complains,
"has arisen to perform what no one but a Spaniard can
entertain the smallest hope of achieving." †   Meanwhile,
however, the German romantic school had laid eager
hands upon the old romantic literature of Spain.   A.
W. Schlegel (1803) and Gries had made translations from
Calderon in assonant verse; and Friedrich Schlegel—
who exalted the Spanish dramatist above Shakspere,
much to Heine's disgust—had written, also in *asonante*,
his dramatic poem "Conde Alarcos" (1802), founded on
the well-known ballad.   Brentano and others of the romantics went so far as to practise assonance in their original as well as translated work.   Jacob Grimm (1815)
and, Depping (1817) edited selections from the "Romancero" which Lockhart made use of in his "Ancient
Spanish Ballads."   With equal delight the French romanticists—Hugo and Musset in particular—seized upon
the treasures of the "Romancero"; but this was somewhat later.

Lockhart's "Spanish Ballads," which were bold and

* Kelly, p. 270.
† The collection of Sanchez (1779) is described as an imitation of the "Reliques" (Edinburgh Review, No. 146).

spirited paraphrases rather than close versions of the originals, enjoyed a great success, and have been repeatedly reprinted. Ticknor pronounced them undoubtedly a work of genius, as much so as any book of the sort in any literature with which he was acquainted.* In the very same year Sir John Bowring published his "Ancient Poetry and Romance of Spain." Hookham Frere, that most accomplished of translators, also gave specimens from the "Romancero." Of late years versions in increasing numbers of Spanish poetry of all kinds, ancient and modern, by Ormsby, Gibson, and others too numerous to name, have made the literature of the country largely accessible to English readers. But to Lockhart belongs the credit of having established for the English public the convention of romantic Spain—the Spain of lattice and guitar, of mantilla and castanet, articles now long at home in the property room of romance, along with the gondola of Venice, the "clock-face" troubadour, and the castle on the Rhine. The Spanish brand of mediævalism would seem, for a number of years, to have substituted itself in England for the German; and doubtless a search through the annuals and gift books and fashionable fiction and minor poetry generally, of the years from 1825 to 1840, would disclose a decided Castilian colouring. To such effect, at least, is the testimony of the Edinburgh reviewer—from whom I have several times quoted—reviewing in January, 1841, the new and sumptuously illustrated edition of "Ancient Spanish Ballads." "Mr. Lockhart's success," he writes, "rendered the subject fashionable; we have, however, no

*He preferred, however, Sir Edmund Head's rendering of the ballad "Lady Alda's Dream" to Lockhart's version.

space to bestow on the minor fry who dabbled in these
. . . fountains. Those who remember their number may
possibly deprecate our re-opening the floodgates of the
happily subsided inundation."

The popular ballad, indeed, is, next after the historical
romance, the literary form to which the romantic movement has given, in the highest degree, a renewal of prosperous life. Every one has written ballads, and the
"burden" has become a burden even as the grasshopper
is such. The very parodists have taken the matter in
hand. The only Calverley made excellent sport of the
particular variety cultivated by Jean Ingelow. And Sir
Frederick Pollock, as though actuated by Lowell's hint,
about "a declaration of love under the forms of a declaration in trover," cast the law reports into ballad phrase in
his "Leading Cases Done into English" (1876):

> "It was Thomas Newman and five his feres
> (Three more would have made them nine),
> And they entered into John Vaux's house,
> That had the Queen's Head to sign.
> The birds on the bough sing loud and sing low,
> What trespass shall be *ab initio.*"

Of course the great majority of these poems in the ballad form, whether lyric or narrative, or a mixture of both,
are in no sense romantic. They are like Wordsworth's
"Lyrical Ballads," idyllic; songs of the affections, of
nature, sentiment, of war, the sea, the hunting field, rus-
tic life, and a hundred other moods and topics. Neither
are the historical or legendary ballads, deriving from
Percy and reinforced by Scott, prevailingly romantic in
the sense of being mediæval. They are such as Macaulay's "Lays of Ancient Rome," in which—with ample
acknowledgment in his introduction both to Scott and

to the " Reliques"—he applies the form of the English minstrel ballad to an imaginative re-creation of the lost popular poetry of early Rome.   Or they continue Scott's Jacobite tradition, like "Aytoun's Lays of the Scottish Cavaliers," Browning's "Cavalier Tunes," Thornbury's "Songs of the Cavaliers and Roundheads" (1857), and a few of Motherwell's ditties.   These last named, except Browning, were all Scotchmen and staunch Tories; as were likewise Lockhart and Hogg; and, for obvious reasons, it is in Scotland that the simpler fashion of ballad writing, whether in dialect or standard English, and more especially as employed upon martial subjects, has flourished longest.   Artifice and ballad preciosity have been cultivated more sedulously in the south, with a learned use of the repetend, archaism of style, and imitation of the quaint mediæval habit of mind.

Of the group most immediately connected with Scott and who assisted him, more or less, in his " Minstrelsy " collection, may be mentioned the eccentric John Leyden, immensely learned in Border antiquities and poetry; and James Hogg, the "Ettrick Shepherd."   The latter was a peasant bard, an actual shepherd and afterward a sheep farmer, a self-taught man with little schooling, who aspired to become a second Burns, and composed much of his poetry while lying out on the hills, wrapped in his plaid and tending his flocks like any Corydon or Thyrsis. He was a singular mixture of genius and vanity, at once the admiration and the butt of the *Blackwood's* wits, who made him the mouthpiece of humour and eloquence which were not his, but Christopher North's.   The puzzled shepherd hardly knew how to take it; he was a little gratified and a good deal nettled.   But the flamboyant figure of him in the *Noctes* will probably do as much as his own verses to keep his memory alive with posterity. Nevertheless, Hogg is one of the best of modern Scotch ballad poets. Having read the first two volumes of the "Border Minstrelsy," he was dissatisfied with some of the modern ballad imitations therein and sent his criticisms to Scott. They were sound criticisms, for Hogg had an intimate knowledge of popular poetry and a quick perception of what was genuine and what was spurious in such compositions. Sir Walter called him in aid of his third volume and found his services of value.

As a Border minstrel, Hogg ranks next to Scott—is, in fact, a sort of inferior Scott. His range was narrower, but he was just as thoroughly saturated with the legendary lore of the countryside, and in some respects he stood closer to the spirit of that peasant life in which popular poetry has its source. As a ballad poet, indeed, he is not always Scott's inferior, though even his ballads are apt to be too long and without the finish and the instinct for selection which marks the true artist. When he essayed metrical romances in numerous cantos, his deficiencies in art became too fatally evident. Scott, in his longer poems, is often profuse and unequal, but always on a much higher level than Hogg. The latter had no skill in conducting to the end a fable of some complexity, involving a number of varied characters and a really dramatic action. "Mador of the Moor," *e.g.*, is a manifest and not very successful imitation of "The Lady of the Lake"; and it requires a strong appetite for the romantic to sustain a reader through the six parts of "Queen Hynde" and the four parts of "The Pilgrims of the Sun." By general consent, the best of Hogg's more am-

bitious poems is " The Queen's Wake," and the best thing
in it is " Kilmeny."   " The Queen's Wake " (1813) com-
bines, in its narrative plan, the framework of " The Lay
of the Last Minstrel " with the song competition in its
sixth canto.   Mary Stuart, on landing in Scotland, holds
a Christmas wake at Holyrood, where seventeen bards
contend before her for the prize of song.   The lays are
in many different moods and measures, but all enclosed
in a setting of octosyllabic couplets, closely modelled
upon Scott; and the whole ends with a tribute to the
great minstrel who had waked once more the long silent
Harp of the North.   The thirteenth bard's song—" Kilmeny "—is of the type of traditionary tale familiar in
" Tam Lin " and " Thomas of Ercildoune," and tells how
a maiden was spirited away to fairyland, where she saw
a prophetic vision of her country's future (including the
Napoleonic wars) and returned after a seven years' absence.

> "Late, late in a gloamin' when all was still,
>   When the fringe was red on the westlin hill,
>   The wood was sere, the moon i' the wane,
>   The reek o' the cot hung o'er the plain,
>   Like a little wee cloud in the world its lane ;
>   When the ingle lowed wi' an eiry leme,
>   Late, late in the gloamin' Kilmeny came hame."

The Ettrick Shepherd's peculiar province was not so
much the romance of national history as the field of Scottish fairy lore and popular superstition.   It was he, rather
than Walter Scott, who carried out the suggestions long
since made to his countryman, John Home, in Collins'
" Ode on the Superstitions of the Highlands."   His
poems are full of bogles, kelpies, brownies, warlocks, and
all manner of " grammarie."   " The Witch of Fife " is

"The Queen's Wake," a spirited bit of grotesque, is repeatedly quoted as authority upon the ways of Scotch witches in the notes to Croker's "Fairy Legends and Traditions of the South of Ireland." Similar themes engaged the poet in his prose tales. Some of these were mere modern ghost stories, or stories of murder, robbery, death warnings, etc. Others, like "The Heart of Eildon," dealt with ancient legends of the supernatural. Still others, like "The Brownie of Bodsbeck: a Tale of the Covenanters," were historical novels of the Stuart times. Here Hogg was on Scott's own ground and did not shine by comparison. He complained, indeed, that in the last-mentioned tale, he had been accused of copying "Old Mortality"; but asserted that he had written his book the first and had been compelled by the appearance of Sir Walter's, to go over his own manuscript and substitute another name for Balfour of Burley, his original hero. Nanny's songs, in "The Brownie of Bodsbeck," are among Hogg's best ballads. Others are scattered through his various collections—"The Mountain Bard," "The Forest Minstrel," "Poetical Tales and Ballads," etc.

Another Scotch balladist was William Motherwell, one of the most competent of ballad scholars and editors, whose "Minstrelsy: Ancient and Modern," was issued at Glasgow in 1827, and led to a correspondence between the collector and Sir Walter Scott.* In 1836 Motherwell was associated with Hogg in editing Burns' works. His original ballads are few in number, and their faults and merits are of quite an opposite nature from his collaborator's. The shepherd was a man of the people, and

* Scott and Motherwell never met in person.

lived, so far as any modern can, among the very conditions which produced the minstrel songs. He inherited
the popular beliefs. His great-grandmother on one side
was a notorious witch; his grandfather on the other side
had "spoken with the fairies." His poetry, such as it
is, is fluent and spontaneous. Motherwell's, on the contrary, is the work of a ballad fancier, a student learned
in lyric, reproducing old modes with conscientious art.
His balladry is more condensed and skilful than Hogg's,
but seems to come hard to him. It is literary poetry
trying to be *Volkspoesie*, and not quite succeeding. Many
of the pieces in the southern English, such as "Halbert
the Grim," "The Troubadour's Lament," "The Crusader's Farewell," "The Warthman's Wail," "The Demon
Lady," "The Witches' Joys," and "Lady Margaret,"
have an echo of Elizabethan music, or the songs of Love-
lace, or, now and then, the verse of Coleridge or Byron.
"True Love's Dirge," *e.g.*, borrows a burden from Shakspere—"Heigho! the Wind and Rain." Others, like
"Lord Archibald: A Ballad," and "Elfinland Wud: An
Imitation of the Ancient Scottish Romantic Ballad," are
in archaic Scotch dialect with careful ballad phrasing.
Hogg employs the broad Scotch, but it is mostly the vernacular of his own time. A short passage from "The
Witch of Fife" and one from "Elfin Wud" will illustrate
two very different types of ballad manner:

> "He set ane reid-pipe till his muthe
>   And he playit se bonnileye,
> Till the gray curlew and the black-cock flew
>   To listen his melodye.

> "It rang se sweit through the grim Lommond,
>   That the nycht-winde lowner blew:

And it soupit alang the Loch Leven,
  And wakenit the white sea-mew.

"It rang se sweit through the grim Lommond,
  Se sweitly but and se shill,
That the wezilis laup out of their mouldy holis,
  And dancit on the mydnycht hill."

"Around her slepis the quhyte muneschyne,
  (Meik is mayden undir kell),
Hir lips bin lyke the blude reid wyne;
  (The rois of flouris hes sweitest smell).

"It was al bricht quhare that ladie stude,
  (Far my luve fure ower the sea).
Bot dern is the lave of Elfinland wud,
  (The Knicht pruvit false that ance luvit me).

"The ladie's handis were quhyte als milk,
  (Ringis my luve wore mair nor ane).
Hir skin was safter nor the silk;
  (Lilly bricht schinis my luve's halse bane)."

Upon the whole, the most noteworthy of Motherwell's original additions to the stores of romantic verse were his poems on subjects from Norse legend and mythology, and particularly the three spirited pieces that stand first in his collection (1832)—"The Battle-Flag of Sigurd," "The Wooing Song of Jarl Egill Skallagrim," and "The Sword Chant of Thorstein Randi." These stand midway between Gray's "Descent of Odin" and the later work of Longfellow, William Morris and others. Since Gray, little or nothing of the kind had been attempted; and Motherwell gave perhaps the first expression in English song of the Berserkir rage and the Viking passion for battle and sea roving.

During the nineteenth century English romance received new increments of heroic legend and fairy lore from the Gaelic of Ireland. It was not until 1867 that Matthew Arnold, in his essay "On the Study of Celtic

Literature," pleading for a chair of Celtic at Oxford, bespoke the attention of the English public to those elements in the national literature which come from the Celtic strain in its blood. Arnold knew very little Celtic, and his essay abounds in those airy generalisations which are so irritating to more plodding critics. His theory, *e.g.*, that English poetry owes its sense for colour to the Celts, when taken up and stated nakedly by following writers, seems too absolute in its ascription of colour-blindness to the Teutonic races. Still, Arnold probably defined fairly enough the distinctive traits of the Celtic genius. He attributes to a Celtic source much of the turn of English poetry for style, much of its turn for melancholy, and nearly all its turn for "natural magic." "The forest solitude, the bubbling spring, the wild flowers, are everywhere in romance. They have a mysterious life and grace there; they are Nature's own children, and utter her secret in a way which makes them something quite different from the woods, waters, and plants of Greek and Latin poetry. Now, of this delicate magic, Celtic romance is so pre-eminent a mistress that it seems impossible to believe the power did not come into romance from the Celts."

In 1825 T. Crofton Croker published the first volume of his delightful "Fairy Legends and Traditions of the South of Ireland." It was immediately translated into German by the Grimm brothers, and was received with enthusiasm by Walter Scott, who was introduced to the author in London in 1826, and a complimentary letter from whom was printed in the preface to the second edition.

Croker's book opened a new world of romance, and

introduced the English reader to novel varieties of elf creatures, with outlandish Gaelic names; the Shefro; the Boggart; the Phooka, or horse-fiend; the Banshee, a familiar spirit which moans outside the door when a death impends; the Cluricaune,* or cellar goblin; the Fir Darrig (Red Man); the Dullahan, or Headless Horseman. There are stories of changelings, haunted castles, buried treasure, the "death coach," the fairy piper, enchanted lakes which cover sunken cities, and similar matters not unfamiliar in the folk-lore of other lands, but all with an odd twist to them and set against a background of the manners and customs of modern Irish peasantry. The Celtic melancholy is not much in evidence in this collection. The wild Celtic fancy is present, but in combination with Irish gaiety and lightheartedness. It was the day of the comedy Irishman— Lover's and Lever's Irishman—Handy Andy, Rory O'More, Widow Machree and the like. It took the famine of '49 and the strenuous work of the Young Ireland Party which gathered about the *Nation* in 1848, to displace this traditional figure in favour of a more earnest and tragical national type. But a single quotation will illustrate the natural magic of which Arnold speaks: "The Merrow (mermaid) put the comb in her pocket, and then bent down her head and whispered some words to the water that was close to the foot of the rock. Dick

---

* Mr. Churton Collins thinks that the lines in "Guinevere "—

"Down in the cellars merry bloated things
    Shouldered the spigot, straddling on the butts
    While the wine ran "—

was suggested by Croker's description of the Cluricaune. ("Illustrations of Tennyson " (1891), p. 152.)

saw the murmur of the words upon the top of the sea,
going out towards the wide ocean, just like a breath of
wind rippling along, and, says he, in the greatest wonder, ' Is it speaking you are, my darling, to the salt
water? '

"' It's nothing else,' says she, quite carelessly; ' I'm
just sending word home to my father not to be waiting
breakfast for me.' " Except for its lack of "high seriousness," this is the imagination that makes myths.

Catholic Ireland still cherishes popular beliefs which
in England, and even in Scotland, have long been merely
antiquarian curiosities. In her poetry the fairies are
never very far away.

> "Up the airy mountain,
>   Down the rushy glen
> We daren't go a-hunting
>   For fear of little men." *

Irish critics, to be sure, tell us that Allingham's fairies
are English fairies, and that he had no Gaelic, though he
knew and loved his Irish countryside. He was a Protestant and a loyalist, and lived in close association with
the English Pre-Raphaelites—with Rossetti especially,
who made the illustration for "The Maids of Elfin-
Mere" in Allingham's volume "The Music Master"
(1855). The Irish fairies, it is said, are beings of a
darker and more malignant breed than Shakspere's
elves. Yet in Allingham's poem they stole little Brid-
get and kept her seven years, till she died of sorrow and
lies asleep on the lake bottom: even as in Ferguson's
weird ballad, "The Fairy Thorn," the good people carry
off fair Anna Grace from the midst of her three compan-

* "The Fairies."   William Allingham.

ions, who "pined away and died within the year and day."

To the latter half of the century belongs the so-called Celtic revival, which connects itself with the Nationalist movement in politics and is partly literary and partly patriotic. It may be doubted whether, for practical purposes, the Gaelic will ever come again into general use. But the concerted endeavour by a whole nation to win back its ancient, wellnigh forgotten speech is a most interesting social phenomenon. At all events, both by direct translations of the Gaelic hero epics and by original work in which the Gaelic spirit is transfused through English ballad and other verse forms, a lost kingdom of romance has been recovered and a bright green thread of Celtic poetry runs through the British anthology of the century. The names of the pioneers and leading contributors to this movement are significant of the varied strains of blood which compose Irish nationality. James Clarence Mangan was a Celt of the Celts; Joseph Sheridan Le Fanu and Aubrey de Vere were of Norman-Irish stock, and the former was the son of a dean of the Established Church, and himself the editor of a Tory newspaper; Sir Samuel Ferguson was an Ulster Protestant of Scotch descent; Dr. George Sigerson is of Norse blood; Whitley Stokes, the eminent Celtic scholar, and Dr. John Todhunter, author of "Three Bardic Tales" (1896), bear Anglo-Saxon surnames; the latter is the son of Quaker parents and was educated at English Quaker schools.

Mangan's paraphrases from the Gaelic, "Poets and Poetry of Munster," appeared posthumously in 1850. They include a number of lyrics, wildly and mournfully beautiful, inspired by the sorrows of Ireland: "Dark

Rosaleen," "Lament for the Princes of Tir-Owen and Tir-Connell," "O'Hussey's Ode to the Maguire," etc. The ballad form was not practised by the ancient Gaelic epic poets. In choosing it as the vehicle for their renderings from vernacular narrative poetry, the modern Irish poets have departed widely from the English and Scottish model, employing a variety of metres and not seeking to conform their diction to the manner of the ballads in the "Reliques" or the "Border Minstrelsy." Ferguson's "Lays of the Western Gael" (1865) is a series of historical ballads, original in effect, though based upon old Gaelic chronicles. "Congal" (1872) is an epic, founded on an ancient bardic tale, and written in Chapman's "fourteener" and reminding the reader frequently of Chapman's large, vigorous manner, his compound epithets and spacious Homeric similes. The same epic breadth of manner was applied to the treatment of other hero legends, "Conary," "Deirdré," etc., in a subsequent volume (1880). "Deirdré," the finest of all the old Irish stories, was also handled independently by the late Dr. R. D. Joyce in the verse and manner of William Morris' "Earthly Paradise." * Among other recent workers in this field are Aubrey de Vere, a volume of selections from whose poetry appeared at New York in 1894, edited by Prof. G. E. Woodberry: George Sigerson, whose "Bards of the Gael and the Gall," a

---

* See vol. i., p. 314. Dr. Joyce was for some years a resident of Boston, where his "Ballads of Irish Chivalry" were published in 1872. His "Deirdré" received high praise from J. R. Lowell. Tennyson's "Voyage of Maeldune" (1880) probably had its source in Dr. P. W. Joyce's "Old Celtic Romances" (1879) (Collins' "Illustrations of Tennyson," p. 163). Swinburne pronounced Ferguson's "Welshmen of Tirawley" one of the best of modern ballads.

volume of translations from the Irish in the original metres, was issued in 1897; Whitley Stokes, an accomplished translator, and the joint editor (with Windisch)
of the "Irische Texte"; John Todhunter, author of "The
Banshee and Other Poems" (1888) and "Three Bardic
Tales" (1896); Alfred Perceval Graves, author of "Irish
Folk Songs" (1897), and many other volumes of national
lyrics; and William Larminie—"West Irish Folk Tales
and Romances" (1893), etc.

The Celtism of this Gaelic renascence is of a much
purer and more genuine character than the Celtism of
Macpherson's "Ossian." Yet with all its superiority in
artistic results, it is improbable that it will make any
such impression on Europe or England as Macpherson
made. "Ossian" was the first revelation to the world
of the Celtic spirit: sophisticated, rhetorical, yet still the
first; and it is not likely that its success will be repeated.
In the very latest school of Irish verse, represented by
such names as Lionel Johnson, J. B. Yeats, George W.
Russell, Nora Hopper, the mystical spirit which inhabits the "Celtic twilight" turns into modern symbolism,
so that some of their poems on legendary subjects bear
a curious resemblance to the contemporary work of Maeterlinck: to such things as "Aglivaine et Salysette" or
"Les Sept Princesses." *

The narrative ballad is hardly one of the forms of high

---

* For a survey of this department of romantic literature the
reader is referred to "A Treasury of Irish Poetry in the English Tongue." Edited by Stopford A. Brooke and T. W. Rolleston (New York, 1900). There are a quite astonishing
beauty and force in many of the pieces in this collection,
though some of the editors' claims seem excessive; as, *e.g.*,
that Mr. Yeats is "the first of living writers in the English
language."

art, like the epic, the tragedy, the Pindaric ode. It is simple and not complex like the sonnet: not of the aristocracy of verse, but popular—not to say plebeian—in its associations. It is easy to write and, in its commonest metrical shape of eights and sixes, apt to run into singsong. Its limitations, even in the hands of an artist like Coleridge or Rossetti, are obvious. It belongs to "minor poetry." The ballad revival has not been an unmixed blessing and is responsible for much slip-shod work. If Dr. Johnson could come back from the shades and look over our recent verse, one of his first comments would probably be: "Sir, you have too many ballads." Be it understood that the *romantic* ballad only is here in question, in which the poet of a literary age seeks to catch and reproduce the tone of a childlike, unself-conscious time, so that his art has almost inevitably something artificial or imitative. Here and there one stands out from the mass by its skill or luck in overcoming the difficulty. There is Hawker's "Song of the Western Men," which Macaulay and others quoted as historical, though only the refrain was old:

> "And shall Trelawney die?
>   Here's twenty thousand Cornish men
>   Will know the reason why!"*

There is Sydney Dobell's "Keith of Ravelston," † which

* Robert Stephen Hawker was vicar of Morwenstow, near "wild Tintagil by the Cornish Sea," where Tennyson visited him in 1848. Hawker himself made contributions to Arthurian poetry, "Queen Gwynnevar's Round" and "The Quest of the Sangreal" (1864). He was converted to the Roman Catholic faith on his death-bed.

† Given in Palgrave's "Golden Treasury," second series. Rossetti wrote of Dobell's ballad in 1868: "I have always regarded that poem as being one of the finest, of its length, in any modern poet; ranking with Keats' 'La Belle Dame sans

haunts the memory with the insistent iteration of its refrain :—

> "The murmur of the mourning ghost
>   That keeps the shadowy kine ;
> Oh, Keith of Ravelston,
>   The sorrows of thy line !"

And again there is Robert Buchanan's "Ballad of Judas
Iscariot" which Mr. Stedman compares for "weird im-
pressiveness and power" with "The Ancient Mariner."
The mediæval feeling is most successfully captured in
this poem. It recalls the old "Debate between the Body
and Soul," and still more the touches of divine compas-
sion which soften the rigours of Catholic theology in the
legends of the saints. It strikes the keynote, too, of that
most modern ballad mode which employs the narrative
only to emphasize some thought of universal application.
There is salvation for all, is the thought, even for the
blackest soul of the world, the soul that betrayed its
Maker.* Such, though after a fashion more subtly intellectual, is the doctrinal use to which this popular form is
put by one of the latest English ballad makers, Mr. John
Davidson. Read, *e.g.*, his "Ballad of a Nun," † the story
of which was told in several shapes by the Spanish poet
Alfonso the Learned (1226–84). A runaway nun returns

Merci' and the other masterpieces of the condensed and
hinted order so dear to imaginative minds." The use of the
family name Keith in Rossetti's "Rose Mary" was a coinci-
dence. His poem was published (1854) some years before
Dobell's. He thought of substituting some other name for
Keith, but could find none to suit him, and so retained it.

* *Cf.* Matthew Arnold's "St. Brandan," suggested by a
passage in the old Irish "Voyage of Bran." The traitor Judas is allowed to come up from hell and cool himself on an
iceberg every Christmas night because he had once given his
cloak to a leper in the streets of Joppa.

† "Ballads and Songs," London, 1895.

in penitence to her convent, and is met at the gate by the Virgin Mary, who has taken her likeness and kept her place for her during the years of her absence.   Or read " A New Ballad of Tannhäuser," * which contradicts "the idea of the inherent impurity of nature" by an interpretation of the legend in a sense quite the reverse of Wagner's.   Tannhäuser's dead staff blossoms not as a sign of forgiveness, but to show him that "there was no need to be forgiven."   The modern balladist attacks the ascetic Middle Age with a shaft from its own quiver.

But it is time to turn from minor poets to acknowledged masters; and above all to the greatest of modern English artists in verse, the representative poet of the Victorian era.   Is Tennyson to be classed with the romantics?   His workmanship, when most truly characteristic, is romantic in the sense of being pictorial and ornate, rather than classically simple or severe.   He assimilated the rich manner of Keats, whose influence is perceptible in his early poems.   His art, like Keats', is eclectic and reminiscent, choosing for its exercise with equal impartiality whatever was most beautiful in the world of Grecian fable or the world of mediæval legend.   But unlike Keats, he lived to add new strings to his lyre; he went on to sing of modern life and thought, of present-day problems in science and philosophy, of contemporary politics, the doubt, unrest, passion, and faith of his own century.   To find work of Tennyson's that is romantic throughout, in subject, form, and spirit alike, we must look among his earlier collections (1830, 1832, 1842). For this was a phase which he passed beyond, as Millais outgrew his youthful Pre-Raphaelitism, or as Goethe

* "New Ballads," London, 1897.

left behind him his " Götz " and " Werther " period and
widened out into larger utterance. Mr. Stedman speaks
of the " Gothic feeling " in " The Lady of Shalott," and
in ballads like " Oriana " and " The Sisters," describing
them as " work that in its kind is fully up to the best of
those Pre-Raphaelites who, by some arrest of development, stop precisely where Tennyson made his second
step forward, and censure him for having gone beyond
them." * This estimate may be accepted so far as it
concerns " The Lady of Shalott," which is known to have
worked strongly upon Rossetti's imagination; but surely
" The Sisters " and " Oriana " do not rank with the best
Pre-Raphaelite work. The former is little better than a
failure; and the latter, which provokes a comparison, not
to Tennyson's advantage, with the fine old ballad, " Helen
of Kirkconnell," is a weak thing. The name Oriana has
romantic associations—it is that of the heroine of " Amadis de Gaul "—but the damnable iteration of it as a
ballad burden is irritating. Mediæval *motifs* are rather
slightly handled in " The Golden Supper " (from the
" Decameron," 4th novel, 10th day); " The Beggar
Maid " (from the ballad of " King Cophetua and the
Beggar Maid " in the " Reliques "); and more adequately
in " Godiva," a blank-verse rendering of the local legend
of Coventry, in which an attempt is made to preserve
something of the antique roughness under the smooth
Vergilian elegance of Tennyson's diction. " The Day
Dream " was a recasting of one of Perrault's fairy tales,
" The Sleeping Beauty," under which title a portion of
it had appeared in the " Poems Chiefly Lyrical " of 1830.

---

* "Victorian Poets." By E. C. Stedman. New York, 1886
(tenth ed.), p. 155.

Tennyson has written many greater poems than this, but few in which the special string of romance vibrates more purely. The tableau of the spellbound palace, with all its activities suspended, gave opportunity for the display of his unexampled pictorial power in scenes of still life; and the legend itself supplied that charmed isolation from the sphere of reality which we noticed as so important a part of the romantic poet's stock-in-trade in " Christabel " and " The Eve of St. Agnes "—

> "The hall-door shuts again and all is still."

Poems like " The Day Dream " and " The Princess " make it evident that Scott and Coleridge and Keats had so given back the Middle Ages to the imagination that any future poet, seeking free play in a realm unhampered by actual conditions—"apart from place, withholding time"—was apt to turn naturally, if not inevitably, to the feudal times. The action of " The Day Dream " proceeds no-where and no-when. The garden—if we cross-examine it—is a Renaissance garden:

> "Soft lustre bathes the range of urns
>   On every slanting terrace-lawn:
> The fountain to its place returns,
>   Deep in the garden lake withdrawn."

The furnishings of the palace are a mixture of mediæval and Louis Quatorze—clocks, peacocks, parrots, golden mantle pegs:—

> "Till all the hundred summers pass,
>   The beams that through the oriel shine
> Make prisms in every carven glass
>   And beaker brimm'd with noble wine."

But the impression, as a whole, is of the Middle Age of

poetic convention, if not of history; the enchanted date-less era of romance and fairy legend.

"St. Agnes" and "Sir Galahad," its masculine counterpart, sound the old Catholic notes of saintly virginity and mystical, religious rapture, the *Gottesminne* of mediæval hymnody. Not since Southwell's "Burning Babe" and Crashaw's "Saint Theresa" had any English poet given such expression to those fervid devotional moods which Sir Thomas Browne describes as "Christian annihilation, ecstasies, exolution, liquefaction, transformation, the kiss of the spouse, gustation of God and ingression into the divine shadow." This vein, we have noticed, is wanting in Scott. On the other hand, it may be noticed in passing, Tennyson's attitude towards nature is less exclusively romantic—in the narrow sense—than Scott's. He, too, is conscious of the historic associations of place. In Tennyson, as in Scott,—

> "The splendour falls on castle walls
> And snowy summits old in story" *—

but, in general, his treatment of landscape, in its human relations, is subtler and more intimate.

"St. Agnes" and "Sir Galahad" are monologues, but lyric and not dramatic in Browning's manner. There is a dramatic falsity, indeed, in making Sir Galahad say of himself—

> "My strength is as the strength of ten
> Because my heart is pure,"

and the poem would be better in the third person. "St. Simeon Stylites" is a dramatic monologue more upon

---

* This famous lyric, one of the "inserted" songs in "The Princess," was inspired by the note of a bugle on the Lakes of Killarney.

268 of English Romanticism.

Browning's model, *i.e.*, a piece of apologetics and self-analysis. But in this province Tennyson is greatly Browning's inferior.

"The Princess" (1847) is representative of that "splendid composite of imagery," and that application of modern ideas to legendary material, or to invented material arbitrarily placed in an archaic setting, which are characteristic of this artist. The poem's sub-title is "A Medley," because it is

> "—made to suit with time and place,
> A Gothic ruin and a Grecian house,
> A talk of college and of ladies' rights,
> A feudal knight in silken masquerade,
> And, yonder, shrieks and strange experiments."

The problem is a modern one—the New Woman. No precise historic period is indicated. The female university is full of classic lore and art, but withal there are courts of feudal kings, with barons, knights, and squires, and shock of armoured champions in the lists.

But the special service of Tennyson to romantic poetry lay in his being the first to give a worthy form to the great Arthurian saga; and the modern masterpiece of that poetry, all things considered, is his "Idylls of the King." Not so perfect and unique a thing as "The Ancient Mariner"; less freshly spontaneous, less stirringly alive than "The Lay of the Last Minstrel," Tennyson's Arthuriad has so much wider a range than Coleridge's ballad, and is sustained at so much higher a level than Scott's romance, that it outweighs them both in importance. The Arthurian cycle of legends, emerging from Welsh and Breton mythology; seized upon by French romancers of the twelfth and thirteenth centuries, who made of Arthur the pattern king, of Lancelot the pattern knight, and of the Table Round the ideal insti- tute of chivalry; gathering about itself accretions like the Grail Quest and the Tristram story; passing by trans- lation into many tongues, but retaining always its scene in Great or Lesser Britain, the lands of its origin, fur- nished the modern English romancer with a groundwork of national, though not Anglo-Saxon epic stuff, which cor- responds more nearly with the Charlemagne epos in France, and the Nibelung hero Saga in Germany, than anything else which our literature possesses. And a national possession, in a sense, it had always remained. The story in outline and in some of its main episodes was familiar. Arthur, Lancelot, Guinivere, Merlin, Modred, Iseult, Gawaine, were well-known figures, like Robin Hood or Guy of Warwick, in Shakspere's time as in Chaucer's. But the epos, as a whole, had never found its poet. Spenser had evaporated Arthur into allegory. Milton had dallied with the theme and put it by.* The Elizabethan drama, which went so far afield in search of the moving accident, had strangely missed its chance here, bringing the Round Table heroes upon its stage only in masque and pageant (Justice Shallow "was Sir Dagonet in Arthur's show"), or in some such perform- ance as the rude old Seneca tragedy of "The Misfortunes of Arthur." In 1695 Sir Richard Blackmore published

---

* See vol. i., pp. 146–47. Dryden, like Milton, had designs upon Arthur. See introduction to the first canto of "Mar- mion":

> "—Dryden, in immortal strain,
> Had raised the Table Round again,
> But that a ribald king and court
> Bade him toil on, to make them sport."

his " Prince Arthur," an epic in ten books and in rimed
couplets, enlarged in 1697 into " King Arthur" in twelve
books. Blackmore professed to take Vergil as his model.
A single passage from his poem will show how much
chance the old chivalry tale had in the hands of a minor
poet of King William's reign. Arthur and his company
have landed on the shores of Albion, where

> "Rich wine of Burgundy and choice champagne
> Relieve the toil they suffered on the main ;
> But what more cheered them than their meats and wine,
> Was wise instruction and discourse divine
> From Godlike Arthur's mouth."

There is no need, in taking a summary view of Tennyson's " Idylls," to go into the question of sources, or to
inquire whether Arthur was a historical chief of North
Wales, or whether he signified the Great Bear (Arcturus)
in Celtic mythology, and his Round Table the circle described by that constellation about the pole star.* Tennyson went no farther back for his authority than Sir
Thomas Malory's " Morte Darthur," printed by Caxton
in 1485, a compilation principally from old French
Round Table romances. This was the final mediæval
shape of the story in English. It is somewhat wandering and prolix as to method, but written in delightful
prose. The story of " Enid," however (under its various
titles and arrangements in successive editions), he took
from Lady Charlotte Guest's translation of the Welsh
" Mabinogion " (1838–49).

* For a discussion of these and similar matters and a bibli-
ography of Arthurian literature, the reader should consult Dr.
H. Oskar Sommer's scholarly reprint and critical edition of
"Le Morte Darthur. By Syr Thomas Malory," three vols.,
London, 1889–91.

Before deciding upon the heroic blank verse and a loosely epic form, as most fitting for his purpose, Tennyson had retold passages of Arthurian romance in the ballad manner and in various shapes of riming stanza. The first of these was "The Lady of Shalott" (1832), identical in subject with the later idyll of "Lancelot and Elaine," but fanciful and even allegorical in treatment. Shalott is from Ascalot, a variant of Astolat, in the old *metrical* romance—not Malory's—of the "Morte Arthur." The fairy lady, who sees all passing sights in her mirror and weaves them into her magic web, has been interpreted as a symbol of art, which has to do properly only with the reflection of life. When the figure of Lancelot is cast upon the glass, a personal emotion is brought into her life which is fatal to her art. She is "sick of shadows," and looks through her window at the substance. Then her mirror cracks from side to side and the curse is come upon her. Other experiments of the same kind were "Sir Galahad" and "Sir Lancelot and Queen Guinevere" (both in 1842). The beauty of all these ballad beginnings is such that one is hardly reconciled to the loss of so much romantic music, even by the noble blank verse and the ampler narrative method which the poet finally adopted. They stand related to the "Idylls" very much as Morris' "Defence of Guenevere" stands to his "Earthly Paradise."

Thoroughly romantic in content, the "Idylls of the King" are classical in form. They may be compared to Tasso's "Gierusalemme Liberata," in which the imperfectly classical manner of the Renaissance is applied to a Gothic subject, the history of the Crusades. The first specimen given was the "Morte d'Arthur" of 1842, set

in a framework entitled "The Epic," in which "the poet,
Everard Hall," reads to his friends a fragment from his
epic, "King Arthur," in twelve books. All the rest he
has burned. For—

> "Why take the style of those heroic times?
> For nature brings not back the Mastodon,
> Nor we those times ; and why should any man
> Remodel models? these twelve books of mine
> Were faint Homeric echoes."

The "fragment" is thus put forward tentatively and
with apologies—apologies which were little needed; for
the "Morte d'Arthur," afterwards embedded in "The
Passing of Arthur," remains probably the best, and certainly the most Homeric passage in the "Idylls." Tennyson's own quality was more Vergilian than Homeric,
but the models which he here remodels were the Homeric epics. He chose for his measure not the Spenserian stanza, nor the *ottava rima* of Tasso, nor the octosyl-
lables of Scott and the chivalry romances, but the heroic
blank verse which Milton had fixed as the vehicle of English classical epic. He adopts Homer's narrative practices: the formulated repetitions of phrase, the pictorial
comparisons, the conventional epithets (in moderation),
and his gnomic habit—

> "O purblind race of miserable men," etc.

The original four idylls were published in 1859.*
Thenceforth the series grew by successive additions and
rearrangements up to the completed "Idylls" of 1888,
twelve in number—besides prologue and epilogue—ac-

---

* Two of them, however, had been printed privately in 1857
under the title of "Enid and Nimuë": the true and the false.
"Nimuë" was the first form of Vivien.

cording to the plan foreshadowed in "The Epic." The story of Arthur had thus occupied Tennyson for over a half century. Though modestly entitled "Idylls," by reason of the episodic treatment, the poem when finished was, in fact, an epic; but an epic that lacked the formal unity of the "Æneid" and the "Paradise Lost," or even of the "Iliad." It resembled the Homeric heroic poems more than the literary epics of Vergil and Milton, in being not the result of a single act of construction, but a growth from the gradual fitting together of materials selected from a vast body of legend. This legendary matter he reduced to an epic unity. The adventures in Malory's romance are of very uneven value, and it abounds in inconsistencies and repetitions. He also redistributed the ethical balance. Lancelot is the real hero of the old "Morte Darthur," and Guinivere—the Helen of romance—goes almost uncensured. Malory's Arthur is by no means "the blameless king" of Tennyson, who makes of him a nineteenth-century ideal of royal knighthood, and finally an allegorical type of Soul at war with Sense. The downfall of the Round Table, that order of spiritual knight-errantry through which the king hopes to regenerate society, happens through the failure of his knights to rise to his own high level of character; in a degree, also, because the emprise is diverted from attainable practical aims to the fantastic quest of the Holy Grail. The sin of Lancelot and the Queen, drawing after it the treachery of Modred, brings on the tragic catastrophe. This conception is latent in Malory, but it is central in Tennyson; and everywhere he subtilises, refines, elevates, and, in short, modernises the *Motivirung* in the old story. Does he thereby also

weaken it? Censure and praise have been freely bestowed upon Tennyson's dealings with Malory. Thus it
is complained that his Arthur is a prig, a curate, who
preaches to his queen and lectures his court, and whose
virtue is too conscious; that the harlot Vivien is a poor
substitute for the damsel of the lake who puts Merlin to
sleep under a great rock in the land of Benwick; that the
gracious figure of Gawain suffers degradation from the
application of an effeminate moral standard to his shining exploits in love and war; that modern *convenances*
are imposed upon a society in which they do not belong
and whose joyous, robust *naïveté* is hurt by them.*

The allegorical method tried in " The Lady of Shalott," but abandoned in the earlier " Idlyls," creeps in
again in the later; particularly in " Gareth and Lynette"
(1872), in the elaborate symbolism of the gates of Camelot, and in the guardians of the river passes, whom
Gareth successively overcomes, and who seem to represent the temptations incident to the different ages of
man. The whole poem, indeed, has been interpreted in
a parabolic sense, Merlin standing for the intellect, the
Lady of the Lake for religion, etc. Allegory was a favourite mediæval mode, and the Grail legend contains an
element of mysticism which invites an emblematic treatment. But the attraction of this fashion for minds of a

---

* Matthew Arnold writes in one of his letters: "I have a
strong sense of the irrationality of that period [the Middle
Ages] and of the utter folly of those who take it seriously and
play at restoring it; still it has poetically the greatest charm
and refreshment possible for me. The fault I find with Tennyson, in his 'Idylls of the King,' is that the peculiar charm
of the Middle Age he does not give in them. There is something magical about it, and I will do something with it before
I have done."

Platonic cast is dangerous to art: the temptation to find a meaning in human life more esoteric than any afforded by the literal life itself. A delicate balance must be kept between that presentation of the concrete which makes it significant by making it representative and typical, and that other presentation which dissolves the individual into the general, by making it a mere abstraction. Were it not for Dante and Hawthorne and the second part of "Faust," one would incline to say that no creative genius of the first order indulges in allegory. Homer is never allegorical except in the episode of Circe; Shakspere never, with the doubtful exception of "The Tempest." The allegory in the "Idylls of the King" is not of the obvious kind employed in the "Faëry Queene"; but Tennyson, no less than Spenser, appeared to feel that the simple retelling of an old chivalry tale, without imparting to it some deeper meaning, was no work for a modern poet.

Tennyson has made the Arthur Saga, as a whole, peculiarly his own. But others of the Victorian poets have handled detached portions of it. William Morris' "Defence of Guenevere" (1858) anticipated the first group of "Idylls." Swinburne's "Tristram of Lyonesse" (1882) dealt at full length, and in a very different spirit, with an epicyclic legend which Tennyson touched incidentally in "The Last Tournament." Matthew Arnold's "Tristram and Iseult" was a third manipulation of the legend, partly in dramatic, partly in narrative form, and in changing metres. It follows another version of Tristram's death, and the story of Vivian and Merlin which Iseult of Brittany tells her children is quite distinct from the one in the "Idylls." Iseult of

Brittany—not Iseult of Cornwall—is the heroine of
Arnold's poem. Thomas Westwood's "Quest of the
Sancgreall" is still one more contribution to Arthurian
poetry of which a mere mention must here suffice.

For our review threatens to become a catalogue. To
such a degree had mediævalism become the fashion, that
nearly every Georgian and Victorian poet of any pretensions tried his hand at it. Robert Browning was not
romantic in Scott's way, nor in Tennyson's. His business was with the soul. The picturesqueness of the external conditions in which soul was placed was a matter
of indifference. To-day was as good as yesterday. Now
and then occurs a title with romantic implications—
"Childe Roland to the Dark Tower Came," *e.g.*, borrowed from a ballad snatch sung by the Fool in "Lear"
(Roland is Roland of the "Chanson"). But the poem
proves to be a weird study in landscape symbolism and
the history of some dark emprise, the real nature of
which is altogether undiscoverable. "Count Gismond,"
again, is the story of a combat in the lists at Aix in
Provence, in which a knight vindicates a lady's honour
with his lance, and slays her traducer at her feet. But
this is a dramatic monologue like any other, and only
accidentally mediæval. "The Heretic's Tragedy: A
Middle Age Interlude," is mediæval without being romantic. It recounts the burning, at Paris, A.D. 1314, of
Jacques du Bourg-Molay, Grand Master of the Templars;
and purports to be a sort of canticle, with solo and
chorus, composed two centuries after the event by a
Flemish canon of Ypres, to be sung at hocktide and festivals. The childishness and devout buffoonery of an
old miracle play are imitated here, as in Swinburne's

"Masque of Queen Bersabe." This piece and "Holy Cross Day" are dramatic, or monodramatic, grotesques; and in their apprehension of this trait of the mediæval mind are on a par with Hugo's "Pas d'armes du Roi Jean" and "La Chasse du Burgrave." But Browning's mousings in the Middle Ages after queer freaks of conscience or passion were occasional. If any historical period, more than another, had special interest for him, it was the period of the Italian Renaissance. Yet Ruskin said: "Robert Browning is unerring in every sentence he writes of the Middle Ages."

Among Mrs. Browning's poems, which, it needs hardly be said, are not prevailingly "Gothic," there are three interesting experiments in ballad romance: "The Romaunt of the Page," "The Lay of the Brown Rosary," and "The Rime of the Duchess May." In all of these she avails herself of the mediæval atmosphere, simply to play variations on her favourite theme, the devotedness of woman's love. The motive is the same as in poems of modern life like "Bertha in the Lane" and "Aurora Leigh." The vehemence of this nobly gifted woman, her nervous and sometimes almost hysterical emotionalism, are not without a disagreeable quality. With greater range and fervour, she had not the artistic poise of the Pre-Raphaelite poetess, Christina Rossetti. In these romances, as elsewhere, she is sometimes shrill and often mannerised. "The Romaunt of the Page" is the tale of a lady who attends her knight to the Holy Land, disguised as a page, and without his knowledge. She saves his life several times, and finally at the cost of her own. A prophetic accompaniment or burden comes in ever and anon in the distant chant of nuns over the dead abbess.

"Beati! beati mortui."

"The Lay of the Brown Rosary" is a charming but uneven piece, in four parts and a variety of measures, about
a girl who, while awaiting her lover's return from the
war, learns in a dream that she must die, and purchases
seven years of life from the ghost of a wicked nun whose
body has been immured in an old convent wall. The
spirit gives the bride a brown rosary which she wears
under her dress, but her kiss kills the bridegroom at the
altar. The most spirited and well-sustained of these
ballad poems is "The Rime of the Duchess May," in
which the heroine rides off the battlements with her husband. "Toll slowly," runs the refrain. Mrs. Browning
employs some archaisms, such as *chapélle, chambére, ladié.*
The stories are seemingly of her own invention, and have
not quite the genuine accent of folk-song.

Even Matthew Arnold and Thomas Hood, representatives in their separate spheres of anti-romantic tendencies, made occasional forays into the Middle Ages. But
who thinks of such things as "The Plea of the Midsummer Fairies" or "The Two Peacocks of Bedfont" when
Hood is mentioned; and not rather of "The Bridge of
Sighs" and "The Song of the Shirt"? Or who, in spite
of "Balder Dead" and "Tristram and Iseult," would
classify Arnold's clean-cut, reserved, delicately intellectual work as romantic? Hood was an artist of the terrible as well as of the comic; witness his "Last Man,"
"Haunted House," and "Dream of Eugene Aram." If
he could have welded the two moods into a more intimate
union, and applied them to legendary material, he might
have been a great artist in mediæval grotesque—a species of Gothic Hoffman perhaps. As it is, his one ro-

mantic success is the charming lyric " Fair Ines." His longer poems in this kind, in modifications of *ottava rima* or Spenserian stanza, show Keats' influence very clearly. The imagery is profuse, but too distinct and without the romantic *chiaroscuro*. " The Water Lady " is a manifest imitation of " La Belle Dame sans Merci," and employs the same somewhat unusual stanza form. Hood—incorrigible punster—who had his jest at everything, jested at romance. He wrote ballad parodies— " The Knight and the Dragon," etc.—and an ironical " Lament for the Decline of Chivalry " :

> "Well hast thou cried, departed Burke,
>   All chivalrous romantic work
>   Is ended now and past !
>   That iron age—which some have thought
>   Of mettle rather overwrought—
>   Is now all overcast."

And finally, " The Saint's Tragedy " (1848) of Charles Kingsley affords a case in which mediæval biography is made the pretext for an assault upon mediæval ideas. It is a *tendenz* drama in five acts, founded upon the " Life of St. Elizabeth of Hungary," as narrated by her contemporary, Dietrich the Thuringian. Its militant Protestantism is such as might be predicted from Kingsley's well-known resentment of the Romanist attitude towards marriage and celibacy; from his regard for freedom of thought; and from that distrust and contempt of Popish priestcraft which involved him in his controversy with Newman. " The Middle Age," says the Introduction, " was, in the gross, a coarse, barbarous, and profligate age. . . . It was, in fact, the very ferocity and foulness of the time which, by a natural revulsion, called forth at the same time the Apostolic holiness and the Manichean asceticism of the mediæval saints. . . . So rough and common a life-picture of the Middle Age will, I am afraid, whether faithful or not, be far from acceptable to those who take their notions of that period principally from such exquisite dreams as the fictions of Fouqué, and of certain moderns whose graceful minds . . . are, on account of their very sweetness and simplicity, singularly unfitted to convey any true likeness of the coarse and stormy Middle Age. . . . But really, time enough has been lost in ignorant abuse of that period, and time enough also, lately, in blind adoration of it. When shall we learn to see it as it was?"

Polemic in its purpose and anti-Catholic in temper, "The Saint's Tragedy" then seeks to dispel the glamour which romance had thrown over mediæval life. Kingsley's Middle Age is not the holy Middle Age of the German "throne-and-altar" men; nor yet the picturesque Middle Age of Walter Scott. It is the cruel, ignorant, fanatical Middle Age of "The Amber Witch" and "The Succube." But Kingsley was too much of a poet not to feel those "last enchantments" which whispered to Arnold from Oxford towers, maugre his "strong sense of the irrationality of that period." The saintly, as well as the human side, of Elizabeth's character is portrayed with sympathy, though poetically the best thing in the drama are the songs of the Crusaders.

Kingsley, in effect, was always good at a ballad. His finest work in this kind is modern, "The Last Buccaneer," "The Sands of Dee," "The Three Fishers," and the like. But there are the same fire and swing in many of his romantic ballads on historical or legendary subjects, such as "The Swan-Neck," "The Red King," "Ballad of Earl Haldan's Daughter," "The Song of the Little Baltung," and a dozen more. Without the imaginative witchery of Coleridge, Keats, and Rossetti, in the ballad of action Kingsley ranks very close to Scott. The same manly delight in outdoor life and bold adventure, love of the old Teutonic freedom and strong feeling of English nationality inspire his historical romances, only one of which, however, "Hereward the Wake" (1866), has to do with the period of the Middle Ages.

CHAPTER VII.

The Pre=Raphaelites.

In the latter half of the century the Italian Middle
Age and Dante, its great exemplar, found new interpreters in the Rossetti family; a family well fitted by its
mixture of bloods and its hereditary aptitudes, literary
and artistic, to mediate between the English genius and
whatever seemed to it alien or repellant in Dante's
system of thought. The father, Gabriele Rossetti, was a
political refugee, who held the professorship of Italian
in King's College, London, from 1831 to 1845, and was
the author of a commentary on Dante which carried the
politico-allegorical theory of the "Divine Comedy" to
somewhat fantastic lengths. The mother was half English and half Italian, a sister of Byron's travelling companion, Dr. Polidori. Of the four children of the marriage, Dante Gabriel and Christina became poets of
distinction. The eldest sister, Maria Francesca, a religious devotee who spent her last years as a member of a
Protestant sisterhood, was the author of that unpretentious
but helpful piece of Dante literature, "A Shadow of
Dante." The younger brother, William Michael, is well
known as a biographer, *littérateur*, and art critic, as an
editor of Shelley and of the works of Dante Gabriel
Rossetti.

Other arts besides the literary art had partaken in the

romantic movement. The eighteenth century had seen the introduction of the new, or English, school of landscape gardening; and the premature beginnings of the Gothic revival in architecture, which reached a successful issue some century later.* Painting in France had been romanticised in the thirties *pari passu* with poetry and drama; and in Germany, Overbeck and Cornelius had founded a school of sacred art which corresponds, in its mediæval spirit, to the Pre-Raphaelite Brotherhood. In England painting was the last of the arts to catch the new inspiration. When the change came, it evinced that same blending of naturalism and Gothicism which defined the incipient romantic movement of the previous century. Painting, like landscape gardening, returned to nature; like architecture, it went back to the past. Like these, and like literature itself, it broke away from a tradition which was academic, if not precisely classic in the way in which David was classic.

In 1848 the Pre-Raphaelite Brotherhood was established by three young painters, Dante Gabriel Rossetti, John Everett Millais, and William Holman Hunt. The name expresses their admiration of the early Italian— and notably the early Florentine—religious painters, like Giotto, Ghiberti, Bellini, and Fra Angelica. In the work of these men they found a sweetness, depth, and sincerity of devotional feeling, a self-forgetfulness and humble adherence to truth, which were absent from the sophisticated art of Raphael and his successors. Even the imperfect command of technique in these " primitives " had a charm. The stiffness and awkwardness of their

---

*See vol. i., chaps. iv. and vii., "The Landscape Poets" and "The Gothic Revival."

figure painting, their defects of drawing, perspective, and light and shade, their lack of anatomical science were like the lispings of childhood or the artlessness of an old ballad. The immediate occasion of the founding of the Brotherhood was a book of engravings which Hunt and Rossetti saw at Millais' house, from the frescoes by Gozzoli, Orcagna, and others in the Campo Santo, at Pisa; the same frescoes, it will be remembered, which so strongly impressed Leigh Hunt and Keats. Holman Hunt—though apparently not his associates—had also read with eager approval the first volume of Ruskin's " Modern Painters," in which the young artists of England are advised to " go to nature in all singleness of heart . . . rejecting nothing, selecting nothing." Pre-Raphaelitism was a practical, as " Modern Painters " was a theoretical, protest against the academic traditions which kept young artists making school copies of Raphael, instructed them that a third of the canvas should be occupied with a principal shadow, and that no two people's heads in the picture should be turned the same way, and asked, " Where are you going to put your brown tree? "

The three original members of the group associated with themselves four others: Thomas Woolner, the sculptor; James Collinson, a painter; F. G. Stephens, who began as an artist and ended as an art critic; and Rossetti's brother William, who was the literary man of the movement. Woolner was likewise a poet, and contributed to *The Germ* * his two striking pieces, " My Beau-

* This was the organ of the Pre-Raphaelites, started in 1850. Only four numbers were issued (January, February, March, April), and in the third and fourth the title was changed to *Art and Poetry*. The contents included, among other things, poems by Dante Gabriel and Christina Ros-

tiful Lady" and "Of My Lady in Death." Among other
artists not formally enrolled in the Brotherhood, but who
worked more or less in the spirit and principles of Pre-
Raphaelitism, were Ford Madox Brown, an older man, in
whose studio Rossetti had, at his own request, been admitted as a student; Walter Deverell, who took Collinson's place when the latter resigned his membership in
order to study for the Roman Catholic priesthood; and
Arthur Hughes.*

But the main importance of the Pre-Raphaelite movement to romantic literature resides in the poetry of Rossetti, and in the inspiration which this communicated to
younger men, like Morris and Swinburne, and through
them tò other and still younger followers. The history
of English painting is no part of our subject, but Rossetti's painting and his poetry so exactly reflect each
other, that some definition or brief description of Pre-
Raphaelitism seems here to be called for, ill qualified as
I feel myself to give any authoritative account of the
matter.†

setti. One of the former's twelve contributions was "The
Blessed Damozel." The *Oxford and Cambridge Magazine*,
which ran through the year 1856 and was edited by William
Morris and Edward Burne-Jones, was also a Pre-Raphaelite
journal and received many contributions from Rossetti.
* The foreign strain in the English Pre-Raphaelites and in
the painters and poets who descend from them is worth not-
ing. Rossetti was three-fourths Italian. Millais' parents
were Channel Islanders—from Jersey—and he had two mother
tongues, English and French. Burne-Jones is of Welsh blood,
and Alma Tadema of Frisian birth. Among Neo-Pre-Ra-
phaelite poets, the names of Theophile Marzials and Arthur
O'Shaughnessy speak for themselves.
† Let the reader consult the large and rapidly increasing
literature on the English Pre-Raphaelites. I do not profess
to be a very competent guide here, but I have found the following works all in some degree enlightening. "Autobio-

And first as to methods: the Pre-Raphaelites rejected the academic system whereby the canvas was prepared by rubbing in bitumen, and the colours were laid upon a background of brown, grey, or neutral tints. Instead of this, they spread their colours directly upon the white, unprepared canvas, securing transparency by juxtaposition rather than by overlaying. They painted their pictures bit by bit, as in frescoes or mosaic work, finishing each portion as they went along, until no part of the canvas was left blank. The Pre-Raphaelite theory was sternly realistic. They were not to copy from the antique, but from nature. For landscape background, they were to take their easels out of doors. In figure painting they were to work, if possible, from a living model and not from a lay figure. A model once selected, it was to be painted as it was in each particular, and without imaginative deviation. "Every Pre-Raphaelite landscape background," wrote Ruskin, "is painted, to the last touch, in the open air from the thing itself. Every Pre-Raphaelite figure, however studied in expression, is a true portrait

graphical Notes of William Bell Scott," two vols., New York, 1892. "English Contemporary Art." Translated from the French of R. de la Sizeranne, Westminster, 1898. "D. G. Rossetti as Designer and Writer." W. M. Rossetti, London, 1889. "The Rossettis." E. L. Cary, New York, 1900. "Dante Rossetti and the Pre-Raphaelite Movement." Esther Wood, New York, 1894. "Pre-Raphaelitism." J. Ruskin, New York, 1860. "The Pre-Raphaelite Brotherhood." Holman Hunt in *Contemporary Review*, vol. xlix. (three articles). "Encyclopædia Britannica," article "Rossetti," by Theodore Watts. Of course the standard lives and memoirs by William Rossetti, Hall Caine, William Sharp, and Joseph Knight, as well as Rossetti's "Family Letters," "Letters to William Allingham," etc., afford criticisms of the movement from various points of view. Lists of Rossetti's paintings and drawings are given by several of these authorities, with photographs or engravings of his most famous masterpieces.

of some living person. Every minute accessory is painted in the same manner." * In this fashion their earliest works were executed. In Rossetti's "Girlhood of Mary Virgin," exhibited in 1849, the figure of St. Anne is a portrait of the artist's mother; the Virgin, of his sister Christina; and Joseph, of a man-of-all-work employed in the family. In Millais' "Lorenzo and Isabella"—a subject from Keats—Isabella's brother, her lover, and one of the guests, are portraits of Deverell, Stephens, and the two Rossettis. But this severity of realism was not long maintained. It was a discipline, not a final method. Even in Rossetti's second painting, "Ecce Ancilla Domini," the faces of the Virgin and the angel Gabriel are blendings of several models; although, in its freedom from convention, its austere simplicity, and endeavour to see the fact as it happened, the piece is in the purest Pre-Raphaelite spirit. Ruskin insisted that, while composition was necessarily an affair of the imagination, the figures and accessories of a picture should be copies from the life. In the early days of the Brotherhood there was an ostentatious conscientiousness in observing this rule. We hear a great deal in Rossetti's correspondence about the brick wall at Chiswick which he copied into his picture " Found," and about his anxious search for a white calf for the countryman's cart in the same composition. But all the Pre-Raphaelites painted from the lay figure as well as from the living model, and Rossetti, in particular, relied quite as much on memory and imagination as upon the object before him. W. B. Scott thinks that his most charming works

* "Lectures on Architecture and Painting." Delivered at Edinburgh in 1853. Lecture iv., "Pre-Raphaelitism."

were the small water-colours on Arthurian subjects, "done entirely without nature and a good deal in the spirit of illuminated manuscripts, with very indifferent drawing and perspective nowhere." As for Millais, he soon departed from rigidly Pre-Raphaelite principles, and became the most successful and popular of British artists in *genre.* In natural talent and cleverness of execution he was the most brilliant of the three; in imaginative intensity and originality he was Rossetti's inferior—as in patience and religious earnestness he was inferior to Hunt. It was Hunt who stuck most faithfully to the programme of Pre-Raphaelitism. He spent laborious years in the East in order to secure the exactest local truth of scenery and costume for his Biblical pieces: "Christ in the Shadow of Death," "Christ in the Temple," and "The Scapegoat." While executing the last-named, he pitched his tent on the shores of the Dead Sea and painted the desert landscape and the actual goat from a model tied down on the edge of the sea. Hunt's "Light of the World" was one of the masterpieces of the school, and as it is typical in many ways, may repay description. Ruskin pronounced it "the most perfect instance of expressional purpose with technical power which the world has yet produced."

In this tall, narrow canvas the figure of Christ occupies nearly half the space. He holds a lantern in his hand and knocks at a cottage door. The face—said to be a portrait of Venables, curate of St. Paul's, Oxford—is quite unlike the type which Raphael has made traditional. It is masculine—even rugged—seamed with lines of care, and filled with an expression of yearning. There is anxiety and almost timidity in his pose as he listens for an answer to his knock. The nails and bolts of the door are rusted; it is overgrown with ivy and the tall stalks and flat umbels of fennel. The sill is choked with nettles and other weeds, emblems all of the long sleep of the world which Christ comes to break. The full moon makes a halo behind his head and shines through the low boughs of an orchard, whose apples strew the dark grass in the foreground, sown with spots of light from the star-shaped perforations in the lantern-cover. They are the apples of Eden, emblems of the Fall. Everything, in fact, is symbolical. Christ's seamless white robe, with its single heavy fold, typifies the Church catholic; the jewelled clasps of the priestly mantle, one square and one oval, are the Old and New Testaments. The golden crown is enwoven with one of thorns, from which new leaves are sprouting. The richly embroidered mantle hem has its meaning, and so have the figures on the lantern. To get the light in this picture right, Hunt painted out of doors in an orchard every moonlight night for three months from nine o'clock till five. While working in his studio, he darkened one end of the room, put a lantern in the hand of his lay-figure and painted this interior through the hole in a curtain. On moonlight nights he let the moon shine in through the window to mix with the lantern light. It was a principle with the Brotherhood that detail, though not introduced for its own sake, should be painted with truth to nature. Hunt, especially, took infinite pains to secure minute exactness in his detail. Ruskin wrote in enthusiastic praise of the colours of the gems on the mantle clasp in "The Light of the World," and said that all the Academy critics and painters together could not have executed one of the nettle leaves at the bottom of the picture. The lizards in the foreground of Millais' " Ferdinand Lured by Ariel " (exhibited in 1850) were studied from life; and Scott makes merry over the shavings on the floor of the carpenter shop in the same artist's " Christ in the House of his Parents," a composition which was ferociously ridiculed by Dickens in " Household Words."

The symbolism which is so pronounced a feature in " The Light of the World " is common to all the Pre-Raphaelite art. It is a mediæval note, and Rossetti learned it from Dante. Symbolism runs through the " Divine Comedy " in such touches as the rush, emblem of humility, with which Vergil girds Dante for his journey through Purgatory; the constellation of four stars—

"Non viste mai fuor ch' alla prima gente "—

typifying the cardinal virtues; the three different coloured steps to the door of Purgatory; * and thickening into the elaborate apocalyptic allegory of the griffin and the car of the church, the eagle and the mystic tree in the last cantos of the " Purgatorio." In Hunt's " Christ in the Shadow of Death," the young carpenter's son is stretching his arms after work, and his shadow, thrown upon the wall, is a prophecy of the crucifixion. In Millais' " Christ in the House of his Parents," the boy has wounded the palm of his hand upon a nail, another foretokening of the crucifixion. In Rossetti's " Girlhood of Mary Virgin," Joseph is training a vine along a piece of trellis in the shape of the cross; Mary is copying in embroidery a three-flowered white lily plant, growing in a flower-pot which stands upon a pile of books lettered

Cf. Milton: " Each stair mysteriously was meant " (" P. L. ").

with the names of the cardinal virtues. The quaint
little child angel who tends the plant is a portrait of a
young sister of Thomas Woolner. Similarly, in " Ecce
Ancilla Domini, ' the lily of the annunciation which
Gabriel holds is repeated in the piece of needlework
stretched upon the 'broidery frame at the foot of Mary's
bed. In "Beata Beatrix" the white poppy brought by
the dove is the symbol at once of chastity and of death;
and the shadow upon the sun-dial marks the hour of
Beatrice's beatification. Again, in "Dante's Dream,"
poppies strew the floor, emblems of sleep and death; an
expiring lamp symbolises the extinction of life; and a
white cloud borne away by angels is Beatrice's departing
soul. Love stands by the couch in flame-coloured robes,
fastened at the shoulder with the scallop shell which is
the badge of pilgrimage. In Millais" "Lorenzo and Isabella " the salt-box is overturned upon the table, signify-
ing that peace is broken between Isabella's brothers and
their table companion. Doves are everywhere in Rossetti's pictures, embodiments of the Holy Ghost and the
ministries of the spirit. Rossetti labelled his early manuscript poems "Poems of the Art Catholic"; and the
Pre-Raphaelite heresy was connected by unfriendly critics
with the Anglo-Catholic or Tractarian movement at Oxford. William Sharp, in speaking of "that splendid
outburst of Romanticism in which Coleridge was the first
and most potent participant," and of the lapse or ebb
that followed the death of Coleridge, Byron, Shelley, and
Keats, resumes: "At last a time came when a thrill of
expectation, of new desire, of hope, passed through the
higher lives of the nation; and what followed thereafter
were the Oxford movement in the Church of England,

the Pre-Raphaelite movement in art, and the far-reaching Gothic revival. Different as these movements were in their primary aims, and still more differing in the individual representations of interpreters, they were in reality closely interwoven, one being the outcome of the other. The study of mediæval art, which was fraught with such important results, was the outcome of the widespread ecclesiastical revival, which in its turn was the outcome of the Tractarian movement in Oxford. The influence of Pugin was potent in strengthening the new impulse, and to him succeeded Ruskin with 'Modern Painters' and Newman with the 'Tracts for the Times.' Primarily the Pre-Raphaelite movement had its impulse in the Oxford religious revival; and however strange it may seem to say that such men as Holman Hunt and Rossetti . . . followed directly in the footsteps of Newman and Pusey and Keble, it is indubitably so." *   Ruskin, too, cautioned his young friends that "if their sympathies with the early artists lead them into mediævalism or Romanism, they will of course come to nothing. But I believe there is no danger of this, at least for the strongest among them. There may be some weak ones whom the Tractarian heresies may touch; but if so, they will drop off like decayed branches from a strong stem." †   One of these weak ones who dropped off was James Collinson, a man of an ascetic and mystical piety—like Werner or Brentano. He painted, among other things, "The Renunciation of St. Elizabeth" from Kingsley's "Saint's Tragedy." "The picture," writes Scott, "resembled the

*"Dante Gabriel Rossetti: a record and a study," London, 1882, pp. 40–41.
†"Pre-Raphaelitism," p. 23, *note*.

feckless dilettanteism of the converts who were then dropping out of their places in Oxford and Cambridge into Mariolatry and Jesuitism. In fact, this James Collinson actually did become Romanist, wanted to be a priest, painted no more, but entered a seminary, where they set him to clean the boots as an apprenticeship in humility and obedience. They did not want him as a priest; they were already getting tired of that species of convert; so he left, turned to painting again, and disappeared." *

M. de la Sizeranne is rather scornful of these metaphysical definitions of Pre-Raphaelitism; "for to characterise a Pre-Raphaelite picture by saying that it was inspired by the Oxford movement, is like attempting to explain the mechanism of a lock by describing the political opinions of the locksmith." † He himself proposes, as the distinguishing characteristics of Pre-Raphaelite art, originality of gesture and vividness of colouring. This is the professional point of view; but the student of literature is less concerned with such technical aspects of the subject than with those spiritual aspects which connect the work of the Pre-Raphaelites with the great mediæval or romantic revival.

When Ruskin came to the rescue of the P.-R. B. in 1851, in those letters to the *Times*, afterwards reprinted in pamphlet form under the title "Pre-Raphaelitism," he recognised the propriety of the name, and the real affinity between the new school and the early Italian schools of sacred art. Mediæval art, he asserted,‡ was

---

* "Autobiographical Notes of William Bell Scott," vol. i., p. 281.
† " English Contemporary Art," p. 58.
‡ " Lectures on Architecture and Painting," 1853.

religious and truthful; modern art is profane and insincere. "In mediæval art, thought is the first thing, execution is the second; in modern art, execution is the first thing and thought is the second. And again, in mediæval art, truth is first, beauty second; in modern art, beauty is first, truth second." Ruskin denied that the Pre-Raphaelites were unimaginative, though he allowed that they had a disgust for popular forms of grace and prettiness. And he pointed out a danger in the fact that their principles confined them to foreground work, and called for laborious finish on a small scale. In "Modern Painters" he complained that the Pre-Raphaelites should waste a whole summer in painting a bit of oak hedge or a bed of weeds by a duck pond, which caught their fancy perhaps by reminding them of a stanza in Tennyson. Nettles and mushrooms, he said, were good to make nettle soup and fish sauce; but it was too bad that the nobler aspects of nature, such as the banks of the castled Rhine, should be left to the frontispieces in the Annuals. Ruskin, furthermore, denied that the drawing of the Pre-Raphaelites was bad or their perspective false; or that they imitated the *errors* of the early Florentine painters, whom they greatly excelled in technical accomplishment. Meanwhile be it remarked that the originality of gesture in Pre-Raphaelite figure painting, which M. de la Sizeranne notices, was only one more manifestation of the romantic desire for individuality and concreteness as against the generalising academicism of the eighteenth century.[*]

As poets, the Pre-Raphaelites derive from Keats rather than from Scott, in their exclusive devotion to beauty, to

[*] See vol. i., p. 44.

art for art's sake; in their single absorption in the passion of love; and in their attraction towards the more esoteric side of mediæval life, rather than towards its broad, public, and military aspects.*

Rossetti's position in the romantic literature of the last half of the ninetenth century is something like Coleridge's in the first half. Unlike Coleridge, he was the leader of a school, the master of a definite group of artists and poets. His actual performance, too, far exceeds

* "The return of this school was to a mediævalism different from the tentative and scrappy mediævalism of Percy, from the genial but slightly superficial mediævalism of Scott, and even from the more exact but narrow and distinctly conventional mediævalism of Tennyson. . . . Moreover, though it may seem whimsical or extravagant to say so, these poets added to the very charm of mediæval literature, which they thus revived, a subtle something which differentiates it from —which, to our perhaps blind sight, seems to be wanting in —mediæval literature itself. It is constantly complained (and some of those who cannot go all the way with the complainants can see what they mean) that the graceful and labyrinthine stories, the sweet snatches of song, the quaint drama and legend of the Middle Ages lack—to us—life; that they are shadowy, unreal, tapestry on the wall, not alive even as living pageants are. By the strong touch of modernness which these poets and the best of their followers introduced into their work, they have given the vivification required" (Saintsbury, "Literature of the Nineteenth Century," p. 439). Pre-Raphaelitism "is a direct and legitimate development of the great romantic revival in England. . . . Even Tennyson, much more Scott and Coleridge and their generation, had entered only very partially into the treasures of mediæval literature, and were hardly at all acquainted with those of mediæval art. Conybeare, Kemble, Thorpe, Madden were only in Tennyson's own time reviving the study of Old and Middle English. Early French and Early Italian were but just being opened up. Above all, the Oxford Movement directed attention to mediæval architecture, literature, thought, as had never been the case before in England, and as has never been the case at all in any other country" ("A Short History of English Literature," by G. Saintsbury, London, 1898, p. 779).

Coleridge's in amount, if not in value. But like Coleridge, he was a seminal mind, a mind rich in original suggestions, which inspired and influenced younger men to carry out its ideas, often with a fluency of utterance and a technical dexterity both in art and letters which the master himself did not possess. Holman Hunt, Millais, and Burne-Jones among painters, Morris and Swinburne among poets, were disciples of Rossetti who in some ways outdid him in execution. His pictures were rarely exhibited, and no collection of his poems was published till 1870. Meanwhile, however, many of these had circulated in manuscript, and " secured a celebrity akin in kind and almost equal in extent to that enjoyed by Coleridge's ' Christabel ' during the many years preceding 1816 in which it lay in manuscript. Like Coleridge's poem in another important particular, certain of Rossetti's ballads, while still unknown to the public, so far influenced contemporary poetry that when they did at length appear, they had all the seeming to the uninitiated of work imitated from contemporary models, instead of being, as in fact they were, the primary source of inspiration for writers whose names were earlier established." * William Morris, *e.g.*, had printed four volumes of verse in advance of Rossetti; and the earliest of these, " The Defence of Guenevere," which contains his most intensely Pre-Raphaelite work and that most evidently done in the spirit of Rossetti's teachings, saw the light (1858) twelve years before Rossetti's own. Swinburne, too, had published three volumes of poetry before 1870, including the " Poems and Ballads " of

* "Recollections of Dante Gabriel Rossetti," by T. Hall Caine, London, 1882, p. 41.

1866, in which Rossetti's influence is plainly manifest; and he had already secured a wide fame at a time when the elder poet's reputation was still esoteric and mainly confined to the *cénacle*. William M. Rossetti, in describing the literary influences which moulded his brother's tastes, tells us that "in the long run he perhaps enjoyed and revered Coleridge beyond any other modern poet whatsoever." *

It is worth while to trace these literary influences with some detail, since they serve to link the neo-romantic poetry of our own time to the product of that older generation which had passed away before Rossetti came of age. It is interesting to find then, that at the age of fifteen (1843) he taught himself enough German to enable him to translate Bürger's "Lenore," as Walter Scott had done a half-century before. This devil of a poem so haunts our history that it has become as familiar a spirit as Mrs. Radcliffe's bugaboo apparitions, and our flesh refuses any longer to creep at it. It is quite one of the family. It would seem, indeed, as if Bürger's ballad was set as a school copy for every young romanticist in turn to try his 'prentice hand upon. Fortunately, Rossetti's translation has perished, as has also his version—some hundred lines—of the earlier portion of the "Nibelungenlied." But a translation which he made about the same time of the old Swabian poet, Hartmann von Aue's "Der Arme Heinrich" (Henry the Leper) is preserved, and was first published in 1886. This poem, it will be remembered, was the basis of Longfellow's "Golden Legend" (1851). Rossetti did

* "The Collected Works of Dante Gabriel Rossetti." Edited by W. M. Rossetti, two vols., London, 1886.

not keep up his German, and in later years he never had much liking for Scandinavian or Teutonic literature. He was a Latin, and he made it his special task to interpret to modern Protestant England whatever struck him as most spiritually intense and characteristic in the Latin Catholic Middle Age. The only Italian poet whom he " earnestly loved" was Dante. He did not greatly care for Petrarch, Boccaccio, Ariosto, and Tasso —the Renaissance poets—though in boyhood he had taken delight in Ariosto, just as he had in Scott and Byron. But that was a stage through which he passed; none of these had any ultimate share in Rossetti's culture. At fifteen he wrote a ballad entitled " Sir Hugh the Heron," founded on a tale of Allan Cunningham, but taking its name and motto from the lines in " Marmion "—

> "Sir Hugh the Heron bold,
> Baron of Twisell and of Ford,
> And Captain of the Hold."

A few copies of this were printed for family circulation by his fond grandfather, G. Polidori. Among French writers he had no modern favourites beyond Hugo, Musset, and Dumas. But like all the neo-romanticists, he was strongly attracted by François Villon, that strange Parisian poet, thief, and murderer of the fifteenth century. He made three translations from Villon, the best known of which is the famous " Ballad of Dead Ladies " with its felicitous rendering of the refrain—

> " But where are the snows of yester year? "
> (Mais où sont les neiges d'antan?)

There are at least three good English verse renderings of this ballad of Villon; one by Andrew Lang; one by

John Payne, and doubtless innumerable others, unknown
to me or forgotten. In fact, every one translates it nowadays, as every one used to translate Bürger's ballad.
It is the "Lenore" of the neo-romanticists. Rossetti
was a most accomplished translator, and his version of
Dante's "Vita Nuova" and of the "Early Italian Poets"
(1861)—reissued as "Dante and His Circle" (1874)—is
a notable example of his skill. There are two other
specimens of old French minstrelsy, and two songs from
Victor Hugo's "Burgraves" among his miscellaneous
translations; and William Sharp testifies that Rossetti
at one time thought of doing for the early poetry of
France what he had already done for that of Italy, but
never found the leisure for it.* Rossetti had no knowledge of Greek, and "the only classical poet," says his
brother, "whom he took to in any degree worth speaking
of was Homer, the 'Odyssey' considerably more than
the 'Iliad.'" This, I presume, he knew only in translation, but the preference is significant, since, as we have
seen, the "Odyssey" is the most romantic of epics.
Among English poets, he preferred Keats to Shelley, as
might have been expected. Shelley was a visionary and
Keats was an artist; Shelley often abstract, Keats always
concrete. Shelley had a philosophy, or thought he had;
Keats had none, neither had Rossetti. It is quite com-
prehensible that the sensuous element in Keats would
attract a born colourist like Rossetti beyond anything
in the English poetry of that generation; and I need not
repeat that the latest Gothic or romantic schools have all
been taking Keats' direction rather than Scott's, or even
than Coleridge's. Rossetti's work, I should say, *e.g.*,

* "Dante Gabriel Rossetti. A Record and a Study," p. 305.

in such a piece as " The Bride's Prelude," is a good deal
more like "Isabella" and "The Eve of St. Agnes" than
it is like "The Ancient Mariner" or "Christabel" or
"The Lay of the Last Minstrel." Rossetti got little
from Milton and Dryden, or even from Chaucer and
Spenser. Wordsworth he valued hardly at all. In the
last two or three years of his life he came to have an
exaggerated admiration for Chatterton. Rossetti's taste,
like his temperament, was tinctured with morbidness.
He sought the intense, the individual, the symbolic, the
mystical. These qualities he found in a supreme degree
in Dante. Probably it was only his austere artistic conscience which saved him from the fantastic—the merely
peculiar or odd—and kept him from going astray after
false gods like Poe and Baudelaire. Chaucer was a
mediæval poet and Spenser certainly a romantic one, but
their work was too broad, too general in its appeal, too
healthy, one might almost say, to come home to Rossetti.* William Rossetti testifies that " any writing

* He wrote to Allingham in 1855, apropos of the latter's
poem "The Music Master": "I'm not sure that it is not too
noble or too resolutely healthy. . . . I must confess to a need
in narrative dramatic poetry . . . of something rather 'exciting,' and indeed, I believe, something of the 'romantic' element, to rouse my mind to anything like the moods produced
by personal emotion in my own life. That sentence is shock-
ingly ill worded, but Keats' narratives would be of the kind I
mean." Theodore Watts ("Encyclopædia Britannica," article "Rossetti") says that "the purely romantic temper was
with Rossetti a more permanent and even a more natural temper than with any other nineteenth-century poet, even including the author of 'Christabel' himself." He thinks that all the
French romanticists together do not equal the romantic feeling in a single picture of Rossetti's; and he somewhat capri-
ciously defines the idea at the core of romanticism as that of
the evil forces of nature assailing man through his sense of
beauty. Analysis run mad! As to Poe, Rossetti certainly

about devils, spectres, or the supernatural generally . . . had always a fascination for him." Sharp remarks that work more opposite than Rossetti's to the Greek spirit can hardly be imagined. "The former [the Greek spirit] looked to light, clearness, form in painting, sculpture, architecture; to intellectual conciseness and definiteness in poetry; the latter [Rossetti] looked mainly to diffused colour, gradated to almost indefinite shades in his art, finding the harmonies thereof more akin than severity of outline and clearness of form; while in his poetry the Gothic love of the supernatural, the Gothic delight in sensuous images, the Gothic instinct of indefiniteness and elaboration, carried to an extreme, prevailed. . . . He would take more pleasure in a design by . . . William Blake . . . than in the more strictly artistic drawing of some revered classicist; more enjoyment in the weird or dramatic Scottish ballad than in Pindaric or Horatian ode; and he would certainly rather have had Shakspere than Æschylus, Sophocles, and Euripides put together."

Rossetti's office in the later and further development of romantic art was threefold: First, to revive and express, both in painting and poetry, the religious spirit of the early Florentine schools; secondly, to give a more intimate interpretation of Dante to the English public, and especially of Dante's life and personality and of his

preferred him to Wordsworth. Hall Caine testifies that he used to repeat "Ulalume" and "The Raven" from memory; and that the latter suggested his "Blessed Damozel." "I saw that Poe had done the utmost it was possible to do with the grief of the lover on earth, and so I determined to reverse the conditions, and give utterance to the yearning of the loved one in heaven" ("Recollections," p. 284).

minor poetry, like the " Vita Nuova," which had not yet
been translated; thirdly, to afford new illustrations of
mediæval life and thought, partly by treating legendary
matter in the popular ballad form, and partly by treating
romantic matter of his own invention with the rich colour
and sensuous imagery which belonged to his pictorial
art.

"Perhaps," writes Mr. Caine,* "Catholicism is itself
essentially mediæval, and perhaps a man cannot possibly
be a 'mediæval artist, heart and soul,' without partaking
of a strong religious feeling that is primarily Catholic—
so much were the religion and art of the Middle Ages
knit each to each. . . . Rossetti's attitude towards spiritual things was exactly the reverse of what we call Protestant. . . . He constantly impressed me during the last
days of his life with the conviction that he was by religious bias of nature a monk of the Middle Ages." All
this is true in a way, yet Rossetti strikes one as being
Catholic, without being religious; as mediæval rather
than Christian. He was agnostic in his belief and not
devout in his practice; so that the wish that he suddenly
expressed in his last illness, to confess himself to a
priest, affected his friends as a singular caprice. It was
the *romantic* quality in the Italian sacred art of the Middle Ages that attracted him; and it attracted him as a
poet and painter, not as a devotee. There was little in
Rossetti of the mystical and ascetic piety of Novalis or
Zacharias Werner; nor of the steady religious devotion
of his friend Holman Hunt, or his own sister Christina.

Rossetti, by the way, was never in Italy, though he made
several visits to France and Belgium. A glance at the

* "Recollections," p. 140.

list of his designs—extending to some four hundred titles—in oil, water-colour, crayon, pen and ink, etc., will show how impartially his interest was distributed over the threefold province mentioned above. There are sacred pieces like "Mary Magdalen at the Door of Simon the Pharisee," "St. Cecily," a "Head of Christ," a "Triptych for Llandaff Cathedral"; Dante subjects such as "Paolo and Francesca," "Beata Beatrix," "La Donna della Finestra," "Giotto Painting the Portrait of Dante"; and, in greater number, compositions of a purely romantic nature—"Fair Rosamond," "La Belle Dame sans Merci," "The Chapel before the Lists," "Michael Scott's Wooing," "Meeting of Sir Tristram and Yseult," "Lady Lilith," "The Damozel of the Sanct Grail," "Death of Breuse sans Pitié," and the like.

It will be noticed that some of these subjects are taken from the Round Table romances. Tennyson was partly responsible for the newly awakened interest in the Arthurian legend, but the purely romantic manner which he had abandoned in advancing from "Sir Galahad" and "The Lady of Shalott" to the "Morte d'Arthur" of 1842 and the first "Idylls" of 1859, continued to characterise the work of the Pre-Raphaelites both in poetry and in painting. Malory's "Morte Darthur" was one of Rossetti's favourite books, and he preferred it to Tennyson, as containing "the *weird* element in its perfection. . . . Tennyson *has* it certainly here and there in imagery, but there is no great success in the part it plays through his 'Idylls.'" * The five wood-engravings from designs furnished by Rossetti for the Moxon Tennyson quarto of 1857 include three Arthurian subjects: "The Lady of

* Caine's "Recollections," p. 266.

Shalott," " King Arthur Sleeping in Avalon," and " Sir
Galahad Praying in the Wood-Chapel." " Interwoven
as were the Romantic revival and the æsthetic movement," writes Mr. Sharp, " it could hardly have been
otherwise but that the young painter-poet should be
strongly attracted to that Arthurian epoch, the legendary
glamour of which has since made itself so widely felt in
the Arthurian idyls of the laureate. . . . Mr. Ruskin
speaks, in his lecture on ' The Relation of Art to Religion ' delivered in Oxford, of our indebtedness to Rossetti as the painter to whose genius we owe the revival
of interest in the cycle of early English legend."

It was in 1857 that Rossetti, whose acquaintance had
been recently sought by three young Oxford scholars,
Edward Burne-Jones, William Morris, and Algernon
Charles Swinburne, volunteered to surround the gallery of
the new Union Club House at Oxford with life-size frescoes from the " Morte Darthur." * He was assisted in
this work by a number of enthusiastic disciples. Burne-
Jones had already done some cartoons in colour for
stained glass, and Morris had painted a subject from the
" Morte Darthur," to wit: " Sir Tristram after his Illness, in the Garden of King Mark's Palace, recognised
by the Dog he had given to Iseult." Rossetti's contribution to the Oxford decorations was " Sir Lancelot
before the Shrine of the Sangreal." Morris' was " Sir
Palomides' Jealousy of Sir Tristram and Iseult," an inci-

* Burne-Jones had been attracted by Rossetti's illustration
of Allingham's poem, " The Maids of Elfinmere," and had
obtained an introduction to him at London in 1856. It was
by Rossetti's persuasion that he gave up the church for the
career of an artist. Rossetti and Swinburne some years later
(1862) became housemates for a time at Chelsea ; and Rossetti
and Morris for a number of years, off and on, at Kelmscott.

dent which he also treated in his poetry. Burne-Jones, Valentine Prinsep, J. H. Pollen, and Arthur Hughes likewise contributed. Scott says that these paintings were interesting as designs; that they were "poems more than pictures, being large illuminations and treated in a mediæval manner." But he adds that not one of the band knew anything about wall painting. They laid their water-colours, not on a plastered surface, but on a rough brick wall, merely whitewashed. They used no adhesive medium, and in a few months the colours peeled off and the whole series became invisible.

A co-partnership in subjects, a duplication of treatment, or interchange between the arts of poetry and painting characterise Pre-Raphaelite work. For example, Morris' poems, "The Blue Closet" and "The Tune of Seven Towers" were inspired by the similarly entitled designs of Rossetti. They are interpretations in language of pictorial suggestions—"word-paintings" in a truer meaning than that much-abused piece of critical slang commonly bears. In one of these compositions—a water-colour, a study in colour and music symbolism— four damozels in black and purple, white and green, scarlet and white, and crimson, are singing or playing on a lute and clavichord in a blue-tiled room; while in front of them a red lily grows up through the floor. To this interior Morris' "stunning picture"—as his friend called it—adds an obscurely hinted love story: the burden of a bell booming a death-knell in the tower overhead; the sound of wind and sea; and the Christmas snows outside. Conversely Rossetti's painting, "Arthur's Tomb," was suggested by Morris' so-named poem in his 1858 volume.

Or, again, compare Morris' poem, "Sir Galahad: A
Christmas Mystery," with the following description of
Rossetti's aquarelle, "How Sir Galahad, Sir Bors, and
Sir Percival were fed with the Sanc Grael; but Sir Percival's sister died by the way": "On the right is painted
the altar, and in front of it the damsel of the Sanc Grael
giving the cup to Sir Galahad, who stoops forward to
take it over the dead body of Sir Percival's sister, who
lies calm and rigid in her green robe and red mantle, and
near whose feet grows from the ground an aureoled lily;
while, with his left hand, the saintly knight leads forward his two companions, him who has lost his sister, and
the good Sir Bors. Behind the white-robed damsel at
the altar, a dove, bearing the sacred casket, poises on
outspread pinions; and immediately beyond the fence
enclosing the sacred space, stands a row of nimbused
angels, clothed in white and with crossed scarlet or flame-
coloured wings." *

Rossetti's powerful ballad, "The King's Tragedy,"
was suggested by the mural paintings (encaustic) with
which William Bell Scott decorated the circular staircase
of Penkill Castle in 1865–68. These were a series of
scenes from "The Kinges Quair" once attributed to
James I. of Scotland. The photogravure reproduction,
from a painting by Arthur Hughes of a section of the
Penkill Castle staircase, represents the king looking
from the window of his prison in Windsor Castle at Lady
Jane Beaufort walking with her handmaidens in a very
Pre-Raphaelite garden. At the left of the picture, Cupid
aims an arrow at the royal lover. Rossetti, Hunt, and
Millais were all great lovers of Keats. Hunt says that

* Sharp's "Dante Gabriel Rossetti," p. 190.

his "Escape of Madeline and Prospero" was the first subject from Keats ever painted, and was highly acclaimed by Rossetti. At the formation of the P.-R B. in 1848, it was agreed that the first work of the Brotherhood should be in illustration of "Isabella," and a series of eight subjects was selected from the poem. Millais executed at once his "Lorenzo and Isabella," but Hunt's "Isabella and the Pot of Basil" was not finished till 1867, and Rossetti's part of the programme was never carried out. Rossetti's "La Belle Dame sans Merci," Mr. J. M. Strudwick's "Madness of Isabella," Arthur Hughes' triptych of "The Eve of St. Agnes," and Millais' great painting, "St. Agnes' Eve," were other tributes of Pre-Raphaelite art to the young master of romantic verse.

Whether this interpenetration of poetry and painting is of advantage to either, may admit of question. Emerson said to Scott: "We [Americans] scarcely take to the Rossetti poetry; it does not come home to us; it is exotic." The sonnets of "The House of Life" have appeared to many readers obscure and artificial, the working out in language of conceptions more easily expressible by some other art; expressed here, at all events, through imagery drawn from a special and even technical range of associations. Such readers are apt to imagine that Rossetti suffers from a hesitation between poetry and painting; as Sidney Lanier is thought by some to have been injured artistically by halting midway between music and verse. The method proper to one art intrudes into the other; everything that the artist does has the air of an experiment; he paints poems and writes pictures.

A department of Rossetti's verse consists of sonnets

written for pictures; pictures by Botticelli, Mantegna, Giorgione, Burne-Jones, and others, and in many cases by himself, and giving thus a double rendering of the same invention. But even when not so occasioned, his poems nearly always suggest pictures. Their figures seem to have stepped down from some fifteenth-century altar piece bringing their aureoles and golden backgrounds with them. This is to be pictorial in a very different sense from that in which Tennyson is said to be a pictorial poet. Hall Caine informs us that Rossetti "was no great lover of landscape beauty." His scenery does not, like Wordsworth's or Tennyson's, carry an impression of life, of the real outdoors. Nature with Rossetti has been passed through the medium of another art before it comes into his poetry; it is a doubly distilled nature. It is nature as we have it in the "Roman de la Rose," or the backgrounds of old Florentine painters: flowery pleasances and orchard closes, gardens with trellises and singing conduits, where ladies are playing at the palm play. In his most popular poem, "The Blessed Damozel"—a theme which he both painted and sang—the feeling is exquisitely and veraciously human. The maiden is "homesick in heaven," and yearns back towards the earth and her lover left behind. Even so, with her symbolic stars and lilies, she is so like the stiff, sweet angels of Fra Angelico or Perugino, that one almost doubts when the poet says

> "—her bosom must have made
> The bar she leaned on warm."

The imagery of the poem is right out of the picture world:

> "The clear ranged, unnumbered heads
> Bowed with their aureoles."

The imaginations are Dantesque:

> "And the souls, mounting up to God,
> Went by her like thin flames."

> "The light thrilled towards her, filled
> With angels in strong, level flight."

Even in "Jenny," one of the few poems of Rossetti that deal with modern life, mediæval art will creep in.

> "Fair shines the gilded aureole
> In which our highest painters place
> Some living woman's simple face.
> And the stilled features thus descried,
> As Jenny's long throat droops aside—
> The shadows where the cheeks are thin
> And pure wide curve from ear to chin—
> With Raffael's, Leonardo's hand
> To show them to men's souls might stand."

The type of womanly beauty here described is characteristic; it is the type familiar to all in "Pandora," "Proserpine," "La Ghirlandata," "The Day Dream," "Our Lady of Pity," and the other life-size, half-length figure paintings in oil which were the masterpieces of his maturer style. The languid pose, the tragic eyes with their mystic, brooding intensity in contrast with the full curves of the lips and throat, give that union of sensuousness and spirituality which is a constant trait of Rossetti's poetry. The Pre-Raphaelites were accused of exaggerating the height of their figures. In Burne-Jones, whose figures are eight and a half heads high, the exaggeration is deliberate. In Morris' and Swinburne's early poems all the lines of the female face and figure are long—the hand, the foot, the throat, the "curve from chin to ear," and above all, the hair.* The hair in these paintings of

* See especially Morris' poem "Rapunzel" in "The Defence of Guenevere."

Rossetti seems a romantic exaggeration, too; immense, crinkly waves of it spreading off to left and right. William Morris' beautiful wife is said to have been his model in the pieces above named.

The first collection of original poems by Rossetti was published in 1870. The manuscripts had been buried with his wife in 1862. When he finally consented to their publication, the coffin had to be exhumed and the manuscripts removed. In 1881 a new edition was issued with changes and additions; and in the same year the volume of "Ballads and Sonnets" was published, including the sonnet sequence of "The House of Life." Of the poems in these two collections which treat directly of Dante the most important is "Dante at Verona," a noble and sustained piece in eighty-five stanzas, slightly pragmatic in manner, in which are enwoven the legendary and historical incidents of Dante's exile related by the early biographers, together with many personal allusions from the "Divine Comedy." But Dante is nowhere very far off either in Rossetti's painting or in his poetry. In particular, the history of Dante's passion for Beatrice, as told in the "Vita Nuova," in which the figure of the girl is gradually transfigured and idealised by death into the type of heavenly love, made an enduring impression upon Rossetti's imagination. Shelley, in his "Epipsychidion," had appealed to this great love story, so characteristic at once of the mediæval mysticism and of the Platonic spirit of the early Renaissance. But Rossetti was the first to give a thoroughly sympathetic interpretation of it to English readers. It became associated most intimately with his own love and loss. We see it in a picture like "Beata Beatrix," and a poem like

"The Portrait," written many years before his wife's death, but subsequently retouched. Who can read the following stanza without thinking of Beatrice and the "Paradiso"?

> "Even so, where Heaven holds breath and hears
>   The beating heart of Love's own breast,—
> Where round the secret of all spheres
>   All angels lay their wings to rest,—
> How shall my soul stand rapt and awed,
>   When, by the new birth borne abroad
> Throughout the music of the suns,
>   It enters in her soul at once
>   And knows the silence there for God!"

Rossetti's ballads and ballad-romances, all intensely mediæval in spirit, fall, as regards their manner, into two very different classes. Pieces like "The Blessed Damozel," "The Bride's Prelude," "Rose Mary," and "The Staff and Scrip" (from a story in the "Gesta Romanorum") are art poems, rich, condensed, laden with ornament, pictorial. Every attitude of every figure is a pose; landscapes and interiors are painted with minute Pre-Raphaelite finish. "The Bride's Prelude"—a fragment—opens with the bride's confession to her sister, in the 'tiring-room sumptuous with gold and jewels and brocade, where the air is heavy with musk and myrrh, and sultry with the noon. In the pauses of her tale stray lute notes creep in at the casement, with noises from the tennis court and the splash of a hound swimming in the moat. In "Rose Mary," which employs the superstition in the old lapidaries as to the prophetic powers of the beryl-stone, the colouring and imagery are equally opulent, and, in passages, Oriental.

On the other hand, "Stratton Water," "Sister Helen," "The White Ship," and "The King's Tragedy" are imi-

tations of popular poetry, done with a simulated roughness and simplicity.   The first of these adopts a common
ballad motive, a lover's desertion of his sweetheart
through the contrivances of his wicked kinsfolk·

> "And many's the good gift, Lord Sands,
>   You've promised oft to me ;
> But the gift of yours I keep to-day
>   Is the babe in my body." . . .

> "Look down, look down, my false mother,
>   That bade me not to grieve :
> You'll look up when our marriage fires
>   Are lit to-morrow eve."

"Sister Helen" is a ballad in dialogue with a subtly
varying repetend, and introduces the popular belief that
a witch could kill a man slowly by melting a wax figure.
Twice Rossetti essayed the historical ballad.   "The
White Ship" tells of the drowning of the son and daughter of Henry I. with their whole ship's company, except
one survivor, Berold, the butcher of Rouen, who relates
the catastrophe.   The subject of "The King's Tragedy"
is the murder of James I. by Robert Graeme and his men
in the Charterhouse of Perth.   The teller of the tale is
Catherine Douglas, known in Scottish tradition as Kate
Barlass, who had thrust her arm through the staple, in
place of a bar, to hold the door against the assassins.
A few stanzas of "The Kinges Quair" are fitted into the
poem by shortening the lines two syllables each, to ac-
commodate them to the ballad metre.   It is generally
agreed that this was a mistake, as was also the introduction of the "Beryl Songs" between the narrative parts of
"Rose Mary."   These ballads of Rossetti compare well
with other modern imitations of popular poetry.   "Sister
Helen," *e.g.*, has much greater dramatic force than Ten-

nyson's "Oriana" or "The Sisters." Yet they impress
one, upon the whole, as less characteristic than the poet's
Italianate pieces; as *tours de force* carefully pitched in
the key of minstrel song, but falsetto in effect. Compared with such things as "Cadyow Castle" or "Jack
o' Hazeldean," they are felt to be the work of an art
poet, resolute to divest himself of fine language and
scrupulously observant of ballad convention in phrase
and accent—details of which Scott was often heedless—
but devoid of that hearty, natural sympathy with the conditions of life from which popular poetry sprang, and
wanting the lyrical pulse that beats in the ballad verse
of Scott, Kingsley, and Hogg. In "The King's Tragedy" Rossetti was poaching on Scott's own preserves,
the territory of national history and legend. If we can
guess how Scott would have handled the same story, we
shall have an object lesson in two contrasted kinds of
romanticism. Scott could not have bettered the grim
ferocity of the murder scene, nor have equalled, perhaps,
the tragic shadow of doom which is thrown over Rossetti's poem by the triple warning of the weird woman.
But the sense of the historic environment, the sense of
the actual in places and persons, would have been stronger
in his version. Graeme's retreat would have been the
Perthshire Highlands, and not vaguely "the land of the
wild Scots." And if scenery had been used, it would
not have been such as this—a Pre-Raphaelite background:

> "That eve was clenched for a boding storm,
>   'Neath a toilsome moon half seen;
> The cloud stooped low and the surf rose high;
> And where there was a line of the sky,
>   Wild wings loomed dark between."

The historical sense was weak in Rossetti. It is not easy to imagine him composing a Waverley novel. The life of the community, as distinct from the life of the individual, had little interest for him. The mellifluous names of his heroines, Aloyse, Rose Mary, Blanchelys, are pure romance. In his intense concentration upon the æsthetic aspects of every subject, Rossetti seemed, to those who came in contact with him, singularly *borné*. He was indifferent to politics, society, speculative thought, and the discoveries of modern science—to contemporary matters in general.* It is to this narrow æstheticism that Mr. Courthope refers when, in comparing Coleridge and Keats with Rossetti and Swinburne, he finds in the latter an "extraordinary skill in the imitation of antique forms," but "less liberty of imagination." † The contrast is most striking in the case of Coleridge, whose intellectual interests had so wide a range. Rossetti cared only for Coleridge's verse; William Morris spoke with contempt of everything that he had written except two or three of his poems; ‡ and Swinburne re-

---

*"I can't say," wrote William Morris, "how it was that Rossetti took no interest in politics; but so it was: of course he was quite Italian in his general turn of thought; though I think he took less interest in Italian politics than in English. . . . The truth is, he cared for nothing but individual and personal matters; chiefly of course in relation to art and literature."

†"The Liberal Movement in English Literature," by W. J. Courthope, London, 1885, p. 230.

‡"Keats was a great poet who sometimes nodded. . . . Coleridge was a muddle-brained metaphysician who, by some strange freak of fortune, turned out a few real poems amongst the dreary flood of inanity which was his wont. . . . I have been through the poems, and find that the only ones which have any interest for me are: (1) 'Ancient Mariner'; (2) 'Christabel'; (3) 'Kubla Khan'; and (4) the poem called 'Love'" (Mackail's "Life of Morris," vol. ii., p. 310).

gretted that he had lost himself in the mazes of theology and philosophy, instead of devoting himself wholly to creative work. Keats, it is true, was exclusively pre-occupied with the beautiful; but he was more eclectic than Rossetti—perhaps also than Morris, though hardly than Swinburne. The world of classic fable, the world of outward nature were as dear to his imagination as the country of romance. Rossetti was not university bred, and, as we have seen, forgot his Greek early. Morris, like Swinburne, was an Oxford man; yet we hear him saying that he "loathes all classical art and literature." * In "The Life and Death of Jason" and "The Earthly Paradise" he treats classical and mediæval subjects impartially, but treats them both alike in mediæval fashion; as Chaucer does, in "The Knightes Tale." † As for Rossetti, he is never classical. He makes Pre-Raphaelite ballads out of the tale of Troy divine and the Rabbinical legends of Adam's first wife, Lilith; ballads with quaint burdens—

> " (O Troy's down,
>   Tall Troy's on fire)";
>
> " (Sing Eden Bower!
>   Alas the hour!)"

and whose very titles have an Old English familiarity— "Eden Bower," "Troy Town," as who says "London Bridge," "Edinboro' Town," etc. Swinburne has given the *rationale* of this type of art in his description of a Bacchus and Ariadne by Lippino Lippi ("Old Masters

* "The Life of William Morris," by W. J. Mackail, London, 1899, vol. ii., p. 171.
† For the Chaucerian manipulation of classical subjects by Pre-Raphaelite artists see "Edward Burne-Jones," by Malcolm Bell, London, 1899.

at Florence "), "an older legend translated and transformed into mediæval shape. More than any others,
these painters of the early Florentine school reproduce
in their own art the style of thought and work familiar
to a student of Chaucer and his fellows or pupils.
Nymphs have faded into fairies, and gods subsided into
men. A curious realism has grown up out of that very
ignorance and perversion which seemed as if it could not
but falsify whatever thing it touched upon. This study
of Fillippino's has all the singular charm of the romantic
school. . . . The clear form has gone, the old beauty
dropped out of sight . . . but the mediæval or romantic
form has an incommunicable charm of its own. . . . Before Chaucer could give us a Pandarus or a Cressida, all
knowledge and memory of the son of Lycaon and the
daughter of Chryses must have died out, the whole poem
collapsed into romance; but far as these may be removed
from the true tale and the true city of Troy, they are not
phantoms."

But of all this group, the one most thoroughly steeped
in mediævalism—to repeat his own description of himself—was William Morris. He was the English equivalent of Gautier's *homme moyen âge;* and it was his endeavour, in letters and art, to pick up and continue the
mediæval tradition, interrupted by four hundred years of
modern civilisation. The sixteenth and seventeenth
centuries did not attract him; and as for the eighteenth,
it simply did not exist for him.* The ugliness of mod-

* "The slough of despond which we call the eighteenth century" ("Hopes and Fears for Art," p. 211). "The English
language, which under the hands of sycophantic verse-makers
had been reduced to a miserable jargon . . . flowed clear,
pure, and simple along with the music of Blake and Coleridge.

ern life, with its factories and railroads, its unpicturesque
poverty and selfish commercialism, was hateful to him as
it was to Ruskin—his teacher. He loved to imagine the
face of England as it was in the time of Chaucer—his
master; to

> "Forget six counties overhung with smoke,
> Forget the snorting steam and piston smoke, . . .
> And dream of London, small and white and clean,
> The clear Thames bordered by its gardens green."

The socialistic Utopia depicted in his "News from Nowhere" (1890) is a regenerated Middle Age, without
feudalism, monarchy, and the mediæval Church, but also
without densely populated cities, with handicrafts substituted for manufactures, and with mediæval architecture,
house decoration, and costume. None of Morris' books
deals with modern life, but all of them with an imaginary future or an almost equally imaginary past. This
same "News from Nowhere" contains a passage of dialogue in justification of retrospective romance. "'How
is it that though we are so interested with our life for the
most part, yet when people take to writing poems or
painting pictures they seldom deal with our modern life,
or if they do, take good care to make their poems or pictures unlike that life? Are we not good enough to paint
ourselves?' . . . 'It always was so, and I suppose always will be,' said he, 'however, it may be explained.
It is true that in the nineteenth century, when there was
so little art and so much talk about it, there was a theory
that art and imaginative literature ought to deal with

Take those names, the earliest in date among ourselves, as a
type of the change that has happened in literature since the
time of George II." (*ibid.*, p. 82).

contemporary life; but they never did so; for, if there was any pretence of it, the author always took care . . . to disguise, or exaggerate, or idealise, and in some way or another make it strange; so that, for all the verisimilitude there was, he might just as well have dealt with the times of the Pharaohs.'" *

The difference between the mediævalism of Rossetti and of Morris illustrates, in an interesting way, the varied results produced by the operation of similar influences on contrasted temperaments. The comparison which Morris' biographer makes between him and Burne-Jones holds true as between Morris and Rossetti: "They received or re-incarnated the Middle Ages through the eyes and brain, in the one case of a Norman, in the other of a Florentine." Morris was twice a Norman, in his love for the romancers and Gothic builders of northern France; and in his enthusiasm for the Icelandic sagas. His visits to Italy left him cold, and he confessed to a strong preference for the art of the North. "With the later work of Southern Europe I am quite out of sympathy. In spite of its magnificent power and energy, I feel it as an enemy; and this much more in Italy, where there is such a mass of it, than elsewhere. Yes, and even in these magnificent and wonderful towns I long rather for the heap of gray stones with a gray roof that we call a house north-away." Rossetti's Italian subtlety and mysticism are replaced in Morris by an English homeliness —a materialism which is Teutonic and not Latin or Celtic, and one surface indication of which is the scrupulously Saxon vocabulary of his poems and prose romances. "His earliest enthusiasms," said Burne-Jones,

* Page 113.

"were his latest. The thirteenth century was his ideal period always"—the century which produced the lovely French romances which he translated and the great French cathedrals which he admired above all other architecture on earth. But this admiration was æsthetic rather than religious. The Catholic note, so resonant in Rossetti's poetry, is hardly audible in Morris, at least after his early Oxford days. The influence of Newman still lingered at Oxford in the fifties, though the Tractarian movement had spent its force and a reaction had set in. Morris came up to the university an Anglo-Catholic, and like his fellow-student and life-long friend, Burne-Jones, had been destined to holy orders. We find them both, as undergraduates, eagerly reading the "Acta Sanctorum," the "Tracts for the Times," and Kenelm Digby's "Mores Catholici," and projecting a kind of monastic community, where celibacy should be practised and sacred art cultivated. But later impressions soon crowded out this early religious fervour. Churchly asceticism and the mediæval "praise of virginity" made no part of Morris' social ideal. The body counted for much with him. In "News from Nowhere," marriage even is so far from being a sacrament, that it is merely a free arrangement terminable at the will of either party. Morris had a passionate love of earth and a regard for the natural instincts. He complains that Swinburne's poetry is "founded on literature, not on nature." His religion is a reversion to the old Teutonic pagan earth-worship, and he had the pagan dread of "quick-coming death." His paradise is an "Earthly Paradise"; it is in search of earthly immortality that his voyagers set sail. "Of heaven or hell," says his prelude, "I have no power

to sing"; and the great mediæval singer of heaven and
hell who meant so much to Rossetti, appealed hardly
more to Morris than to Walter Scott.

Moreover, Morris' work in verse was the precise equivalent of his work as a decorative artist, who cared little
for easel pictures, and regarded painting as one method
out of many for covering wall spaces or other surfaces.*
His poetry is mainly narrative, but whether epical or
lyrical in form, is always less lyric in essence than Rossetti's.   In its objective spirit and even distribution of
emphasis, it contrasts with Rossetti's expressional intensity very much as Morris' wall-paper and tapestry designs contrast with paintings like "Beata Beatrix" and
"Proserpina."   Morris—as an artist—cared more for
places and things than for people; and his interest was
in the work of art itself, not in the personality of the
artist.

Quite unlike as was Morris to Scott in temper and
mental endowment, his position in the romantic literature of the second half-century answers very closely to
Scott's in the first.   His work resembled Scott's in volume, and in its easiness for the general reader.   For the
second time he made the Middle Ages *popular*.   There
was nothing esoteric in his art, as in Rossetti's.   It was

* "Sir Edward Burne-Jones told me that Morris would have
liked the faces in his pictures less highly finished, and less
charged with the concentrated meaning or emotion of the
painting . . . and he thought that the dramatic and emotional interest of a picture ought to be diffused throughout it
as equally as possible.   Such, too, was his own practice in the
cognate art of poetry ; and this is one reason why his poetry
affords so few memorable single lines, and lends itself so little
to quotation" (Mackail's "Life of William Morris," vol. ii.,
p. 272).

English and came home to Englishmen. His poetry, like his decorative work, was meant for the people, and "understanded of the people." Moreover, like Scott, he was an accomplished *raconteur*, and a story well told is always sure of an audience. His first volume, "The Defence of Guenevere" (1858), dedicated to Rossetti and inspired by him, had little popular success. But when, like Millais, he abandoned the narrowly Pre-Raphaelite manner and broadened out, in "The Life and Death of Jason" (1867) and "The Earthly Paradise" (1868–70), into a fashion of narrative less caviare to the general, the public response was such as met Millais.

Morris' share in the Pre-Raphaelite movement was in the special field of decorative art. His enthusiasm for Gothic architecture had been aroused at Oxford by a reading of Ruskin's chapter on "The Nature of Gothic" in "The Stones of Venice." In 1856, acting upon this impulse, he articled himself to the Oxford architect G. E. Street, and began work in his office. He did not persevere in the practice of the profession, and never built a house. But he became and remained a *connois-seur* of Gothic architecture and an active member of the Society for the Protection of Ancient Buildings. His numerous visits to Amiens, Chartres, Reims, Soissons, and Rouen were so many pilgrimages to the shrines of mediæval art. Indeed, he always regarded the various branches of house decoration as contributory to the master art, architecture.

A little later, under the dominating and somewhat overbearing persuasions of Rossetti, he tried his hand at painting, but never succeeded well in drawing the human face and figure. The figure designs for his stained glass, tapestries, etc., were usually made by Burne-Jones, Morris furnishing floriated patterns and the like. In 1861 was formed the firm of Morris & Company, which revolutionised English household decoration. Rossetti and Burne-Jones were among the partners in this concern, which undertook to supply the public with high art work in wall painting, paper hangings, embroidery, carpets, tapestries, printed cottons, stamped leather, carved furniture, tiles, metals, jewelry, etc. In particular, Morris revived the mediæval arts of glass-staining, illumination, or miniature painting, and tapestry-weaving with the high-warp loom. Though he chose to describe himself as a "dreamer of dreams born out of my due time," and "the idle singer of an empty day," he was a tireless practical workman of astonishing cleverness and versatility. He taught himself to dye and weave. When, in the last decade of the century, he set up the famous Kelmscott Press, devoted to artistic printing and book-making, he studied the processes of type-casting and paper manufacture, and actually made a number of sheets of paper with his own hands. It was his favourite idea that the division of labour in modern manufactures had degraded the workman by making him a mere machine; that the divorce between the art of the designer and the art of the handicraftsman was fatal to both. To him the Middle Ages meant, not the ages of faith, or of chivalry, or of bold and free adventure, but of popular art—of "The Lesser Arts"; when every artisan was an artist of the beautiful and took pleasure in the thing which his hand shaped; when not only the cathedral and the castle, but the townsman's dwelling-house and the labourer's cottage was a thing of beauty. He believed that in

those times there was, as there should be again, an art
by the people and for the people. It was the democratic
and not the aristocratic elements of mediæval life that
he praised. "From the first dawn of history till quite
modern times, art, which nature meant to solace all, fulfilled its purpose; all men shared in it; that was what
made life romantic, as people call it, in those days; that
and not robber-barons and inaccessible kings with their
hierarchy of serving-nobles and other such rubbish." *
One more passage will serve to set in sharp contrast the
romanticism of Scott and the romanticism of Ruskin and
Morris. "With that literature in which romance, that is
to say humanity, was re-born, there sprang up also a feeling for the romance of external nature, which is surely
strong in us now, joined with a longing to know something real of the lives of those who have gone before us;
of these feelings united you will find the broadest expression in the pages of Walter Scott; it is curious, as
showing how sometimes one art will lag behind another
in a revival, that the man who wrote the exquisite and
wholly unfettered naturalism of 'The Heart of Midlo-
thian,' for instance, thought himself continually bound to
seem to feel ashamed of, and to excuse himself for, his
love of Gothic architecture; he felt that it was romantic,
and he knew that it gave him pleasure, but somehow he
had not found out that it was art, having been taught in
many ways that nothing could be art that was not done
by a named man under academical rules." †

It is worth while to glance at Morris' culture-history
and note the organic filaments which connect the later

* "Hopes and Fears for Art," p. 79.
† *Ibid.*, p. 83.

with the earlier romanticism. He had read the Waverley
novels as a child, and had even snatched a fearful joy
from Clara Reeve's "Old English Baron." * He knew
his Tennyson before he went up to Oxford, but reserved
an unqualified admiration only for such things as
"Oriana" and "The Lady of Shalott." He was greatly
excited by the woodcut engraving of Dürer's "Knight,
Death and the Devil" in an English translation of
Fouqué's "Sintram." † Rossetti was first made known
to him by Ruskin's Edinburgh lectures of 1854 and by
the illustration to Allingham's "Maids of Elfin Mere,"
over which Morris and Burne-Jones "pored continually."
Morris devoured greedily all manner of mediæval chronicles and romances, French and English; but he read
little in Elizabethan and later authors. He disliked
Milton and Wordsworth, and held Keats to be the foremost of modern English poets. He took no interest in
mythology, or Welsh poetry or Celtic literature generally, with the exception of the "Morte Darthur," which,
Rossetti assured him, was second only to the Bible. The
Border ballads had been his delight since childhood.
An edition of these; a selection of English mediæval
lyrics; and a "Morte Darthur," with a hundred illustrations from designs by Burne-Jones, were among the un-
fulfilled purposes of the Kelmscott Press.

Morris' first volume, "The Defence of Guenevere and
Other Poems," was put forth in 1858 (reprint in 1875);
"a book," says Saintsbury, "almost as much the herald
of the second school of Victorian poetry as Tennyson's
early work was of the first." ‡ "Many of the poems,"

---

* See vol. i., pp. 241–43.   † *Vide supra*, p. 152.
‡ "A Short History of English Literature," p. 783.

wrote William Bell Scott, "represent the mediæval spirit
in a new way, not by a sentimental, nineteenth-century-
revival mediævalism, but they give a poetical sense of a
barbaric age strongly and sharply real." * These last
words point at Tennyson. The first four pieces in the
volume are on Arthurian subjects, but are wholly different in style and conception even from such poems as
"The Lady of Shalott" and "Sir Lancelot and Queen
Guinevere." They are more mannerised, more in the
spirit of Pre-Raphaelite art, than anything in Morris'
later work. If the name-poem is put beside Tennyson's
idyl "Guinevere"; or "Sir Galahad, a Christmas Mystery," beside Tennyson's "Sir Galahad," the difference
is striking. In place of the refined ethics and sentiment, and purely modern spiritual ideals which find a
somewhat rhetorical expression in Tennyson, Morris endeavours to render the genuine Catholic mediæval materialistic religious temper as it appears in Malory;
where unquestioning belief, devotion, childish superstition, and the fear of hell coexist with fleshly love and
hate—a passion of sin and a passion of repentance.
Guenevere's "defence" is, at bottom, the same as
Phryne's:

> "See through my long throat how the words go up
>   In ripples to my mouth; how in my hand
> The shadow lies like wine within a cup
>   Of marvellously colour'd gold."

>   "Dost thou reck
> That I am beautiful, Lord, even as you
> And your dear mother?" †

Morris criticised Tennyson's Galahad, as "rather a

* "Recollections of Rossetti," vol. ii., p. 42.
† "King Arthur's Tomb."

mild youth." His own Galahad is not the rapt seer of
the vision beatific, but a more flesh-and-blood character,
who sometimes has cold fits in which he doubts whether
the quest is not a fool's errand; and whether even Sir
Palomydes in his unrequited love, and Sir Lancelot in
his guilty love, do not take greater comfort than he.

Other poems in the book were inspired by Froissart's
" Chronicle " or other histories of the English wars in
France: " Sir Peter Harpdon's End," " Concerning Gef-
fray Teste Noire," " The Eve of Crecy," etc.* Still
others, and these not the least fascinating, were things of
pure invention, lays of " a country lit with lunar rainbows
and ringing with fairy song." † These have been thought
to owe something to Edgar Poe; but they much more
nearly resemble the work of the latest symbolistic
schools. When reading such poems as " Rapunzel,"
" Golden Wings," and " The Tune of Seven Towers,"
one is frequently reminded of " Serres Chaudes" or " Pel-
léas et Mélisande "; and is at no loss to understand why
Morris excepted Maeterlinck from his general indifference to contemporary writers—Maeterlinck, like himself,
a student of Rossetti. There is no other collection of
English poems so saturated with Pre-Raphaelitism. The
flowers are all orchids, strange in shape, violent in colouring. Rapunzel, *e.g.*, is like one of Maeterlinck's
spellbound princesses. She stands at the top of her
tower, letting down her hair to the ground, and her lover
climbs up to her by it as by a golden stair. Here is
again the singular Pre-Raphaelite and symbolistic scen-

---

* One of these, "The Haystack in the Floods," has a tragic
power unexcelled by any later work of Morris.
† Saintsbury, p. 785.

ery, with its images from art and not from nature. Tall
damozels in white and scarlet walk in garths of lily and
sunflower, or under apple boughs, and feed the swans in
the moat.

> "Moreover, she held scarlet lilies, such
>   As Maiden Margaret bears upon the light
>   Of the great church walls." *

> "Lord, give Mary a dear kiss,
>   And let gold Michael, who look'd down,
>   When I was there, on Rouen town,
> From the spire, bring me that kiss
>   On a lily!" †

The language is as artfully quaint as the imaginations
are fantastic:

> "Between the trees a large moon, the wind lows
>   Not loud, but as a cow begins to low." ‡

> "Pale in the green sky were the stars, I ween,
>   Because the moon shone like a star she shed
>   When she dwelt up in heaven a while ago,
>   And ruled all things but God." §

> "Quiet groans
> That swell out the little bones
> Of my bosom." ‖

> "I sit on a purple bed,
>   Outside, the wall is red,
>   Thereby the apple hangs,
>   And the wasp, caught by the fangs,
>   Dies in the autumn night.
>   And the bat flits till light,
>   And the love-crazed knight
>   Kisses the long, wet grass." ¶

A number of these pieces are dramatic in form, monologues or dialogues, sometimes in the manner of the

* "King Arthur's Tomb."   † "Rapunzel."
‡ "King Arthur's Tomb."   § *Ibid.*
‖ "Rapunzel."   ¶ "Golden Wings."

mediæval mystery plays.*   Others are ballads, not of the popular variety, but after Rossetti's fashion, employing burdens, English or French:

> "Two red roses across the moon";
> "Hah! hah! la belle jaune giroflée";
> "Ah! qu'elle est belle La Marguerite"; etc.

The only poem in the collection which imitates the style of the old minstrel ballad is "Welland Water." The name-poem is in *terza rima;* the longest, "Sir Peter Harpdon's End," in blank verse; "Golden Wings," in the "In Memoriam" stanza.

When Morris again came before the public as a poet, his style had undergone a change akin to that which transformed the Pre-Raphaelite painter into the decorative artist. The skeins of vivid romantic colour had run out into large-pattern tapestries. There was nothing eccentric or knotty about "The Life and Death of Jason" and "The Earthly Paradise." On the contrary, nothing so facile, pellucid, pleasant to read had appeared in modern literature—a poetic lubberland, a "clear, un-wrinkled song." The reader was carried along with no effort and little thought on the long swell of the verse, his ear lulled by the musical lapse of the rime, his eye soothed—not excited—by ever-unrolling panoramas of an enchanted country "east of the sun and west of the moon." Morris wrote with incredible ease and rapidity. It was a maxim with him, as with Ruskin, that all good work is done easily and with pleasure to the workman; and certainly that seems true of him which Lowell said of Chaucer—that he never "puckered his brow over an

*See "Sir Galahad," "The Chapel in Lyoness," "A Good Knight in Prison."

unmanageable verse." Chaucer was his avowed master,* and perhaps no English narrative poet has come so near to Chaucer. Like Chaucer, and unlike Scott, he did not invent stories, but told the old stories over again with a new charm. His poetry, as such, is commonly better than Scott's; lacking the fire and nervous energy of Scott in his great passages, but sustained at a higher artistic level. He had the copious vein of the mediæval chroniclers and romancers, without their tiresome prolixity and with finer resources of invention. He had none of Chaucer's humour, realism, or skill in character sketching. In its final impression his poetry resembles Spenser's more than Chaucer's. Like Spenser's, it grows monotonous—without quite growing languid—from the steady flow of the metre and the exhaustless profusion of the imagery. The reader becomes, somewhat ungratefully, surfeited with beauty, and seeks relief in poetry more passionate or intellectual. Chaucer and, in a degree, Walter Scott, have a way of making old things seem near to us. In Spenser and Morris, though bright and clear in all imagined details, they stand at an infinite remove, in a world apart—

> "—a little isle of bliss
> Midmost the beating of the steely sea"

which typifies the weary problems and turmoil of contemporary life.

"Jason" was a poem of epic dimensions, on the winning of the Golden Fleece; "The Earthly Paradise," a series of twenty-four narrative poems set in a framework of the poet's own. Certain gentlemen of Norway, in the

---

*See "Jason," Book xvii., 5–24, and the *Envoi* to "The Earthly Paradise."

reign of Edward III. of England, set out—like St. Brandan—on a voyage in search of a land that is free from death. They cross the Western ocean, and after long years of wandering, come, disappointed of their hope, to a city founded centuries since by exiles from ancient Greece. There being hospitably received, hosts and guests interchange tales in every month of the year; a classical story alternating with a mediæval one, till the double sum of twelve is complete. Among the wanderers are a Breton and a Suabian, so that the mediæval tales have a wide range. There are Norse stories like "The Lovers of Gudrun"; French Charlemagne romances, like "Ogier the Dane"; and late German legends of the fourteenth century, like "The Hill of Venus," besides miscellaneous travelled fictions of the Middle Age.* But the Hellenic legends are reduced to a common term with the romance material, so that the reader is not very sensible of a difference. Many of them are selected for their marvellous character, and abound in dragons, monsters, transformations, and enchantments: "The Golden Apples," "Bellerophon," "Cupid and Psyche," "The Story of Perseus," etc. Even "Jason" is treated as a romance. Of its seventeen books, all but the last are devoted to the exploits and wanderings of the Argonauts.

* Some of Morris' sources were William of Malmesbury, "Mandeville's Travels," the "Gesta Romanorum," and the "Golden Legend." "The Man Born to be King" was derived from "The Tale of King Constans, the Emperor" in a volume of French romances ("Nouvelles françaises en prose du xiii.ième Siècle," Paris, 1856) of which he afterwards (1896) made a prose translation. The collection included also "The Friendship of Amis and Amile"; "King Florus and the Fair Jehane"; and "The History of Over Sea"; besides "Aucassin and Nicolete," which Morris left out because it had been already rendered into English by Andrew Lang.

Medea is not the wronged, vengeful queen of the Greek tragic poets, so much as she is the Colchian sorceress who effects her lover's victory and escape. Her romantic, outweighs her dramatic character. Sea voyages, emprizes, and wild adventures, like those of his own wanderers in " The Earthly Paradise," were dearer to Morris' imagination than conflicts of the will; the νόστος or home-coming of Ulysses, *e.g.* He preferred the " Odyssey " to the " Iliad," and translated it in 1887 into the thirteen-syllabled line of the " Nibelungenlied." * Of the Greek tales in " The Earthly Paradise," " The Love of Alcestis " has, perhaps, the most dramatic quality.

Like Chaucer and like Rossetti,† Morris mediævalised classic fable. " Troy," says his biographer, " is to his imagination a town exactly like Bruges or Chartres; spired and gabled, red-roofed, filled (like the city of King Æetes in ' The Life and Death of Jason ') with towers and swinging bells. The Trojan princes go out, like knights in Froissart, to tilt at the barriers." ‡   The distinction between classical and romantic treatment is well illustrated by a comparison of Theocritus' idyl " Hylas," with the same episode in " Jason."   " Soon was he 'ware of a spring," says the Syracusan poet, " in a hollow land, and the rushes grew thickly round it, and dark swallow-wort, and green maiden-hair, and blooming parsley and deer-grass spreading through the marshy land. In the midst of the water the nymphs were arraying their dances, the sleepless nymphs, dread goddesses of the country people, Eunice, and Malis, and Nycheia, with

* His Vergil's " Æneid," in the old fourteener of Chapman, was published in 1876.
† *Vide supra*, p. 315.   ‡ Mackail, i., p. 168.

her April eyes. And now the boy was holding out the wide-mouthed pitcher to the water, intent on dipping it; but the nymphs all clung to his hand, for love of the Argive lad had fluttered the soft hearts of all of them. Then down he sank into the black water."* In "Jason," where the episode occupies some two hundred and seventy lines, one of the nymphs meets the boy in the wood, disguised in furs like a northern princess, and lulls him to sleep by the stream side with a Pre-Raphaelite song:

> "I know a little garden close
> Set thick with lily and red rose";

the loveliest of all the lyrical passages in Morris' narrative poems except possibly the favourite two-part song in "Ogier the Dane":

> "In the white-flower'd hawthorne brake,
> Love, be merry for my sake:
> Twine the blossoms in my hair,
> Kiss me where I am most fair—
> Kiss me, love! for who knoweth
> What thing cometh after death?"

This is the strain which recurs in all Morris' poetry with the insistence of a burden, and lends its melancholy to every season of "the rich year slipping by."

Three kinds of verse are employed in "The Earthly Paradise": the octosyllabic couplet; the rime royal, which was so much a favourite with Chaucer; and the heroic couplet, handled in the free, "enjambed" fashion of Hunt and Keats.

"Love is Enough," in the form of a fifteenth-century morality play, and treating a subject from the "Mabino-

---

* Lang's translation.

gion," appeared in 1873. Mackail praises its delicate
mechanism in the use of "receding planes of action"
(Love is prologue and chorus, and there is a musical
accompaniment); but the dramatic form only emphasises
the essentially undramatic quality of the author's genius.
What is the matter with Morris' poetry? For something
is the matter with it. Beauty is there in abundance, a
rich profusion of imagery. The narrative moves without a hitch. Passion is not absent, passionate love
and regret; but it speaks a sleepy language, and the
final impression is dream-like. I believe that the singular lack which one feels in reading these poems comes
from Morris' dislike of rhetoric and moralising, the two
main nerves of eighteenth-century verse. Left to themselves, these make sad work of poetry; yet poetry includes
eloquence, and life includes morality. The poetry of
Morris is sensuous, as upon the whole poetry should be;
but in his resolute abstention from the generalizing habit
of the previous century, the balance is lost between the
general and the concrete, which all really great poetry
preserves. Byron declaims and Wordsworth moralises,
both of them perhaps too much; yet in the end to the
advantage of their poetry, which is full of truths, or of
thoughts conceived as true, surcharged with emotion and
uttered with passionate conviction. One looks in vain
in Morris' pages for such things as

"There's not a joy the world can give like that it takes away";

or   "—the good die first,
    ——And they whose hearts are dry as summer dust,
    Burn to the socket."

Such coin of universal currency is rare in Morris, as
has once before been said. Not that quotability is an

absolute test of poetic value; for then Pope would rank higher than Spenser or Shelley. But its absence in Morris is significant in more than one way.

While " The Earthly Paradise " was in course of com- position, a new intellectual influence came into Morris' life, the influence of the Icelandic sagas. Much had been done to make Old Norse literature accessible to English readers since the days when Gray put forth his Runic scraps and Percy translated Mallet.* Walter Scott, *e.g.*, had given an abstract of the " Eyrbyggja Saga." Amos Cottle had published at Bristol in 1797 a metrical version of the mythological portion of the " Elder Edda " (" Icelandic Poetry, or the Edda of Sae- mund "), with an introductory verse epistle by Southey. Sir George Dasent's translation of the " Younger Edda " appeared in 1842; Laing's " Heimskringla " in 1844; Dasent's " Burnt Nial " in 1861; his " Gisli the Outlaw," and Head's " Saga of Viga-Glum " in 1866. William and Mary Howitt's " Literature and Romance of Northern Europe " appeared in 1852. Morris had made the ac- quaintance of Thorpe's " Northern Mythology " (1851) and " Yuletide Stories " (1853) at Oxford; two of the tales in " The Earthly Paradise " were suggested by them: " The Land East of the Sun " and " The Fostering of Aslaug." These, however, he had dealt with independ- ently and in an ultra-romantic spirit. But in 1869 he took up the study of Icelandic under the tuition of Mr. Erick Magnusson; in collaboration with whom he is- sued a number of translations.† " The Lovers of Gud- run " in " The Earthly Paradise " was taken from the

* See vol. i., pp. 190–92.
† The " Grettis Saga " (1869) : the " Völsunga Saga " (1870) ; " Three Northern Love Stories " (1875).

"Laxdaela Saga," and is in marked contrast with the other poems in the collection. There is no romantic glamour about it. It is a grim, domestic tragedy, moving among the homeliest surroundings. Save for the lawlessness of a primitive state of society which gave free play to the workings of the passions, the story might have passed in Yorkshire or New England. A book like "Wuthering Heights," or "Pembroke," occasionally exhibits the same obstinate Berserkir rage of the tough old Teutonic stock, operating under modern conditions. For the men and women of the sagas are hard as iron; their pride is ferocious, their courage and sense of duty inflexible, their hatred is as enduring as their love. The memory of a slight or an injury is nursed for a lifetime, and when the hour of vengeance strikes, no compunction, not even the commonest human instincts—such as mother love—can avert the blow. Signy in the "Völsunga Saga" is implacable as fate. To avenge the slaughter of the Volsungs is with her an obsession, a fixed idea. When incest seems the only pathway to her purpose, she takes that path without a moment's hesitation. The contemptuous indifference with which she hands over her own little innocent children to death is more terrible than the readiness of the fierce Medea to sacrifice her young brothers to Jason's safety; more terrible by far than the matricide of Orestes.

The colossal mythology of the North had impressed Gray's imagination a century before. Carlyle in his "Hero Worship" (1840) had given it the preference over the Greek, as an expression of race character and imagination. In the preface to his translation of the "Völsunga Saga," Morris declared his surprise that no version of the story yet existed in English. He said that it was one of the great stories of the world, and that to all men of Germanic blood it ought to be what the tale of Troy had been to the whole Hellenic race. In 1876 he cast it into a poem, " Sigurd the Volsung," in four books in riming lines of six iambic or anapæstic feet. "The Lovers of Gudrun " drew its material from one of that class of sagas which rest upon historical facts. The family vendetta which it narrates, in the Iceland of the eleventh century, is hardly more fabulous—hardly less realistic—than any modern blood feud in the Tennessee mountains. The passions and dramatic situations are much the same in both. The " Völsunga Saga " belongs not to romantic literature, strictly speaking, but to the old cycle of hero epics, to that earlier Middle Age which preceded Christian chivalry. It is the Scandinavian version of the story of the Niblungs, which Wagner's music-dramas have rendered in another art. But in common with romance, it abounds in superhuman wonders. It is full of Eddaic poetry and mythology. Sigmund and Sinfiotli change themselves into were wolves, like the people in "William of Palermo": Sigurd slays Fafnir, the dragon who guards the hoard, and his brother Regni, the last of the Dwarf-kin; Grimhild bewitches Sigurd with a cup of evil drink; Sigmund draws from the hall pillar the miraculous sword of Odin, and its shards are afterwards smithed by Regni for the killing of the monster.

Morris was so powerfully drawn to the Old Norse literature that he made two visits to Iceland, to verify the local references in the sagas and to acquaint himself with the strange Icelandic landscapes whose savage sublimity is reflected in the Icelandic writings. " Sigurd the Volsung" is probably the most important contribution of Norse literature to English poetry; but it met with no such general acceptance as "The Earthly Paradise." The spirit which created the Northern mythology and composed the sagas is not extinct in the English descendants of Frisians and Danes. There is something of it in the minstrel ballads; but it has been so softened by modern life and tempered with foreign culture elements, that these old tales in their aboriginal, barbaric sternness repel. It is hard for any blossom of modern poetry to root itself in the scoriæ of Hecla.

An indirect result of Morris' Icelandic studies was his translation of Beowulf (1897), not a success; another was the remarkable series of prose poems or romances, which he put forth in the last ten years of his life.* There is nothing else quite like these. They are written in a peculiar archaic English which the author shaped for himself out of fifteenth- and early sixteenth-century models, like the "Morte Darthur" and the English translation of the "Gesta Romanorum," but with an anxious preference for the Saxon and Danish elements of the vocabulary. It is a dialect in which a market town is called a "cheaping-stead," a popular assembly a "folk-mote," foresters are "wood-abiders," sailors are "ship-carles," a family is a "kindred," poetry is "song-craft," † and

---

* These, in order of publication, were "The House of the Wolfings" (1889) ; "The Roots of the Mountains" (1890) ; "The Story of the Glittering Plain (1891) ; "The Wood Beyond the World" (1894) ; "The Well at the World's End" (1896) ; "The Water of the Wondrous Isles" (1897) ; and "The Sundering Flood" (1898).

† Morris became so intolerant of French vocables that he detested and would "fain" have eschewed the very word literature.

any kind of enclosure is a "garth." The prose is frequently interchanged with verse, not by way of lyrical outbursts, but as a variation in the narrative method, after the manner of the Old French *cantefables*, such as "Aucassin et Nicolete"; but more exactly after the manner of the sagas, in which the azoic rock of Eddaic poetry crops out ever and anon under the prose strata. This Saxonism of style is in marked contrast with Scott, who employs without question the highly latinised English which his age had inherited from the last. Nor are Morris' romances historical in the manner of the Waverley novels. The first two of the series, however, are historical in the sense that they endeavour to reproduce in exact detail the picture of an extinct society. Time and place are not precisely indicated, but the scene is somewhere in the old German forest, and the period is early in the Christian era, during the obscure wanderings and settlements of the Gothic tribes. "The House of the Wolfings" concerns the life of such a community, which has made a series of clearings in "Mirkwood" on a stream tributary to the Rhine. The folk of Midmark live very much as Tacitus describes the ancient Germans as living. Each kindred dwells in a great common hall, like the hall of the Niblungs or the Volsungs, or of King Hrothgar in "Beowulf." Their herding and agriculture are described, their implements and costumes, feasts in hall, songs, rites of worship, public meetings, and finally their warfare when they go forth against the invading Romans. In "The Roots of the Mountains" the tribe of the Wolf has been driven into the woods and mountains by the vanguard of the Hunnish migrations. In time they make head against these, drive them back,

and retake their fertile valley. In each case there is a
love story and, as in Scott, the private fortunes of the
hero and heroine are enwoven with the ongoings of public events. But it is the general life of the tribe that is of
importance, and there is little individual characterisation.
There is a class of thralls in "The House of the Wolfings," but no single member of the class is particular-
ised, like Garth, the thrall of Cedric, in "Ivanhoe."

The later numbers of the series have no semblance of
actuality. The last of all, indeed, "The Sundering
Flood," is a war story which attains an air of geograph-
ical precision by means of a map—like the plan of Egdon
Heath in "The Return of the Native"—but the region
and its inhabitants are alike fabulous. Romances such
as "The Water of the Wondrous Isles" and "The Wood
beyond the World" (the names are not the least imaginative feature of these curious books) are simply a new
kind of fairy tales. Unsubstantial as Duessa or Armida
or Circe or Morgan le Fay are the witch-queen of the Wood
beyond the World and the sorceress of the enchanted Isle
of Increase Unsought. The white Castle of the Quest,
with its three champions and their ladies, Aurea, Atra,
and Viridis; the yellow dwarfs, the magic boat, the wicked
Red Knight, and his den, the Red Hold; the rings and
spells and charms and garments of invisibility are like
the wilder parts of Malory or the Arabian Nights.

Algernon Charles Swinburne was an early adherent of
the Pre-Raphaelite school, although such of his work
as is specifically Gothic is to be found mainly in the
first series of "Poems and Ballads" (1866); * a volume

* This collection is made up of Swinburne's earliest work,
but is antedated in point of publication by "The Queen

which corresponds to Morris' first fruits, "The Defence of Guenevere." If Morris is prevailingly a Goth—a heathen Norseman or Saxon—Swinburne is, upon the whole, a Greek pagan. Rossetti and Morris inherit from Keats, but Swinburne much more from Shelley, whom he resembles in his Hellenic spirit, as well as in his lyric fervour, his shrill radicalism—political and religious—and his unchastened imagination. Probably the cunningest of English metrical artists, his art is more closely affiliated with music than with painting. Not that there is any paucity of imagery in his poetry; the imagery is superabundant, crowded, but it is blurred by an iridescent spray of melodious verbiage. The confusion of mind which his work often produces does not arise from romantic vagueness, from the dreamlike and mysterious impression left by a ballad of Coleridge's or a story of Tieck's; but rather, as in Shelley's case, from the dizzy splendour and excitement of the diction. His verse, like Shelley's, is full of foam and flame, and the result upon the reader is to bewilder and exhaust. He does not describe in pictures, like Rossetti and Morris, but by metaphors, comparisons, and hyperboles. Take the following very typical passage—the portrait of Iseult in "Tristram of Lyonesse" (1882):

> "The very veil of her bright flesh was made
> As of light woven and moonbeam-colored shade
> More fine than moonbeams; white her eyelids shone
> As snow sun-stricken that endures the sun,
> And through their curled and coloured clouds of deep,
> Luminous lashes, thick as dreams in sleep,

Mother, and Rosamond" (1861) dedicated to Rossetti; and "Atalanta in Calydon" (1865). "Poems and Ballads" was inscribed to Burne-Jones.

Shone, as the sea's depth swallowing up the sky's,
The springs of unimaginable eyes.
As the wave's subtler emerald is pierced through
With the utmost heaven's inextricable blue,
And both are woven and molten in one sleight
Of amorous colour and implicated light
Under the golden guard and gaze of noon,
So glowed their aweless amorous plenilune,
Azure and gold and ardent grey, made strange
With fiery difference and deep interchange
Inexplicable of glories multiform ;
Now, as the sullen sapphire swells towards storm
Foamless, their bitter beauty grew acold,
And now afire with ardour of fine gold.
Her flower-soft lips were meek and passionate,
For love upon them like a shadow sate
Patient, a foreseen vision of sweet things,
A dream with eyes fast shut and plumeless wings
That knew not what man's love or life should be,
Nor had it sight nor heart to hope or see
What thing should come ; but, childlike satisfied,
Watched out its virgin vigil in soft pride
And unkissed expectation ; and the glad
Clear cheeks and throat and tender temples had
Such maiden heat as if a rose's blood
Beat in the live heart of a lily-bud."

What distinct image of the woman portrayed does one carry away from all this squandered wealth of words and tropes? Compare the entire poem with one of Tennyson's Arthurian "Idyls," or even with Matthew Arnold's not over-prosperous "Tristram and Iseult," or with any of the stories in "The Earthly Paradise," and it will be seen how far short it falls of being good verse narrative —with its excesses of language and retarded movement. Wordsworth said finely of Shakspere that he could not have written an epic: "he would have perished from a plethora of thought." It is not so much plethora of thought as lavishness of style which clogs the wheels in Swinburne. Too often his tale is

> "Like a tale of the little meaning,
>   Though the words are strong. "

But his narrative method has analogies, not only with things like Shelley's "Laon and Cythna," but with Elizabethan poems such as Marlowe and Chapman's "Hero and Leander." If not so conceited as these, it is equally encumbered with sticky sweets which keep the story from getting forward.

The symbolism which characterises a great deal of Pre-Raphaelite art is not conspicuous in Swinburne, whose spirit is not mystical. But two marks of the Pre-Raphaelite—and, indeed, of the romantic manner generally—are obtrusively present in his early work. One of these is the fondness for microscopic detail at the expense of the obvious, natural outlines of the subject. Thus of Proserpine at Enna, in the piece entitled "At Eleusis,"

> "—she lying down, red flowers
> Made their sharp little shadows on her sides."

"Endymion " is, perhaps, partly responsible for this exaggeration of the picturesque; and in Swinburne, as in Keats, the habit is due to an excessive impressibility by all forms of sensuous beauty. It is a sign of riches, but of riches which smother their possessor. It is impossible to fancy Chaucer or Goethe, or any large, healthy mind dealing thus by its theme. Or, indeed, contrast the whole passage from "At Eleusis " with the mention of the rape of Proserpine in the "Winter's Tale " and in " Paradise Lost."

Another Pre-Raphaelite trait is that over-intensity of spirit and sense which was not quite wholesome in Rossetti, but which manifested itself in Swinburne in a

morbid eroticism.   The first series of " Poems and Ballads" was reprinted in America as "Laus Veneris."
The name-poem was a version of the Tannhäuser legend,
a powerful but sultry study of animal passion, and it set
the key of the whole volume.   It is hardly necessary to
say of the singer of the wonderful choruses in " Atalanta "
and the equally wonderful hexameters of "Hesperia,"
that his imagination has turned most persistently to the
antique, and that a very small share of his work is to be
brought under any narrowly romantic formula.   But there
are a few noteworthy experiments in mediævalism included among these early lyrics.   "A Christmas Carol "
is a ballad of burdens, suggested by a drawing of Rossetti's, and full of the Pre-Raphaelite colour.   The inevitable damsels, or bower maidens, are combing out the
queen's hair with golden combs, while she sings a song
of God's mother;   how she, too, had three women for her
bed-chamber—

> "The first two were the two Maries,
> The third was Magdalen," *

who " was the likest God "; and how Joseph, who, likewise had three workmen, Peter, Paul, and John, said to
the Virgin in regular ballad style:

> "If your child be none other man's,
>   But if it be very mine,
> The bedstead shall be gold two spans,
>   The bedfoot silver fine."

> * "Where the lady Mary is,
>   With her five handmaidens whose names
> Are five sweet symphonies,
>   Cecily, Gertrude, Magdalen,
> Margaret and Rosalys."
>   —"The Blessed Damozel."

"The Masque of Queen Bersabe" is a miracle play, and imitates the rough *naïveté* of the old Scriptural drama, with its grotesque stage directions and innocent anachronisms. Nathan recommends King David to hear a mass. All the *dramatis personæ* swear by Godis rood, by Paulis head, and Peter's soul, except "Secundus Miles" (*Paganus quidam*), a bad man—a species of Vice—who swears by Satan and Mahound, and is finally carried off by the comic devil:

> "*S. M.* I rede you in the devil's name,
> Ye come not here to make men game;
> By Termagaunt that maketh grame,
> I shall to-bete thine head.
> *Hic Diabolus capiat eum.*" *

Similarly "St. Dorothy" reproduces the childlike faith and simplicity of the old martyrologies.† Theophilus addresses the Emperor Gabalus with "Beau Sire, Dieu vous aide." The wicked Gabalus himself, though a heathen, curses by St. Luke and by God's blood and bones, and quotes Scripture. Theophilus first catches sight of Dorothy through a latticed window, holding a green and red psalter among a troop of maidens who play upon short-stringed lutes. The temple of Venus where he does his devotions is a "church" with stained-glass windows. Heaven is a walled pleasance, like the Garden of Delight in the "Roman de la Rose,"

> "Thick with companies
> Of fair-clothed men that play on shawms and lutes."

Swinburne has also essayed the minstrel ballad in various forms. There were some half-dozen pieces of the

---

* *Cf.* Browning's "The Heretic's Tragedy," *supra*, p. 276.
† This was the subject of Massinger's "Virgin Martyr."

sort in the "Laus Veneris" volume, of which several, like "The King's Daughter" and "The Sea-Swallows," were imitations of Rossetti's and Morris' imitations, artistically overwrought with elaborate Pre-Raphaelite refrains; others, like "May Janet" and "The Bloody Son," are closer to popular models. The third series of "Poems and Ballads" (1889) contains nine of these in the Scotch dialect, two of them Jacobite songs. That Swinburne has a fine instinct in such matters and holds the true theory of ballad imitation is evident from his review of Rossetti's and Morris' work in the same kind.* "The highest form of ballad requires, from a poet," he writes, "at once narrative power, lyrical and dramatic. . . . It must condense the large, loose fluency of romantic tale-telling into tight and intense brevity. . . . There can be no pause in a ballad, and no excess; nothing that flags, nothing that overflows." He pronounces "Sister Helen" the greatest ballad in modern English; but he thinks that "Stratton Water," which is less independent in composition, and copies the formal as well as the essential characteristics of popular poetry, is "a study after the old manner too close to be no closer. It is not meant for a perfect and absolute piece of work in the old Border fashion, . . . and yet it is so far a copy that it seems hardly well to have gone so far and no farther. On this ground Mr. Morris has a firmer tread than the great artist by the light of whose genius and kindly guidance he put forth the first fruits of his work, as I did afterwards. In his first book, the ballad of 'Welland River,' the Christmas carol in 'The Land East of the Sun and West of the Moon,' etc., . . . are examples of

* "Essays and Studies," pp. 85–88.

flawless work in the pure early manner. Any less absolute and decisive revival of mediæval form . . . rouses some sense of failure by excess or default of resemblance."

Swinburne's own ballads are clever and learned experiments, but he does not practise the brevity which he recommends; some of them, such as "The Bloody Son," "The Weary Wedding," and "The Bride's Tragedy," otherwise most impressive, would be more so if they were shorter or less wordy. Though his genius is more lyrical than dramatic, the fascination which the dramatic method has had for him from the first is as evident in his ballads as in his series of verse dramas, which begins with "The Queen Mother," and includes the enormous "Mary Stuart" trilogy. Several of these are mediæval in subject; the "Rosamond" of his earliest volume—Fair Rosamond of the Woodstock Maze—the other "Rosamund, Queen of the Goths" (1899) in which the period of the action is 573 A.D.; and "Locrine" (1888), the hero of which is that mythic king of Britain whose story had been once before dramatised for the Elizabethan stage; and whose daughter, "Sabrina fair," goddess of the Severn, figures in "Comus." But these are no otherwise romantic than "Chastelard" or "The Queen Mother." The dramatic diction is fashioned after the Elizabethans, of whom Swinburne has been an enthusiastic student and expositor, finding an attraction even in the morbid horrors of Webster, Ford, and Tourneur.*

Once more the poet touched the Round-Table romances

---

* See "A Study of Ben Jonson"; "John Ford" (in "Essays and Studies"); and the introductions to "Chapman" and "Middleton" in the Mermaid Series.

in "The Tale of Balen" (1896), written in the stanza of
"The Lady of Shalott," and in a style simpler and more
direct than "Tristram of Lyonesse." The story is the
same as Tennyson's "Balin and Balan," published with
"Tiresias and Other Poems" in 1885, as an introduction
to "Merlin and Vivien." Here the advantage is in
every point with the younger poet. Tennyson's version
is one of the weakest spots in the "Idylls." His hero is
a rough Northumberland warrior who looks with admiration upon the courtly graces of Lancelot, and borrows a
cognisance from Guinevere to wear upon his shield, in
hope that it may help him to keep his temper. But having once more lost control of this, he throws himself
upon the ground

"Moaning 'My violences, my violences!'"—

a bathetic descent not unexampled elsewhere in Tennyson.
This episode of the old "Morte Darthur" has fine
tragic possibilities. It is the tale of two brothers who
meet in single combat, with visors down, and slay each
other unrecognised. It has some resemblance, therefore,
to the plan of "Sohrab and Rustum," but it cannot be
said that either poet avails himself of the opportunity for
a truly dramatic presentation of his theme. Tennyson,
as we have seen, aimed to give epic unity to the wandering and repetitious narrative of Malory, by selecting and
arranging his material with reference to one leading conception; the effort of the king to establish a higher social
state through an order of Christian knighthood, and his
failure through the gradual corruption of the Round
Table. He subdues the history of Balin to this purpose,
just as he does the history of Tristram which he relates

incidentally only, and not for its own sake, in "The Last
Tournament." Balin's simple faith in the ideal chivalry
of Arthur's court is rudely dispelled when he hears from
Vivien, and sees for himself, that the two chief objects of
his reverence, Lancelot and the queen, are guilty lovers
and false to their lord; and in his bitter disappointment,
he casts his life away in the first adventure that offers.
Moreover, in consonance with his main design, Tennyson seeks, so far as may be, to discard whatever in
Malory is merely accidental or irrational; whatever is
stuff of romance rather than of epic or drama—whose
theatre is the human will. To such elements of the
wonderful as he is obliged to retain he gives, where possible, an allegorical or spiritual significance. There are
very strange things in the story of Balin, such as the invisible knight Garlon, a "darkling manslayer"; and the
chamber in the castle of King Pellam, where the body of
Joseph of Arimathea lies in state, and where there are a
portion of the blood of Christ and the spear with which
his heart was pierced; with which spear Sir Balin smites
King Pellam, whereupon the castle falls and the two adversaries lie among its ruins three days in a deathlike
trance. All this wild magic—which Tennyson touches
lightly—Swinburne gives at full length; following Malory
closely through his digressions and the roving adventures
—most of which Tennyson suppresses entirely—by which
he conducts his hero to his end. This is the true romantic method.

As Rossetti for the Italian and Morris for the Scandinavian, Swinburne stands for the spirit of French romanticism. At the beginning of the nineteenth century
France, the inventor of "Gothic" architecture and chiv-

alry romance, whose literature was the most influential
of mediæval Europe, still represented everything that is
most anti-mediæval and anti-romantic. Gérard de Nerval
thought that the native genius of France had been buried
under two ages of imported classicism; and that Perrault, who wrote the fairy tales, was the only really original mind in the French literature of the eighteenth century. M. Brunetière, on the contrary, holds that the true
expression of the national genius is to be found in the
writers of Louis XIV.'s time—that France is instinctively
and naturally classical. However this may be, in the
history of the modern return to the past, French romanticism was the latest to awake. Somewhat of the chronicles, fabliaux, and romances of old France had dribbled
into England in translations; * but Swinburne was perhaps the first thoroughpaced disciple of the French romantic school. Victor Hugo is the god of his idolatry,
and he has chanted his praise in prose and verse, in
" ode and elegy and sonnet." † Gautier and Baudelaire
have also shared his devotion.‡ The French songs in
" Rosamond " and " Chastelard " are full of romantic
spirit. " Laus Veneris " follows a version of the tale
given in Maistre Antoine Gaget's " Livre des grandes
merveilles d'amour " (1530), in which the Venusberg is
called " le mont Horsel "; and " The Leper," a very

* *Vide supra*, pp. 90, 109, 330, and vol. i., pp. 221–22, 301.
† See especially " A Study of Victor Hugo " (1886) ; the articles on " L'Homme qui Rit " and " L'Année Terrible " in
" Essays and Studies " (1875) ; and on Hugo's posthumous
writings in " Studies in Prose and Poetry " (1886) ; " To Victor Hugo " in " Poems and Ballads " (first series) ; *Ibid.* (second series) ; " Victor Hugo in 1877," *Ibid.*
‡ See " Ave atque Vale " and the memorial verses in English, French, and Latin on Gautier's death in " Poems and
Ballads " (second series).

characteristic piece in the same collection, is founded on a passage in the "Grandes Chroniques de France" (1505). Swinburne introduced or revived in English verse a number of old French stanza forms, such as the ballade, the sestina, the rondel, which have since grown familiar in the hands of Dobson, Lang, Gosse, and others. In the second series of "Poems and Ballads" (1878) he gave translations of ten of the ballads of that musical old blackguard

"Villon, our sad, bad, glad, mad brother's name."*

The range of Swinburne's intellectual interests has been wider than that of Rossetti and Morris. He is a classical scholar, who writes easily in Latin and Greek. Ancient mythology and modern politics divide his attention with the romantic literatures of many times and countries. Rossetti made but one or two essays in prose criticism, and Morris viewed the reviewer's art with contempt. But Swinburne has contributed freely to critical literature, an advocate of the principles of romantic art in the last quarter of the nineteenth century, as Coleridge, Lamb, and Hazlitt had been in the first. The manner of his criticism is not at all judicial. His prose is as lyrical as his verse, and his praise and blame both in excess—dithyrambic laudation or affluent billingsgate. In particular, he works the adjective "divine" so hard that it loses meaning. Yet stripped of its excited superlatives, and reduced to the cool temperature of ordinary speech, his critical work is found to be full of insight, and his judgment in matters of poetical technique almost always right. I may close this chapter with a few sen-

* "A Ballad of François Villon." *Vide supra*, pp. 298–99.

tences of his defence of retrospective literature.* "It is but waste of breath for the champions of the other party to bid us break the yoke and cast off the bondage of that past, leave the dead to bury their dead, and turn from the dust and rottenness of old-world themes, epic or romantic, classical or feudal, to face the age wherein we live. . . . In vain, for instance, do the first poetess of England and the first poet of America agree to urge upon their fellows or their followers the duty of confronting and expressing the spirit and the secret of their own time, its meaning, and its need. . . . If a poem cast in the mould of classic or feudal times, of Greek drama or medi-æval romance, be lifeless and worthless, it is not because the subject or the form was ancient, but because the poet was inadequate. . . . For neither epic nor romance of chivalrous quest or classic war is obsolete yet, or ever can be; there is nothing in the past extinct . . . [Life] is omnipresent and eternal, and forsakes neither Athens nor Jerusalem, Camelot nor Troy, Argonaut nor Crusader, to dwell, as she does with equal good will, among modern appliances in London and New York."

* "Essays and Studies," pp. 45–49.

CHAPTER VIII.

Tendencies and Results.

IT has been mentioned that romanticism was not purely a matter of æsthetics, without relation to the movement of religious and political thought.* But it has also been pointed out that, as compared with what happened in Germany, English romanticism was almost entirely a literary or artistic, and hardly at all a practical force; that there was no such *Zusammenhang* between poetry and life as was asserted by the German romantic school to be one of their leading principles. Walter Scott, *e.g.*, liked the Middle Ages because they were picturesque; because their social structure rested on a military basis, permitted great individual freedom of action and even lawlessness, and thus gave chances for bold adventure; and because classes and callings were so sharply differentiated—each with its own characteristic manners, dialect, dress—that the surface of society presented a rich variety of colour, in contrast with the drab uniformity of modern life. Perhaps to Scott the ideal life was that of a feudal baron, dwelling in a Gothic mansion, surrounded by retainers and guests, keeping open house, and going a-hunting; and he tried to realise this ideal—so far as it was possible under modern conditions—at Abbotsford. He respected rank and pedigree, and liked to

* See vol. i., pp. 31–32.

own land. He was a Tory and, in Presbyterian Scotland, he was an Episcopalian. But his mediæval enthusiasms were checked by all kinds of good sense. He
had no wish to restore mediæval institutions in practice,
In spite of the glamour which he threw over feudal life.
he knew very well what that life must have been in reality: its insecurity from violence and oppression, its barbarous discomfort; the life of nobles in unplumbed stone
castles; the life of burghers in walled towns, without
lighting, drainage, or police; the life of countrymen who
took their goods to market over miry roads impassable
half the year for any wheeled vehicle. As to the English poets whom we have passed in review, from Coleridge to Swinburne, not one of them joined the Catholic
Church; and most of them found romantic literary tastes
quite consistent with varying shades of political liberalism and theological heterodoxy.

THE ANGLO-CATHOLIC MOVEMENT.—Still even in England, the mediæval revival in art and letters was not
altogether without influence on practice and belief in
other spheres of thought. Thus the Oxford Tractarians of
1833 correspond somewhat to the throne-and-altar party
in Germany. At Newcastle in 1845, William Bell Scott
visited a painted-glass manufactory where he found his
friend, Francis Oliphant—afterwards husband of Margaret Oliphant, the novelist—engaged as a designer. He
describes Oliphant as no artist by nature, but a man
of pietistic feelings who had "thrown himself into the
Gothic revival which was, under the Oxford movement,
threatening to become a serious antagonist to our present
freedom from clerical domination." Scott adds that the
master of this glass-making establishment was an un-

cultivated tradesman, who yet had the business shrewd-
ness to take advantage of "the clerical and architectural
proclivities of the day," and had visited and studied the
French cathedrals.   "These workshops were a surprise
to me.   Here was the Scotch Presbyterian working-artist,
with a short pipe in his mouth, cursing his fate in having
to elaborate continual repetitions of saints and virgins—
Peter with a key as large as a spade, and a yellow plate
behind his head—yet by constant drill in the groove
realising the sentiment of Christian art, and at last able
to express the abnegation of self, the limitless sadness
and even tenderness, in every line of drapery and every
twist of the lay figure."

Here is one among many testimonies to the influence
of the Oxford movement on the fine arts.   It would be
easy to call witnesses to prove the reverse—the influence
of romance upon the Oxford movement.   Newman *
quotes an article contributed by him to the *British Critic*
for April, 1839, in which he had spoken of Tractarian-
ism "as a reaction from the dry and superficial character
of the religious teaching and the literature of the last
generation, or century. . . . First, I mentioned the literary influence of Walter Scott, who turned men's minds to
the direction of the Middle Ages.   ' The general need,' I
said, ' of something deeper and more attractive than what
had offered itself elsewhere may be considered to have
led to his popularity; and by means of his popularity he
reacted on his readers, stimulating their mental thirst,
feeding their hopes, setting before them visions which,
when once seen, are not easily forgotten, and silently in-
doctrinating them with nobler ideas, which might after-

* "Apologia pro Vita Sua," p. 139.

wards be appealed to as first principles.'" Of Coleridge
he spoke, in the same paper, as having laid a philosophical basis for church feelings and opinions; and of
Southey and Wordsworth as "two living poets, one of
whom in the department of fantastic fiction, the other in
that of philosophical meditation, have addressed themselves to the same high principles and feelings, and carried forward their readers in the same direction." Newman, like Ruskin, was fond of Scott's verse as well as of
his prose.*

Professor Gates has well recognised that element in
romantic art which affiliates with Catholic tendencies.
"Mediævalism . . . was a distinctive note of the Romantic spirit, and, certainly, Newman was intensely alive
to the beauty and the poetic charm of the life of the
Middle Ages. One is sometimes tempted to describe
him as a great mediæval ecclesiastic astray in the nineteenth century and heroically striving to remodel modern
life in harmony with his temperamental needs. His imagination was possessed with the romantic vision of the
greatness of the Mediæval Church—of its splendour and
pomp and dignity, and of its power over the hearts and
lives of its members; and the Oxford movement was in
its essence an attempt to reconstruct the English Church

---

* "It would require the . . . magic pen of Sir Walter to
catalogue and to picture . . . that most miserable procession" ("Callista: a Sketch of the Third Century," 1855;
chapter, "Christianos ad Leones"). It is curious to compare
this tale of the early martyrs, Newman's solitary essay in
historical romance, with "Hypatia." It has the intellectual
refinement of everything that came from its author's pen; and
it has strong passages like the one describing the invasion of
the locusts. But, upon the whole, Newman was as inferior to
Kingsley as a novelist as he was superior to him in the dia-
lectics of controversy.

in harmony with this romantic ideal. . . . As Scott's imagination was fascinated with the picturesque paraphernalia of feudalism—with its jousts, and courts of love, and its coats of mail and buff-jerkins—so Newman's imagination was captivated by the gorgeous ritual and ceremonial, the art and architecture of mediæval Christianity. . . . Newman sought to revive in the Church a mediæval faith in its own divine mission and the intense spiritual consciousness of the Middle Ages; he aimed to restore to religion its mystical character, to exalt the sacramental system as the divinely appointed means for the salvation of souls, and to impose once more on men's imaginations the mighty spell of a hierarchical organisation, the direct representative of God in the world's affairs. . . . Both he and Scott substantially ruined themselves through their mediævalism. Scott's luckless attempt was to place his private and family life upon a feudal basis and to give it mediæval colour and beauty; Newman undertook a much nobler and more heroic but more intrinsically hopeless task—that of re-creating the whole English Church in harmony with mediæval conceptions." *

All this is most true, and yet it is easy to exaggerate the share which romantic feeling had in the Oxford movement. In his famous apostrophe to Oxford, Matthew Arnold personifies the university as a " queen of romance," an "adorable dreamer whose heart has been so romantic," " spreading her gardens to the moonlight, and whispering from her towers the last enchantments of the Middle Age," and " ever calling us nearer to . . .

* See the entire section "Selections from Newman," by Lewis G. Gates, New York, 1895. Introduction, pp. xlvi–lix.

beauty." Newman himself was a poet, as well as one of
the masters of English prose. The movement left an
impress upon general literature in books like Keble's
"Christian Year" (1827) and "Lyra Innocentium"
(1847); in Newman's two novels, "Callista" and "Loss
and Gain" (1848), and his "Verses on Various Occasions" (1867); and even found an echo in popular fiction. Grey in Hughes' "Tom Brown at Oxford" represents the Puseyite set. Miss Yonge's "Heir of Redcliffe"
and Shorthouse's "John Inglesant" are surcharged with
High-Church sentiment. Newman said that Keble made
the Church of England poetical. "The author of 'The
Christian Year' found the Anglican system all but destitute of this divine element [poetry]; . . . vestments
chucked off, lights quenched, jewels stolen, the pomp
and circumstances of worship annihilated; . . . the royal
arms for the crucifix; huge ugly boxes of wood, sacred to
preachers, frowning on the congregation in place of the
mysterious altar; and long cathedral aisles unused, railed
off, like the tombs (as they were) of what had been and
was not." * Newman praises in "The Christian Year"
what he calls its "sacramental system"; and to the unsympathetic reader it seems as though Keble saw all
outdoors through a stained-glass window. The movement had its æsthetic side, and coincided with the revival
of church Gothic and with the effort to make church
music and ritual richer and more impressive. But, upon
the whole, it was more intellectual than æsthetic, an
affair of doctrine and church polity rather than of ecclesiology; while the later phase of ritualism into which it
has tapered down appears to the profane to be largely a

* "Essays Critical and Historical" (1846).

matter of upholstery, given over to people who concern themselves with the carving of lecterns and the embroidery of chasubles and altar cloths; with Lent lilies, antiphonal choirs, and what Carlyle calls the "singular old rubrics" of the English Church and the "three surplices at All-Hallowmas."

Newman was, above all things, a theologian; a subtle reasoner whose relentless logic led him at last to Rome. "From the age of fifteen," he wrote, "dogma has been the fundamental principle of my religion; I know no other religion; I cannot enter into the idea of any other sort of religion; religion, as a mere sentiment, is to me a dream and a mockery." Discussions concerning church ceremonies, liturgy, ritual, he put aside with some impatience. His own tastes were simple to asceticism. Mozley says that Newman and Hurrell Froude induced several of the Oriel fellows to discontinue the use of wine in the common room. "When I came up at Easter, 1825, one of the first standing jokes against the college all over the university was the Oriel tea-pot." * Dean Church testifies to the plainness of the services at St. Mary's.† Aubrey de Vere reports his urging Newman to make an expedition with him among the Wicklow Mountains, and the latter's "answering with a smile that life was full of work more important than the enjoyment of mountains and lakes. . . . The ecclesiastical imagination and the mountain-worshipping imagination are two very different things. Wordsworth's famous 'Tintern Abbey' describes the river Wye, etc. . . . The one thing which it did not see was the great monastic ruin;

* "Reminiscences," Thomas Mozley, Boston, 1882.
† "Life and Letters of Dean Church," London, 1894.

. . . and now here is this great theologian, who, when within a few miles of Glendalough Lake, will not visit it." *

There is much gentle satire in "Loss and Gain" at the expense of the Ritualistic set in the university who were attracted principally by the external beauty of the Roman Catholic worship. One of these is Bateman, a solemn bore, who takes great interest in "candlesticks, ciboriums, faldstools, lecterns, ante-pendiums, piscinas, roodlofts, and sedilia": wears a long cassock which shows absurdly under the tails of his coat; and would tolerate no architecture but Gothic in English churches, and no music but the Gregorian. Bateman is having a chapel restored in pure fourteenth-century style and dedicated to the Royal Martyr. He is going to convert the chapel into a chantry, and has bought land about it for a cemetery, which is to be decorated with mediæval monuments in sculpture and painting copied from the frescoes in the Campo Santo at Pisa, of which he has a portfolio full of drawings. "It will be quite sweet," he says, "to hear the vesper-bell tolling over the sullen moor every evening." Then there is White, a weak young æsthete who shocks the company by declaring: "We have no life or poetry in the Church of England; the Catholic Church alone is beautiful. You would see what I mean if you went into a foreign cathedral, or even into one of the Catholic churches in our large towns. The celebrant, deacon and sub-deacon, acolytes with lights, the incense and the chanting all combine to one end, one act of worship." White is much exercised by the question whether a sacristan should wear the short or the long

* "Recollections of Aubrey de Vere," London, 1897.

cotta. But he finally marries and settles down into a fat preferment.

Newman's sensitiveness to the beauty of Catholic religion is acute. "Her very being is poetry," he writes. But equally acute is his sense of the danger under which religion lies from the ministration of the arts, lest they cease to be handmaids, and "give the law to Religion." Hence he praises, from an ecclesiastical point of view, the service of the arts in their rudimental state—the rude Gothic sculpture, the simple Gregorian chant.* A similar indifference to the merely æsthetic aspects of Catholicism is recorded of many of Newman's associates; of Hurrell Froude, *e.g.*, and of Ward. When Pugin came to Oxford in 1840 to superintend some building at Balliol, he saw folio copies of St. Buonaventura and Aquinas' "Summa Theologiæ" lying on Ward's table, and exclaimed, "What an extraordinary thing that so glorious a man as Ward should be living in a room without mullions to the windows!" This being reported to Ward, he asked, "What are mullions? I never heard of them." Ward cared nothing about rood-screens and lancet windows; Newman and Faber preferred the Palladian architecture to the Gothic.† Pugin, on the other hand, who had been actually converted to the Roman Church through

* "Idea of a University" (1852). See also in "Parochial and Plain Sermons" the discourse on "The Danger of Accomplishments," and that on "The Gospel Palaces." In the latter he writes, speaking of the cathedrals: "Unhappy they who, while they have eyes to admire, admire them only for their beauty's sake; . . . who regard them as works of art, not fruits of grace."

† Cardinal Wiseman had a decided preference for Renaissance over Gothic, and the churches built under his authority were mostly in Italian styles.

his enthusiasm for pointed architecture; and who, when asked to dinner, stipulated for Gothic puddings, for which he enclosed designs, was greatly distressed at the carelessness about such matters which he found at Oxford. A certain Dr. Cox was going to pray for the conversion of England, in an old French cope. "What is the use," asked Pugin, "of praying for the Church of England in that cope?" *

Of the three or four hundred Anglican clergymen who went over with Newman in 1845, or some years later with Manning, on the decision in the Gorham controversy, few were influenced in any assignable degree by poetic motives. "As regards my friend's theory about my imaginative sympathies having led me astray," writes Aubrey de Vere, "I may remark that they had been repelled, not attracted, by what I thought an excess of ceremonial in the churches and elsewhere when in Italy. . . . It seemed to me too sensuous." † Indeed, at the outset of the movement it was not the mediæval Church, but the primitive Church, the Church of patristic discipline and doctrine, that appealed to the Tractarians. It was the Anglican Church of the seventeenth century, the Church of Andrewes and Herbert and Ken, to which Keble sought to restore the "beauty of holiness"; and those of the Oxford party who remained within the establishment continued true to this ideal. "The Christian Year" is the genuine descendant of George Herbert's "Temple" (1632). What impressed Newman's imagination in the Roman Catholic Church was not so much the

---

* "William George Ward and the Oxford Movement," London, 1889, pp. 153–55.
† "Recollections," p. 309.

romantic beauty of its rites and observances as its imposing unity and authority.   He wanted an authoritative standard in matters of belief, a faith which had been held *semper et ubique et ab omnibus.*   The English Church was an Elizabethan compromise.   It was Erastian, a creature of the state, threatened by the Reform Bill of 1832, threatened by every liberal wind of opinion.   The Thirty-nine Articles meant this to one man and that to another, and there was no court of final appeal to say what they meant.   Newman was a convert not of his imagination, but of his longing for consistency and his desire to believe.

There is nothing romantic in either temper or style about Newman's poems, all of which are devotional in subject, and one of which—"The Pillar of the Cloud" ("Lead, Kindly Light") (1833)—is a favourite hymn in most Protestant communions.   The most ambitious of these is "The Dream of Gerontius," a sort of mystery play which Sir Henry Taylor used to compare with the "Divine Comedy."   Indeed, none but Dante has more poignantly expressed the purgatorial passion, the desire for pain, which makes the spirits in the flames of purification unwilling to intermit their torments even for a moment.   The "happy, suffering soul" of Gerontius lies before the throne of the Crucified and sings:

> "Take me away, and in the lowest deep
> There let me be,
> And there in hope the lone night-watches keep
> Told out for me." *

* Frederick William Faber, one of the Oxford men who went over with Newman in 1845, and became Superior of the Oratory of St. Philip Neri, was a religious poet of some distinction.   A collection of his hymns was published in 1862.

Some dozen years before the "Tracts for the Times" began to appear at Oxford, a sporadic case of conversion at the sister university offers a closer analogy with the catholicising process among the German romantics. Kenelm Henry Digby, who took his degree at Trinity College in 1819, and devoted himself to the study of mediæval antiquities and scholastic philosophy, was actually led into the Catholic fold by his enthusiasm for the chivalry romances, as Pugin was by his love of Gothic architecture. His singular book, "The Broad Stone of Honour," was first published in 1822, and repeatedly afterwards in greatly enlarged form. In its final edition it consists of four books entitled respectively "Godefridus," "Tancredus," "Morus" (Sir Thomas More), and "Orlandus," after four representative paladins of Christian chivalry. The title of the whole work was suggested by the fortress of Ehrenbreitstein, the "Gibraltar of the Rhine." Like Fouqué, Digby was inspired by the ideal of knighthood, but he emphasises not so much the gallantry of the knight-errant as his religious character as the champion of Holy Church. The book is, loosely speaking, an English "Génie du Christianisme," less brilliantly rhetorical than Chateaubriand, but more sincerely devout. It is poetic and descriptive rather than polemical, though the author constantly expresses his dislike of modern civilisation, and complains with Burke that this is an age of sophists, calculators, and economists. He quotes profusely from German and French reactionaries, like Busching,* Fritz Stolberg, Görres, Friedrich Schlegel, Lamennais, and Joseph de Maistre; and illustrates his topic at every turn from mediæval

* "Ritterzeit und Ritterwesen."

chronicles, legendaries, romances, and manuals of chivalry; from the lives of Charlemagne, St. Louis, Godfrey of Bouillon, the Chevalier Bayard, St. Anselm, King René, etc., and above all, from the " Morte Darthur." He defends the Crusades, the Templars, and the monastic orders against such historians as Muller, Sismondi, and Hume; is very contemptuous of the Protestant concessions of Bishop Hurd's " Letters on Chivalry and Romance "; * and, in short, fights a brave battle against the artillery of " the moderns " with weapons borrowed from " the armoury of the invincible knights of old." The book is learned, though unsystematic and discursive, but its most interesting feature is its curiously personal note, its pure spirit of honour and Catholic piety. The enthusiasm of the author extends itself from the institutes of chivalry and the Church to the social and political constitution of the Middle Ages. He is anti-democratic as well as anti-Protestant; upholds monarchy, nobility, the interference of the popes in the affairs of kingdoms, and praises the times when the doctrines of legislation and government all over Europe rested on the foundations of the Church.

A few paragraphs from " The Broad Stone of Honour " will illustrate the author's entrance into the Church through the door of beauty, and his identification of romantic art with " the art Catholic." " It is much to be lamented," he writes, " that the acquaintance of the English reader with the characters and events of the Middle Ages should, for the most part, be derived from the writings of men who were either infidels, or who wrote on every subject connected with religion, with the feel-

* See vol. i., pp. 221–26.

ings and opinions of Scotch Presbyterian preachers of the last century." * " A distinguishing characteristic of everything belonging to the early and Middle Ages of Christianity is the picturesque. Those who now struggle to cultivate the fine arts are obliged to have recourse to the despised, and almost forgotten, houses, towns, and dresses of this period. As soon as men renounced the philosophy of the Church, it was inevitable that their taste, that the form of objects under their control, should change with their religion; for architects had no longer to provide for the love of solitude, of meditation between sombre pillars, of modesty in apartments with the lancet-casement. They were not to study duration and solidity in an age when men were taught to regard the present as their only concern. When nothing but exact knowledge was sought, the undefined sombre arches were to be removed to make way for lines which would proclaim their brevity, and for a blaze of light which might correspond with the mind of those who rejected every proposition that led beyond the reach of the senses. . . . So completely is it beyond the skill of the painter or the poet to render bearable the productions of the moderns, . . . and so fast are the poor neglected works of Christian antiquity falling to ruin, that it is hard to conceive how the fine arts can be cultivated after another century has elapsed; for when children are taught in infant schools to love accounts from their cradle, and to study political economy before they have heard of the Red Cross Knight or the Wild Hunter, the manner and taste of such an age will smother the sparks of nature." † The Church sum-

* Vol. ii., p. 44 (ed. 1846).
† *Ibid.*, pp. 315–16.

moṇed all natural beauty to the ministry of religion. "Flowers bloomed on the altars; men could behold the blue heaven through those tall, narrow-pointed eastern windows of the Gothic choir as they sat at vespers. . . . The cloud of incense breathed a sweet perfume; the voice of youth was tuned to angelic hymns; and the golden sun of the morning, shining through the coloured pane, cast its purple or its verdant beam on the embroidered vestments and marble pavement." * Or read the extended rhapsody which closes the first volume, where, to counteract the attractions of classic lands, the author passes in long review the sites and monuments of romance in England, Germany, Spain, Italy, and France. Aubrey de Vere says that nothing had been so "impressive, suggestive, and spiritually helpful" to him as Newman's "Lectures on Anglican Difficulties" (1850), "with the exception of the 'Divina Commedia' and Kenelm Digby's wholly uncontroversial 'Mores Catholici'" (1831–40).

THE STUDY OF MEDIÆVAL ART.—The correlation of romantic poetry, Catholic worship, and mediæval art has been indicated in the chapter upon the Pre-Raphaelites, as well as in the foregoing section of the present chapter. But the three departments have other tangential points which should not pass without some further mention. The revival of Gothic architecture which began with Horace Walpole † went on in an unintelligent way through the eighteenth century. One of the queerest monuments of this new taste—a successor on a larger scale to Strawberry Hill—was Fonthill Abbey, near Salisbury, that

* *Ibid.*, p. 350.
† See vol. i., chap. vii., "The Gothic Revival."

prodigious folly to which Beckford, the eccentric author of "Vathek," devoted a great share of his almost fabulous wealth. It was begun in 1796, took nearly thirty years in building, employed at one time four hundred and sixty men, and cost over £273,000. Its most conspicuous feature was an octagonal tower 278 feet high, so ill constructed that it shortly tumbled down into a heap of ruins.*

The growing taste for mediæval architecture was powerfully reinforced by the popularity of Water Scott's writings. But Abbotsford is evidence enough of the superficiality of his own knowledge of the art; and during the first half of the nineteenth century, Gothic design was applied not to churches, but to the more ambitious classes of domestic architecture. The country houses of the nobility and landed gentry were largely built or rebuilt in what was known as the castellated style.† Meanwhile a truer understanding of the principles of pointed architecture was being helped by the publication of archæological works like Britton's "Cathedral Antiquities" (1814–35), Milner's "Treatise on Ecclesiastical Architecture" (1811), and Rickman's "Ancient Examples of Gothic Architecture" (1819). The parts of individual buildings, such as Westminster Abbey and Lin-

---

* A view of Fonthill Abbey, as it appeared in 1822, is given in Fergusson's "History of Modern Architecture," vol. ii., p. 98 (third ed.).

† For Scott's influence on Gothic see Eastlake's "Gothic Revival," pp. 112-16. A typical instance of this castellated style in America was the old New York University in Washington Square, built in the thirties. This is the "Chrysalis College" which Theodore Winthrop ridicules in "Cecil Dreeme" for its "mock-Gothic" pepper-box turrets, and "deciduous plaster." Fan traceries in plaster and window traceries in cast iron were abominations of this period.

coln Cathedral, were carefully studied and illustrated with plans and sections drawn to scale; and measurement was substituted for guesswork. But the real restorer of ecclesiastical Gothic in England was Augustus Welby Northmore Pugin, an enthusiast, nay, a fanatic, in the cause; whose "Contrasts" (1836) is not only a landmark in the history of the revival of mediæval art, but a most instructive illustration of the manner in which an æsthetic admiration of the Middle Ages has sometimes involved an acceptance of their religious beliefs and social principles. Three generations of this family are associated with the rise of modern Gothic. The elder Pugin (Augustus Charles) was a French *emigré*, who came to England during the Revolution, and gained much reputation as an architectural draughtsman, publishing, among other things, "Specimens of Gothic Architecture," in 1821. The son of A. W. N. Pugin, Edward Welby (1834–73), also carried on his father's work as a practical architect and a writer.

Pugin joined the Roman Catholic Church just about the time when the "Tracts for the Times" began to be issued. His "Contrasts: or a Parallel between the Architecture of the Fifteenth and Nineteenth Centuries" is fiercely polemical, and displays all the zeal of a fresh convert. In the preface to the second edition he says that "when this work was first brought out [1836], the very name of Christian art was almost unknown"; and he affirms, in a footnote, that in the whole of the national museum, "there is not even one room, one *shelf*, devoted to the exquisite productions of the Middle Ages." The book is a jeremiad over the condition to which the cathedrals and other remains of English ecclesiastical architecture had been reduced by the successive spoliations and mutilations in the times of Henry VIII., Edward VI., and Cromwell, and by the "vile" restorations of later days. It maintains the thesis that pointed architecture is not only vastly superior artistically, but that it is the only style appropriate to Christian churches; "in it alone we find the faith of Christianity embodied and its practices illustrated." Pugin denounces alike the Renaissance and the Reformation, "those two monsters, revived Paganism and Protestantism." There is no chance, he thinks, for a successful revival of Gothic except in a return to Catholic faith. "The mechanical part of Gothic architecture is pretty well understood, but it is the principles which influenced ancient compositions, and the soul which appears in all the former works, which is so lamentably deficient. . . . 'Tis they alone that can restore pointed architecture to its former glorious state; without it all that is done will be a tame and heartless copy." He points out the want of sympathy between "these vast edifices" and the Protestant worship, which might as well be carried on in a barn or conventicle or square meeting-house. Hence, the nave has been blocked up with pews, the choir or transept partitioned off to serve as a parish church, roodloft and chancel screen removed, the altar displaced by a table, and the sedilia scattered about in odd corners. The contrast between old and new is strikingly presented, by way of object lessons, in a series of plates, arranged side by side, and devised with a great deal of satirical humour. There is, *e.g.*, a Catholic town in 1440, rich with its ancient stone bridge, its battlemented wall and city gate, and the spires and towers of St. Marie's Abbey, the Guild Hall, Queen's

Cross, St. Cuthbert's Church, and the half-timbered, steep-roofed, gabled houses of the burgesses. Over against it is the picture of the same town in 1840, hideous with the New Jail, Gas Works, Lunatic Asylum, Wesleyan Chapel, New Town Hall, Iron Works, Quaker Meeting-house, Socialist Hall of Science, and other abominations of a prosperous modern industrial community. Or there is the beautiful old western doorway of St. Mary Overies, destroyed in 1838. The door stands invitingly open, showing the noble interior with kneeling worshippers scattered here and there over the unobstructed pavement. Opposite is the new door, grimly closed, with a printed notice nailed upon it: "Divine Service on Sundays. Evening lecture." A separate plate exhibits a single compartment of the old door curiously carved in oak; and beside it a compartment of the new door in painted deal and plain as a pike-staff.

But the author is forced to confess that the case is not much better in Catholic countries, where stained windows have been displaced by white panes, frescoed ceilings covered with a yellow wash, and the "bastard pagan style" introduced among the venerable sanctities of old religion. English travellers return from the Continent disgusted with the tinsel ornament and theatrical trumperies that they have seen in foreign churches. "I do not think," he concludes, "the architecture of our English churches would have fared much better under a Catholic hierarchy. . . . It is a most melancholy truth that there does not exist much sympathy of idea between a great portion of the present Catholic body in England and their glorious ancestors. . . . Indeed, such is the total absence of solemnity in a great portion of modern

Catholic buildings in England, that I do not hesitate to say that a few crumbling walls and prostrate arches of a religious edifice raised during the days of faith will convey a far stronger religious impression to the mind than the actual service of half the chapels in England."

In short, Pugin's Catholicism, though doubtless sincere, was prompted by his professional feelings. His reverence was given to the mediæval Church, not to her —æsthetically—degenerate daughter; and it extended to the whole system of life and thought peculiar to the Middle Ages. "Men must learn," he wrote, "that the period hitherto called dark and ignorant far excelled our age in wisdom, that art ceased when it is said to have been revived, that superstition was piety, and bigotry faith." In many of his views Pugin anticipates Ruskin. He did not like St. Peter's at Rome, and said: "If those students who journey to Italy to study art would follow the steps of the great Overbeck,* . . . they would indeed derive inestimable benefit. Italian art of the thirteenth, fourteenth, and fifteenth centuries is the beau ideal of Christian purity, and its imitation cannot be too strongly inculcated; but when it forsook its pure, mystical, and ancient types, to follow those of sensual Paganism, it sunk to a fearful state of degradation."

As a practising architect Pugin naturally received and executed many commissions for Catholic churches. But the Catholic Church in England did much less, even in proportion to its resources, than the Anglican establishment towards promoting the Gothic revival. Eastlake says that Pugin's "strength as an artist lay in the design of ornamental detail"; and that he helped importantly in

* *Vide supra,* p. 153.

the revival of the mediæval taste in stained glass, metal work, furniture, carpets, and paper-hangings. Several of his works have to do with various departments of ecclesiology; chancel-screens, roodlofts, church ornaments, symbols and costumes, and the like. But the only one that need here be mentioned is the once very influential "True Principles of Pointed or Christian Architecture" (1841). This revival of ecclesiastical Gothic fell in with the reform of Anglican ritual, which was one of the features or sequences of the Oxford movement, and the two tendencies afforded each other mutual support.

Evidence of a newly awakened interest in mediæval art is furnished by a number of works of a more systematic character which appeared about the middle of the century, dealing not only with architecture, but with the early schools of sculpture and painting. One of these was "Sketches of the History of Christian Art" (3 vols., 1847) by Alexander William Crawford Lindsay, twenty-fifth Earl of Crawford. In the preface to the reprint of this book in 1885, Lady Crawford speaks of it as a pioneer in an "early time of unawakened interest." Ruskin refers to it repeatedly—always with respect—and acknowledges in "Præterita" that Lord Lindsay knew a great deal more about Italian art than he himself did. The book reviews in detail the works of Christian builders, sculptors and painters, both in Italy and north of the Alps, from the time of the Roman catacombs and basilicas down to the Renaissance. It gives likewise a history of Christian mythology, iconography and symbolism; all that great body of popular beliefs about angels, devils, saints, martyrs, anchorites, miracles, etc., which Protestant iconoclasm and the pagan spirit of the *cinque-*

cento had long ago swept into the dust-bin as sheer idol-atry and superstition. Lord Lindsay's treatment of these matters is reverential, though his own Protestantism is proof against their charm. His tone is moderate; he has no quarrel with the Renaissance, and professes re-spect for classical art, which seems to him, however, on a lower spiritual plane than the Christian. He remarks that all mediæval art was religious; the only concession to the secular being found in the illuminations of some of the chivalry romances. Gothic architecture was the expression of Teutonic genius, which is realistic and stands for the reason, while Italian sacred painting was idealistic and stands for the imagination. In the most perfect art, as in the highest type of religion, reason and imagination are in balance. Hence, the influence of Van Eyck, Memling, and Dürer on Italian painters was wholesome; and the Reformation, the work of the rea-soning Teutonic mind, is not to be condemned. Reason is to blame only when it goes too far and extinguishes imagination.*

"The sympathies of the North, or of the Teutonic race, are with Death, as those of the Southern, or classic, are with Life. . . . The exquisitely beautiful allegorical tale of ' Sintram and His Companions' by La Motte Fouqué, was founded on the 'Knight and Death' of

* "A blast from the icy jaws of Reason, the wolf Fenris of the Teutonic mind, swept one and all into the Limbo of ob-livion—that sole ante-chamber spared by Protestantism in spoiling Purgatory. Perhaps this was necessary and inevi-table. If we would repair the column, we must cut away the ivy that clings around the shaft, the flowers and brushwood that conceal the base; but it does not follow that, when the repairs are completed, we should isolate it in a desert,—that the flowers and brushwood should not be allowed to grow up and caress it as before" (vol. ii., p. 380, second ed.).

Albert Dürer, and I cannot but think that Milton had the 'Melancholy' in his remembrance while writing 'Il Penseroso.'"* The author thinks that, whatever may be true of Gothic architecture—an art less national than ecclesiastical—"sculpture and painting, on the one hand, and the spirit of chivalry on the other, have usually flourished in an inverse ratio one to the other, and it is not therefore in England, France, or Spain, but among the free cities of Italy and Germany that we must look for their rise." † I give these conclusions—so opposite to those of Catholic mediævalists like Digby and Pugin— because they illustrate the temper of Lindsay's book. One more quotation I will venture to add for its agreement with Uvedale Price's definition of the picturesque : ‡ "The picturesque in art answers to the romantic in poetry; both stand opposed to the classic or formal school —both may be defined as the triumph of nature over art, luxuriating in the decay, not of her elemental and everlasting beauty, but of the bonds by which she had been enthralled by man. It is only in ruin that a building of pure architecture, whether Greek or Gothic, becomes picturesque." §

Lord Lindsay's "Sketches" contained no illustrations. Mrs. Jameson's very popular series on "Sacred and Legendary Art" was profusely embellished with woodcuts and etchings. The first number of the series, "Legends of the Saints and Martyrs," was begun in 1842, but issued only in 1848. "Legends of the Monastic Orders"

* Vol. ii., p. 364, *note;* and *vide supra*, p. 152.
† *Ibid.*, p. 289.
‡ *Vide supra*, p. 34.
§ *Ibid.*, p. 286, *note.*

followed in 1850; "Legends of the Madonna" in 1852; and the "History of Our Lord" (completed by Lady Eastlake) in 1860. Mrs. Jameson had an imperfect knowledge of technique, and her work was descriptive rather than critical. But it probably did more to enlist the interest of the general reader in Christian art than Lord Lindsay's more learned volumes; or possibly even than the brilliant but puzzling rhetoric of Ruskin.

With Pugin's "Contrasts" began the "Battle of the Styles." This was soon decided in Pugin's favour, so far as ecclesiastical buildings were concerned. Fergusson, who is hostile to Gothic, admits that wherever clerical influence extended, the style came into fashion. The Cambridge Camden Society was founded in 1839 for the study of church architecture and ritual, and issued the first number of its magazine, *The Ecclesiologist*, in 1841. But the first national triumph for secular Gothic was won when Barry's design for the new houses of Parliament was selected from among ninety-seven competing plans. The corner-stone was laid at Westminster in 1840, and much of the detail, as the work went on, was furnished by Pugin.

It was not long before the Gothic revival found an ally in the same great writer who had already come forward as the champion of Pre-Raphaelite painting. The masterly analysis of "The Nature of Gothic" in "The Stones of Venice" (vol. i., 1851; vols. ii. and iii., 1853), and the eloquence and beauty of a hundred passages throughout the three volumes, fascinated a public which cared little about art, but knew good literature when they saw it. Eastlake testifies that Ruskin had some practical influence on English building. Young artists went to Venice to study the remains of Italian Gothic, and the results of their studies were seen in the surface treatment of many London façades, especially in the cusped window arches, and in the stripes of coloured bricks which give a zebra-like appearance to the architecture of the period. But, in general, working architects were rather contemptuous of Ruskin's fine-spun theories, which they ridiculed as fantastic, self-contradictory, and super-subtle; rhetoric or metaphysics, in short, and not helpful art criticism.

Ruskin's adhesion to Gothic was without compromise. It was "not only the best, but the *only rational* architecture." "I plead for the introduction of the Gothic form into our domestic architecture, not merely because it is lovely, but because it is the only form of faithful, strong, enduring, and honourable building, in such materials as come daily to our hands." * On the other hand, Roman architecture is essentially base; the study of classical literature is "pestilent"; and most modern building is the fruit of "the Renaissance poison tree." "If . . . any of my readers should determine . . . to set themselves to the revival of a healthy school of architecture in England, and wish to know in few words how this may be done, the answer is clear and simple. First, let us cast out utterly whatever is connected with the Greek, Roman, or Renaissance architecture, in principle or in form. . . . The whole mass of the architecture, founded on Greek and Roman models, which we have been in the habit of building for the last three centuries, is utterly devoid of all life, virtue, honourableness, or power of doing good. It is base, unnatural, unfruitful,

* "Stones of Venice," vol. ii., p. 295 (American ed. 1860).

unenjoyable, and impious. Pagan in its origin, proud and unholy in its revival, paralysed in its old age." *

Ruskin loved the religious spirit of the mediæval builders, Byzantine, Lombard, or Gothic; and the pure and holy faith of the early sacred painters like Fra Angelico, Orcagna, and Perugino. He thought that whatever was greatest even in Raphael, Leonardo, and Michelangelo came from their training in the old religious school, not from the new science of the Renaissance. "Raphael painted best when he knew least." He deplored the harm to Catholic and Protestant alike of the bitter dissensions of the Reformation. But he sorrowfully acknowledged the corruption of the ancient Church, and had no respect for modern Romanism. Against the opinion that Gothic architecture was fitted exclusively for ecclesiastical uses, he strongly protested. On the contrary, he advised its reintroduction, especially in domestic building. "Most readers . . . abandon themselves drowsily to the impression that Gothic is a peculiarly ecclesiastical style. . . . The High Church and Romanist parties . . . have willingly promulgated the theory that, because all the good architecture that is now left is expressive of High Church or Romanist doctrines, all good architecture ever has been and must be so— a piece of absurdity. . . . Wherever Christian Church architecture has been good and lovely, it has been merely the perfect development of the common dwelling-house architecture of the period. . . . The churches were not separated by any change of style from the buildings round them, as they are now, but were merely more finished and full examples of a universal style. . . . Be-

* *Ibid.*, vol. iii., p. 213.

cause the Gothic and Byzantine styles are fit for churches, they are not therefore less fit for dwellings. They are in the highest sense fit and good for both, nor were they ever brought to perfection except when they were used for both." *

The influence of Walter Scott upon Ruskin is noteworthy. As a child he read the Bible on Sundays and the Waverley Novels on week-days, and he could not recall the time when either had been unknown to him. The freshness of his pleasure in the first sight of the frescoes of the Campo Santo he describes by saying that it was like having three new Scott novels.† Ruskin called himself a "king's man," a "violent illiberal," and a "Tory of the old-fashioned school, the school of Walter Scott." Like Scott, he was proof against the religious temptations of mediævalism. "Although twelfth-century psalters are lovely and right," he was not converted to Catholic teachings by his admiration for the art of the great ages; and writes, with a touch of contempt, of those who are "piped into a new creed by the squeak of an organ pipe." If Scott was unclassical, Ruskin was anti-classical. The former would learn no Greek; and the latter complained that Oxford taught him all the Latin and Greek that he would learn, but did not teach him that fritillaries grew in Iffley meadow.‡ Even that fondness for costume which has been made a reproach

---

* *Ibid.*, vol. ii., pp. 109–14.
† See the final instalment of "Præterita" for an extended eulogy of Scott's verse and prose.

‡ "I know what white, what purple fritillaries
   The grassy harvest of the river-fields
   Above by Ensham, down by Sandford, yields."
                        —Matthew Arnold, "Thyrsis."

against Scott finds justification with Ruskin. "The essence of modern romance is simply the return of the heart and fancy to the things in which they naturally take pleasure; and half the influence of the best romances, of 'Ivanhoe,' or 'Marmion,' or 'The Crusaders,' or 'The Lady of the Lake,' is completely dependent upon the accessories of armour and costume." * Still Ruskin had the critical good sense to rate such as they below the genuine Scotch novels, like "Old Mortality" and "The Heart of Mid-Lothian"; and he is quite stern towards the melodramatic Byronic ideal of Venice. "The impotent feelings of romance, so singularly characteristic of this century, may indeed gild, but never save the remains of those mightier ages to which they are attached like climbing flowers; and they must be torn away from the magnificent fragments, if we would see them as they stood in their own strength. . . . The Venice of modern fiction and drama is a thing of yesterday, a mere efflorescence of decay, a stage dream." † For it cannot be too often repeated that the romance is not in the Middle Ages themselves, but in their strangeness to our imagination. The closer one gets to them, the less romantic they appear.

MEDIÆVAL SOCIAL IDEALS.—It is obvious how a fondness for the Middle Ages, in a man of Scott's conservative temper, might confirm him in his attachment to high Tory principles and to an aristocratic-feudal ideal of society; or how, in an enthusiastic artist like Pugin, and a gentleman of high-strung chivalric spirit like Sir Kenelm Digby, it might even lead to an adoption of

* "Stones of Venice," vol. iii., p. 211.
† *Ibid.*, vol. ii., p. 4.

the whole mediæval religious system.   But it is not so easy, at first sight, to understand why the same thing should have conducted Ruskin and William Morris to opinions that were more "advanced" than those of the most advanced Liberal.   Orthodox economists looked upon the theories put forward in Ruskin's "Unto this Last" (1860), "Munera Pulveris" (1862–63), and "Fors Clavigera" (1871–84), as the eccentricities of a distinguished art critic, disporting himself in unfamiliar fields of thought.   And when in 1883 the poet of "The Earthly Paradise" joined the Democratic Federation, and subsequently the Socialist League, and was arrested and fined one shilling and costs for addressing open-air meetings, obstructing public highways, and striking policemen, amusement was mingled with disapproval.   What does this dreamer of dreams and charming decorative artist in a London police court?

But Socialism, though appearing on the face of it the most modern of doctrines, is in a sense reactionary, like Catholicism, or knight-errantry, or Gothic architecture. That is, those who protest against the individualism of the existing social order are wont to contrast it unfavourably with the principle of association which is found everywhere in the Middle Ages.   No mediæval man was free or independent; all men were members one of another.   The feudal system itself was an elaborate network of interdependent rights and obligations, in which service was given in return for protection.   The vassal did *homage* to his lord—became his *homme* or man—and his lord was bound to take care of him.   In theory, at least, every serf was entitled to a living.   In theory, too, the Church embraced all Christendom.   None save Jews were outside it or could get outside it, except by excommunication; which was the most terrible of penalties, because it cut a man off from all spiritual human fellowship. The same principle of co-operation prevailed in mediæval industry and commerce, organised into guilds of craftsmen and trading corporations, which fixed the prices and quality of goods, the number of apprentices allowed, etc. The manufacturer was not a capitalist, but simply a master workman. Government was paternal and interfered continually with the freedom of contract and the rights of the individual. Here was where Carlyle took issue with modern Liberalism, which proclaims that the best government is that which governs least. According to the *laissez-faire* doctrine, he said, the work of a government is not that of a father, but of an active parish constable. The duty of a government is to govern, but this theory makes it its duty to refrain from governing. Not liberty is good for men, but obedience and stern discipline under wise rulers, heroes, and heaven-sent kings. Carlyle took no romantic view of the Middle Ages. He is rather contemptuous of Scott's mediæval-picturesque,* and his Scotch Calvinism burns fiercely against the would-be restorers of mediæval religious formularies and the mummeries of "the old Pope of Rome"—a ghastly survival of a dead creed.† He said that Newman had the brain of a good-sized rabbit. But

---

* *Vide supra*, p. 35.

† "I reckon him the remarkablest Pontiff that has darkened God's daylight. . . . Here is a Supreme Priest who believes God to be—what, in the name of God, *does* he believe God to be?—and discerns that all worship of God is a scenic phantasmagory of wax-candles, organ-blasts, Gregorian chants, mass-brayings, purple monsignori, etc." ("Past and Present," Book iii., chap. i.).

in this matter of collectivism *versus* individualism, Carlyle was with the Middle Ages. "For those were rugged, stalwart ages. . . . Gurth, born thrall of Cedric, it is like, got cuffs as often as pork-parings; but Gurth did belong to Cedric; no human creature then went about connected with nobody; left to go his way into Bastilles or worse, under *Laissez-faire.* . . . That Feudal Aristocracy, I say, was no imaginary one. . . . It was a Land Aristocracy; it managed the Governing of this English People, and had the reaping of the Soil of England in return. . . . Soldiering, Police and Judging, Church-Extension, nay, real Government and Guidance, all this was actually *done* by the Holders of Land in return for their Land. How much of it is now done by them; done by anybody? Good Heavens! '*Laissez faire,* Do ye nothing, eat your wages and sleep,' is everywhere the passionate half-wise cry of this time." *

From 1850 onwards, in which year Ruskin made Carlyle's acquaintance, the former fell under the dominion of these ideas, and began to preach a species of Aristocratic Socialism.† He denounced competition and profit-seeking in commerce; the factory system; the capitalistic organisation of industry. His scheme of a regenerated society, however, was by no means so democratic as that imagined by Morris in "News from Nowhere." It was a "new feudalism" with a king at the head of it and a rural nobility of "the great old families," whose relations to their tenantry are not very clearly defined.‡   Ruskin

---

* *Ibid.,* Book iv., chap. i.

† With Morris, too, when an Oxford undergraduate, "Carlyle's 'Past and Present,'" says his biographer, "stood alongside of 'Modern Painters' as inspired and absolute truth."

‡ For a systematic exposition of Ruskin's social and politi-

took some steps towards putting into practice his plans for a reorganisation of labour under improved conditions. "Fors Clavigera" consisted of a series of letters to workingmen, inviting them to join him in establishing a fund for rescuing English country life from the tyranny and defilement of machinery. In pursuance of this project, the St. George's Guild was formed, about 1870, Ruskin devoting to it £7,000 of his own money. Trustees were chosen to administer the fund; a building was bought at Walkley, in the suburbs of Sheffield, for use as a museum; and the money subscribed was employed in promoting co-operative experiments in agriculture, manufacturing, and education.

In 1848 the widespread misery among the English working class, both agricultural labourers and the operatives in cities, broke out in a startling way in the Chartist movement. Sympathy with some of the aims of this movement found literary expression in Charles Kingsley's novels, "Yeast" and "Alton Locke"; in his widely circulated tract, "Cheap Clothes and Nasty"; in his letters in *Politics for the People* over the signature "Parson Lot"; in some of his ballads like "The Three Fishers"; and in the writings of his friends, F. D. Maurice and Thomas Hughes. But the Christian Socialism of these Broad Churchmen was by no means of the mediæval type. Kingsley was an exponent of "Muscular Christianity." He hated the asceticism and sacerdotalism of the Oxford set, and challenged the Tractarian movement with all his might.* Neither was this Christian Socialism of a

cal philosophy, the reader should consult "John Ruskin, Social Reformer," by J. A. Hobson, London, 1898.

* *Vide supra*, pp. 279, 280.

radical nature, like Morris'. It limited itself to an endeavour to alleviate distress by an appeal to the good
feeling of the upper classes; and by setting on foot trade-
unions, co-operative societies, and workingmen's col-
leges. Kingsley himself, like Ruskin, believed in a
landed gentry; and like both Ruskin and Carlyle, he
defended Governor Eyre of Jamaica against the attacks
of the radical press.*

Ruskin and Morris travelled to Socialism by the pathway of art. Carlyle had early begun his complaints
against the mechanical spirit of the age, and its too great
reliance on machinery in all departments of thought and
life.† But Ruskin made war on machinery for different
reasons. As a lover of the beautiful, he hated its ugly
processes and products. As a student of art, he mourned
over the reduction of the handicraftsman to a slave
of the machine. Factories had poisoned the English
sky with their smoke, and blackened English soil
and polluted English rivers with their refuse. The rail-
road had spoiled Venice and vulgarised Switzerland.
He would like to tear up all the railroads in Wales and
most of those in England, and pull down the city of New
York. He could not live in America two months—a
country without castles. Modern architecture, modern
dress, modern manufactures, modern civilisation, were
all utterly hideous. Worst of all was the effect on the
workman, condemned by competitive commercialism to
turn out cheap goods; condemned by division of labour
to spend his life in making the eighteenth part of a pin.

---

*For a number of years, beginning with 1854, Ruskin
taught drawing classes in Maurice's Working Man's College.
† See "Characteristics" and "Signs of the Times."

Work without art, said Ruskin, is brutalising. To take
pleasure in his work, said Morris, is the workman's best
inducement to labour and his truest reward. In the
Middle Ages every artisan was an artist; the art of the
Middle Ages was popular art. Now that the designer
and the handicraftsman are separate persons, the work of
the former is unreal, and of the latter merely mechanical.

This point of view is eloquently stated in that chapter
on "The Nature of Gothic" in "The Stones of Venice,"
which made so deep an impression on Morris when he
was in residence at Oxford.* "It is verily this degradation of the operative into a machine which, more than
any other evil of the times, is leading the mass of the
nations everywhere into vain, incoherent, destructive
struggling for a freedom of which they cannot explain the
nature to themselves. Their universal outcry against
wealth and against nobility is not forced from them
either by the pressure of famine or the sting of mortified
pride. These do much, and have done much in all ages;
but the foundations of society were never yet shaken as
they are at this day. It is not that men are ill-fed, but
that they have no pleasure in the work by which they
make their bread, and therefore look to wealth as the
only means of pleasure. It is not that men are pained
by the scorn of the upper classes, but they cannot endure
their own; for they feel that the kind of labour to which
they are condemned is verily a degrading one, and makes
them less than men. . . . We have much studied and
much perfected, of late, the great civilised invention of
the division of labour; only we give it a false name.
It is not, truly speaking, the labour that is divided; but

* *Vide supra*, p. 321.

the men—divided into mere segments of men—broken into small fragments and crumbs of life, so that all the little piece of intelligence that is left in a man is not enough to make a pin, or a nail, but exhausts itself in making the point of a pin, or the head of a nail. . . . And the great cry that rises from all our manufacturing cities, louder than their furnace blast, is all, in very deed, for this—that we manufacture everything there except men. . . . And all the evil to which that cry is urging our myriads can be met only . . . by a right understanding, on the part of all classes, of what kinds of labour are good for men, raising them, and making them happy; by a determined sacrifice of such convenience, or beauty, or cheapness as is to be got only by the degradation of the workman." *

Morris' contributions to the literature of Socialism include, besides his romance, " News from Nowhere," two volumes of verse, " Poems by the Way " (1891) and " The Dream of John Ball "; together with " Socialism: Its Growth and Outcome " (1893), an historical sketch of the subject written in collaboration with Mr. E. Belfort Bax. Mackail also describes a satirical interlude, entitled " The Tables Turned, or Nupkins Awakened," which was acted thrice at Farringden Road in the autumn of 1887—a Socialistic farce in the form of a mediæval miracle play—a conjunction quite typical of the playwright's political principles and literary preferences. Morris' ideal society, unlike Ruskin's, included no feudal elements; there was no room in it for kings, or nobles, or great cities, or a centralised government. It was prim-

* Vol. ii., chap. vi., §§ xv., xvi. Morris reprinted the whole chapter on the Kelmscott Press.

itive Teutonic rather than mediæval; resembling the communal type described in "The House of the Wolf-ings." There were to be no more classes—no rich or poor. To ordinary Socialists the reform means a fairer distribution of the joint product of capital and labour; higher wages for the workingman, shorter hours, better food and more of it, better clothes, better houses, more amusements—in short, "beer and skittles" in reasonable amount. The Socialism of Ruskin and Morris was an outcome of their æsthetic feeling. They liked to imag-ine the work people of the future as an intelligent and artistic body of handicraftsmen, living in pretty Gothic cottages among gardens of their own, scattered all over England in small rural towns or villages, and joyfully engaged in making sound and beautiful objects of use, tools, furniture, woven goods, etc. To the followers of Mr. Hyndman these motives, if not these aims, must have seemed somewhat unpractical. And in reading "Fors Clavigera," one sometimes has a difficulty in understand-ing just what sort of person Ruskin imagined the British workman to be.

THE NEO-ROMANTICISTS.—The literature of each new generation is apt to be partly an imitation of the last, and partly a reaction against it. The impulse first given by Rossetti was communicated, through Mor-ris and Swinburne, to a group of younger poets whom Mr. Stedman distinguishes as "Neo-Romanticists." *
The most noteworthy among these are probably Arthur O'Shaughnessy,† John Payne,‡ and Théophile Mar-

---

* "Victorian Poets," chap. vii., § vi.
† "An Epic of Women" (1870) ; "Lays of France" (1872) ;
"Music and Moonlight" (1874) ; "Songs of a Worker" (1881).
‡ "A Masque of Shadows" (1870) : "Intaglios" (1871) ;

zials;* though mention (want of space forbids more)
should also be made of George Augustus Simcox, whose
"Poems and Romances" (1869) are in the Pre-Raphaelite tradition.   The work of each of these has pronounced
individuality; yet, as a whole, it reminds one continually
now of Rossetti, now of Morris, and again of Swinburne;
not infrequently, too, of Keats or Leigh Hunt; but never
of the older romanticism, never of Scott nor even of
Coleridge or Tennyson.   The reminder comes sometimes
through a turn of phrase or the trick of the verse; but more
insistently in the choice of subject and the entire attitude
of the poet towards art and life, an attitude that may be
vaguely described as "æsthetic."   Even more distinctly
than in Swinburne, English romanticism in these latest
representatives is seen to be taking a French direction.
They show the influence not only of Hugo and Gautier,
but of those more recent schools of "decadents" which
exhibit French romanticism in its deliquescent stage;
writers like Théodore de Banville and Charles Baudelaire; books like Aloysius Bertrand's "Gaspard de la
Nuit."   Morbid states of passion; the hectic bloom of
fever; heady perfumes of the Orient and the tropics;
the bitter-sweet blossom of love; forced fruits of the hot-
house (*serres chaudes*); the iridescence of standing pools;
the fungoidal growths of decay; such are some of the
hackneyed metaphors which render the impression of
this neo-romantic poetry.

Marzials was born at Brussels, of French parents.
His "Gallery of Pigeons" is inscribed to the modern

"Songs of Life and Death" (1872) ; "Lautrec" (1878) ; "New
Poems" (1880).
    *"A Gallery of Pigeons" (1873).

Provençal poet Aubanel, and introduced by a French sonnet. O'Shaughnessy "was half a Frenchman in his love for, and mastery of, the French language"; * and on his frequent visits to Paris, made close acquaintance with Victor Hugo and the younger school of French poets. O'Shaughnessy and Payne were intimate friends, and dedicated their first books to each other. In 1870–72 they were members of the literary circle that assembled at the house of Ford Madox Brown, and there they met the Rossettis, Morris, Swinburne, and William Bell Scott. O'Shaughnessy emerges most distinctly from the group by reason of his very original and exquisite lyrical gift—a gift not fully recognised till Mr. Palgrave accorded him, in the second series of his "Golden Treasury" (1897), a greater number of selections than any Victorian poet but Tennyson: a larger space than he gave either to Browning or Rossetti or Matthew Arnold.†
Comparatively little of O'Shaughnessy's work belongs to the department of mediæval-romantic. His "Lays of France," five in number, are founded upon the *lais* of

* "Arthur O'Shaughnessy." By Louise Chandler-Moulton, Cambridge and Chicago, 1894.
† Swinburne, as a living author, is not represented in the "Treasury." O'Shaughnessy's metrical originality is undoubted. But one of his finest lyrics, "The Fountain of Tears," has an echo of Baudelaire's American master, Edgar Poe, as well as of Swinburne;

> "Very peaceful the place is, and solely
>   For piteous lamenting and sighing,
>   And those who come living or dying
> Alike from their hopes and their fears:
>   Full of cypress-like shadows the place is,
>   And statues that cover their faces;
> But out of the gloom springs the holy
> And beautiful Fountain of Tears."

Marie de France, the Norman poetess of the thirteenth
century whose little fable, "Du coq et du werpil," Chaucer expanded into his "Nonne Prestes Tale." O'Shaughnessy's versions are not so much paraphrases as independent poems, following Marie's stories merely in
outline.

The verse is the eight-syllabled couplet with variations
and alternate riming; the style follows the graceful,
fluent simplicity of the Old French; and in its softly
articulated, bright-coloured prolixity, the narrative frequently suggests "The Earthly Paradise" or "The Story
of Rimini." The most remarkable of these pieces is
"Chaitivel," in which the body of a bride is carried away
by a dead lover, while another dead lover comes back
from his grave in Palestine and fights with the bridegroom for possession of her soul. The song which the
lady sings to the buried man is true to that strange mediæval materialism, the cleaving of "soul's love" to
"body's love," the tenderness intense that pierces the
"wormy circumstance" of the tomb, and refuses to let
the dead be dead, which was noted in Keats' "Isabella":

> "Hath any loved you well, down there,
>   Summer or winter through?
> Down there, have you found any fair
>   Laid in the grave with you?
> Is death's long kiss a richer kiss
>   Than mine was wont to be—
> Or have you gone to some far bliss
>   And quite forgotten me?"

Of similar inspiration, but more pictorially and exter-
nally Gothic, are such tales as "The Building of the
Dream" and "Sir Floris" in Payne's volume, "The
Masque of Shadows." The former of these, introduced

by a quotation from Jehan du Mestre, is the history of a
certain squire of Poitou, who devotes himself to necro-
mancy and discovers a spell in an old Greek manuscript,
whereby, having shod his horse with gold and ridden
seven days into the west, he comes to the enchanted land
of Dame Venus and dwells with her a season.   But the
bliss is insupportable by a mortal, and he returns to his
home and dies.   The poem has analogies with " The
Earthly Paradise " and the Tannhäuser legend.   The
ancient city of Poitou, where the action begins, is elabo-
rately described, with its " lazy grace of old romance " :

> " Fair was the place and old
> Beyond the memory of man, with roofs
>   Tall-peak'd and hung with woofs
> Of dainty stone-work, jewell'd with the grace
>   Of casements, in the face
> Of the white gables inlaid, in all hues
>   Of lovely reds and blues.
> At every corner of the winding ways
>   A carven saint did gaze,
> With mild sweet eyes, upon the quiet town,
>   From niche and shrine of brown ;
> And many an angel, graven for a charm
>   To save the folk from harm
> Of evil sprites, stood sentinel above
>   High pinnacle and roof."

" Sir Floris " is an allegorical romaunt founded on a passage in " Le Violier des Histoires Provenciaux."   The
dedication, to the author of " Lohengrin," praises Wolf-
ram von Eschenbach, the poet of " Parzival," as " the
sweetest of all bards."   Sir Floris, obeying a voice heard
in sleep, followed a white dove to an enchanted garden,
where he slew seven monsters, symbolic of the seven
deadly sins; from whose blood sprang up the lily of
chastity, the rose of love, the violet of humility, the
clematis of content, the marigold of largesse, the mystic

marguerite, and the holy vervain "that purgeth earth's desire." Sir Galahad then carries him in a magic boat to the Orient city of Sarras, where the Grail is enshrined and guarded by a company of virgin knights, Percival, Lohengrin, Titurel, and Bors. Sir Floris sees the sacred chalice—a single emerald—lays his nosegay upon the altar, witnesses the mystery of the eucharist, and is kissed upon the mouth by Christ. This poet is fond of introducing old French words "to make his English sweet upon his tongue"; *accueillade, valiantise, faineant, allegresse, gentilesse, forte et dure,* and occasionally a phrase like *dieu vous doint felicité.* Payne's ballads are less characteristic.* Perhaps the most successful of them is "The Rime of Redemption"—in "The Masque of Shadows" volume. Sir Loibich's love has died in her sins, and he sits by the fire in bitter repentance. He hears the voice of her spirit outside in the moonlight, and together they ride through the night on a black steed, first to Fairyland, then to Purgatory, and then to the gate of Heaven. Each of these in turn is offered him, but he rejects them all—

> "With thee in hell, I choose to dwell"—

and thereby works her redemption. The wild night ride has an obvious resemblance to "Lenore":

> "The wind screams past; they ride so fast,
>   Like troops of souls in pain
> The snowdrifts spin, but none may win
>   To rest upon the twain."

Very different from these, and indeed with no pretensions

* See especially "Sir Erwin's Questing," "The Ballad of May Margaret," "The Westward Sailing," and "The Ballad of the King's Daughter" in "Songs of Life and Death."

to the formal peculiarities of popular minstrelsy, is
O'Shaughnessy's weird ballad "Bisclaveret," * suggested
by the superstition concerning were-wolves:

"The splendid fearful herds that stray
     By midnight "—
"The multitudinous campaign
  Of hosts not yet made fast in Hell."

Bisclaveret is the Breton word for *loup garou ;* and the
poem is headed with a caption to this effect from the
"Lais" of Marie. The wild, mystical beauty of which
the Celtic imagination holds the secret is visible in this
lyrist; but it would perhaps be going too far to attribute
his interest in the work of Marie de France to a native
sympathy with the song spirit of that other great branch
of the Celtic race, the ancient Cymry.

Payne's volume of sonnets, "Intaglios" (a title perhaps prompted by the chiselled workmanship of Gautier's
"Emaux et Camées ") bears the clearest marks of Rossetti's influence—or of the influence of Dante through
Rossetti. The inscription poem is to Dante, and the
series named "Madonna dei Sogni " is particularly full
of the imagery and sentiment of the "Purgatorio" and
the "Vita Nuova." Several of the sonnets in the collection are written for pictures, like Rossetti's. Two are
on Spenserian subjects, "Belphœbe " and "The Garden
of Adonis "; and one, "Bride-Night" is suggested by
Wagner's "Tristram und Isolde." Payne's work as a
translator is of importance, and includes versions of the
"Decameron," "The Thousand and One Nights," and
the poems of François Villon, all made for the Villon
Society.

* In "An Epic of Women."

Jewels and flowers are set thickly enough in the pages of all this school; but it is in Théophile Marzials' singular, yet very attractive, verses that the luxurious colour in which romance delights, and the decorative features of Pre-Raphaelite art run into the most *bizarre* excesses. He wantons in dainty affectations of speech and eccentricities of phantasy. Here we find again the orchard closes, the pleached pleasances, and all those queer picture paradises, peopled with tall lilied maidens, angels with peacock wings and thin gold hoops above their heads, and court minstrels thrumming lutes, rebecks, and mandolins—

> "I dreamed I was a virginal—
> The gilt one of Saint Cecily's."

The book abounds in nocturnes, arabesques, masquerades, bagatelles, rococo pastorals. The lady in "The Gallery of Pigeons" sits at her broidery frame and works tapestries for her walls. At night she sleeps in the northern tower where

> "Above all tracery, carven flower,
> And grim gurgoil is her bower-window";

and higher up a griffin clings against a cornice,

> "And gnashes and grins in the green moonlight,"

and higher still, the banderolle flutters

> "At the top of the thinnest pinnacle peak."

In a Pre-Raphaelite heaven the maidens sit in the blessed mother's chamber and spin garments for the souls in Limbo, or press sweet wine for the sacrament, or illuminate missals with quaint phantasies. Mr. Stedman quotes a few lines which he says have the air of parody:

"They chase them each, below, above,—
  Half madden'd by their minstrelsy,—
    Thro' garths of crimson gladioles;
And, shimmering soft like damoisels,
The angels swarm in glimmering shoals,
    And pin them to their aureoles,
And mimick back their ritournels."

This reads, indeed, hardly less like a travesty than the well-known verses in *Punch :*

"Glad lady mine, that glitterest
  In shimmer of summer athwart the lawn ;
Canst tell me whether is bitterest,
  The glamour of eve, or the glimmer of dawn?"

This stained-glass imagery was so easy to copy that, before long, citoles and damoisels and aureoles and garths and glamours and all the rest of the picturesque furniture grew to be a burden. The artistic movement had invaded dress and upholstery, and Pre-Raphaelitism tapered down into æstheticism, domestic art, and the wearing of sunflowers. Du Maurier became its satirist; Bunthorn and Postlethwaite presented it to the philistine understanding in a grotesque mixture of caricature and quackery.

THE REACTION.—Literary epochs overlap at the edges, and contrasting literary modes coexist. There was some romantic poetry written in Pope's time; and in the very heat and fury of romantic predominance, Landor kept a cool chamber apart, where incense was burned to the ancient gods.* But it is the master current which gives

---

* "From time to time bright spirits, intolerant of the traditional, try to alter the bournes of time and space in these respects, and to make out that the classical, whatever the failings on its part, was always in its heart rather Romantic, and that the Romantic has always, at its best, been just a little classical. . . . But such observations are only of use as guards against a too wooden and matter-of-fact classification ; the

tinge and direction to lesser confluents; and romanticism may be said to have had everything its own way down to the middle of the century. Then reaction set in and the stream of romantic tendency ceased to spread itself over the whole literary territory, but flowed on in the narrower and deeper channels of Pre-Raphaelitism and its allied movements. This reaction expressed itself in different ways, of which it will be sufficient here to mention three: realistic fiction, classical criticism, and the Queen Anne revival.

The leading literary form of the past fifty years has been the novel of real life. The failure of "Les Burgraves" in 1843 not more surely signalised the end of French romanticism, than the appearance of "Vanity Fair" in 1848 announced that in England, too, the reign of romance was over. Classicism had given way before romanticism, and now romanticism in turn was yielding to realism. Realism sets itself against that desire of escape from actual conditions into an ideal world, which is a note of the romantic spirit in general; and consequently it refuses to find the past any more interesting than the present, and has no use for the Middle Ages. The temperature, too, had cooled; not quite down to the Augustan grade, yet to a point considerably below the fever heat registered by the emotional thermometer of the late Georgian era. Byron's contemporaries were shocked by his wickedness and dazzled by his genius. They remonstrated admiringly with him; young ladies wept over his poetry and prayed for the poet's conver-

great general differences of the periods remain, and can never be removed in imagination without loss and confusion " ("A Short History of English Literature," Saintsbury, p. 724).

sion. But young university men of Thackeray's time discovered that Byron was a *poseur ;* Thackeray himself describes him as " a big, sulky dandy."   " The Sorrows of Werther," which made people cry in the eighteenth century, made Thackeray laugh; and he summed it up in a doggerel ballad:

> "Charlotte was a married woman
>   And a moral man was Werther,
> And for nothing in creation
>   Would do anything to hurt her."
>
> .   .   .   .   .   .
>
> "Charlotte, having seen his body
>   Borne before her on a shutter,
> Like a well-conducted woman,
>   Went on cutting bread and butter."

Mr. Howells in Venice sneers at Byron's theatrical habit of riding horesback on the Lido in "conspicuous solitude," as recorded in "Julian and Maddalo."   He notices the local traditions about Byron—a window from which one of his mistresses was said to have thrown herself into the canal, etc.—and confesses that these matters interest him very little.

As to the Walter Scott kind of romance, we know what Mr. Howells thinks of it; and have read " Rebecca and Rowena," Thackeray's travesty of " Ivanhoe."   Thackeray took no print from the romantic generation; he passed it over, and went back to Addison, Fielding, Goldsmith, Swift.   His masters were the English humourists of the eighteenth century.   He planned a literary history of that century, a design which was carried out on other lines by his son-in-law, Leslie Stephen.   If he wrote historical novels, their period was that of the Georges, and not of Richard the Lion Heart.   It will not do, of course, to lay too much stress on Thackeray, whose profession was satire and whose temper purely anti-romantic. But if we turn to the leaders of the modern schools of fiction, we shall find that some of them, like George Eliot and Anthony Trollope, are even more closely realistic than Thackeray—who, says Mr. Howells, is a caricaturist, not a true realist—and of others such as Dickens and Meredith, we shall find that, in whatever way they deviate from realism as strictly understood, it is not in the direction of romance.

In Matthew Arnold's critical essays we meet with a restatement of classical principles and an application of them to the literature of the last generation. There was something premature, he thinks, about the burst of creative activity in the first quarter of the nineteenth century. Byron was empty of matter, Shelley incoherent, Wordsworth wanting in completeness and variety. He finds much to commend in the influence of a literary tribunal like the French Academy, which embodies that ideal of authority so dear to the classical heart. Such an institution acts as a salutary check on the lawlessness, eccentricity, self-will, and fantasticality which are the besetting intellectual sins of Englishmen. It sets the standard and gives the law. "Work done after men have reached this platform is *classical;* and that is the only work which, in the long run, can stand." For want of some such organ of educated opinion, to take care of the qualities of order, balance, measure, propriety, correctness, English men of genius like Ruskin and Carlyle, in their national impatience of prescription and routine, run on into all manner of violence, freak, and extravagance.

Again, in the preface of the 1853 edition of his poems,

Arnold asserts the superiority of the Greek theory of poetry to the modern. "They regarded the whole; we regard the parts. With them the action predominated over the expression of it; with us the expression predominates over the action. . . . We have poems which seem to exist merely for the sake of single lines and passages; not for the sake of producing any total impression."

"Faust" itself, judged as a whole, is defective. Failing a sure guide, in the confusion of the present times, the wisest course for the young writer is to fix his attention upon the best models. But Shakspere is not so safe a model as the ancients. He has not their purity of method, and his gift of expression sometimes leads him astray. "Mr. Hallam, than whom it is impossible to find a saner and more judicious critic, has had the courage (for at the present day it needs courage) to remark, how extremely and faultily difficult Shakspere's language often is." Half a century earlier it would have needed courage to question Hallam's remark; but the citation shows how thoroughly Coleridge and Hazlitt and Lamb had shifted the centre of orthodoxy in matters of Shaksperian criticism. *Now* the presumption was against any one who ventured a doubt of Shakspere's impeccability. The romantic victory was complete. "But, I say," pursues the essayist, "that in the sincere endeavour to learn and practise . . . what is sound and true in poetical art, I seemed to myself to find the only sure guidance, the only solid footing, among the ancients." All this has a familiar look to one at all read in eighteenth-century criticism; but in 1853 it sounds very much like heresy.

As an instance of the inferiority of romantic to classical method in narrative poetry, Arnold refers to Keats'

"Isabella." *   "This one short poem contains, perhaps, a greater number of happy single expressions which one could quote than all the extant tragedies of Sophocles. But the action, the story? The action in itself is an excellent one; but so feebly is it conceived by the poet, so loosely constructed, that the effect produced by it, in and for itself, is absolutely null. Let the reader, after he has finished the poem of Keats, turn to the same story in the ' Decameron '; he will then feel how pregnant and interesting the same action has become in the hands of a great artist who, above all things, delineates his object; who subordinates expression to that which it is designed to express."

A sentence or two from Arnold's essay on Heinrich Heine, and we may leave this part of our subject. " Mr. Carlyle attaches, it seems to me, far too much importance to the romantic school of Germany—Tieck, Novalis, Jean Paul Richter. . . . The mystic and romantic school of Germany lost itself in the Middle Ages, was overpowered by their influence, came to ruin by its vain dreams of renewing them. Heine, with a far profounder sense of the mystic and romantic charm of the Middle Age than Görres, or Brentano, or Arnim; Heine, the chief romantic poet of Germany, is yet also much more than a romantic poet; he is a great modern poet, he is not conquered by the Middle Age, he has a talisman by which he can feel, along with but above the power of the fascinating Middle Age itself, the power of modern ideas."

And, finally, the oscillation of the pendulum has brought us back again for a moment to the age of gayety, and to that very Queen Anne spirit against which the

* *Vide supra*, pp. 123–25.

serious and sentimental Thomson began the revolt.
There is not only at present a renewed appreciation of
what was admirable in the verse of Pope and the prose
of Swift, but we discover a quaint attractiveness in the
artificiality of Augustan manners, dress, and speech.
Lace and brocade, powder and patch, Dutch gardens,
Reynolds' portraits, Watteau fans, Dresden china, the
sedan chair, the spinet, the hoop-skirt, the *talon rouge*—
all these have receded so far into the perspective as to
acquire picturesqueness.   To Scott's generation they
seemed eminently modern and prosaic, while buff jerkins
and coats of mail were poetically remote.   But so the
whirligig of time brings in its revenges, and the old-
fashioned, as distinguished from the antique, begins to
have a romanticness of its own.   It is now some quarter
century since people took to building Queen Anne cottages, and gentlemen at costume parties to treading
minuets in small clothes and perukes, with ladies in high-
cushioned hair and farthingales.   Girl babies in large
numbers were baptised Dorothy and Belinda.   Book illustrators like Kate Greenaway, Edwin Abbey, and Hugh
Thomson carried the mode into art.   The date of the Queen
Anne revival in literature and the beginnings of the *bric-à-
brac* school of verse are marked with sufficient precision by
the publication of Austin Dobson's " Vignettes in Rhyme "
(1873), "Proverbs in Porcelain" (1877), and the other
delightful volumes of the same kind that have followed.
Mr. Dobson has also published, in prose, lives of Steele,
Fielding, Hogarth, and Goldsmith ; " Eighteenth-Century
Vignettes," and the like.   But his particular ancestor
among the Queen Anne wits was Matthew Prior, of whose
metrical tales, epigrams, and *vers de société* he has made

a little book of selections; and whose gallantry, lightness, and tone of persiflage, just dashed with sentiment, he has reproduced with admirable spirit in his own original work.

It was upon the question of Pope that romantics and classics first joined issue in the time of Warton, and that the critical battle was fought in the time of Bowles and Byron; the question of his real place in literature, and of his title to the name of poet. Mr. Dobson has a word to say for Pope, and with this our enquiries may fittingly end:

> "Suppose you say your Worst of POPE, declare
> His Jewels Paste, his Nature a Parterre,
> His Art but Artifice—I ask once more
> Where have you seen such artifice before?
> Where have you seen a Parterre better grac'd,
> Or gems that glitter like his Gems of Paste?
> Where can you show, among your Names of Note,
> So much to copy and so much to quote?
> And where, in Fine, in all our English Verse,
> A Style more trenchant and a Sense more terse?"

> "So I, that love the old Augustan Days
> Of formal courtesies and formal Phrase ;
> That like along the finish'd Line to feel
> The Ruffle's Flutter and the Flash of Steel ;
> That like my Couplet as Compact as Clear ;
> That like my Satire sparkling tho' severe,
> Unmix'd with Bathos and unmarr'd by trope,
> I fling my Cap for Polish—and for POPE !" *

But ground once gained in a literary movement is never wholly lost; and a reversion to an earlier type is never complete. The classicism of Matthew Arnold is not at all the classicism of the eighteenth century; Thackeray's realism is not the realism of Fielding. It is what it is, partly just because Walter Scott had written his Wa-

---

* "A Dialogue to the Memory of Mr. Alexander Pope."

verley Novels in the mean while. Apart from the works for which it is directly responsible, the romantic movement had enriched the blood of the literature, and its results are seen even in writings hostile to the romantic principles. As to the absolute value of the great romantic output of the nineteenth century, it may be at once acknowledged that, as "human documents," books which reflect contemporary life have a superior importance to the creations of the modern imagination, playing freely over times and places distant, and attractive through their distance; over ancient Greece or the Orient or the Middle Age. But that a very beautiful and quite legitimate product of literary art may spring from this contact of the present with the past, it is hoped that our history may have shown.

THE END.

BIBLIOGRAPHY.

Allingham, William. "Irish Songs and Poems." London and New York, 1893.
Arnim, Ludwig Joachim von. Selections in Koch's "Deutsche National Litteratur." Stuttgart, 1891. Vol. cxlvi.
Arnim, Ludwig Joachim [and Brentano]. "Des Knaben Wunderhorn." Wiesbaden and Leipzig, 1874–76. 2 vols.
Arnold, Matthew. "Essays in Criticism." London, 1895.
———— "On the Study of Celtic Literature." London, 1893.
———— Poems. London, 1877. 2 vols.
Austin, Sarah. "Fragments from German Prose Writers." London, 1841.

Balzac, Honoré de. "Les Contes Drolatiques." Paris, 1855.
Baring-Gould, S. "The Vicar of Morwenstow" [life of R. S. Hawker]. New York, 1879.
Bell, Malcolm. "Edward Burne-Jones." London, 1899.
Bertrand, L. "La Fin du Classicisme." Paris, 1897.
Bowles, W. L. Introduction and Life in "Works of Alexander Pope." London, 1806. 10 vols.
———— Poetical Works. (Gilfillan's ed.) Edinburgh, 1855. 2 vols.
———— See p. 73 for pamphlets in Pope Controversy.
Boyd, Henry. "The Divina Comedia." (Trans.) London, 1802. 3 vols.
Boyesen, H. H. "Essays on German Literature." New York, 1892.
Brandes, Georg M. C. "Die Hauptströmungen der Literatur des Neunzehnten Jahrhunderts." (Trans.) Berlin, 1872–76. 4 vols.
Brandl, Alois. "Samuel Taylor Coleridge and the English Romantic School." (Trans.) London, 1887.
———— "Thomas of Erceldoune." Berlin, 1880.
Brentano, Clemens. Selections in Koch's "Deutsche National Litteratur." Stuttgart, 1891. Vol. cxlvi.
———— See *Arnim.*

Brooke, Stopford A. [and T. W. Rolleston]. "A Treasury of Irish Poetry." New York, 1900.
Brunetière, Ferdinand. "A Manual of the History of French Literature." (Trans.) New York, 1898.
Byron, George Noel Gordon, Lord. Works. London, 1832–33. 15 vols.

Caine, T. Hall. "Recollections of Dante Gabriel Rossetti." London, 1882.
Campbell, Thomas. "Specimens of the British Poets." London, 1841.
Carlyle, Thomas. Works. London, 1869–72. 31 vols.
Cary, E. L. "The Rossettis." New York, 1894.
Cary, Henry F. "The Vision of Dante." (Trans.) New York, 1861.
Chateaubriand, Vicomte F. A. R. de. "The Beauties of Christianity." (Trans.) Philadelphia, 1815.
Coleridge, S. T. "Anima Poetæ." Boston, 1895.
——— Works. New York, 1884. 7 vols.
Collins, J. Churton. "Illustrations of Tennyson." London, 1891.
Colvin, Sidney. "Keats." (English Men of Letters Series.) New York, 1887.
Courthope, W. J. "The Liberal Movement in English Literature." London, 1885.
Croker, T. Crofton. "Fairy Legends and Traditions of the South of Ireland." London, 1870.
Cross, W. L. "The Development of the English Novel." New York, 1899.
Davidson, John. "Ballads and Songs." London, 1895.
De Quincey, Thomas. Works. New York, 1878. 12 vols.
Digby, Sir Kenelm H. "The Broad Stone of Honour." London, 1844–48. 3 vols.
Dobson, H. Austin. "Poems on Several Occasions." London, 1895. 2 vols.

Eastlake, Sir Charles L. "A History of the Gothic Revival." London, 1872.

Fergusson, James. "History of Architecture." London, 1865–76. 4 vols.
Ford, R. "The Ancient Ballads of Spain." *Edinburgh Review,* January, 1841.
Fouqué, F. H. K., Baron de la Motte. "The Four Seasons: Undine and Other Tales." (Trans.) New York, 1875.
——— "The Magic Ring." (Trans.) Edinburgh, 1825.
——— "Thiodolf the Icelander." (Trans.) Philadelphia, 1863.

Gates, Lewis E. "Selections from Newman." New York, 1895.
———— "Studies and Appreciations." New York, 1890.
Gautier, Théophile. "Histoire du Romantisme." Paris, 1884.
Görres, J. J. von. Selections in Koch's "Deutsche National Litteratur." Stuttgart, 1891. Vol. cxlvi.
Gosse, Edmund. "From Shakespere to Pope." London, 1885.
Grimm, Jakob L. K., and Wilhelm K. "Household Tales." (Trans.) London, 1884. 2 vols.

Heine, Heinrich. "The Romantic School in Germany." (Trans.) New York, 1882.
Herford, C. H. "The Age of Wordsworth." London, 1897.
Hettner, H. J. T. "Litteraturgeschichte." Braunschweig, 1827.
Hewlett, Maurice. "The Forest Lovers." New York and London, 1898.
Hillebrand, Karl. "German Thought." (Trans.) New York, 1880.
Hobson, J. A. "John Ruskin, Social Reformer." London, 1898.
Hogg, James. Works. London, 1873. 2 vols.
Howitt, William and Mary. "Literature and Romance of Northern Europe." London, 1852. 2 vols.
Hugo, Victor Marie. Œuvres Complètes. Paris, 1863.
Hunt, J. H. Leigh. Autobiography. London, 1870.
———— Poetical Works. London, 1832.
———— "Stories from the Italian Poets." New York, 1846.
———— "The Seer." Boston, 1865. 2 vols.
Hunt, W. Holman. "The Pre-Raphaelite Brotherhood. *Contemporary Review.* Vol. xlix.
Hutton, R. H. "Essays, Theological and Literary." London, 1880. 2 vols.

Jameson, Anna. "Sacred and Legendary Art." London, 1870. 2 vols.
Joyce, R. D. "Deirdrè. Boston, 1876.
Jullien, A. "Le Romantisme et l'Editeur Renduel." Paris, 1897.

Keats, John. Poetical Works. (Rossetti's ed.) London, 1876.
Keble, John. "The Christian Year." Philadelphia, 1834.
Kelly, J. F. M. "A History of Spanish Literature." New York, 1898.
Ker, W. P. "Epic and Romance." London, 1897.

Kingsley, Charles. "Hereward, the Last of the English." New York, 1888.

———— Poems. London, 1884. 2 vols.

Kingsley, F. E. G. "Charles Kingsley: His Letters and Memories of his Life." London, 1877. 2 vols.

Lindsay, A. W. C., Earl of Crawford. "Sketches of the History of Christian Art." London, 1885. 2 vols.

Lockhart, J. G. "Ancient Spanish Ballads." New York, 1842.

———— "Life of Scott." Boston and Philadephia, 1837–38. 7 vols.

Longfellow, H. W. "Hyperion." Boston, 1875.

———— Poetical Works. Boston, 1889. 6 vols.

———— "Poets and Poetry of Europe." Philadelphia, 1845.

———— "The Divine Comedy of Dante." (Trans.) Boston, 1867. 3 vols.

Macaulay, T. B. "Milton." *Edinburgh Review,* August, 1825.

Mackail, W. J. "The Life of William Morris." London, 1899.

McLaughlin, E. T. "Studies in Mediæval Life and Literature." New York and London, 1894.

Maigron, Louis. "Le Roman Historique à l'Epoque Romantique." Paris, 1898.

Marzials, Théophile. "The Gallery of Pigeons." London, 1873.

Meinhold, J. W. "Mary Schweidler, the Amber Witch." (Trans.) New York, 1845.

Milnes, R. M., Lord Houghton. "Life and Letters of John Keats." New York, 1848.

Morris, William. "Hopes and Fears for Art." Boston, 1882.

———— "Love is Enough." Boston, 1873.

———— "News from Nowhere." London, 1891.

———— "Old French Romances." (Trans.) New York, 1896.

———— [and E. B. Bax]. "Socialism." London, 1896.

———— "The Defence of Guenevere." London, 1875.

———— "The Earthly Paradise." Boston, 1868–71. 3 vols.

———— "The Life and Death of Jason." Boston, 1867.

———— "The Story of Sigurd the Volsung." Boston, 1877.

———— See p. 337 for list of prose romances.

Motherwell, William. "Minstrelsy, Ancient and Modern." Glasgow, 1827.

Moulton, L. C. "Arthur O'Shaughnessy." Cambridge and Chicago, 1894.

Musset, L. C. A. de. Œuvres Complètes. Paris, 1881.

Newman, J. H. "Callista." London, 1873.
———— "Essays, Critical and Historical." London, 1872.
2 vols.
———— "Loss and Gain." London, 1881.
———— "Parochial and Plain Sermons." London, 1873–91.
8 vols.
———— "Verses on Various Occasions." London, 1883.
Novalis (F. L. von Hardenberg). "Henry of Ofterdingen."
(Trans.) Cambridge, 1842.
———— "Hymns to the Night," etc. (trans. of George Mac-
Donald), in "Rampolli." London and New York, 1897.

O'Shaughnessy, Arthur. "An Epic of Women." London,
1870.
———— "Lays of France." London, 1874.
———— "Music and Moonlight." London, 1874.

Palgrave, F. T. "The Golden Treasury of Songs and Lyri-
cal Poems." Cambridge, 1863. Second Series, New
York, 1897.
Parsons, T. W. "The Divine Comedy of Dante." (Trans.)
Boston, 1893.
Pater, Walter. "Appreciations." London, 1889.
Payne, John. "Intaglios." London, 1884.
———— "Lautrec." London, 1878.
———— "New Poems." London, 1880.
———— "Songs of Life and Death." London, 1884.
———— "The Masque of Shadows." London, 1884.
Petit de Julleville, Louis. "Histoire de la Littérature Fran-
çaise." Paris, 1896–99. 8 vols.
Price, Sir Uvedale. "Essays on the Picturesque." London,
1810. 3 vols.
Pugin, A. N. W. "Contrasts." Edinburgh, 1898.
———— "The True Principles of Pointed Architecture,"
Edinburgh, 1895.

Reade, Charles. "The Cloister and the Hearth." New York,
1894. 2 vols.
Robertson, J. M. "New Essays toward a Critical Method."
London, 1897.
Roscoe, William. Preface to "Works of Alexander Pope."
London, 1824. 10 vols.
Rossetti, Christina G. "The Goblin Market." London,
1865.
Rossetti, D. G. The Collected Works of Dante Gabriel Ros-
setti. Edited by William M. Rossetti. London, 1886.
2 vols.

4

Rossetti, D. G. Family Letters, with Memoir by W. M. Rossetti. Boston, 1895.

Rossetti, Maria F. "A Shadow of Dante." Boston, 1872.

Rossetti, W. M. "Dante Gabriel Rossetti as Designer and Writer." London, 1889.

Ruskin, John. "Fors Clavigera." New York, 1871–72. 2 vols.

———— "Modern Painters." New York, 1857–60. 5 vols.

———— "Munera Pulveris." New York, 1872.

———— "Præterita." London, 1899. 3 vols.

———— "Pre-Raphaelitism." New York, 1860.

———— "Stones of Venice." New York, 1860. 3 vols.

———— "Unto this Last." London, 1862.

Saintsbury, George. "A Primer of French Literature." Oxford, 1880.

———— "A Short History of English Literature." London, 1898.

Scherer, W. "A History of German Literature." (Trans.) New York, 1886. 2 vols.

Schlegel, A. W. von. "Lectures on Dramatic Art and Literature." (Trans.) London, 1846.

Schmidt, Julian. "Geschichte der Deutschen Litteratur." Berlin, 1890.

Scott, Sir Walter. "Critical and Miscellaneous Essays." Philadelphia, 1841. 3 vols.

———— Journal. New York, 1891.

———— Poetical Works. (Dennis' ed.) London, 1892. 5 vols.

———— "The Waverley Novels." (Dryburgh ed.) Edinburgh, 1892–93. 25 vols.

Scott, W. B. "Autobiographical Notes." New York, 1892. 2 vols.

Shairp, J. C. "Aspects of Poetry." Boston, 1882.

Sharp, William. "Dante Gabriel Rossetti." London, 1882.

Shelley, Percy Bysshe. Poetical Works. (Centenary ed.) Boston, 1892. 4 vols.

Shorthouse, J. H. "John Inglesant." New York, 1882.

Sizeranne, R. de la. "English Contemporary Art." (Trans.) Westminster, 1898.

Smith, Charlotte. "Elegiac Sonnets." London, 1800–06. 2 vols.

Southey, Robert. "Chronicle of the Cid." (Trans.) Lowell, 1846. (1st Am. ed.)

———— Poetical Works. London, 1838. 10 vols.

Staël-Holstein, Mme. A. L. G. de. "Germany." (Trans.) London, 1814. 3 vols.

Stedman, E. C. "Victorian Poets." Boston, 1876.

Stendhal, De (Marie Henri Beyle). "Racine et Shakspere."
  Paris, 1854.
Stevenson, R. L. B. "Familiar Studies of Men and Books."
  London, 1882.
Swinburne, A. C. "Essays and Studies." London, 1875.
————— "Poems and Ballads." London, 1866. Second
  Series, 1878. Third Series, 1889.
————— "Studies in Prose and Poetry." New York, 1894.
————— "The Tale of Balen." New York, 1896.
————— "Tristram of Lyonesse." London, 1882.
————— "Victor Hugo." New York, 1886.

Tennyson, Alfred. Works. London, 1892. (Globe ed.)
Thorpe, Benjamin. "Northern Mythology." London, 1851–
  52. 3 vols.
————— "Yuletide Stories." London, 1875.
Ticknor, George. "History of Spanish Literature." New
  York, 1849. 3 vols.
Tieck, J. Ludwig. "Phantasus." Berlin, 1844–45. 2 vols.
————— "Tales" (trans.) in the works of Thomas Carlyle.
  2 vols. London, 1869–72.
Tighe, Mary. "Psyche, with Other Poems." London, 1812.

Uhland, J. Ludwig. Gedichte. Stuttgart, 1875.

Vere, Aubrey Thomas de. "Recollections." London, 1897.

Ward, Wilfrid. "William George Ward and the Oxford
  Movement." London, 1889.
Watts, Theodore. "Rossetti." *Encyclopædia Britannica*.
Wood, Esther. "Dante Rossetti and the Pre-Raphaelite
  Movement." New York, 1894.
Wordsworth, William. Poetical Works. (Centenary ed.)
  London, 1870. 6 vols.

Yonge, Charlotte M. "The Heir of Redcliffe." New York,
  1871. 2 vols.

INDEX.